LITERATURE
AND An Anthology of Sixty Years of
The New Republic
LIBERALISM

LITERATURE
AND
An Anthology of Sixty Years of
The New Republic
LIBERALISM

Edited by Edward Zwick

With an Introduction by
Irving Howe

THE NEW REPUBLIC BOOK COMPANY, INC.

Washington, D.C.

Library of Congress Cataloging in Publication Data
Main entry under title:

Literature and liberalism.

   1. American literature—20th century. 2. Criticism—United States. I. Zwick, Edward. II. The New Republic.
PS535.5.L56   810'.8'005   76-2448
ISBN 0-915220-06-7

Contents

Literature and Liberalism —
An Introduction by Irving Howe   xi

Editor's Note   xxv

PROSE

Second Mortgage	*Irwin Shaw*	3
The Teaser	*John Cheever*	6
Six Years After	*Katherine Mansfield*	9
Handy: A Story	*Erskine Caldwell*	12
Like the Sad Heart of Ruth	*Peter Taylor*	17
A Loaf of Bread	*Robert Gibbons*	19
Vag	*John Dos Passos*	27
The Campers at Kitty Hawk	*John Dos Passos*	29
As a Soldier Thinks of War	*Alan Seeger*	33
Day in Spain	*Lillian Hellman*	36
Communists and Cops	*Edmund Wilson*	39
Connecticut Valley	*Malcolm Cowley*	44
Pageant of Birds	*Eudora Welty*	47
Italy, 1927	*Ernest Hemingway*	51
I Have a Thing to Tell You: III	*Thomas Wolfe*	57
Factory Town	*Sherwood Anderson*	67
The Good Year	*William Saroyan*	70
Me and the Babe	*Hamilton Basso*	74
The Sexes	*Dorothy Parker*	77
The Scrolls	*Woody Allen*	80
Dinner Bridge	*Ring Lardner*	83
Landscape	*Edmund Wilson*	87
The Muffled Ship	*John Galsworthy*	88
The Threshold	*I. Turgenieff*	89

POETRY

Sic Semper	Maxwell Anderson	93
The Revolutionary	D.H. Lawrence	94
Invocation to the Social Muse	Archibald MacLeish	96
Ballad of Roosevelt	Langston Hughes	97
The Excavation	Max Endicoff	98
Ode for School Convocation	John Ciardi	99
Two Poems	e.e. cummings	100
Roosters	Elizabeth Bishop	101
Painted Head	John Crowe Ransom	103
In Memory of W.B. Yeats	W.H. Auden	104
Requiem for the Dead in Spain	Kenneth Rexroth	106
For a Friend Parting	Robert Penn Warren	107
Troop Train	Karl Shapiro	108
The Waltz of the Twenty-Year Olds	Louis Aragon	109
Soldier (T.P.)	Randall Jarrell	110
The Roman Soldier	Richmond Lattimore	111
Promise of Peace	Robinson Jeffers	111
Assignment	Marya Mannes	112
The Haunting Fingers	Thomas Hardy	113
About Hell	Babette Deutsch	114
The Conversation of Prayers	Dylan Thomas	115
The Lost Wife	Stephen Vincent Benét	116
The Death of the Hired Man	Robert Frost	116
The Mill	Edwin Arlington Robinson	120
The Second-Fated	Robert Graves	121
Sonnet	Edna St. Vincent Millay	122
Ecce Puer	James Joyce	122
Prelude	Conrad Aiken	123
The Broken Tower	Hart Crane	123
Gold Morning, Sweet Prince	Delmore Schwartz	124
Cracked Mary and the Bishop	W.B. Yeats	126
Cracked Mary Reproved	W.B. Yeats	127
Another Dream Song	John Berryman	127
Dilemma	Mark Van Doren	128
The Monstrous Marriage	William Carlos Williams	128
Angel of Little Neck Clams	Anne Sexton	129
Angel of Clean Sheets	Anne Sexton	130
Subway Love	John Updike	130
Subway	Oscar Williams	131

A Lion Named Passion   John Hollander   132
The Windy City   Carl Sandburg   134
Billboards and Galleons   Vachel Lindsay   142
Elegy   Allen Tate   147
Dunbarton   Robert Lowell   148

CRITICISM

The Duty of Harsh Criticism   Rebecca West   153
The Motive of the Critic   H.L. Mencken   156
The Curse of Official
  Culture   Robert Brustein   159
The Word Became Flesh   Hallie Flanagan and
                                     Philip Davis   165
Irrational Elements in Art
  and Politics   Lewis Mumford   169
The New Realism   Kenneth Evett   175
Warhol   Stephen Koch   177
Matisse and Picasso   Clive Bell   181
Pictures   Virginia Woolf   184
Renoir and the Impressionists   Leo Stein   187
Wilder: Prophet of the
  Genteel Christ   Michael Gold   190
The Literary Class War   Edmund Wilson   194
To a Revolutionary Critic   Malcolm Cowley   202
"The Education of Henry
  Adams"   Louis Kronenberger   205
Nearer My Land to Thee   Alfred Kazin   211
Exile's Return   Malcolm Cowley   218
Gertrude Stein Comes Home   T. S. Matthews   223
Alice B. Toklas   Gilbert Harrison   225
In Search of a Moral Style   Irving Howe   229
A Preface to Modern
  Literature   Edmund Wilson   235
The Novel Démeublé   Willa Cather   244
Beyond the Talking   William Faulkner   247
A Bolt from the Blue   Mary McCarthy   249
Gogol   Robert Littell   258
The Springs of Poetry   Louise Bogan   260
How to Criticize a Poem   Theodore Spencer   262
The Art of Translation   Vladimir Nabokov   264
Miss Lowell and Things   Walter Lippmann   270
The World of Robert Frost   Granville Hicks   271

Shakespeare: Made in
  America   *George Santayana*   274
Ibsen the Romantic   *E. M. Forster*   277
Willa Cather   *Lionel Trilling*   281
Bernhardt   *Stark Young*   285
Duse Now   *Stark Young*   287
Strawinsky   *Paul Rosenfeld*   289
Progress in Music   *Robert Evett*   295
The Movies   *Francis Hackett*   301
Land of Dreams, and
  Nightmares   *Otis Ferguson*   303
Saccharine Symphony   *Manny Farber*   307
Orson Welles: There Ain't
  No Way   *Pauline Kael*   309
Diary of a Mad Housewife   *Stanley Kauffmann*   314
Stripped Bare at the Follies   *Robert Coles*   317

Notes on the Contributors   323

IRVING HOWE

Literature and Liberalism

It is now a quarter of a century since Lionel Trilling remarked upon the difficulties faced by educated Americans in reconciling their political ideas with their literary tastes. Most of "us," he wrote, "are in our social and political beliefs consciously liberal," yet the writers we most admire—and he named the great figures of European modernism—"are indifferent to, even hostile to, the tradition of democratic liberalism . . ."

The problem was aggravated for Mr. Trilling by the fact that those works of recent American literature presenting themselves as "patently liberal" could seldom excite our deepest loyalties. We could not gain from them "the sense of largeness, of cogency, of the transcendence which largeness and cogency can give, the sense of being reached in our secret and primitive minds." Mr. Trilling was referring here to the damage wrought by fellow-traveling ideology, but still more, he was deploring a tendency of liberal writing to congeal into set formulas such as the simplistic notion that "the life of man can be nicely settled by a correct social organization, or short of that, by the election of high moral attitudes."

In these reflections Mr. Trilling was consciously echoing the complaint that John Stuart Mill had made a century earlier. Mill had felt dismay at seeing his favored ideas turn rigid and life-denying, and in his resulting confusion had gained unexpected nourishment from the poetry of Wordsworth and the prose of Coleridge. Neither Wordsworth's poetry nor Coleridge's prose won Mill's full intellectual acquiescence, yet he valued them for what Mr. Trilling calls "a sense of variousness and possibility," that richness of feeling that the dry, overly programmatic liberalism of the utilitarians could not yield.

The passage of a quarter of a century has not lessened the force of Mr. Trilling's argument, though one might add that his judgment of liberalism could be made with equal strength against other systems of contemporary thought: against Christianity, Marxism, and conservatism, which have all become sterile or sentimental. What has characterized the literature of our lifetime has been an absence of sustaining belief, or more to the point, an absence of even provisional belief, the kind that writers can conditionally employ or seriously pit themselves against. And since the dominant intellectual tendency of twentieth-century

America has been one or another kind of liberalism, the result of this breakdown has been to arouse scorn, irritation, and boredom with the claims of liberalism.

Our literature and our thought have never, to be sure, been aligned in a simple flow of harmony: it is naive to suppose that such an untroubled relation could ever exist. Even with regard to the Christian centuries, it is only popularized history that proposes an untroubled, "organic" relation between belief and imagination. Once we take a closer look at particular Christian works we find them complicated by tension, heresy, perhaps even a masked skepticism. Nevertheless, later generations may pardon us for supposing that our own time is one in which, partly as a consequence of the exhausting fanaticisms of fascism and communism, there has occurred a radical sundering between belief and imagination. Sometimes a sundering so extreme, that serious writers have been provoked into feeling that imaginative survival depends on a refusal of all beliefs.

It has not always been so. Whatever criticisms we may wish to make of twentieth-century liberalism, it is desperately useful to remind ourselves that liberalism in its heroic phase—toward the end of the eighteenth and a good part of the nineteenth century—enabled and perhaps even inspired a large portion of Western literature. Being utterly obvious, this proposition has been mostly ignored; and largely ignored, it might now have some freshness and force. What I have in mind is liberalism not as a mere program for social change or a political movement advancing that program; what I have in mind is liberalism as a new historical temper, a turning of minds to openness of idea and variousness of sentiment.

Liberalism in its heroic phase constitutes one of the two or three greatest revolutionary experiences in human history, comparable with the ethic of the Old Testament and the word of Jesus in its power to transform the imagination. Whether or not a given writer calls himself a liberal or can be said to "reflect" the outlook of liberalism, matters hardly at all. What does matter is that the richness and multiplicity of modern culture would simply have been impossible without the animating liberal idea. The root terms and values of modern literature would be inconceivable without the thought of the Enlightenment or the new image of human potentiality cast up by Romanticism—and both the Enlightenment and Romanticism, with whatever complications, contribute to liberalism in its heroic phase. The very idea of "the self," a central convention of modern literature, simply could not have come into being had there not been the earlier, fructifying presence of liberalism. The dynamics of plot that characterize the nineteenth-century novel, based as these are on new assumptions about mobility and freedom, are quite inconceivable without the shaping premises of liberalism.

To say this isn't, of course, to suggest that literature of the modern era has no other or older sources; it is only to account, somewhat, for distinctive new energies. "The deepest driving force of the liberal ideas of the Enlightenment," writes Karl Mannheim, "lay in the fact that it appealed to the free will and kept alive the feeling of being indeterminate and unconditioned . . . ." Without such feelings, how could the modern novelist so much as have conceived of a *Bildungsroman,* with its progress through society and growth of the self, or of an escape from the locked frames of social role and class perspective? I don't mean to suggest that these typical patterns of modern literature have no analogues in earlier, more traditional literatures; only that the moral and psychological contents we recognize as distinctively our own depend crucially on that complex of ideas and impulses we identify as liberalism. And insofar as these truisms are actually true, they hold for writers as various in opinion as Dickens and Dostoevsky, Zola and Lawrence, Proust and Dreiser, all of whom respond to, find sustenance in, turn sharply against, and express disgust with the values of a liberalism they cannot escape. Even the conservative counter-Enlightenment, which coexists with major portions of modernist literature, is able to reach definition because of privileges that liberalism had secured as rights.

It is a great moral and imaginative power, this liberalism that begins to blossom in eighteenth-century Europe. It promises a dismissal of intolerable constraints; it speaks for previously unimagined rights; it declares standards of sincerity and candor; it offers the promise that each man shall have his voice, and that each voice will be heard. For the whole of European and American literature from, say, the last third of the eighteenth century, liberalism helps release energies of assertion, but, more important, energies of opposition—opposition to privilege and vulgarity, to the imprisonment of the body and denial of the spirit. If the nineteenth-century novel is frequently organized as a comedy of conflict between fading aristocracy and oncoming bourgeoisie, that novel takes emotive sharpness from the vision of human possibility that, more than any program, is the great contribution of classical liberalism.

For how could Julien Sorel make his gesture without the strain of liberalism in Stendhal's outlook? Or Pip break past the accumulated snobbisms of his England without the strain of liberalism in Dickens's outlook? Or Jude Fawley stumble toward his vision of the ennobled life without that strain in Hardy? And how, for that matter, could a writer like D.H. Lawrence, self-declared enemy of liberalism, suppose himself to be moving beyond its limits had not the luxury of that option been provided by liberalism?

Nor is it only for its energizing role of opposition that liberalism matters here. With some nineteenth-century writers liberalism also becomes the substance of a deeply serious and humane moral vision. What Mill invokes in his essays, George Eliot realizes in her fiction. Eliot, it is true, brings to her novels affections for English country life and received churchly pieties that contribute to that fullness of spirit we admire in her work. But what is distinctive in her work is the transfiguration of liberal opinion into moral sensibility. Respect for all living beings, belief in human potential, appreciation of differences among us that go deep and differences that merely amuse, and an awareness of the need for compassionate solidarity in facing the terribleness of life—these values are realized in George Eliot's work, values of liberalism made warm and vibrant.

But need we suppose that such values are unique to liberalism? I certainly would not wish to claim a monopoly of virtue for any political outlook. Yet it must be said that over the past two centuries it has been mainly liberalism, at least liberalism in its times of early freshness, that has done the most to advance such values. Perhaps it is in the nature of liberalism that it can gain social strength only when allied with other world-views, say, the ethical substance of Christianity or the political promise of democratic socialism. George Eliot's outlook has often been summarized as a "religion of humanity," as if thereby to acknowledge the still-vibrant residue of faith that sustains her novels. And that seems to me very well, for a true liberalism makes no demand for exclusiveness or even hegemony. It is always ready to welcome amiable partners.

Liberalism proves to be enabling for literature, especially the novel, in still another and more distinctively "literary" way. It provides an organizing principle through which nineteenth-century novelists can bound their worlds; it helps them locate the jostling plurality of groups and interests that comprises modern society; and it improvises linkages between the increasingly irksome and repressive actualities of our life and those unsubdued yearnings for transcendence that linger among sensitive people. *Jude the Obscure* seems a crucial instance, the pathos of its leading figures being inseparable from those visions of a truthful life that reached Hardy through writers like John Stuart Mill. But even when we turn to a novelist like Trollope, less fine-grained than either Eliot or Hardy and sometimes marred by that English complacency that takes the guise of heartiness, we find that his actions and characters are focused through the lens of a whiggish liberalism—it is his way of comprehending the world in which men must live and act.

II

Torn from the rib of John Locke, America presents a more complicated relation between literature and liberalism. When Locke says, "In the beginning all the world was America," he is saying more about America than "the beginning"; he has in mind, one supposes, that America began as an idea of Europe. Whatever may be reformative in European culture, and a modest part of whatever is revolutionary, finds a locus of desire in the *idea* of America. That our national experience diverges from this idea everyone has noticed, and the act of making that discovery soon becomes an essential part of the national experience. Through the cautions of our historians and the pain of our history, we have come to recognize as mere foolishness any claim for America as pure emanation of liberal virtue—there is plenty in our origins and still more in our development that is anything but liberal. Nevertheless, America as a distinctive civilization does emerge at least partly out of a Europe enlivened by the ferment of liberal thought. And this holds for both our institutions—the republic itself, our civil freedoms, the development of the party system—and our myths—America as a new Israel, the second chance for a fallen humanity.

Even in so illiberal a culture as New England Puritanism one can already see some of the reformative European energies at work. If the Puritans, in Perry Miller's striking phrase, regarded themselves as embarked on an errand into the wilderness, it was an errand shaped both by the changes under way in Europe and by the Nature they encountered in America. In its "incessant drive to learn how and how most ecstatically . . . to hold any sort of communion" with the unsullied Nature of the New World, this errand would be gradually transformed by the wilderness itself. Miller traces, from the early Puritan divines through Jonathan Edwards and then to the heretical Emerson, a continuity of search "to confront, face to face, the image of a blinding divinity in the physical universe"; but what is here most striking is how the Puritan errand was transformed by the wilderness it sought to transform, how that Nature that was to be graced by God's mission came to be seen as the source of grace. And in this change one can see the course of American myth itself, to be intertwined with our institutions as both complement and contrast.

This relationship between institutions and myth is crucial for an understanding of what happens to the sentiment of liberalism in nineteenth-century America—I say "sentiment" because the fate of liberalism in nineteenth-century America seems very much to be a gradual diffusion from original doctrine to shared feeling. "The great advantage of Americans," writes de Tocqueville, "is that they have arrived at a state of democracy without having to endure a democratic revolution." There is really no long-settled weight of reactionary traditions to throw over or guard against. Except perhaps when railing against the decadence of Europe, which soon becomes a kind of popular sport, liberalism in America cannot define itself as a force of opposition, a movement intent upon breaking down the barriers of the past. For the past is far away, across the ocean, or it lives secretively within the present, afflicting the consciousness of those who suppose it a sign of freedom that they wish to be rid of the past. The very prevalence of liberal assumptions, shared in part even by the more conservative thinkers among the Founding Fathers, seems to remove or lessen the need for a highly focused articulation of the liberal idea. What all accept, none feels obliged to argue. The major political groupings are to be distinguished not by whether they favor or reject the premises of a liberal polity, but by the degree of fervor or caution with which they advance them.*

The one large exception, of course, is to be heard among Southern ideologues trying to justify slavery. But even there it seems to be mainly a defensive impulse, a scraping together of bits and pieces of argument in behalf of the "peculiar institution." Slavery is a cancer in the body politic, but it does not radically deflect American thought from its democratic course. One can see a certain appropriateness in Henry Adams' description of America in the 1820s: "Except for Negro slavery, it was sound and healthy in every part. Stripped for the hardest work, every muscle firm and elastic, every ounce of brain ready for use, and not a trace of superfluous flesh on his nervous and supple body, the American stood in the world as a new order." Not the least interest of this passage is that it centers on that moment in the national experience when social reality and cultural myth are probably more harmonious than ever before or since.

It is a moment, as we also know, of rather severe social conflict. The Jacksonian upsurge represents an effort to extend the social promise of the republic; yet whatever terms we may wish to use for it—populist, plebeian, petty bourgeois— we aren't spontaneously inclined to think of it as an instance of liberalism. Nor of anything contrary to liberalism. It seems a phase in the transformation of received liberal values into that quasi-religious ethos of democratic individualism that dominates nineteenth-century American experience.

---

*The term "liberal" as a political designation that large numbers of Americans, especially educated ones, apply to themselves, is rarely to be found (so far as I can discover) in nineteenth-century American usage. "Liberal" as qualifying adjective, as in "liberal Christianity" or "liberal sentiments," yes; but "liberal" as a substantive political category, no.

But let us turn back for a moment, to the Founding Fathers, and ask ourselves what the authors of *The Federalist Papers* might have made of Locke's sentence, "In the beginning all the world was America." I imagine a dialogue between Madison and Hamilton. With a touch of asperity, Hamilton remarks that in trying to work out the foundations for a new republic they aren't, after all, composing by-laws for paradise—which by its very nature wouldn't require any. And Madison replies, yes, he had already suggested as much in a controversial *Federalist Paper*; yet it would be well for Mr. Hamilton to remember that Locke's remark had been a shrewd one, since without acknowledgment of the paradisal yearning in the imagination of our fellow Americans, we would hardly be in a position to work out the foundations of a new republic.

Hardheaded men, these Founding Fathers were proposing a political experiment largely in accord with Locke's prescription for a limited constitutional government; they believed in imposing restraints upon the very government to which they yielded powers; they were not romantic about either the New World or its inhabitants. Yet their entire enterprise presupposed *some* romanticism, some sense of the hold America had established upon the European imagination (otherwise, why would Lafayette have bothered to help?) and thereby on the American too. That romanticism seems to have been present, if only as a force to be confined, in the awareness of men like Madison and Hamilton. The former writes in *The Federalist Papers* a classical statement of the doctrine of countervailing powers:

> Ambition must be made to counteract ambition. . . .It may be a reflection on human nature that such devices should be necessary to control the abuses of government. But what is government itself but the greatest of all reflections on human nature? If men were angels, no government would be necessary. . . .

And Hamilton touches on the same theme in a more caustic style:

> Reflections of this kind [in behalf of a balance of power]may have trifling weight with men who hope to see realized in America the halcyon scenes of the poetic or fabulous age; but those who believe we are likely to experience a common portion of the vicissitudes and calamities which have fallen to the lot of other nations . . . etc., etc.

Now what seems most striking about these passages is the polemic against unspecified opponents, those who might suppose men to be angels or want to see realized in the New World halcyon scenes. Who could they be? Jeffersonians, no doubt, but also, perhaps, a good many Americans wearing no political tag. Writing such polemics, Madison and Hamilton were responding to something urgent and authentic in the American imagination, something they too must have felt if only in order to repudiate. And the question that must be faced is this: Could the principles upon which the American government was founded and the expectations that had arisen with the beginning of American settlement be reconciled? Can one bring together the worldly realism of *The Federalist Papers* with the Edenic nostalgia coursing through American literature?*

---

*This question as well as a few of the following paragraphs, are borrowed from an earlier essay of mine, "Anarchy and Authority in American Literature."

Much depends on what we mean by "bring together." Reconciling into a unity—no. But that the worldly realism and Edenic nostalgia could coexist in some subterranean relation of complicity and tension, I take to be a fact. The mundane workability of the republican arrangement enabled our literature to rise to that imaginative autonomy that distinguishes it in the nineteenth century. There is a close relation between the constraints of power built into the American system and the soaring of the American imagination toward visions of bliss where nature and spirit, individual and society find an ultimate harmony. The sturdiness and roominess of a stable liberal polity allow literature the freedom to "transcend" it and even oppose it in the name of higher values.

At least insofar as it yields itself to visions of democratic transcendence, the literary imagination of nineteenth-century America finds release through two channels: the thought of the Emersonians and the fiction of those writers who summon, through fables of solitary friendship, brief and fragile versions of anarchic community.

In Emersonian thought a major driving force is the wish to find a religious sanction for democratic sentiment, or, perhaps more accurately, to find a strategy for elevating democratic sentiment to religious emotion. The young Transcendentalists of the 1840s proposed, in Emerson's words, "to cast behind you all conformity, and acquaint men at first hand with Deity." And the best place, as it turned out, for making that acquaintance was within the self.

Emerson and his friends, in what amounted to a restatement of an old Christian heresy, raised the I to a quasi-divine status, so that man would now be seen not merely as a being like God but as a being that shares directly in the substance of divinity. Lending an air of sanctity to the persuasions of individualism, this outlook provided a new vision of man for a culture seeking to define itself as a new home for man. The culture that had arisen on the site of mankind's second beginning was declared, not yet a paradise, but a paradise in potential—or of potentiality.

All this was very stirring and served our literature wonderfully well. Not only did it stimulate Whitman to his vision of democratic man as one who exalts the glories of the autonomous self while, out of sheer exuberance, shuffling a supply of replaceable selves, it also provoked Hawthorne and Melville to their various embodyings of dissent. But—I repeat a point essential to my argument—even as the Emersonian view of man was released by the creation of a liberal polity, it is also a view that in crucial respects diverges from the assumptions of that polity.

The point may be illustrated by turning to Thoreau. For most of his life, though apparently less so toward the end, he looked upon freedom as an absolute state of being, which might be reached by men who shook off the torpor of convention and penetrated the roots of self. He was openly contemptuous of those who saw freedom as an arrangement between authority and citizens that necessarily involved social constraints. His vision of freedom was asocial; except by way of preliminary it did not depend on collective effort or established government; it was a state of being that each man could reach for himself, perhaps to be described as a romantic equivalent to the religious state of beatitude.

Now this is a powerful vision, and it has a permanent value, especially for those of us who reject it in principle because we accept the limits of a liberal society.

Thoreau, however, cared rather little about such a society or its limits; his commitment to an absolute selfhood—at its least attractive, a private utòpia for anarchic curmudgeons—implies an antipathy not only to the idea of government but to the very nature and necessary inconveniences of liberal government. Ultimately derived from liberalism, the Emersonian ethos has here been driven toward an antiliberal extreme.*

A somewhat similar pattern can be seen in major fictions written by Americans in the nineteenth century: Cooper, Twain, Melville. In their work the wish to break past the limits of society—perhaps even the limits of the human condition—manifests itself through images of space. They chart journeys not so much in order to get their heroes out of America but to transport the idea of America into a new and undefiled space. The urge to transcendence appears as accounts of men who move away, past frontiers and borders, into the "territory" or out to sea, in order to sustain images of communal possibility. For the enticements of space offer hopes of a new beginning, so that, for a time, an individual hero can be seen as reenacting, within or beyond society, the myth upon which the society rests but that it cannot fulfill. And in America this start is seen not so much as the liberal idea of reordering the social structure, but as a leap beyond the edge of society itself—a wistful ballet of transcendence.

A special kind of politics is at stake here: not the usual struggle among contending classes nor the interplay and mechanics of power, but a politics concerned with the *idea* of society itself, a politics that dares consider whether society is good and—still more wonderful question—whether society is necessary. These are the questions ultimately posed by the stories of Natty Bumppo and Chingachgook, Huck Finn and Nigger Jim, Ishmael and Queequeg—stories in which the search for transcendence shifts its locus from God to friendship and friendship becomes an emblem for an apolitical politics. A literature that on any manifest level seems hardly to be political at all, becomes the one to raise the most fundamental problems in political thought: what is the rationale for society, the justification for the state?

And if we agree for a moment so to regard nineteenth-century American writing, we discover running through it a strong if subterranean current of anarchism. Not anarchism as it is known to Europe, but anarchism as a social vision arising in preindustrial America, encouraged by the apparently secured triumph of the liberal polity and thereby resurgent fantasies of paradisal fulfillment.

Anarchism here signifies a vision of a human community beyond the social

---

*The point has been nicely argued by Heinz Eulau: "Thoreau was incapable of recognizing those distinctions of degree which are politically decisive. He could not recognize them because he fell back, again and again, on the principle of individual conscience as the sole valid guide in political action . . . [But]individual conscience as a political principle was too obviously in conflict with the democratic principle of majority rule, even for Thoreau. . . . His only way out was, once more, a paradox: 'Any man more right than his neighbors constitutes a majority of one already.' Consequently, Thoreau had to postulate a (by democratic standards) curious distinction between law and right, with the explanation that one has to have faith in man, that each man can determine for himself what is right and just. Hence, no conflict is possible, so the argument goes, because law is law only if identical with right. Thoreau could not demonstrate, however, that there is, in case the majority is wrong, an objective criterion for assaying the correctness of an individual's or a minority's judgment."

calculation of good and evil, beyond the need for the state as an apparatus of law and suppression, beyond the yardsticks of moral measurement, beyond the constraints of authority. It envisages a community of autonomous—one might almost say, Emersonian—persons, each secure in his own self. What is novel here is the assumption that because of our blessed locale we could find space in which to return, backward and free, to a stateless fraternity supposed to be anterior to and surely better than the liberal polity.

The oppressive system of laws, oppressive because they are laws, gives way to a self-ordering discipline of persons in a fraternal relationship. While this relationship is seen as enabled by and perhaps only possible within an unsullied nature, it is not so much the thought of pastorale that excites the major nineteenth-century American writers as it is a vision of human ease and comradeship being fulfilled within the pastoral setting. And thereby the problem of authority, perhaps the most difficult that can be faced in political thought, is imaginatively dissolved: a solution as inadequate as it is entrancing.

But even as the dream of paradise is lodged deeply in the imaginations of our nineteenth-century writers, they must live in a society Madison helped to form, Jackson to reform, and the expansion of American business to transform. The conviction that injustice and vulgarity grow stronger is shared by many of our nineteenth-century writers—a conviction that, finally, an America is being created that frustrates both the dream of a new Eden and the political idea of a liberal democracy. Neither in practice nor thought can our writers find a way of coping with this disenchantment. In their bitterness with the social reality and their growing sense of helplessness before it, American writers seek to get round the intractability of what they encounter. They summon poignant images of utopia—fragile, evanescent—on the borders of the forest, on rafts drifting down the Mississippi, on ships ruled by monomaniacal captains. Whatever they cannot change, they will turn away from, clinging meanwhile to the anarchic vision that seems all the more beautiful as it reaches into the distance of lost possibilities.

In the career of Herman Melville this pattern takes on a tragic and archetypal character. Speaking of the "democratic parable" as a major theme in Melville's work, Harold Kaplan has summarized its development:

> In its first step . . . the theme criticizes the obtuse tyrannies of cultural forms and exhibits the primary value of the person, equipped with nothing much more than the strong impulse to life. But it is equally critical in its second step, as it exposes the resourcelessness of mere freedom and the destructiveness of nature. . . . On its third level of understanding, it combines negatives and positives in order to safeguard freedom against the threat of order, and order against the threat of freedom.

Melville's early writings, up to and including *Moby Dick*, are suffused with visions of anarchic bliss. How deeply the paradisal dream remained lodged in his imagination we can gather from a poem, "To Ned," which he published in 1888, three years before his death. It is a poem addressed to Richard Tobias Green, Melville's companion in the South Pacific adventures recorded in his first book, *Typee*. The tone is nostalgic: "Where is the world we roved, Ned Bunn?" In the Marquesas that Melville and Ned had known in their youth, they "breathed primeval balm/From Eden's eye yet overrun," but now the author must marvel whether mortals can twice, "Here and hereafter, touch a Paradise." One can only envv a man who supposed he had touched it once.

Taipi as a tempting if also threatening Arcadia, the comely friendship between Ishmael and Queequeg before they submit to Ahab's compulsive authoritarianism—these are stages in Melville's celebration of a roaming freedom that leads, and perhaps must lead, to a final, saddened recognition of "the resourcelessness of mere freedom and the destructiveness of nature." The early books—though with clear anticipations of the doubts and cautions that will crowd the later ones—release Melville's distaste for those "forms," those arthritic regulations that in *Billy Budd* finally achieve their dubious victory. The young Melville exudes a plebeian hopefulness; he is utterly American in his democratic impatience with liberal constraints. Even in *Billy Budd* there is much social irony— muted, wary, despairing. Billy is an archetype of innocence, imaginable only as a creature of a utopian yearning so intense and yet so untenable in the life we must lead that Melville's mature imagination has no choice but fondly to destroy him. *Billy Budd* reflects Melville's weary disenchantment with the radical utopianism, the anarchism of his youth; by the time he came to write this story Melville could do no more than be the Abraham to his imaginary Isaac, sending to the sacrificial altar the boy who in gesture if not speech summoned the dream of his youth. He had come round, one might say, to a resigned perception of liberal necessities, those limits and injustices entailed by the mere fact of society.

Less stark yet rather similar in direction is the turning of the later Whitman, especially in his essays, "Democracy" and "Personalism," written in the late 1860s and fused into "Democratic Vistas" in 1871. In these prose writings we can still see Whitman the Emersonian, clinging to "sovereignty and sacredness of the individual" and finding "in the absolute Soul" of "each single individual something so transcendent" that it "places all beings on a common level." But there is also a new Whitman fumbling his way toward a stance of liberalism, trying to cope with a noisy mass culture and justifying his adherence to democracy not "on the ground that the People, the masses, even the best of them, are . . . essentially sensible or good," but simply because democracy seems "the only safe and preservative" mode of political life. These linked vocabularies speak of a tension between two styles of thought: the earlier quasi-religious democratic individualism and the emerging liberalism of the post-Civil War years. This liberalism—what I would call modern or social liberalism—tries to bring together a traditional liberal concern for personal rights and liberties with a belief that the very government long regarded as suspect must now actively reign in the excesses of industrial capitalism.

It is a liberalism that carries an air of puzzlement and disenchantment, a liberalism signifying a reluctant surrender of myth and dream. Emotionally still attached to the more innocent varieties of democratic faith, the writers who, like William Dean Howells, begin to move toward social liberalism (or socialism) seem to understand that they are being swept up as part of a reaction to American failures. The liberalism to which they now turn implies that America must share the destiny of other nations, the burdens and failures of history; it is a politics of making do.

From the high-minded individualism of E. L. Godkin, the editor of the *Nation* in the 1880s and 1890s, to the progressivism of Herbert Croly, who founds the *New Republic* in 1914 as an explicit advocate of a strong national government that is to serve as a kind of social umpire—this is to put into political terms what I have been trying to sketch as a shift of literary sentiment. The progressivism of a man like Croly, linked with the career and vagaries of Theodore Roosevelt, is by no means a simple matter, but it moves toward the essentials of twentieth-century American liberalism: an impatience with "the energetic and selfish individualism" that Croly saw as the heritage of the Jeffersonian past; a belief in the need for a strong reforming, central government; a commitment to social change that would right the imbalances cast up by *laissez faire*. This is a liberalism that accepts society as a given, struggles to tame large secondary institutions like the corporations and the trade unions, and cares more about controls and limits than transcendence and myth. It may not deny the uniqueness of the American tradition, but it insists that any effort to cling to the views or language of Jefferson, Jackson, and Emerson is simply self-deluding.

The early *New Republic* is especially important here, for even as it provides a major articulation of social liberalism it also opens its pages to a great many new writers, including the earliest American defenders of cultural modernism, who either have no politics at all or find liberalism inadequate or uninteresting. The magazine does not seek to recreate that intimate, flowing relationship between collective myth and literary expression that makes nineteenth-century America seem so remarkable; it accepts the likelihood that between liberalism and literature there will now be a distance, even a decided coolness. Yet it assumes that liberalism has the responsibility for creating conditions of freedom and generosity in which literature may flourish, even if one result is that literature will pain and shock the liberal mind. This relationship is nicely reflected in the practice of the *New Republic*, during its best early days and later under Edmund Wilson's literary editorship, of granting the "back of the book," where poetry and criticism appear, a latitude of opinion and sensibility not always tolerated in its political pages. Admirable as this arrangement seems, it constitutes a mode of coexistence rather than of fraternity. Thus one finds in this anthology of literary material from the *New Republic* a number of very distinguished names—Frost, Auden, Nabokov, Lawrence, Yeats—that are not usually associated with the main lines of twentieth-century American liberalism. Some of these writers have scorned and openly attacked liberalism, usually from the right. If one brings to bear upon this problem the customary liberal value of tolerance, it is possible to say that the recurrent presence of such writers has been a source of intellectual strength, perhaps even a sign that the magazine has had enough self-confidence in its own tradition to allow a wide range of cultural voices to speak through its pages. But admirable as such an arrangement may be, there is —one had better acknowledge—another possible way of looking at it: as a kind of intellectual self-limitation, a tacit recognition that the relation between liberalism and literature in the twentieth century seems, at best, closer to wary coexistence than fruitful friendship. It indicates a profound limitation in the reach of liberalism—for no longer can there be a serious claim that it advances a world-view capable of inspiring the whole of society and culture.

III

In twentieth-century American writing—we will merely glance at it—the influence of social liberalism is obviously large, though I doubt that any serious reader would challenge my impression that the influence of Emersonianism remains considerably larger. In the work of almost every significant novelist following Dreiser, the criticism of commercial values that liberalism develops as a major theme, finds both echo and embodiment. A writer like Frost who clings to a brittle native individualism, seems driven in his inferior work to mere ideological posturing—there is an ungainly wilfulness in that New Hampshire mask of his. In the early Hemingway traditional American individualism has been burnished to a fine stoical defense, later to yield to a grudging recognition of those communal sentiments prompted by liberalism. In the work of Fitzgerald an exquisite balance is struck between the American democratic myth and the later liberal critique. *The Great Gatsby* brings together the theme of utopian yearning (that receding green light) and the theme of social waste, as if to span two eras of American understanding. And even in the work of William Faulkner, a professed opponent of liberalism, its influence remains powerful. A book like *Light in August* stems from a conscious, if despairing, adherence to traditional Southern values, but the energy of anger, the thrust of violence represented by Joe Christmas suggests that the liberal critique of modern society had registered on Faulkner's imagination—registered against his will, perhaps, but powerfully nonetheless, since he was a deeply honest writer who could not help acknowledging truths not his own.

I have flitted past some of the major figures of twentieth-century American writing, but if one considers the names of other, scarcely less distinguished writers whose work appears in these pages, the influence of social liberalism seems equally evident. For Edmund Wilson, liberalism takes on a rockier, more native cast, it figures as an American memory, a residual integrity. Only, by the late 1920s, it seems to have failed. He lurches briefly "leftward," toward Stalinism, then for a time toward the fragile groupings of the anti-Stalinist radical intellectuals, and finally into a stance of personal opposition, a truculent resistance to the cant of our time—all of these being developments that reflect an original bafflement and disappointment with the liberal heritage. For a writer like Robert Penn Warren, self-consciously emerging as a Southern figure, liberalism at first seems emotionally thin, much too rationalistic, excessively interlocked with the mechanism of the industrial city; yet in his deepest feelings, in his instinctive sympathies for underdogs and his growing awareness of the claims of the blacks, he too has been deeply affected by the liberalism that, in theory, he may still declare himself to reject. And so it goes for a great many American writers in our century: For those who may sneer at liberalism, as John Dos Passos did in the late 1920s when, for a little while, he became a contributor to the communist *New Masses*; for those who declare liberalism to be philosophically superficial, as Lewis Mumford has from time to time, and as, in a different way, the Southern writers have frequently done; and for those who have attacked it for timorousness, an unwillingness to move toward a radical social program (as have any number of *New Republic* contributors, including the present writer, over the years). Yet what seems so remarkable is that it is liberalism, in its large American orbit and its continued hold upon the language and limits of our politics, that remains the central force—central morally, intellectually, politically—toward which so many of our writers have had to orient themselves, sometimes in affection, sometimes repulsion, sometimes an uncomfortable mixture of the two.

Still, things are very different from what they were in the "classical" moment of American romanticism a century earlier. The relationship between liberal belief and literary work is at best uneasy and tense; there is mutual influence, but also incomplete sympathy and entangled opposition.

IV

In the past, then, there were times when liberalism and literature could strike up a fruitful intimacy, sometimes marriage and sometimes liaison. This usually occurred when liberalism had become clenched into a force of opposition to entrenched privilege or power, or when, in unexpected security, it had become diffused into a quasi-religious myth or mystique. The second of these options now seems unavailable: this is hardly an age for a Whitman. The first is being reenacted in the world of Eastern Europe where the most courageous writers gain their energy from the vision of a liberalized society. Some of these writers, to be sure, do not think of themselves as liberals; others, like Solzhenitsyn, now declare themselves to be opponents of liberalism, scorning it in ways that remind one of Dostoevsky and Tolstoy. But the logic of their situation, as social and moral critics of the authoritarian state, presses them to offer as a vibrant counterimage the possibility of a society where men are free to speak, and dissidence will not lead to the camps. No matter what Solzhenitsyn's formal declarations or later ideological turnings, his two major novels, *The First Circle* and *The Cancer Ward*, rest upon this vision as it might enable his Nerzhins and Rubins and Sologdins to live as free men. When struggling for elementary rights in the claustrophobic spaces of authoritarianism, the liberal vision can again take on historical urgency and moral force.

But with us in the West, where liberalism is more or less accepted as the common ground of public life and where, by now, it has taken many bruises, many stains, it has to accept a decidedly more modest relation to the life of culture. It probably has to forgo tragic and heroic themes, since precisely its public virtues—doubt, hesitation and irony—make those themes largely inaccessible. But comedy remains a major possibility, especially if the writer touched by liberalism can turn upon its snobbisms and affectations, while still finding in it some strands of virtue. If we glance at the greatest work of fiction composed in English during our century, we find at its center a roly-poly pacific Jew, a small figure of tolerance, muddle, and affection, a creature quite the opposite of the hero, a man liberal almost by default, as if he could not be anything else. Yet in these comic limitations there are values to be honored, a precious sediment of civilization.

Between liberalism and literature there must now be a relation of uneasiness, suspicion, disaffection. Modernist literature has strained toward extreme instances, impatience before compromise and commonplace, and a vision of the agonistic, the ultimate. Modernist literature has shown little taste or capacity for "balance." The legend of modernist literature has inclined the great writers of the last century to see themselves as heroes, acknowledged or neglected, while liberalism, except when summoning men to resist tyranny, works on a smaller scale. By now liberalism does not have much glamour and self-assurance; it is likely to be cut off from the great myths of tradition; it feels decidedly uneasy before the allurements of transcendence. But when we look back at the murderous intoxications of our century, we may find it in our hearts to feel kindlier to these moderate virtues.

If, then, we finally turn again to Mr. Trilling's complaint against liberalism—that it "has not been able to produce a body of literature which can strongly engage our emotions"—I think it reasonable to say that he was perhaps asking too much from liberalism, demanding from it powers that at this point in history it cannot have. Liberalism (and in some European countries, one might add, social democracy) is now committed to a defense and extension of the welfare state, and whatever the practical uses of this politics may be, it is not likely to yield large images of dramatic possibility or heroic challenge.

The great virtue of liberalism is that it creates the conditions that enable writers to take a measure of its failings, to rail against its deficiencies of vision, to cry out that a merely tolerable world is not enough. They are right: it is not enough. But let them also be certain that in so crying out, they do not repeat the terrible mistake of a good many writers sixty and seventy years ago, which was to help create an intolerable world.

Editor's Note

This anthology covers sixty years. It may be read as a chronicle of the literary life of America; but it is also, and perhaps more tellingly, a chronicle of the literary life of a single magazine. It was my intention as editor that this selection from among thousands of essays, narratives, reviews, stories, poems, be even in quality or rather consistent in its high quality. But the reader will quickly recognize that what is here reprinted is not an equal representation of the decades: Genuine literary and aesthetic standards pay no special heed to an imputed democracy of time, which is why most of what I have chosen clusters into discernible (and definable) periods.

The earliest of these spans the years between what was then still the one Great War and the Great Crash. A liberal magazine, quite certain of its politics, less certain of its views on culture and the arts, demonstrated a remarkable openness to contradictory or at least disparate visions. Frost, Lawrence, Yeats, Mencken, Santayana, who did not share *TNR's* social convictions, appeared in its pages, as did Shaw, who might have seemed to share some of them. This was the era in which Clive Bell and Leo Stein wrote on the new painting, Paul Rosenfeld on the new music, Willa Cather on the novel, Stark Young and Francis Hackett on theater and the newest of the forms, the movies. If *TNR's* politics predisposed it to what was fresh or innovative in the culture, there remained nonetheless a tension and disjunction between the magazine's rational liberal mind and its artistic imagination.

The Depression, however, evoked a harmony of concern, and the passions of politics became the obsessions of literature. This was an especially rich period for *TNR*: The distinctions between the "back of the book" and its front began to erode. Both had become radicalized. But again, its literary pages were freer, less predictable than its political ones, which often seemed precariously poised between program and dogma, the alternating responses of liberalism to the pressures of economic collapse, the Spanish Civil War, and the rise of Hitlerism. Both Edmund Wilson and Malcolm Cowley as literary editors regarded social issues as within their proper domain, drawing to the magazine the most articulate and most talented of the politically engaged. Better able to avoid the dubious disciplines of fellow traveling than their colleagues with explicit political responsibilities, they established *TNR* as a controversial forum in which such diverse writers as Louis Kronenberger, Granville Hicks, and Allen Tate struggled with the dissonant demands of craft and ideals. The debates over Humanism were fought in their pages, including Michael Gold's vicious attack on Thornton Wilder. A full-scale literary class war was waged over Archibald MacLeish's "Invocation to the Social Muse."

At this time also the genre of reportage emerged. A curious new prose style, rooted in muckraking journalism and the naturalism of Zola and Norris, it was all at once intensely personal and intensely political. Lillian Hellman, Ernest

Hemingway, Sherwood Anderson, were among its most noted adepts, both commentators and participants creating a role for themselves in headlines and history.

These quite different clusters, then, are the literary high points of *TNR's* past. The war years that followed were not a notably creative period, a poverty mirrored in the magazine. But even the more interesting cultural modes of the 1950s and 1960s were only spottily reflected in *The New Republic*, which had been thrust into a new political universe and remained settled into a literary one that had lost its vitality. The new criticism prospered in the smaller magazines and the scholarly journals; the beats and the more resilient experimentalists found tribunes and interpreters elsewhere. Fiction all but disappeared from *TNR* and in the last few years, especially, poetry was published almost as filler.

Retrospectively, the 1950s symbolized the isolation of programmatic liberalism from the intellectual and creative life. No one has yet adequately appraised the deadening of sensibility induced by McCarthyism, but it was evident everywhere. Moreover, the politics of incremental reform did not, as it turned out, have a very soulful side. And fighting the Cold War—or even fighting against it—tended to be a hortatory enterprise, not hospitable to the refinements of the tradition or the enticements of the vanguard. Specialization, which took over in the professions and the universities, was ascendant in the magazines, and this magazine as well: The essay gave way to the review, the general to the precise. No Edmund Wilson would then grope toward *Axel's Castle* and *To the Finland Station* in the pages of *The New Republic*; no Malcolm Cowley toward *Exile's Return*; no Alfred Kazin toward *On Native Ground*. Wilson could "rhapsodize" in a thousand words on a summer breeze in Paris or a streetcar in Manhattan; would some rising young assistant professor of English somewhere, anywhere, find that serious? Lippmann could write of Amy Lowell's poems; would Arthur Schlesinger?

And yet, and yet ... a forum no longer, the magazine still remained a platform for distinctive voices, singularly vigorous in their own standards and also insistent on social meanings in literature: Irving Howe and Mary McCarthy, Lionel Trilling and Leon Edel, Eric Bentley and Pauline Kael, among others. And despite such distinguished literary editors as Richard Gilman and Reed Whittemore, such eminent regulars as Stanley Kauffmann and Robert Brustein and their influence, the magazine itself appeared to be on the margins of our literary life. Reading (and writing for)*The New Republic* was for someone committed to literature or art, no longer compelling.

The New Republic, then as now, had an impact, largely political. This was best reflected in the satisfaction felt by the magazine's editors when a newspaper photograph showed John Kennedy boarding the presidential plane with a current issue of *TNR* clutched tightly under his arm. They knew that he was reading them. At that moment, it would seem, the "back of the book" not only came second, but became, quite without anyone's regret, secondary.

Will a later anthologist find clusters of literary and artistic excellence in the seventh or eighth decades? It will depend, perhaps primarily, on what happens in our literature but also on whether the editors of *The New Republic* find the "back of the book" as central to their concerns, and indeed related to the deeper politics of America, as is the front.

Washington, D.C.   EDWARD ZWICK
January 1976

PROSE

Second Mortgage

The bell rang and I went to the window to see who it was.

"Don't answer it," my father called. "It may be a summons."

"They can't serve summonses on Sunday," I said, parting the curtains cautiously.

"Don't answer it, anyway." My father came into the living-room. He didn't know how to handle bill collectors. They bullied him and he made wild promises, very seriously, to pay, and never did and they'd come and hound him terribly. When he was home alone he never answered the doorbell. He never even went to look to see who it was. He just sat in the kitchen reading the paper while the bell clanged over his head. Even the postman couldn't get the front door opened when my father was home alone.

The bell rang again. "What the hell," I said, "it's only a little old lady. She's probably selling something. We can open the door."

"What for?" my father asked. "We can't buy anything."

I opened the door anyway. The little old lady jumped when the door swung back. Her hands fluttered. They were plump little hands, swollen, without gloves. "I'm Mrs. Shapiro," she said, waiting.

I waited. She tried to smile. I waited sternly. Strangers are never friends at the doors of the poor. I was only seventeen but I had learned that anyone who rang our doorbell might turn out to be the Edison Electric Company or the Brooklyn Borough Gas Company, intent on shutting off the electricity or the gas.

Mrs. Shapiro hunched inside her shapeless little coat. "I own the second mortgage," she said.

Still I waited, sternly. Another enemy.

Her hand came out, cold, plump and pleading. "I want to speak to your father, maybe," she said.

My father had retreated to the kitchen and the Sunday Times, hoping that nothing would happen at the front door that would require his tearing himself out of that peaceful welter of journalism.

"Pop!" I called. I heard him sigh and the rustle of the Sunday Times as he put down the editorial page. Mrs. Shapiro came in and I closed the door. My father came in, wiping his glasses, longing for the kitchen.

"This is Mrs. Shapiro, Pop," I said. "She owns the second mortgage."

3

"Yes." Mrs. Shapiro was eager and bright and apologetic for a moment. She moved into the middle of the room. There were runs in her fat little stockings and her shoes were shapeless. "I came because. . . ."

"Yes," my father said, with his imitation of a businesslike attitude, that he always tried on bill collectors and which he lost as soon as they started to bully him. "Yes. Of course. Just a moment. . . . My wife . . . my wife knows more about this than . . . Oh . . . Helen! Helen!"

My mother came downstairs, fixing her hair.

"Mrs. Shapiro," my father said. "The second mortgage. . . ."

"It's this way," Mrs. Shapiro said, moving toward my mother." In 1929, I. . . ."

"Won't you sit down?" My mother pointed to a chair. She glanced at my father, tightening her mouth. My mother was always contemptuous if my father proved unequal to the task of beating off the representatives of our poverty.

Mrs. Shapiro sat on the very edge of the chair, leaning forward, her knees together. "The second mortgage is eight hundred dollars," Mrs. Shapiro said. We all sat silent. Mrs. Shapiro was disheartened by the silence, but she went on, her fat gray cheeks moving anxiously over her words. "Eight hundred dollars is a lot of money," she said.

We didn't contradict her.

"In 1929," Mrs. Shapiro said, "I had eight thousand dollars." She looked to our faces for pity, envy, anything. We sat there expressionless, with the faces of people who have become used to owing money. "Eight thousand dollars. I worked all my life for it. I had a vegetable store. It's hard to make money in vegetables nowadays. Vegetables are expensive and they spoil and there is always somebody else who sells them cheaper than you can. . . ."

"Yes," my mother said, "vegetables are very expensive. I paid twenty cents for a head of cauliflower yesterday. . . ."

"It wasn't any good, either," my father said. "I don't like cauliflower. It reminds me of cabbage, somehow."

"When Mr. Shapiro died of cancer, it took him two years to die," Mrs. Shapiro went on, trying to please us. "I had eight thousand dollars. I had rheumatism and high blood pressure and I couldn't take care of the store any more." Once more she begged our faces for that crumb of pity. "I took the eight thousand dollars out of the bank and I went to Mr. Mayer and I said, 'Mr. Mayer, you're a big man, you have a fine reputation, I am giving you a widow's life savings, invest it for me so that I have enough to live on. I don't need much, Mr. Mayer,' I told him, 'just a few dollars a week until I die, that's all,' I said, 'just a few dollars.'"

"I know Mayer," my father said. "He's not doing so well now. The Trust Company's in receivership now."

"Mr. Mayer," Mrs. Shapiro said with passion, her fists quivering on her little thighs, "is a crook! He took my money and he put it out in second mortgages. Eight thousand dollars' worth of second mortgages!"

She stopped. For the moment she could not say another word.

"Today," my father said, "even first mortgages are no good. Nothing's any good any more."

"In the last two years," Mrs. Shapiro said, her eyes brimming with tears, "I haven't got a penny out of them . . . out of eight thousand dollars' worth of second mortgages, not a penny." A little rag of handkerchief came out and wiped at her eyes. "I used to go to Mr. Mayer and he'd tell me I'd have to wait. How long can I wait? I don't have with what to eat now, as it is! Can I wait longer than that?" Triumphantly she wept. "Now Mr. Mayer won't see me anymore. They tell me he's out when I go there. It doesn't do any good to go there." She stopped, wiping her eyes. We sat, uncomfortable and still.

"I'm going to the houses where I have the second mortgages," Mrs. Shapiro said. "Nice houses, they are, like this. With rugs and curtains and steam heat and something cooking on the stove that you can smell inside. I have the second mortgage on houses like that, and I don't have enough to eat. . . ." Her tears soaked through the rag of a handkerchief. "Please," she cried, "please—give me something. I don't want the eight hundred dollars, but something. It's my money . . . I have nobody. I have rheumatism and there's no heat in my room and there're holes in my shoes. I walk on my bare feet. Please. . . . Please. . . ."

We tried to stop her but she kept on, crying, "Please . . . please . . . just a little bit. A hundred dollars. Fifty. My money. . . ."

"All right, Mrs. Shapiro," my father said. "Come back next Sunday. I'll have it for you then."

The tears stopped. "Oh, God bless you," Mrs. Shapiro said. Before we knew what she was about, she flung herself across the room and was on her hands and knees in front of my father and was kissing his hand wildly. "God bless you, God bless you," she cried over and over again. My father sat through it nervously, trying to pick her up with his free hand, looking pleadingly at my mother.

Finally my mother could bear it no longer. "Mrs. Shapiro," she said, breaking in over the "God bless you's," "listen to me! Stop that! Please stop it! We can't give you anything! Next Sunday or any Sunday. We haven't got a cent."

Mrs. Shapiro dropped my father's hand. She stayed on her knees in front of him, though, looking strange there in the middle of our living room. "But Mr. Ross said. . . ."

"Mr. Ross is talking nonsense!" my mother said. "We have no money and we're not going to have any. We expect to be thrown out of the house any day now! We can't give you a penny, Mrs. Shapiro."

"But next Sunday. . . ." Mrs. Shapiro tried to make my mother understand that she didn't expect it now, not for another week.

"We won't have any more next Sunday than we have today. And we have eighty-five cents in the house right now, Mrs. Shapiro!" My mother stood up, went over to Mrs. Shapiro, where she was kneeling on the floor. Before my mother could touch her, Mrs. Shapiro keeled over onto the floor, hitting it heavily, like a packed handbag that's been dropped.

It took us ten minutes to pull her out of her faint. My mother gave her tea, which she drank silently. She didn't seem to recognize us as she drank her tea and made ready to go. She told us that this was the fifth time in two months that she had fainted like that. She seemed ashamed of herself, somehow. My mother gave her the address of a doctor who would wait for his money and Mrs. Shapiro went out, her fat, shabby stockings shaking as she went down the steps. My mother and I watched her as she shambled down the street and disappeared around the corner, but my father went into the kitchen and The New York Times.

She was back the next Sunday and two Sundays after that, ringing the bell, but we didn't open the door. She rang for almost a half-hour each time, but we all sat quietly in the kitchen, waiting for her to go away.

JOHN CHEEVER   SEPTEMBER 8, 1937

The Teaser

After that last week in Boston, Harcourt decided to fire Beatrice. She was through. Even the gallery didn't clap for encores, whatever she gave them. Harcourt didn't want to do it, but she was fifty-two years old and she would have to realize sometime that younger women were going to take her place. He didn't want to do it because he knew it would nearly kill her. No one else would give her a job; at least not on the stage doing teasers and that was the only thing she could do. On the night he put the notice in her pay envelope, he watched her from the back of the house. It confirmed his decision. Her face and figure were still good, but she had lost the trick. In growing older she had grown more confident and proud until she didn't make any effort to put it over. She made the house feel like dirt. After the intermission he went downtown. He wasn't going to be around when she got the news. She was a strong woman, still handsome, and she'd put up a fight. So he went downtown to a movie.

That was on Saturday night. After the show there was a rehearsal. The two leading comedians knew that Beatrice was through and somehow the girls had found out about it. After they were paid they stood around the stage waiting for Cohen to call the rehearsal and waiting for Beatrice to climb the iron stairs that wound up from the dressing-rooms and make the noise everyone expected her to make. For once there was no jealousy. They were not only sorry; they were frightened. None of the girls liked Beatrice. She never got along with the other women and never called the girls by their names. They stood around waiting, with their coats over their costumes, their tarnished dancing shoes showing. They felt as if they were responsible for her middle age. As if they ought to apologize.

They heard her running up the iron treads as she always came up those stairs. She was dressed in street clothes and she looked nice. She was carrying a big leather purse under one arm. Instead of saying anything she walked right through the wings, right by the mail rack and out the door. From the window someone saw her hailing a cab. She looked as if she meant business. She might have something on Harcourt that would make him keep her. Cohen called the rehearsal and the girls lined up. A little after midnight Harcourt came back and went up to Cohen, who was standing by the piano.

"What did Beatrice do?" he asked.

"She didn't do anything. She just got into her street clothes and went out."

"Oh, God. That's worse," Harcourt said. "She probably thinks she can sue me. She probably thinks she has something on me. But she hasn't. She hasn't anything on me."

On Sunday the whole show moved up to Portland by bus and they opened with a matinee on Monday. All the time Harcourt kept expecting to hear from Beatrice, but nothing happened. He didn't believe she would take it quietly. Her place was being taken by a younger girl named Marie Badu. She was a dark French-Canadian with a long build and swarthy skin. The orchestra played muted, rapid music and after the first encore she raced around the stage giving them all of it before they knew what they were seeing.

It was in January and there was a heavy snow on the ground. The girls were complaining about the snow and the cold all the time. They couldn't seem to heat the theatre and the air in the dressing-rooms and on the stage was stale and cold. It was an old house that was only opened two or three times a season and it smelt of camphor and disinfectant. After the first two nights the audience fell off. The gallery was always full but across the foot-lights and through the smoke you could see blocks of empty seats on the floor and no one ever sat in the boxes.

Marie Badu was leaving the theatre after the last show on Wednesday. She was quiet and she took her work seriously and she didn't talk with the line girls. She was walking up the alley that led from the stage door to the street. The eaves of the theatre overhung the sidewalk and the melting snow from the roof had frozen again on the paving. She stepped carefully in her high-heeled shoes, but halfway down on the walk she slipped. Her left foot went forward and she fell, bending her right leg backwards from the knee. Some of the girls, coming out a few minutes later, found her there by the wall.

"Oh, for God's sake," she said softly, when they stopped. "Oh, for God's sake, don't stand around like a lot of saps, do something. I'm sorry," she added quickly, "but it hurts, it hurts. It hurts." One of the girls called a cab and they took her to a hospital. Her right leg was broken.

Harcourt didn't know what to do. They only had one other teaser in the show and one wasn't enough. It would take a girl a day and a night to come on from New York. There was no one in Boston but Beatrice. He didn't want to see her again. He was afraid to see her. He decided to try out one of the line girls. He took the prettiest one, a plump, fresh-looking blonde and rehearsed her all morning. She was anxious to get ahead and she was willing to do anything. But she couldn't seem to fall into it. She was slow and even shy. Harcourt stood in the back of the dark, dead theatre and shouted at her until he was hoarse.

"Give it to 'em. Shake it up. You're not here to embarrass them."

"Yes, Mr. Harcourt."

He put her on for the matinee, but when he went back to the office he wired Beatrice's hotel and called her to Portland.

They were buying tickets for the last show when she came into the office. She was wearing her black street clothes and she looked smart. Her face was pale and just enough bleached hair showed under her hat.

"What do you want?" she said.

"Now listen, Beatrice. I'm in a bad way. Sit down, sit down. Marie broke her leg on the ice in the alley and I'm short a girl. I want you to go on for me."

"You mean you want me to go on for the rest of the week?"

"That's it."

"Well, I'm not going to," she said quietly.

"Now listen, Beatrice. I'm in a bad way. With only one other girl we'll go so much in the red that it'll take us a month to pull out. I've done some bad things to you. I've done some good things. If you'll just do this for me."

"I'm not signing up for any three-day appearances. I'm not a substitute yet. The round trip up here cost six dollars. That's on you. Give me the money and I'll take the train back tonight."

"Now listen, Beatrice."

"If you want me to sign up for the rest of the season it's all right. But not for any three days. I know you think I'm through. You think I'm an old woman, don't you? But I'm not. I can give it to them as well as any other girl on this circuit."

"How about a hundred dollars for the three days?"

"I tell you I'm not signing up for any three-day appearances whatever you pay me. Give me the six dollars. If you keep me here arguing I'll miss the train and it'll cost you a hotel bill."

Although Harcourt had pushed a chair toward her she was still standing.

"Well, suppose we call the three days a trial, then. You go on for three days and if they like you I'll keep you on for the rest of the season."

"If I make good I'll be on for the rest of the season?"

"Yes, you'll be on for the rest of the season."

She looked straight at him. Her eyes were clear and her features were firm and pleasant. She looked fifty-two, but she was still attractive. Her figure was mature and athletic. The black dress gave her dignity. She looked like a widow.

"I won't make you sign any papers," she said. "I'll take your word for it. If you'll show me where the dressing-rooms are I'll go on before the intermission."

When she went on Harcourt was standing in the wings watching her and so were all the girls. They knew that something like a trial was up. She came in from the right on slow music. She was wearing a white evening dress that trailed on the floor. Her bleached hair shone in the light. She came up to the footlights and sang her song and then, to slower music, began to walk idly, proudly around the stage, loosening the dress at her breasts. She had a quiet, wise smile on her face as if she knew everything in the world.

When she came off the indifferent applause sounded from backstage like someone spilling a pail of water. She went on again, under a pink light, her head lifted, the quiet, wise smile on her face. She knew her stuff and each exit was timed perfectly. On the third encore she had taken off everything but her skirt and she had this draped tightly around her body like a shawl. She came up to the footlights and dropped this onto the floor. The house was dead silent. A couple of men lighted cigarettes. Then she walked to the back of the stage and turned around. Harcourt was watching her all the time. The orchestra leader knew what she wanted and the drum began a brutal, monotonous beat. She lifted her arms, locked her hands at the back of her neck and began to buck.

It brought the house down. Harcourt had never heard a noise like that. From the wings it sounded like a heavy rain and thunder and above it you could hear them whistling from the gallery. He didn't know what she was doing until Cohen, who had been standing in the back of the house, came running up to him.

"God, she's wonderful," he said. He was laughing and breathing so heavily that he could hardly speak. "She's had someone paint a coupla red hands on her fanny. She's wonderful."

Instead of laughing with Cohen, Harcourt acted as if he hadn't heard, and walked away. He walked through the flats, out by the mail-rack, away from the clapping and the stamping. He walked out into the cold alley and stood there feeling as if he had sat beside her on all those desperate days and nights when she had sat in her hotel room, thinking it up, watching the traffic below her window.

KATHERINE MANSFIELD   MARCH 28, 1923

Six Years After*

It was not the afternoon to be on deck—on the contrary. It was exactly the afternoon when there is no snugger place than a warm cabin, a warm bunk. Tucked up with a rug, a hot water bottle and a piping hot cup of tea, she would not have minded the weather in the least. But he hated cabins, hated to be inside anywhere more than was absolutely necessary. He had a passion for keeping, as he called it, above board, especially when he was travelling. And it wasn't surprising, considering the enormous amount of time he spent cooped up in the office. So, when he rushed away from her as soon as they got on board and came back five minutes later to say he had secured two deck chairs on the lee side and the steward was undoing the rugs, her voice through the high sealskin collar murmured "Good": and because he was looking at her, she smiled with bright eyes and blinked quickly, as if to say, "Yes, perfectly all right—absolutely." And she meant it.

"Then we'd better—" said he, and he tucked her hand inside his arm and began to rush her off to where their chairs stood. But she had just time to breathe, "Not so fast, Daddy, please," when he remembered too and slowed down.

---

* There is good reason to believe that this unfinished story is the last to which Katherine Mansfield set her hand. A first draft of it was written in 1921. With this she was evidently dissatisfied. Her papers show that she took it up again many times. The final version apparently written about November 1922, breaks off abruptly at the words: "Can one do nothing for the dead? And for a long time the answer had been—Nothing!" The two final paragraphs are taken from an earlier version.

J. Middleton Murry

Strange! They had been married twenty-eight years, and it was still an effort to him, each time, to adapt his pace to hers.

"Not cold, are you?" he asked, glancing sideways at her. Her little nose, geranium pink above the dark fur, was answer enough. But she thrust her free hand into the velvet pocket of her jacket and murmured gaily, "I shall be glad of my rug."

He pressed her tighter to his side—a quick nervous pressure. He knew, of course, that she ought to be down in the cabin; he knew that it was no afternoon for her to be sitting on deck, in this cold and raw mist, lee side or no lee side, rugs or no rugs, and he realized how she must be hating it. But he had come to believe that it really was easier for her to make these sacrifices than it was for him. Take their present case, for instance. If he had gone down to the cabin with her, he would have been miserable the whole time, and he couldn't have helped showing it. At any rate, she would have found him out. Whereas, having made up her mind to fall in with his ideas, he would have betted anybody she would even go so far as to enjoy the experience. Not because she was without personality of her own. Good Lord! She was absolutely brimming with it. But because . . . but here his thoughts always stopped. Here they always felt the need of a cigar, as it were. And looking at the cigar-tip, his fine blue eyes narrowed. It was a law of marriage, he supposed. . . . All the same, he always felt guilty when he asked these sacrifices of her. That was what the quick pressure meant. His being said to her being: "You do understand, don't you?" and there was an answering tremor in her fingers, "I *understand*."

Certainly, the steward—good little chap—had done all in his power to make them comfortable. He had put up their chairs in whatever warmth there was and out of the smell. She did hope he would be tipped adequately. It was on occasions like these (and her life seemed to be full of such occasions) that she wished it was the woman who controlled the purse.

"Thank you, steward. That will do beautifully."

"Why are stewards so often delicate-looking?" she wondered, as her feet were tucked under. "This poor little chap looks as though he'd got a chest, and yet one would have thought . . . the sea air. . . ."

The button of the pigskin purse was undone. The tray was tilted. She saw sixpences, shillings, half-crowns.

"I should give him five shillings," she decided, "and tell him to buy himself a good nourishing—"

He was given a shilling, and he touched his cap and seemed genuinely grateful.

Well, it might have been worse. It might have been sixpence. It might, indeed. For at that moment Father turned towards her and said, half-apologetically, stuffing the purse back, "I gave him a shilling. I think it was worth it, don't you?"

"Oh, quite! Every bit!" said she.

It is extraordinary how peaceful it feels on a little steamer once the bustle of leaving port is over. In a quarter of an hour one might have been at sea for days. There is something almost touching, childish, in the way people submit themselves to the new conditions. They go to bed in the early afternoon, they shut their eyes and "it's night" like little children who turn the table upside down and cover themselves with the tablecloth. And those who remain on deck—they seem to be always the same, those few hardened men travellers—pause, light their pipes, stamp softly, gaze out to sea, and their voices are subdued as they walk up and down. The long-legged little girl chases after the red-checked boy, but soon both are captured; and the old sailor, swinging an unlighted lantern, passes and disappears. . . .

He lay back, the rug up to his chin and she saw he was breathing deeply. Sea air! If any one believed in sea air, it was he. He had the strongest faith in its tonic qualities. But the great thing was, according to him, to fill the lungs with it the moment you came on board. Otherwise, the sheer strength of it was enough to give you a chill. . . .

She gave a small chuckle, and he turned to her quickly. "What is it?"

"It's your cap," she said. "I never can get used to you in a cap. You look such a thorough burglar."

"Well, what the deuce am I to wear?" He shot up one gray eyebrow and wrinkled his nose. "It's a very good cap, too. Very fine specimen of its kind. It's got a very rich white satin lining." He paused. He declaimed as he had hundreds of times before at this stage, "Rich and rare were the gems she wore."

But she was thinking he really was childishly proud of the white satin lining. He would like to have taken off his cap and made her feel it. "Feel the quality!" How often had she rubbed between finger and thumb his coat, his shirt cuff, tie, sock, linen handkerchief, while he said that.

She slipped down more deeply into her chair.

And the little steamer pressed on, pitching gently, over the gray, unbroken, gently moving water, that was veiled with slanting rain.

Far out, as though idly, listlessly, gulls were flying. Now they settled on the waves, now they beat up into the rainy air, and shone against the pale sky like the lights within a pearl. They looked cold and lonely. "How lonely it will be when we have passed by," she thought. "There will be nothing but the waves and those birds and rain falling!"

She gazed through the rust-spotted railing along which big drops trembled, until suddenly she shut her lips. It was as if a warning voice inside her had said, "Don't look!"

"No, I won't," she decided. "It's too depressing, much too depressing."

But immediately, she opened her eyes and looked again. Lonely birds, water lifting, white pale sky—how were they changed?

And it seemed to her there was a presence far out there, between the sky and the water; someone very desolate and longing watched them pass and cried as if to stop them—but cried to her alone.

"Mother!"

"Don't leave me," sounded in the cry. "Don't forget me! You are forgetting me, you know you are!" And it was as though from her own breast there came the sound of childish weeping.

"My son—my precious child—it isn't true!"

Sh! How was it possible that she was sitting there on that quiet steamer beside Father, and at the same time she was hushing and holding a little slender boy—so pale—who had just woken out of a dreadful dream?

"I dreamed I was in a wood—somewhere far away from everybody—and I was lying down and a great blackberry vine grew over me. And I called to you—and you wouldn't come—you wouldn't come—so I had to lie there forever."

What a terrible dream! He had always had terrible dreams. How often, years ago, when he was small, she had made some excuse and escaped from their friends in the dining-room or the drawing-room to come to the foot of the stairs and listen. "Mother!" And when he was asleep, his dream had journeyed with her back into the circle of lamplight; it had taken its place there like a ghost. And now—

Far more often—at all times—in all places—like now, for instance—she never settled down, she was never off her guard for a moment but she heard him. He wanted her. "I am coming as fast as I can! As fast as I can!" But the dark stairs have no ending, and the worst dream of all—the one that is always the same—goes forever and ever uncomforted.

This is anguish! How is it to be borne? Still, it is not the idea of her suffering which is unbearable—it is his. Can one do nothing for the dead? And for a long time the answer had been—Nothing.

. . . But softly without a sound the dark curtain has rolled down. There is no more to come. That is the end of the play. But it can't end like that—so suddenly. There must be more. No it's cold, it's still. There is nothing to be gained by waiting.

But—did he go back again? Or, when the war was over, did he come home for good? Surely, he will marry—later on—not for several years. Surely one day I shall remember his wedding and my first grandchild—a beautiful dark-haired boy born in the early morning—a lovely morning—spring!

"Oh, Mother, it's not fair to put these ideas into my head! Stop, Mother, stop! When I think of all I have missed, I can't bear it."

"I can't bear it!" She sits up breathing the words and tosses the dark rug away. It is colder than ever, and now the dusk is falling, falling like ash upon the pallid water.

And the little steamer, growing determined, throbbed on, pressed on, as if at · the end of the journey there waited. . . .

ERSKINE CALDWELL   SEPTEMBER 23, 1940

Handy: A Story

Nobody knew where Handy came from, and nobody knew where he would go if he left, but if he had not killed Grandpa Price, he could have stayed another ten years or more.

Grandpa Price was old, and he was peevish, and he did nothing but fuss and find fault all day long. If he had been let alone, he would not have lived much longer, anyway.

But Handy hit Grandpa Price with a windlass, and the old man died that night. Handy had to pack up the little that belonged to him and get ready to go somewhere else to live.

"You ought to have had better sense," Harry Munford told him.

"It wasn't sense that had to do with it," Handy said.

"Just the same, it wasn't a good thing to do."

"A man oughtn't be an out-and-out trouble-maker," Handy said. "People who spend their lives making things don't have time to find fault with others."

"Even so," Harry said, "you shouldn't have done what you did to Grandpa Price."

A whole day could be spent counting up the downright trouble-making things Grandpa Price had said and done during the past ten or fifteen years. When he ran out of the ordinary things to find fault with, such as not enough gravy on the chicken or too much sweetening in the custard, he would go around quarreling about the time of day it happened to be. Sometimes when it was morning, he would say it ought to be afternoon, and when it was noon, he would say it ought to be dawn, and then rant and rave if anybody said noon was as good as anything else for it to be. Only a few days before he died, he got after Harry because the chimney might not be in plumb. That made Harry so mad he almost lost his head. "What if it ain't?" he shouted at the old man. "Because if it ain't, it ought to be," Grandpa Price said. Harry was so mad by then that he went for a plumb line and dropped it on the chimney. The chimney was only an eighth of an inch out of plumb. "That ought to make you shut your mouth from now on!" Harry shouted at him. "I won't shut my mouth, because the chimney is out of plumb and you know it. It ought to be torn down and built up again right," Grandpa Price said. "Over my dead body," Harry told him. Grandpa Price fussed about the chimney being out of plumb all the rest of the day and even through supper until he went to bed that night. He called Harry and all the Munfords lazy, good-for-nothing and slipshod. He followed Harry around the place saying anybody who would take up for an out-of-plumb chimney was not a good citizen.

"The more I think about it, Handy, the more I think you shouldn't have done it," Harry said. "Any number of times I've felt like picking up a brick or a crowbar and doing the thing myself, but a man can't go around the world hitting old men like that, no matter how provoked he is. The law's against it."

"I just couldn't stand it no longer, Mr. Harry," Handy said. "I'm sorry about it now, but it just couldn't be helped at the time."

Handy had lived there ten or twelve years. When he walked into the front yard for the first time, it was in the middle of the cotton-picking season. He came in and said he was looking for something to do. It was a time when Harry needed cotton pickers if he ever needed them. Harry was all ready to hire Handy. He told Handy he was paying 60 cents a hundred in the fields.

Handy shook his head as though he knew exactly what he wanted. Cotton picking was not it. "No sirree bob. I don't pick no cotton," Handy said. "I haven't got any need for anybody else these days," Harry told him. "The cotton is falling on the ground, going to waste faster every day, and that's all I'm concerned about now." "You always got need for something new, or something made of something old." "What do you mean?" "I make things," Handy said. "I just take what's thrown away and make it useful. Sometimes I like to make a thing just because it's pretty, though."

He picked up a stick of wood about a foot long and two or three inches thick. Nobody paid much attention to what he was doing, and Harry was sizing him up to be a tramp. He asked Handy if he had ever worked in the fields, and Handy said he had not. He asked him if he had ever worked on the river steamers, and Handy said no. In the cotton mills. Not ever. Railroads. No. Harry shook his head. He put Handy down a tramp. Handy scraped the wood with the knife blade and handed it to Harry. It was the smoothest-whittled wooden spoon anybody had ever seen. It looked as if it had been sandpapered and polished. It had taken Handy only the length of time he was standing there to do it. Harry turned the spoon over and over in his hands, felt of it, and smiled at Handy. Anybody who could do a thing like that deserved a better jacknife than Handy had. Harry took his own out of his pocket and gave it to him.

Nobody said anything more to him about picking cotton in the fields. Handy walked around the yard looking at things for a while, and then he went around to the back of the house and looked inside the barn, the woodshed, the smokehouse and the chicken-run. He looked in all the hen nests, and then he began carving nest-eggs out of some blocks of wood he found in barn. They were smooth and brown, and the laying hens liked them better than any other kind.

After he had made six or eight nest-eggs, he found something else to do. He never asked Harry or anybody if it was all right for him to do a thing, or if they wanted something made; he just went ahead and made whatever he felt like doing. The chairs Handy made were the most comfortable in the house, the plowstocks were the strongest on the farm, and the weathervanes were the prettiest in the country.

"The trouble with Grandpa Price, he wasn't like me and you, Handy," Harry said. "The reason me and you are alike is that I crave to get things growing in the fields and you to make things with your hands. Grandpa Price didn't have that feeling in him. All he wanted was to find fault with what other people grow or make."

Handy was sad and dejected. He knew it would take him a long time to find another place where the people would let him stay and make things. He would be able to stop along the road now and then, of course, and make a chicken coop for somebody or build a pigpen; but as soon as he finished it, they would give him a leftover meal or a pair of old pants and tell him to go on away. He knew all about the trouble he was going to have finding somebody who would let him stay and just make things. Some of them would offer him a job plowing in the fields, or working on a river steamer. "I want to make things out of pieces of wood," Handy said. "I want to build things with my fingers." The people were going to back away from him; they would shut the door in his face. He could not sit still. His hands began to tremble.

"What's the matter, Handy?" Harry asked him. "What makes you shake like that? Don't let what happened to Grandpa Price untie you."

"It's not that, it's something else."

"What else?"

"I'm going to find it hard not having a place to live where I can make things."

"I hate like everything to see you go," Harry said. "Somehow or other it don't seem right at all." It hurt him so much to think about Handy's leaving that he tried not to look at him. "But," he said, "the sheriff will make it hard for me if I fail to tell him what happened." It was already the day after Grandpa Price had died, and the sheriff had to be told about it before Grandpa Price could be buried in the cemetery. "But I don't want to do it, just the same," Harry said sadly. "It means driving you off, Handy, and I'd drive you off a dozen times before I'd let the sheriff find you here when he comes."

It hurt so much to think about it he could not sit there and look at Handy. He got up and walked away by himself.

When he came back, Handy was not there. But presently he saw Handy's head bobbing up and down behind the barn fence, and he was relieved. After a while he went into the house to change into clean overalls and shirt. He had to change before he could go into town, anyway. There was nothing to stop him from taking as much time as he wanted, though. He looked at two or three pairs of overalls before deciding which to put on. He liked to have a person like Handy around, because Handy was always making something, or getting ready to make something. That was what he liked about Handy. He was like the children when they came home from school, or on holidays. They were busy at something, play or work, every minute they were awake. He was afraid, though, that when they grew up they would get to be like Grandpa Price, that they would spend their time finding fault instead of making things.

When Harry finally came out into the yard, it was late in the afternoon.

"I don't like to go to town at this time of the day," he said, looking towards the barn where Handy was, up at the sky, and back again towards the barn. "It would mean coming back long after dark."

Harry walked around the house, to the garden several times, and finally towards the barnyard. He wondered more and more all the time what Handy was spending so much time down there for. Several times he had seen Handy come to the barn door, throw some trash and shavings outside, and then disappear again.

It grew dark soon, and he did not see Handy again until the next morning. Handy was at the table eating breakfast when Harry came in and sat down.

"What's this?" Harry asked, standing up again suddenly.

"A little present for Grandpa Price," Handy said.

"But Grandpa Price is dead—"

"I only made it to hang around his neck in the grave," Handy said. "I wanted to make something for him, but I thought he'd find so much fault with it if he was alive that I went ahead and made it all wrong just to please him."

It was a wooden chain about two feet long, each link about the size of a fingernail, and each one a different object. Handy had carved it from beginning to end since the afternoon before, sitting up all night to finish it.

"If Grandpa Price was alive, he'd be so tickled to get it he wouldn't want to find any fault with it, Handy. As it is, I don't know that I've ever seen a finer-looking present."

Harry sat down and picked up the chain to look at it more closely. The first link he looked at was a miniature chair with three legs shorter than the fourth one.

"I didn't think anybody but me remembered about that time when Grandpa Price quarreled so much about one of the chairs having one leg shorter than the others. I said one leg was shorter. Grandpa Price said three were short and one was long. Up to that time, that was about the biggest quarrel me and him ever had, wasn't it, Handy?"

Handy nodded.

Harry bent over to see what some of the other objects were. One was carved to look like a piece of the sky with the sun and stars shining at the same time. Another was a picture in a frame that looked upside down no matter which way it was turned.

Handy pushed back his chair and got up.

"This is too fine a thing to put in a grave, Handy," Harry said. "It would be a sin to bury a thing like this in the ground where nobody could ever see it again."

"I made it for a present to hang around Grandpa Price's neck," Handy said. "That's why I made it."

"Well," Harry said, shaking his head, "that being the case—I guess you've got the right to say— But it does seem a shame—"

Handy went out through the kitchen, down the steps, and across the yard to the barn. As soon as he got inside the barn door, he fired the shotgun.

Harry jumped to his feet, carrying the chain for Grandpa Price's neck with him.

"What did Handy shoot for?" he said. Then he went down to the barn.

When he came back, he was slow about it. He looked sad, but there was another look on his face at the same time. One moment he appeared as if he might cry; the next moment it was as though he felt so good he had to grin about it. "Handy won't have to go now, after all." He grinned all over his face. "If Handy had stayed alive, I'd never have seen him again," he said to himself. He walked up on the porch and began looking at the chain again, picking out a link here and a link there to stare at and feel with his fingers.

"Grandpa Price can be buried in the cemetery if he wants to," he said aloud, "but Handy is going to be buried right here in the backyard."

He felt the chain with all the fingers of both hands and held it up to gaze at in the sunlight.

"I want to have him around," he said.

Like the Sad Heart
of Ruth

No, Memphis in autumn has not the moss-hung oaks of Natchez. Nor, my dear young man, have we the exotic, the really exotic orange and yellow and rust foliage of the maples at Rye or Saratoga. When our five-month summer season burns itself out, the foliage is left a cheerless brown. Observe that Catawba tree beyond the wall; and the leaves under your feet here on the terrace are mustard and khaki colored; and the air, the atmosphere (who would dare to breathe a deep breath!) is virtually a sea of dust. But we do what we can. We've walled ourselves in here with these evergreens and box and jasmine. You must know, yourself, young man, that no beauty is native to us but the verdure of early summer. And it's as though I've had to take my finger, just so, and point out to Kate the lack of sympathy that there is in the climate and in the eroded countryside of this region. I have had to build this garden and say, "See, my child, how nice and sympathetic everything can be." But now she does see it my way. You understand, my daughter has finally made her life with me in this little garden plot, and year by year she has come to realize how little else there is.

And you, you know nothing of flowers? A young man who doesn't know the zinnia from the aster! How curious that you and my daughter should have made friends. I don't know under what circumstances you two may have met, but my daughter now has most of her friends among the flower-minded people. She makes so few friends nowadays outside of our little circle, sees so few people outside our own garden here, really, that I find it quite strange for there to be someone who doesn't know flowers.

No, nothing, we've come to feel, is ever very lovely, really lovely, I mean, in this part of the nation, nothing *but* this garden; and you can well imagine what even this little bandbox of a garden once was. I created it out of a virtual chaos of a back yard—Kate's playground, I might say. For three years I nursed that little magnolia there, for one whole summer did nothing but water the ivy on the east wall of the house; if only you could have seen the scrubby hedge and the unsightly servants' quarters of our neighbors that are beyond my serpentine wall (I suppose, at least, they're still there). In those days it was all very different, you understand, and Kate's father was about the house, and Kate was a child. But now in the spring we have what is truly a sweet garden here, modeled on my mother's at Rye; for three weeks in March our hyacinths are an inspiration to Kate and to me and to all those who come to us regularly; the larkspur and marigold are heavenly in May over there beside the roses.

17

But you do not know the zinnia from the aster, young man? How curious that you two should have become friends. And now you are impatient of her, and you mustn't be; I don't mean to be too indulgent, but she'll be along presently. Only recently she's become incredibly painstaking in her toilet again. Whereas in the last few years she's not cared so much for the popular fads of dress. Gardens and floral design have occupied her—with what guidance I could give—have been pretty much her life, really. Now in the old days, I confess, before her father was taken from us—I lost Mr. Ross in the dreadfully hot summer of '30, the summer of the nationwide drought when all my flowers died in June (*All* of them, though not one from neglect. Young man, I worked my flowers the very day Mr. Ross passed away. A dreadful summer)—why, she used then to run here and there with people of every sort, it seemed. I put no restraint upon her, understand. How many times I've said to my Kate, "You must make your own life, my child, as you would have it." Yes, in those days she used to run here and there with people of every sort and variety, it seemed to me. Where was it you say you met, for she goes so few places that are really *out* any more? But Mr. Ross would let me put no restraint upon her. I still remember the strongheadedness of her teens that had to be overcome and the testiness in her character when she was nearer to twenty than thirty. And you should have seen her as a tot of twelve when she would be somersaulting and rolling about on this very spot. Honestly, I see that child now, the mud on her middy-blouse and her straight yellow hair in her eyes.

When I used to come back from visiting my people at Rye, she would grit her teeth at me and give her confidence to the black cook. I would find my own child become a mad little animal. It was through this door here from the sun-room that I came one September afternoon—just such an afternoon as this, young man— still wearing my traveling suit, and called to my child across the yard for her to come and greet me. I had been away for the two miserable summer months, but at the sight of me the little Indian turned and with a whoop she ran to hide in the scraggly privet hedge which was at the far end of the yard. I called her twice to come from out that filthiest of shrubs. "Ellen Katherine!" We used to call her by her full name when her father was alive. But she didn't stir. She crouched at the roots of the hedge and spied at her travel-worn mother between the leaves.

I pleaded with her at first quite indulgently and good-naturedly and described the new ruffled dress and the paper cut-outs I had brought from her grandmother at Rye. Then at last I threatened to withhold my presents until Thanksgiving or Christmas. The cook in the kitchen may have heard some change in my tone, for she came to the kitchen door over beyond that lattice work which we've since put up, and looked out first at me and then at the child. While I was threatening thus, my daughter crouched in the dirt and began to mumble things to herself which I could not hear, and the noises she made were like those of an angry little cat. It seems that it was a warmer afternoon than this one—but my garden does deceive—and I had been moving about in my heavy traveling suit. In my exasperation I stepped out into the rays of the sweltering sun, and into the yard which I so detested; and I uttered in a scream the child's full name, "Ellen Katherine Ross!" Just then the black cook stepped out onto the back porch, but I ordered her to return to the kitchen. I began to cross the yard toward Ellen Katherine—that frowning little girl who was *incredibly* the same Kate you've met—and simultaneously she began to crawl along the hedgerow toward the wire fence that divided my property from the neighbor's.

I believe it was the extreme heat that made me speak so very harshly and with such swiftness as to make my words incomprehensible. When I saw that the child had reached the fence and intended climbing it, I pulled off my hat, tearing my veil to pieces as I hurried my pace. I don't actually know what I was saying—I probably couldn't have told you even a moment later—and I didn't even feel any pain from the turn which I gave my ankle in the gulley across the middle of the yard. But the child kept her nervous little eyes on me and her lips continued to move now and again. Each time her lips moved I believe I must have raised my voice in more intense rage and greater horror at her ugliness. And so, young man, striding straight through the hedge I reached her before she had climbed to the top of the wire fencing. I think I took her by the arm above the elbow, about here, and I said something like, "I shall have to punish you, Ellen Katherine." I did not jerk her. I didn't jerk her one bit, as she wished to make it appear, but rather, as soon as I touched her, she relaxed her hold on the wire and fell to the ground. But she lay there—in her canniness—only the briefest moment looking up and past me through the straight hair that hung over her face like an untrimmed mane. I had barely ordered her to rise when she sprang up and moved with such celerity that she soon was out of my reach again. I followed—running in those high heels—and this time I turned my other ankle in the gulley, and I fell there on the ground in that yard, this garden. You won't believe it—pardon, I must sit down—you won't believe it: she didn't come to aid me with childish apologies, but instead she deliberately climbed into her swing that hung from the dirty old poplar that was here formerly (I have had it cut down and the roots dug up) and she began to swing, not high and low, but only gently, and stared straight down at her mother through her long hair—which, you may be sure, young man, I had cut the very next day at my own beautician's and curled into a hundred ringlets.

ROBERT GIBBONS   DECEMBER 8, 1941

A Loaf of Bread

About this time in October, some leaves, windblown from the sycamore tree that stands near the courthouse, go sliding, with a dry slithering sound, down the pavement of Jefferson Avenue. At the corner of Jefferson Avenue and Main they come to a stop in an aged and unexpecting huddle near the curb. The feet of many folks—folks with cotton money and folks without any kind of money—go back and forth along Jefferson until the leaves are ragged and tattered like the clothes of little children. A farmer or a woman might drop a dime there among the taggy leaves; and it might lie hidden until a passing wind, stirring in the trashiness, would let it peek out like a full moon half-shut in by a broken cloud.

Loxey Cunningham saw that dime, and before he jumped for it, something went running through him as if a rabbit were in his muscles. He wanted that dime—wanted it so bad that he could feel himself tingling in between his legs.

Even when he could feel it hard and round and thin between thumb and finger, like a little wheel, he wasn't able to believe that he had found it and that it was his dime.

He stirred around in the leaves with his other hand. He didn't find any more money, only leaves and dirt and trash. But he did see a good, long stub of a cigarette; and, as he picked it up, somebody standing right over him said, "Loxey, do your Paw know you done started smoking?"

Loxey squatted lower, flinched, and a cold something was heavy in his belly. He looked up at Uncle Jake in the one-eyed way a chicken looks up. He could see by the slant of Uncle Jake's eye that the dime was not seen; Uncle Jake was seeing the cigarette. Fast as he could do it without Uncle Jake seeing, Loxey closed his right hand. Then he let the cigarette dribble off the fingers of his left.

Uncle Jake was pig-eyed—and fat, too, like a hog; his face was red; and stubby bristles made him look more and more like a big boar-hog. Seeing him, seeing the pig-facedness of Uncle Jake, was always to see in memory all the hurting times the face had made.

They used to be sent over to Uncle Jake's and Aunt Millie's every time a baby came to Maw. Paw used to send them over, telling them before they left, "The Book says, 'Honor thy father and mother.' When yawl go over to Millie's it's like she's yer own maw, and Jake's like yer own paw. An' yawl do like they says, er I'll tan yuh in an inch uh yer lives. Unnerstan'?"

They heard, but they could not understand. Paw had a curious God, who stood back of Paw and Uncle Jake. Backing up Paw was not as curious as backing up Uncle Jake. Paw did go to church. He was big in the Gum Bay church. But Uncle Jake never went to church.

And when they were sent over, Uncle Jake said things they couldn't understand. That was when they were little. When they were older, they understood. Uncle Jake used to say, "Dammit to hell, your paw sure do go after it. His old lady oughter be like mine—without no insides." And he said once, "That one makes five of you already, Loxey. And it's what keeps Joe so thin and measley. Lookit me! Fat and no houseful of kids."

Uncle Jake said to him as he stood, "You oughter be ashamed, Loxey, a-sneaking around picking up butts when your paw is a good Christian member of the church."

Loxey said, "I thought I seen a marble down there in the trash."

"Where's your Paw?"

"He went up towards the courthouse a while back."

Uncle Jake spat a big, brown blob close to Loxey and grunted, "You're a lying scoundrel! I seen him down the street near Tucker's just now. Maybe I won't tell him on you though."

"You can tell him what you want to, I don't give a damn."

Uncle Jake spat again, so close to Loxey that one little, brown speck hopped up on to Loxey's big toenail and sat there. Uncle Jake said, "Yeah, I'll tell him you cussed me, too. He'll beat your butt-end raw for that. He ain't churchified for nothing."

Loxey said nothing. He dug his hands deep into the pockets of faded denim overalls, and turned away, making as if to leave. Making to leave was plenty now, because Loxey Cunningham had a dime and was in the middle of town and didn't care how many times Uncle Jake had said, "God damn you kids, I done kept you up all your life! So, when I say, 'Pick cotton,' I mean do that thing!"

It wasn't until he was across Jefferson and on the other corner that he looked backwards over his shoulder. Uncle Jake was going away, down the street toward Tucker's. The galluses of Uncle Jake's overalls came over his shoulders like buggy-harness on a big mule. They met each other in the middle of Uncle Jake's back. Loxey watched the broad blue-shirted back move away. He grinned a little grin to himself and brought his hand out of his pocket and opened it.

The dime was dirty. Loxey spat on it. It shined more after he had rubbed it on his overalls.

Loxey walked up Main toward the depot; there was such a crowd around the station that Paw and Uncle Jake wouldn't be able to find him, if they looked. Everybody around the station was laughing, frolicky-like, and telling jokes and yelling to each other. Loxey climbed onto one of the high, red and little-wheeled baggage wagons; he sat there watching the people and thinking about his dime and about what, of all the things there were, he would buy with his dime. A kid sucking a piece of red-and-white candy went by. The dime would buy candy. But there ought to be something bigger and better than candy.

A reason they liked to go to Uncle Jake's, he thought, was that Aunt Millie always put more stuff on the table than their Maw did at home. Maw tried awfully hard, and she nearly aways managed to get some salt meat and pone-bread or something like that. Sometimes it wasn't enough for two helpings, but it generally went around once. At Uncle Jake's, though, they had ham a lot of times, and sausage, and grits and gravy. The gravy that Aunt Millie fixed was thickening-gravy. It had flour in it. They used to have gravy at home, only it was grease from the fatback. They mixed it with syrup and sopped it. It made good victuals whenever they were hungry—and that was every time—but the things Aunt Millie fixed made better ones.

And one night Uncle Jake wasn't there for supper. He was in town, Aunt Millie said. She sat in Uncle Jake's place and said the blessing. When she finished, everybody reached for something. Loxey got a piece of ham in one hand and a piece of white bread in the other, and the stuff looked so good that he could nearly already taste it.

There were Aunt Millie and all of the kids—and just afterwards there was Uncle Jake, too. It seemed that he might have been floating around on a minute and, when the minute came toward them, he floated in on it, so that Loxey half-expected to see him go backward out the door when the minute was over and gone.

But he stayed. He swayed a little as he stood there, his pig eyes looking in quick, little jumps from one to the other of them. His face was redder than usual. He said, "Well, I'll be God-damned, Millie! Every blessed little scutter of 'em is setting there ready to eat before I even get home. I'll say, that's a hell of a note!"

Aunt Millie went on up to Uncle Jake, and her hands went to his galluses. She was nearly about crying when she said, "But, Jake, it got so late, I got to thinking you was held up in town. And all the kids was sleepy. That's the only reason."

Uncle Jake wouldn't let her say any more. He took one of his great, hairy hands and caught both of Aunt Millie's wrists just like they were a pair of reins. He clamped down hard. Aunt Millie said, "Oh!" That was all. It was one short sound, sucked in and jumping down her throat like a scared mouse. Then she fell away to one side against the wall, and when Uncle Jake turned her loose, she just stood there, her hands and arms wilting down from her like corn on a hot day.

Every one of them, except Betty Lee, maybe, was wishing that babies never would come to Maw even if it did mean they wouldn't ever get a bait of victuals. They were afraid to look straight at Uncle Jake, but they could feel him as he stood watching, while he worked on the mad place that was deep inside him. Finally he yelled, "God-amighty damn! Git out of my sight, you little bitches and son-of-a-bitches! Git to bed! Now!"

There were six of the kids, five of them and Betty Lee. Uncle Jake was her uncle, too, but she was Uncle Jake's sister's girl and wasn't any kin to them. But she used to come over to Uncle Jake's now and again.

Uncle Jake came charging around the table to where Loxey was. He stood over Loxey, and he was swaying like a big wagonload of hay on a rough road. Something knotted up inside Loxey at the place where his breastbone left off and his belly began. Uncle Jake's two hands reached down, took the bread and ham that Loxey was still holding, and flung it onto the table. Then something heavy and meaty hit Loxey and knocked him out of the chair. He lay on the floor trying to think and to feel. He tried not to cry. Two or three of the kids began to whimper, so Loxey pulled himself off the floor and said, "Let's go home."

Uncle Jake's arm went up. He said, "You ain't going nowhere tonight excepting up to bed. So git!"

They went on, but Betty Lee went back. Her papa owned a place that was almost as big as Uncle Jake's.

Later on that night Loxey lay on the pallet with his two brothers watching the moon, red-orange and bloody, go down in the west. There was no light to the moon, and all outdoors was dead and ghostly and full of deep devilishness. It was a time to think about dying, even God's dying. Then, far-off and lonesome, a train whistle blew; and Loxey wondered, when he heard it, whether, if he had been dead, he could have heard.

And now, on that Saturday afternoon, as a train came down the grade to the station and whistled in a far-off and lonesome way, he thought of that night at Uncle Jake's, the time Uncle Jake came in drunk on a minute.

Suddenly, it came to him what he wanted to buy with the dime. Suddenly, the picture of the ham and the white bread, lying on the table where Uncle Jake had flung it, came to him. A loaf of white bread—that was what he would get with his dime, and have it all to himself—a loaf of white bread.

He didn't wait any longer to watch the people or to see the train. He hopped down from the baggage wagon and started down the street toward Mr. Ben Darley's grocery store.

Loxey was out of town and half the way home before he began to wonder where he would go to eat the bread. He had to have some water, or else the bread would lump up and choke him. He didn't want to go home. All of his brothers and sisters were there to tell on him unless he gave them some of the bread, and he meant to have all of it for himself. Anyway, one loaf of white bread wouldn't be enough to go around. None of them could get a bait of it. So he knew he'd have to slip down by the spring and eat the bread before he ever went home.

He couldn't let Paw know. Paw never believed in white bread unless it was bought with hard-earned cotton money. The Book said man should make bread by the sweat of his brow. That made pone-bread Christian bread. So, for Loxey, there wasn't anything except to eat the bread and let nobody know about it.

As he passed by Ed Jurneyman's, there on the porch sat Aunt Millie talking with Ed's mama.

Aunt Millie called to him, and asked, "What you got in that there sack, Loxey?"

He hated to lie to Aunt Millie, but, if he told the truth, Ed's mama would be sure to blab to his folks. So he thought fast and answered Aunt Millie: "It's just an old pair of shoes a man give me in town."

Ed's mama said, "Heh, heh, well, why don't you put them on?"

"I'm saving them for Sunday," he told her.

Aunt Millie said, "That's right, Loxey. You're getting old enough almost to catch a gal now."

He said, "Shucks," and picked up speed. He could hear them laughing, but he didn't look back. He was thinking about two other things already. The first was what he'd say about the shoes he didn't have when Aunt Millie made mention of them around his folks. He decided he'd tell everybody that he was fooling, and didn't have any shoes at all, just a sack of leaves. He could fill the empty sack with leaves and make out the whole tale. The other thing that he thought about had come to him when he knew that Uncle Jake and Aunt Millie weren't at home. And, as he really began to think about it, things rushed in on him so that he didn't have time to think about a lot of other things.

He could see already the icebox in Aunt Millie's kitchen. There, in the icebox, yellow specks of butter floated at the top of a half-gallon jar of buttermilk—a big, green jar full to the brim with thick, tongue-stinging buttermilk, ice-cold. When, all of a sudden, something like that hit him, the long months of pone-bread and syrup and grease-gravy went flabby where, he guessed, his soul ought to have been; and his mouth watered in what seemed to be a sinfully warm sort of way.

The front door at Uncle Jake's wasn't locked. Aunt Millie never locked up, no matter how much Uncle Jake bellowed. The tingling he had known when he found the dime became a sharpness trying to find the inside of him. It cut a twanging string and turned things loose inside him.

Bread on the table across the kitchen from the icebox. Cold air out against him—his own breath hot between his teeth. The block of ice, cool and clear and deep as a shady creek, and, alongside, a green jar of buttermilk. The plate of butter, beside the milk. He had come for milk only and had to hurry. A knife to cut butter. A sharp knife in the drawer across the room.

Time inside him crawling like a long freight train on an uphill grade; and time outside, plunging down a square-built chute toward a door, behind which door he stood, full of feeling and full of a rawness of sense.

Butter melted from the heat of the hand, a small glass in the cupboard. Butter in glass, glass in hand with knife, bread under arm. Green jar of buttermilk, cold, chilly cold, in the other hand.

The sound of running feet! And Betty Lee cried through the house, "Aunt Millie! Aunt Millie!"

Part of his breath going in and part coming out fought in his throat. He would try to get away. Both hands full, he couldn't open the kitchen door that led to the back porch. So, when Betty Lee came into the kitchen, he was standing there.

Betty Lee's hand went up to her mouth as if to stop the sound of "Oh!" Then she said, "The door was open. I thought Aunt Millie was here."

He said, "She ain't here, I don't reckon."

Betty Lee looked at the things in his hands.

She looked at them, one by one, before she said, "Did Aunt Millie—?"

"It ain't no business of yours!" he broke in on her. Then he decided he'd better play up to her. He said, "Listen here, Betty Lee, I'll tell you what: let's me and you go and eat this together, and you can have half."

Betty Lee frowned and put her finger in the corner of her mouth. "Mother sent me over to borry some eggs."

He said, "Shucks, we'll have this et up in no time. Then you can run back and tell her that Aunt Millie ain't at home. That wouldn't be no story, either." He shoved the butter and the knife toward her, and when she took it, kind of unconsciously, he knew she was going to come. Even when she said, "But we'd be stealing," he knew he had her.

He said, "Aw, it might be hooking, but not stealing. Ain't we kin to Aunt Millie? Don't she git plenty of milk and butter? And this here loaf-bread, it's mine. I found a dime and bought it."

Betty Lee's face got brighter, and maybe a little more evil, too. She wasn't as hungry as he was, but the idea of doing something that ought not to be done got her. Still Betty Lee was afraid they'd get caught.

She asked, "But that knife and jar and glass?"

He said, "Aw, the devil, Betty Lee, you're a fraidy-cat, like girls always is. We can leave this stuff in the barn where Uncle Jake'll find it. He'll blame it on one of the niggers. Come on, and let's go."

So she went with him. He had to promise her as they went toward the barn that if they got caught, he'd take all the blame.

They were settled in the nearly empty, west corncrib, when, in just the way he'd done once before, Uncle Jake floated in on his minute and stayed.

For a second, things were so still that Loxey thought he could hear the weevils crackling in the last few ears of corn. Then Betty Lee said, "Oh!" Loxey couldn't see her, but he knew her hand was over her mouth.

Uncle Jake stepped up into the crib, easily and slowly like a spider tracking a fly. The corners of his mouth began to drop until they became two sharp, tobacco-juice-brown points hanging down his chin. Loxey edged away, knocked against a little hill of corn. One ear bumped hollowly on the floor, while the remainder slid across each other during a little space. The sound they made was a whispering.

Uncle Jake stood over Loxey. Loxey's looking went up from Uncle Jake's red-brown brogans and along his legs to where his belly came out, fat and pillowy and round. So far, Uncle Jake's hands hung by his sides, but the fingers were working in the joints.

Betty Lee whimpered, "It wasn't me done it, Uncle Jake. It was Loxey."

Uncle Jake whipped around and made like he would hit Betty Lee. Betty Lee's breath jumped into her, and Loxey could hear it go. Then she screamed a long scream, loud and sharp; finally Uncle Jake bent over and shook her. He said, "Shut up! I ain't going to hit you!"

Loxey saw his chance; he jumped up and broke for the door. Uncle Jake whirled, fast like a rat-terrier, and hit him in the chest with a fist. Loxey lay there on the floor, his breath gone; but Uncle Jake didn't stop. He started kicking and kept kicking for a long time, it seemed. Loxey's whole left leg went dead. He couldn't feel the last two kicks.

Uncle Jake started talking in the low voice the preacher used when the text was on the evilness of sin. All the while, Betty Lee was scroonched up into a little ball, crying without sound; and Loxey was hurting like raw meat and gristle.

"Wasn't looking for me home, was you? Robbing me of house and home, jus' taking over, wasn't you? Didn't count on me a-coming in early from town, didn't know this here new pair of shoes would git to hurting my corns, did you? Never counted on that, did you? Naw! Jus' aimed to have yourselfs a feed! And then what was you aiming to do? Like I don't know! Goddam your soul, Loxey! And Betty Lee almost your own sister. That's a nasty sinful thing to think of."

Uncle Jake hit Loxey twice on the side of the head. "That maybe'll learn you to grow up to be a Christian like your paw, and not be no kin-robbing, kin-raping little bastard!"

By the way Uncle Jake ended in a shout Loxey knew he was ready to start beating again. Loxey put his head down and took most of it on his back. And all through it Loxey didn't say anything. He guessed he had done wrong to steal, even if it didn't seem like stealing. But, now, the beating was over, and Uncle Jake was ready to go. Uncle Jake said to Betty Lee, "Get up, and go on to the house." Just after Uncle Jake said this Loxey looked up; and he had to say something. He yelled crazily, "You can have all the rest, but that's my loaf-bread."

Uncle Jake had gathered all the stuff together, in his hands or under his arm, and he stood looking down at Loxey, his eyes, his lips, the angle of his head, all one big sneer. "Hanh! Hanh!" he laughed. "Where'n hell would you get a loaf of bread!"

Loxey made to run at him, but Uncle Jake poked with his foot. Loxey yelled again, "It's mine! I bought it with a dime I found! You seen me when I found it, too."

Betty Lee was standing outside the crib now. Her eyes were level with Loxey's; and they were little black marbles. She cried stridently, "He didn't, Uncle Jake! He stole that bread, and when I caught him he made me come!"

Loxey began to feel hot with tears around the eyes. "She's a-lying!" he shouted at her.

Uncle Jake gave another kick. Some of the buttermilk sloshed out of the jar and made a little white circle on the crib floor. Uncle Jake said, "Don't call her no lie! And lookit what you made me do!"

They turned their backs on Loxey. The crib was a cell, and Loxey was the prisoner being left alone. He was crying like a kid now, and talking at the same time. "It was my dime! It was my bread! I found it; it was mine!"

They weren't in the doorway of the crib any longer. They were going away from him. He got to his feet and jumped out of the crib. He stood there on the ground inside the barn and watched Uncle Jake and Betty Lee go outside and into the sunlight.

Their shadows bobbed to the left of them, bobbed up and down, a shorter shadow in front of a longer shadow, both of them going away from Loxey.

Just inside the barn and leaning against the walls, prongs down, was a pitchfork. A wheel somewhere within him began to whirl. As it whirled, it slung salt-tears through him. They stung in his blood and in his soul. He set the fork in his hands, left hand forward on the handle and his right arm crooked at the elbow and the right hand back a little on the handle. The end of the handle was hard against his ribs. He ran forward, madly.

The sharp prongs, bright with haying, shone in the sun as Uncle Jake's back floated toward them. The spot where the galluses crossed in the middle of the back floated in on a minute, curving down like a swooping bird and—a jolt in Loxey's ribs. Something gave way, because the points were sharper than the handle.

Uncle Jake groaned in a tired sort of way.

The full ploshy clink of something breaking on the ground. Uncle Jake stood stock-still in his tracks. Loxey was away from the handle, watching his loaf of white bread hit the ground, roll, and stop. And every time Uncle Jake coughed, or tried to cough, the handle of the pitchfork jerked stiffly and poked like a long finger at Loxey.

Betty Lee's voice, full of wonderment, said, "Loxey, blood's coming out of Uncle Jake's mouth; and he can't see me." Then Betty Lee screamed.

Uncle Jake fell slowly like a heavy tree. He couldn't double-up in the middle, because of the prongs in him. He fell; and he was straight and treelike when he fell. The fork stayed in him, leaning to one side like a rotten fencepost.

Betty Lee's screaming grew less loud as she ran into the house.

The ground sloped where Uncle Jake lay. A brook of buttermilk streaked with red ran from under Uncle Jake. Loxey picked up his loaf of white bread. For a moment, he stood motionless, the way a wild animal pauses. Then he ran back behind the barn, across the fields, and into Mattison's Swamp. Down in the swamp, he pulled the wrapper off the bread and saw that the loaf was moulded. When he saw that, he just sat there in the half-darkness of the swamp and listened to the sounds come within the night. He was tired and wearied in the way the world grows old. He sat there with the loaf on his knees. Far away he could hear people shouting as they set out to hunt him. He sat there, quietly, waiting for them. After a while he grew hungry and ate a piece of his bread, mould and all.

Vag

The young man waits at the edge of the concrete, with one hand he grips a rubbed suitcase of phony leather, the other hand almost making a fist, thumb up,

that moves in ever so slight an arc when a car slithers past, a truck roars, clatters; the wind of cars passing ruffles his hair, slaps grit in his face.

Head swims, hunger has twisted the belly tight,

he has skinned a heel through the torn sock, feet ache in the broken shoes, under the threadbare suit carefully brushed off with the hand, the torn drawers have a crummy feel, the feel of having slept in your clothes, in the nostrils lingers the staleness of discouraged carcasses crowded into a transient camp, the carbolic stench of the jail, on the taut cheeks the shamed flush from the boring eyes of cops and deputies, railroad bulls (they eat three squares a day, they are buttoned into wellmade clothes, they have wives to sleep with, kids to play with after supper, they work for the big men who buy their way, they stick their chests out with the sureness of power behind their backs). Get the hell out, scram. Know what's good for you, you'll make yourself scarce. Gittin' tough, eh? I think you kin take it, eh?

The punch in the jaw, the slam on the head with the nightstick, the wrist grabbed and twisted behind the back, the big knee brought up sharp into the crotch,

the walk out of town with sore feet to stand and wait at the edge of the hissing speeding string of cars where the reek of ether and lead and gas melts into the silent grassy smell of the earth.

Eyes black with want seek out the eyes of the drivers, a hitch, a hundred miles down the road.

Overhead in the blue a plane drones. Eyes follow the silver Douglas that flashes in the sun and bores its smooth way out of sight into the blue.

(The transcontinental passengers sit pretty, big men with bankaccounts, highlypaid jobs, who are saluted by doormen; telephonegirls say goodmorning to them. Last night after a fine dinner, drinks with friends, they left Newark. Roar of climbing motors slanting up into the inky haze. Lights drop away. An hour staring along a silvery wing at a big lonesome moon hurrying west through curdling scum. Beacons flash in a line across Ohio.

At Cleveland the plane drops banking in a smooth spiral, the string of lights along the lake swings in a circle. Climbing roar of the motors again; slumped in the soft seat drowsing through the flat moonlight night.

Chi. A glimpse of the dipper. Another spiral swoop from cool into hot air thick with dust and the reek of burnt prairies.

Beyond the Mississippi dawn creeps up behind through the murk over the great plains. Puddles of mist go white in the Iowa hills, farms, fences, silos, steel glint from a river. The blinking eyes of the beacons reddening into day. Watercourses vein the eroded hills.

Omaha. Great cumulus clouds, from coppery churning to creamy to silvery white, trail brown skirts of rain over the hot plains. Red and yellow badlands, tiny horned shapes of cattle.

Cheyenne. The cool high air smells of sweetgrass.

The tightbaled clouds to westward burst and scatter in tatters over the strawcolored hills. Indigo mountains jut rimrock. The plane breasts a huge crumbling cloudbank and toboggans over bumpy air across green and crimson slopes into the sunny dazzle of Salt Lake.

The transcontinental passenger thinks contracts, profits, vacationtrips, mighty continent between Atlantic and Pacific, power, wires humming dollars, cities jammed, hills empty, the indiantrail leading into the wagonroad, the macadamed pike, the concrete skyway; trains, planes, history the billiondollar speedup,

and in the bumpy air over the desert ranges towards Las Vegas

sickens and vomits into the carton container the steak and mushrooms he ate in New York. No matter, silver in the pocket, greenbacks in the wallet, drafts, certified checks, plenty restaurants in L.A.)

The young man waits on the side of the road; the plane has gone; thumb moves in a small arc when a car tears hissing pass. Eyes seek the driver's eyes. A hundred miles down the road. Head swims, belly tightens, wants crawl over his skin like ants:

went to school, books said opportunity, ads promised speed, own your house, shine bigger than your neighbor, the radiocrooner whispered girls, ghosts of platinum girls coaxed from the screen, millions in winnings were chalked up on the board in the offices, paychecks were for hands willing to work, the cleared desk of an executive with three telephones on it;

waits with swimming head, needs knot the belly, idle hands numb, beside the speeding traffic.

A hundred miles down the road.

The Campers at Kitty Hawk

O n December 17, 1903, Bishop Wright of the United Brethren, onetime editor of The Religious Telescope, received in his frame house on Hawthorn Street in Dayton, Ohio, a telegram from his boys Wilbur and Orville who'd gotten it into their heads to spend their vacations in a little camp out on the dunes of the North Carolina coast tinkering with a mancarrying kite they'd knocked together themselves. The telegram read:

SUCCESS FOUR FLIGHTS THURSDAY MORNING ALL AGAINST TWENTYONE MILE WIND STARTED FROM LEVEL WITH ENGINEPOWER ALONE AVERAGE SPEED THROUGH AIR THIRTYONE MILES LONGEST FIFTYSEVEN SECONDS INFORM PRESS HOME CHRIST-MAS.

The figures were a little wrong because the telegraph operator misread Orville's hasty penciled scrawl
but the fact remains
that a couple of young bicycle mechanics from Dayton, Ohio,
had designed constructed and flown
for the first time ever a practical airplane.

After running the motor a few minutes to heat it up I released the wire that held the machine to the track and the machine started forward into the wind. Wilbur ran at the side of the machine holding the wing to balance it on the track. Unlike the start on the 14th, made in a calm, the machine, facing a twenty-seven-mile wind, started very slowly. . . . Wilbur was able to stay with it until it lifted from the track after a forty-foot run. One of the lifesaving men snapped the camera for us, taking a picture just as it reached the end of the track and the machine had risen to a height of about two feet. . . . The course of the flight up and down was extremely erratic, partly due to the irregularities of the air, partly to lack of experience in handling this machine. A sudden dart when a little over a hundred and twenty feet from the point at which it rose in the air ended the flight. . . . This flight lasted only twelve seconds but it was nevertheless the first in the history of the world in which a machine carrying a man had raised itself by its own power into the air in full flight, had sailed forward without reduction of speed and had finally landed at a point as high as that from which it started.

A little later in the day the machine was caught in a gust of wind and turned over and smashed, almost killing the coastguardsman who tried to hold it down;
it was too bad
but the Wright brothers were too happy to care;
they'd proved that the damn thing flew.

When these points had been definitely established we at once packed our goods and returned home, knowing that the age of the flying machine had come at last.

They were home for Christmas in Dayton, Ohio, where they'd been born into a family settled west of the Alleghenies since 1814; in Dayton, Ohio, where they'd been to grammarschool and highschool and joined their father's church and played baseball and hockey and worked out on the parallel bars and the flying swing and sold newspapers and built themselves a printing press out of odds and ends from the junkheap and flown kites and tinkered with mechanical contraptions and gone around town as boys doing odd jobs to turn an honest penny.

The folks claimed it was the Bishop's bringing home a helicopter, a fifty-cent mechanical toy made of two fans worked by elastic bands that was supposed to hover in the air, that had gotten his two youngest boys hipped on the subject of flight.

so that they stayed home instead of marrying like the other boys did, and puttered all day about the house picking up a living with job printing,

bicycle repair work,

sitting up late nights reading books on aerodynamics.

Still they were sincere churchmembers,

their bicycle business was prosperous,

a man could rely on their word. They were well thought of in Dayton.

In those days flying machines were the chuckle of all the crackerbarrel philosophers.

Langley's and Chanute's unsuccessful efforts had been jeered down with an I-told-you-so that rang from coast to coast.

The Wrights' big problem was to find a place secluded enough to carry on their experiments without being the horse laugh of the countryside. Then they had no money to spend;

they were practical mechanics; when they needed anything they built it themselves.

They hit on Kitty Hawk,

on the great dunes and sandy banks that stretch south towards Hatteras seaward of Albemarle Sound,

a vast stretch of seabeach

empty except for coastguard stations, a few fishermen's shacks and the swarms of mosquitoes and the ticks and chiggers in the crabgrass behind the dunes

and overhead the gulls and swooping terns, in the evening fishhawks and cranes flapping across the saltmarshes, occasionally eagles

that the Wright brothers followed soaring with their eyes

as Leonardo watched them centuries before

straining his sharp eyes to apprehend

the laws of flight.

Four miles across the loose sand from the scattering of shacks the Wright brothers built themselves a camp and a shed for their gliders. It was a long way to pack their groceries, their tools, anything they happened to need; in summer it was hot as blazes, the mosquitoes were hell;

but they were alone there

and they'd figured out that the loose sand was as soft as anything they could find to fall in.

There with a glider made of two planes and a tail in which they lay flat on their bellies and controlled the warp of the planes by shimmying their hips, taking off again and again all day from a big dune named Kill Devil Hill,

they learned to fly.

Once they'd managed to hover for a few seconds and soar ever so slightly on a rising aircurrent

they decided the time had come to put in a motor.

Back in their shop in Dayton, they had build an air tunnel (their first great contribution to the science of flying) and tried out model planes in it.

They couldn't interest any builders of gasoline engines so they had to build their own motor. It worked.

After that Christmas of 1903 the Wright brothers weren't doing it for fun any more; they gave up their bicycle business, got the use of a big old cowpasture belonging to the local banker for practice flights, spent all the time when they weren't working on their machine in promotion, worrying about patents, infringements, spies, trying to interest government officials, to make sense out of the smooth, involved, heartbreaking remarks of lawyers.

In two years they had a plane that would cover twenty-four miles at a stretch round and round the cowpasture.

People on the interurban car used to crane their necks out of the windows when they passed along the edge of the field, startled by the clattering pop pop of the old Wright motor and the sight of the white biplane like a pair of ironingboards, one on top of the other, chugging along a good fifty feet in the air. The cows soon got used to it.

As the flights got longer

the Wright brothers got backers

engaged in lawsuits,

lay in their beds at night sleepless with the whine of phantom millions, worse than the mosquitoes at Kitty Hawk.

In 1907 they went to Paris,

allowed themselves to be outfitted in dressuits and silk hats,

learned to tip waiters

talked with government experts, got used to gold braid and postponements and Vandyke beards and the outspread palms of politicos. For amusement

they played diabolo in the Tuileries gardens.

They gave publicized flights at Fort Myers, where they had their first fatal crackup, St. Petersburg, Paris, Berlin; at Pau they were all the rage

such an attraction that the hotelkeeper

wouldn't charge them for their room.

Alfonso of Spain shook hands with them and was photographed sitting in the machine,

King Edward watched a flight,

the Crown Prince insisted on being taken up,

the rain of medals began.
They were congratulated by the Tsar
and the King of Italy and the amateurs of sport, and the society climbers and the papal titles
and decorated by a society for universal peace.
Aeronautics became the sport of the day.
The Wrights don't seem to have been impressed by the upholstery and the braid and the gold medals and the parades of plush horses,
they remained practical mechanics
and insisted on doing all their own work themselves,
even to filling the gasoline tank.

In 1911 they were back on the dunes
at Kitty Hawk with a new glider
Orville stayed up in the air for nine and a half minutes, which remained a long time the record for motorless flight.
The same year Wilbur died of typhoid fever in Dayton.
In the rush of new names: Farnum, Blériot, Curtiss, Ferber, Esnault-Peletrie, Delagrange;
in the snorting impact of bombs and the whine and rattle of shrapnel and the sudden stutter of machineguns after the motor's been shut off overhead,
and we flatten into the mud
and make ourselves small, cowering in the corners of ruined walls,
the Wright brothers passed out of the headlines;
but not even headlines or the bitter smear of newsprint or the choke of smokescreen and gas or chatter of brokers on the stockmarket or barking of phantom millions or oratory of brasshats laying wreaths on new monuments
can blur the memory
of the chilly December day
two shivering bicycle mechanics from Dayton, Ohio,
first felt their homemade contraption,
whittled out of hickory sticks,
gummed together with Arnstein's bicycle cement,
stretched with muslin they'd sewn on their sister's sewing machine in their own backyard on Hawthorn Street, in Dayton, Ohio,
soar into the air
above the dunes and the wide beach
at Kitty Hawk.

As a Soldier Thinks of War

The winter's trials are about over. Already the larks are singing in the dawn that every week seems earlier, and whenever the cloudbanks roll away there is real warmth in the sunshine. The season of good weather that will bring great events and precipitate the action which all winter has been more or less in suspense will at the same time make the business of fighting harder to those of us in whom spring will wake other thoughts and other impulses. For war seemed perfectly proper when the fields were sere and nature abounded in images of death. But the bursting shells that hitherto have only sent the crows clamoring out of the bare forests will seem a strange anomaly when they scatter the cherry blossoms that will soon cloud the hillsides here where our trenches run.

They are the young soldier's worst enemy, these moments when the greatness of his renunciation is brought home to him by a song, a perfume, a memory:

> "J'aimerai toujours le temps des cerises,
> Et le souvenir que j'en garde au coeur."

It is when someone near the campfire begins to sing as only a Latin can—the feeling that wells so naturally from his heart touching in his listeners the spring of all that is fondest in memory and desire; it is in the long nights at the outposts when the grim irony comes over him that he should be there praying for the dawn where once it was *Lente, lente, currite noctis equi*—it is then that Youth in its tragic brevity and beauty slips by, and the sense of its vanishing opportunities for happiness plagues his heart with a poignancy of regret that at times becomes almost intolerable.

When he feels this way, the best remedy is to look a moment on the other side of the picture. Let him fancy himself liberated, lounging on the Riviera, or sipping his liqueur along the boulevards. Let him picture himself for a moment in the Venusberg of his dreams. Would he really be content? Would he not soon sing the same song as the minstrel knight? The vision would rise before him of young men who had been his companions in many a happy night in the Latin Quarter or Montmartre. Spurred less by the thought of any military ostentation or glory than that another generation might live free of the menace that had hung over their lives, quietly, uncomplainingly, they had marched forth. Who that had shared their hours of rejoicing could feel now in their hour of trial that, other things being equal, his place was not all the more at their side, that the burden that unsought had been laid on their shoulders should not rightfully be his too? No one of any imagination; no one of any conscience.

I have talked with so many of the young volunteers here. Their case is little known, even by the French, yet altogether interesting and appealing. They are foreigners on whom the outbreak of war laid no formal compulsion. But they had stood on the *butte* in springtime perhaps, as Julian and Louise stood, and looked out over the myriad twinkling lights of the beautiful city. Paris—mystic, maternal, personified, to whom they owed the happiest moments of their lives—Paris was in peril. Were they not under a moral obligation, no less binding than their comrades were bound legally, to put their breasts between her and destruction? Without renouncing their nationality they had yet chosen to make their homes here beyond any other city in the world. Did not the benefits and blessings they had received point them a duty that heart and conscience could not deny?

"Why did you enlist?" In every case the answer was the same. That memorable day in August came. Suddenly the old haunts were desolate, the boon companions had gone. It was unthinkable to leave the danger to them and accept only the pleasures oneself, to go on enjoying the sweet things of life in defence of which they were perhaps even then shedding their blood in the north. Some day they would return, and with honor—not all, but some. The old order of things would have irrevocably vanished. There would be a new comradeship whose bond would be the common danger run, the common sufferings borne, the common glory shared. "And where have you been all the time, and what have you been doing?" The very question would be a reproach, though none were intended. How could they endure it?

Face to face with a situation like that a man becomes reconciled, justifies easily the part he is playing, and comes to understand, in a universe where logic counts for so little and sentiment and the impulses of the heart for so much, the inevitableness and naturalness of war. Suddenly the world is up in arms. All mankind takes sides. The same faith that made him surrender himself to the impulses of normal living and of love forces him now to make himself the instrument through which a greater force works out its inscrutable ends through the impulses of terror and repulsion. And with no less a sense of moving in harmony with a universe where masses are in continual conflict and new combinations are engendered out of eternal collisions, he shoulders arms and marches forth with haste.

If no more serious argument can be brought against war than those inconveniences and sacrifices resulting to a man from his break with merely comfortable living, I confess I cannot see the contention of the pacifist, nor am I able to understand how war can be any more reasonably objected to than parturition, for example. That, too, is painful; only, being a phenomenon of common occurrence and one to which no alternative has ever been imagined even by the visionary, its inevitableness is universally accepted. It would be well if war were equally so—the supreme demand that nature makes upon the male, as the other iş the supreme demand made upon the female. Wars are the birthpangs of new eras. And he who, ready to assume the burden and share the anguish, makes himself the instrument through which this vast power operates, is playing the largest part a man can play. Though he perish while the sweetness of youth is still in him and his capacities for earthly happiness are still unexhausted, I imagine that he does so with infinitely more assurance than any hypothetical reward of a supernatural religion can afford its votary. For his comfort is the sense of his life's blood flowing close to the heart of that cosmic entity of which he feels himself a fraction, and in whose movements it is his measure of his life's success to play the most essential, the most intimate part.

This view of war in its sublimity is one that will not easily occur to the distant spectator. It takes long nights at the outposts, nights such as the last we have been spending half way up the hillside to the enemy's trenches, when the cannon thundered all along the line down toward Rheims, and, mounting toward the meteors that fell out of the morning skies, the slow-curving rockets marked the course of the battlefront across the vast, misty lowlands and into the starlit distances. Not the sense of the bestiality and inutility of it all, but rather of its entire harmoniousness in a universe properly understood is the emotion that possesses the spectator of such a scene. The easygoing pacifist will continue to talk of the horrors of militarism and the clock of civilization being set back a hundred years. This is because he is unable to conceive of evolution except as an orderly progress toward the realization of some arbitrary ideal based upon considerations of individual human wellbeing. The philosophic mind, on the other hand, does not think of evolution in terms of anything so relative as the principles of human morality at all, but rather as an increasing complexity of phenomena—of the possibilities for happiness as well as of all else—a process which works out through destructive influences quite as much as through inventive and creative.

In B———the other day I watched the children playing in the streets, for, reassured by the long deadlock on this part of the front, many families have returned to the little towns here within the very zone of artillery fire, living in the caves of their houses, where they run to shelter whenever the "marmites" begin to tumble about their roofs or the sudden buzzing of an aeroplane is heard overhead. They were playing soldier, which is natural enough for children in any part of the world, only their games had a little touch of realism that was amusing, for they were imitating with their childish voices the whistling of the shells that even to them has become a sound so familiar as to cause no emotion. It was a little thing, but it made me think of the opening paragraph of de Musset's "Confessions," where he attributes so much of the character of his genius to the spirit of that age in which he was born. And I had visions of distant compensations when the generation that is growing up under the stress of this present cataclysm is ripe to bear its spiritual fruits.

Sometimes through the doors of our dugouts here on the firing line a batch of American papers and periodicals is handed in with the mail that under the most abnormal conditions is delivered with laudable regularity. It is amusing to read these distant commentaries on the war, here where the postman that brings them to us has to crouch to shelter himself from the enemy's fire. In them are arranged all the errors of the antimilitarists which such a juxtaposition renders all the more transparent—the exaggerated notion of the importance of human life, the inability to understand international relations as being conducted upon any other basis than that which subsists between individuals. Especially there is the tendency to forget that peace in America is accidentally due to the very condition which Germany is trying to produce in Europe—that is, an hegemony of one people so powerful that no neighbor is able to contest it—and to attribute it to some quality of superiority in American civilization which thereby gives us the right to evangelize to the older nations. Let America beware of the hour when her long isolation from the currents of world politics shall be at an end, when, her most vital interests suddenly brought into conflict with those of a powerful rival, she must play her part among nations that have not had the leisure to dwell much upon prospects of what is most comfortable and agreeable to humanity, but having from time immemorial been forced to accept the grim inevitableness of the ultimate resort to armed force, have from time immemorial taken their precautions to meet it. Let her beware of that hour lest the alternative to war be not peace but dishonor. For that hour will certainly come.

I for my part find more beautiful the vistas that unfold through the windows of common everyday reality than through the portals of any premature Palace of Peace. The games of the children in the streets of B——— arouse speculations more interesting to me than those of the pacifist visionary. In so far as civilization means complexity in all the devices for material comfort and convenience, America can claim first place. But it seems to me that Europe will continue for some time yet to sing the world's great songs and make the world's great poems. For she has vibrated to all ranges of emotion. She has known great élans, and from the pinnacles of enthusiasm visions will have been revealed to her more wonderful than have ever yet been dreamed of. She has suffered greatly, and her heart has been tried with that kind of affliction that alone can unfold the profundities of the human spirit.

LILLIAN HELLMAN   APRIL 13, 1938

Day in Spain

The article appearing below was written by Miss Lillian Hellman at the request of Walter Winchell, to be published in Mr. Winchell's widely syndicated column. After it was prepared, however, the King Features Syndicate, owned by W. R. Hearst, refused to permit it to be distributed to the newspapers taking Mr. Winchell's column.—THE EDITORS

At twelve o'clock on an October day in Valencia it is usually warm and sunny. I stopped at the flower market and bought a bunch of flowers and some green leaves I had never seen before. I went around the corner and down the street and felt good walking in the hot sunshine. Ahead of me was a cat and I don't think I paid any attention to what happened until I saw the cat suddenly sit down in the middle of the street. While I stood there looking at him, I began to hear the sirens. A woman with a pushcart suddenly picked up a little girl, threw the child on the cart, and wheeled it swiftly away. I think a few people began to run, but most people stopped, suddenly, and then moved on again more swiftly. I knew afterwards, by the way my jaw felt, that I had been pressing my teeth together too hard. I turned, too, and began to walk, and told myself over and over again that as long as the sirens sounded the planes had not yet arrived. I didn't really believe that, but people were standing quietly in the open square, looking up. I went through the square quickly and towards my hotel and when I first heard the noise of the motors I didn't want to turn to see where they were. I thought: in that hotel room is a toothbrush, a clean nightgown, a cake of soap, an old coat and a box of lousy candy. Yet I am hurrying to it, it is where I am trying to go, it is the place where I have what belongs to me. And I knew, suddenly, why even the poorest women in Madrid wanted to stay with what was theirs.

But when I got to the corner of the hotel, the noise of the planes was close. I stopped at the corner and leaned against the wall. The planes were high in the east and flying fast. Next to me were two soldiers. One of them had a bunch of grapes in his hand. In a minute he said something to his friend and pointed in another direction. From the south four planes were flying towards us. They came up, swung around. Suddenly the soldier touched my arm and shouted, "They are ours." "There go ours." Then he pulled off some grapes, wiped them clean on his coat, and handed them to me. He said, "Our planes are up. It's all right, now." It wasn't all right. In the section around the port, three minutes later, the Italian bombers killed sixty-three people. But as we ate the grapes and smiled at each other, we didn't know that.

I drove up to the base hospital at Benacasim with Gustav Regler. Regler, who is a Jesuit-trained Catholic, was a fairly well known novelist until Hitler came in. He was a captain in the World War and had been badly injured in this, the "little war," when his car was bombed to pieces going up to the front lines. Driving fast towards Benacasim, we talked about writers and writing and got excited and argued and had fun. We got to Benacasim at dinner time, and the Germans and the Americans were eating at one large table. Some of their wives were there with them and I thought what good-looking people they all were and how generous they were with their food and cigarettes. (There wasn't much food and it was very bad.) Later that night, lying on a straw bed next to the wife of a Czech army officer, I thought that these foreigners from everywhere were noble people. I had never used the word noble before, and it came hard, even to say it to myself. They had come a long way to Spain, most of them making the cruel sixteen-hour walk across the Pyrenees. When it was over, if they came out alive, or with enough arms and legs to seem alive, there would be no glory and no reward. They had come because they thought that if a man believed in democracy he ought to do something about it. That's all they would go home with— wherever home was. Lying there, I prayed, for the first time in many years, that they would get what they wanted.

The next morning the American, Dr. Busch, Regler, the political commissar and I went on a round of visits. In the third room we visited, there were two men. One was a Canadian. One was a New York boy with that small, pinched, pale face that is so common among poor people in New York. The Canadian had lost his foot and didn't know it yet. The American boy was lying on his left side, his face twitching with pain. He was so bad that I couldn't look at him and, as Busch went over to the bed to examine him, I moved away. The political commissar was a fat little man who had just recovered from a bad spine wound. I heard the New York boy cry out in pain and I said to the political commissar, "What's the matter with him?" He said, "He was shot through the kidneys and through the thigh. The thigh wound is open." I said, "Can't you give him dope? Listen to him scream." The commissar nodded, "Sure. Busch will give him something. But don't mind the boy too much: he's a bad hypochondriac."

In the courtyard of the press office in Madrid, somebody has put a great many big statues. Nobody is very clear about how they got there, or what they are, or why they are there, but everybody agrees they are very bad statues indeed. Wednesday night, at about seven o'clock, a newspaper man said to me, "They're pretty awful. If they've got to shell, why can't they ever hit these things?" We reached the door to the street, "Can you find your way in the dark?" and I laughed and said sure, I was old enough not to be afraid of the dark. But when I opened the door and came out on the sidewalk, I knew that was a foolish thing to have said.

Without meaning to, I gasped. It is a terrible thing to see a city in complete darkness. A modern city is not meant to be without light at night: the buildings meet at the top in distorted triangles, and the sky seems too close to the earth. I went down the street, trying not to stumble, trying to find the curb of the sidewalks, trying not to step in holes. Twice I got lost, and once I turned my ankle and fell, and when I got up I was crying, and thought I was crying because my ankle hurt. But when I finally got to the hotel, I ran through it, feeling safe again. That was at seven o'clock. At eight-fifteen there was a sudden, whistling noise and then a far-off, muffled crash. A few minutes later, an English girl who worked in the Blood Transfusion Institute opened my door and came in to ask what I had done that day, did I like Madrid, did I want a drink, couldn't she—and stopped to listen and then to talk again quickly.

They were dropping forty shells a minute into Madrid and the whistling noise was growing very close. She turned to me, "Do you know what that is?" "Yes," I said, "shelling." "All right," she said. "I came up because I knew it was your first time. Come in the bathroom and you'll be able to tell how close it is." We went into the bathroom and she sat on the tub and watched me. In a few minutes the whistling went straight by the corner window and the crash this time was heavy, not sharp, and very close. She got up. "I'll go see if I can do anything. Go down to the dining room. It's in the center of the building." I said, "What good does that do?" She laughed, "Not much," and went out. I stood there looking out into the darkness. There were no sounds but the whistling, the flight of the shell and then a sharp or a dull crash. Suddenly there was a long heavy sound in the darkness—I think it was from a man—and through it a second sound. When the sound from the man ceased, the second sound came clear: a child was screaming, shrilly. In the hour and a half that Madrid was shelled that night there were many other sounds. Some of those sounds have no name in English.

This was the damage done that night: eighty people had been killed, two hotels had been hit, one grocery store and some houses in the poorest section of the town were gone, the press office had three shells in it, and the gentleman who didn't like the statues had been there to see two of the statues get two shells. In a kitchen back of my hotel, a blind woman was holding the bowl of soup that she came to get each night. She was killed eating the bowl of soup. Afterwards an Englishman said to me, "Not much sense to this kind of killing. They don't even try for military objectives any more, or for men. When I was on the Franco side, a few months ago, I heard the German technicians call this 'the little war.' They're practising. They're testing, testing the guns. They're finding the accuracy of the guns, they're finding the range." Finding the range on a blind woman eating a bowl of soup is a fine job for a man.

EDMUND WILSON   FEBRUARY 11, 1931

Communists and Cops

The Communists have announced their intention of leading a "Hunger March" on January 20. The city administration has agreed to receive a delegation at City Hall, but has not unreasonably refused a request to allow the Communists to make speeches from the steps.

In consequence, from ten o'clock on, a cordon of two hundred policemen are on guard around City Hall and the little park in front of it. You can't get anywhere near the building without running the gauntlet of the cops and presenting unimpeachable credentials. It is like some scene on an old-fashioned German parade grounds. The only human figures in the park are the immobile policemen, equestrian and on foot, with their blue coats and flat blue military caps and the great snow-white booby Civic Virtue with his thick trunk and his sulky Irish face, trampling on confused female bodies.

About one o'clock the Communists arrive, and the demonstration which has caused the city administration to fortify itself as if for a siege, commences. The demonstration consists of making speeches and of marching around City Hall Park. A good many of the Communists are Jews and some are Negroes—they are mostly small scrubby zealous people wearing red neckties, red hats or red dresses: there are a good many women with glasses. They have also recruited from the employment agencies and the breadlines a considerable number of seedy unemployed, Negroes, micks, old men, anomalous, miscellaneous people whom they have been able to persuade to take part in the demonstration as a means of getting unemployment insurance. They carry placards: "We Want No Charity," "No Evictions for the Unemployed," "We Demand Armories and Public Buildings for the Unemployed." They concentrate at the foot of the park opposite the Federal Building, and speakers get up on the iron dustbins. A crowd gathers—the newspaper photographers climb on the roofs of the Coca-Cola and Orange Drink stands on either side and dominate the scene with their cameras.

The first speaker is a young Negro named Newton, the editor of the Communist Negro paper and secretary of the League of Struggle for Negro Rights, who was one of the Communists arrested last May in Atlanta for circulating radical leaflets. Newton had never been in the South before: he is an educated Negro fom Boston. Some years ago, while working in a hotel, he got a two-weeks' vacation and arranged to go to a Y.M.C.A. camp; but when he arrived there, they wouldn't have him and gave him his money back. Later on, he met a Negro Communist, who told him that the Communists were out to abolish race discrimination, and joined the party. Like many of the Communist leaders, he is fine-looking, with large sensitive black eyes, skin closer to coffee than mahogany and a thick but straight and rather unnegroid nose. He is almost immediately joined by other speakers, among them a Negro of a quite different type, blacker, with a round face and an old soft hat, whose voice sounds falsetto above the rest. Speaker after speaker leaps onto the dustbin until there is only a babel of yelling— then speechmaking is given up: the group on the dustbin begins rousing the crowd with methods like those of college cheerleaders—"We—want—*work-or-wages!* We—want—*work-or-wages!*" The harsh fanatic rhythm goes on and on—the people in the crowd get caught up into it and begin to shout with the leaders. The street is packed and impassable, and now the crowd is packing the road. The taxis and the mail trucks can't get by, and the police decide to break things up. Coming behind the speakers' stand, they push the people along the sidewalk. "Oh-oh!" exclaims a gaping bystander. "He's hittin' 'em on the head!" From the road a mounted policeman starts out to ride into the crowd. As he does so, he screws up one side of his mouth: he is a clean-cut young man with his mind on holding in his horse. He scarcely does more than turn the horse's head in the direction of the overthronged sidewalk and go through the motions of riding into it. "That's right!—go after 'em!" a young man among the bystanders eggs him on.

The crowd becomes liquefied and begins to move. A nice-looking boy of about ten, Comrade Charley, a Young Pioneer from Brighton Beach, wearing an old red-plaid mackinaw, shouts from above the heads of the crowd with a voice that sounds strangely fresh and vigorous amid the systematic shouting of the grown people. He is being carried on the shoulders of a very tall Negro, another worker in the League of Struggle for Negro Rights, who has recently served a sentence of three months for breaking up an anti-lynching meeting of the Pullman porters' association: the Pullman porters' association are socialists but, according to the Negro Communists, on the right side of white respectability, and guilty on this occasion of deliberately suppressing the evidence in regard to the lynching of a Pullman porter in Georgia.

The demonstration pushes slowly around the park. "Aw, that's a lotta—!" yells one of the spectators. "Oh, yeah?" retorts a fierce little Communist. "What the hell do you know about it?"—"We want bread!" another Communist is declaring—"Try and get it!" says another spectator, grim but sympathetic. A very shabby Jew of mature age who speaks English very thickly distributes leaflets on unemployment insurance and repeats conscientiously again and again: "Dis has got to become a law vedder de bosses like it or not!" The police watch from behind the iron posts that prevent people from driving in to City Hall: some are Negroes, brought down from Harlem for the occasion, but they have almost the same Prussian military stature, the same square faces and mail-slot mouths as their white fellows. The policemen seem to fall into two classes: the husky good-natured kind who accomplish their disciplinary duties, though with satisfaction, without heat, and the more stupid staring-eyed type hired frankly as mobilizable brutes. Some of these are evidently Jews, specially provided like the Negroes to deal with agitators of their own race. In any case, the police offer a curious contrast to everybody else present: if the Communists seem mostly stunted, the office workers out for lunch are hardly better; and the cops seem the only healthy full-sized people and the only people decently dressed in these choked-up streets of milling human beings, bewildered, determined, half-scared, or angry at not being able to get more quickly to their destinations, but all looking undersized, undernourished, dingy-featured, drearily dressed. Only when the Communists sing "The International" or a Communist song to the tune of "John Brown's Body" is one aware of any capacity among them for normal human enthusiasm or warmth.

> It's the final conflict!
>   Let each stand in his place!
> The International Soviet
>   Shall be the human race!

The bald words, the banal tune, for all they have come to mean that the anthems of nations are ceasing to mean, lift the heart as the marching Communists raise their arms and wave them to the refrain. Some of the leaders have themselves carried on the shoulders of their companions and try to revive the "We want work or wages!" cry. All around them under the gray winter sky rise the high ugly walls of the buildings of downtown New York, keeping the marchers, the crowd and the traffic crammed into the tight little space, the only open space at this end of the island, between the buildings and the rigorously guarded park: the men's-wear shops, Schrafft's soda fountains, Liggett's drug stores and cafeterias of Nassau Street and Broadway, the rusty green dome of the World Building, the green trimmings on dingy red brick of the Sun Building, topping their awkward perpendicular fragments still standing narrow and precarious from the last century as if the structure they were to have belonged to had never been finished, a corner with cheap chop-suey signs over cheap investment-loan signs, a brick office building from whose flat cold red every suggestion of color seems to have departed beyond any possibility of revival by the sun, the somewhat handsomer gray cliff of the Woolworth Building eroded and lined like a giant butte and diminishing in tiers toward the top, the squashed-out, square-sided dome of the Federal Building spotted with little portholes like moles above a vast bulk of gray machine-made public dignity. In that cramped and inhospitable arena, the Communists produce simply confusion—a confusion which gets worse and worse. From the other side of the park, a dreadful woman's scream is heard.

In the meantime, the delegation, under police escort, has been presenting its demands at City Hall. The Mayor is sick in bed—according to the Communists, afraid to face them and malingering—and they are received by the incomparably affable Mr. Kerrigan. F.G. Biedenkapp, the principal spokesman, demands unemployment insurance, free gas, electricity and coal and no evictions for the unemployed, and free clothing and food for their children, reduced rents, the throwing open of vacant apartments and public buildings and the use of schools and public halls for meeting places, the distribution of unemployment relief through a board composed entirely of workers and Communists, which shall also take over all the employment-agency work now being done by the State Labor Department, the Y.M.C.A. and all the other organizations, no discrimination between workers because of race, color, nationality or sex, and the immediate release of comrades now in jail as a result of previous demonstrations. To this Mr. Kerrigan replies that "the city is constituted according to law and a number of your demands would be illegal if carried out," that "if the city officials tried to carry them out they would be immediately removed," that the city officials are contributing out of their salaries for unemployment relief, that the city employment fund is to be increased, that the city is going to try to bring pressure to bear at Albany to amend the law so as to make it possible to stop evictions, that the city has set up a free employment agency which will have the effect of suppressing the private agencies and eliminating "the deception and dishonesty practised by some of them," that the Board of Education is already doing what it can to feed the children of the unemployed. "I don't want to say," he concludes, "that if you don't like it here, you can go back to Russia, because many of you were born here—but I will say that I will pay the full fare, one way, of any ten of you who want to go there. That is about all we can do under the present system." F.G. Biedenkapp, in reply to this, declares that the committee is "entirely dissatisfied with your explanations and excuses"—and the Communists, under escort, withdraw.

Once outside, they make haste to climb on the statue of Benjamin Franklin just below the Sun Building and shout that their demands have been refused: "We saw the acting mayor and told him our demands and he said that it was against the law to grant them. The unemployed workers must change the laws!" This is a signal for the demonstration to swarm. They hang their placards all over the statue, which stands with a discolored green bronze crown, with one hand extended as if in patriarchal blessing, and at its feet a garland of large funereal wreaths presented by the Sons of the American Revolution. Comrade Charley, full of pep in his red mackinaw, climbs up on to the great bourgeois's shoulders and displays a placard which says: "We Demand Free Food for Our Children!" A crowd gathers on the opposite curbs. The statue stands on a little lozenge of pavement between Nassau Street and Park Row and is so situated that any disturbance around it causes a maximum jam of the traffic to and from Brooklyn Bridge: the Communists have picked a strategic point for obstructing the downtown life of the city. Taxis bawl and street cars clang—curious office workers overflow the sidewalks, asking one another what is going on. Somebody from a high floor of the Sun Building drops a paper bag full of water down upon the crowd around the statue; it comes apart in the air and people watch the whirl of water fall.

The police decide to put an end to the demonstration. They force their way into the crowd and begin pulling down the placards and the speakers from the statue. An unintelligible melee ensues. The Communists flee before the police and the by-standers get mixed up with them. One has a glimpse of a last indomitable speaker with a wild livid insane face still vituperating alone on the statue—a second later he has disappeared. People yell, "Look out!" Mounted cops begin galloping along the sidewalks and everybody runs in terror before them, demonstrators and innocent pedestrians both. A Communist, grabbing apples from an unemployed apple-vendor, soaks the policemen with them and finally crowns one of the horses with the crate. Another seizes a horse by the tail—a detective clutches him by the collar and beats him—two women rush to his rescue and almost pull the policeman off his horse. The traffic are sore; the spectators dismayed; the unemployed have scattered like autumn leaves. The Communists rally, shouting "Close up ranks!" and rush up the entrance of the flat raised tunnel which leads to the Brooklyn Bridge subway, completely filling the wide steps and booing the police as if from bleachers. The police stretch a rope along the back of the park and excitedly patrol the paths. In one place, quite remote from the disturbance, there is a shoe-shining stand, with a row of men peacefully sitting in the chairs and reading the tabloids as they have their shoes shined—but at the sudden appearance of charging mounted cops, they all spring out of their seats simultaneously and leap over the iron fence. A gray flight of pigeons rise from the park, the only free living things in sight. The Communists, routed again from the bridge entrance, shouting "We want bread, not horses' hoofs!" rally around short-lived speakers on the curbs in persistent but ever dwindling groups. A patrol wagon and an ambulance arrive; a stretcher is carried out of City Hall. One reads in the papers the next morning that there are demonstrators with broken arms, teeth knocked out, fractured skulls and all sorts of wounds, an auditor in the comptroller's office with his head cut open against the Municipal Building and a policeman who fell into the hands of the demonstrators in the hospital from having been kicked in the stomach.

The Communists, pursued into the labyrinth of the more than Roman pillars and vaults of the Municipal Building, lurk awhile and then return. Driven down Centre Street, they come back up Elm. Among the passers-by behind the park, a small plump sharp-beaked Jewess in red—great wrath in a tiny body like one of Virgil's bees—wanders all alone shouting, "Down with the police!" At the corner of Centre Street, a little dingy man pauses as a spattering on the sidewalk turns out to be too thick, too red and too profuse for spit—he says in a foolish way to no one in particular and with a combination of surprise and awe: "Blood!"

Now the streets are completely cleared—the suction pumps of the downtown buildings have pulled up their population again. The people are emerging from the subway, going up the steps to Brooklyn Bridge, unimpeded—the taxis drive down to Wall Street, the trucks drive across from the docks. The pretzel man with his basket and the roast-chestnut man have come out. The battle has been completely obliterated. None of these people has even heard of it. Many of the people who witnessed or became involved in it never even knew what it was about. They are neither sympathetic with the Communists nor indignant at them—they are not even indignant at having been chased by the police. They feel no stake in the city as a community and consequently take very little interest in the city administration. If they have jobs in these hard times, they are satisfied to hang on to them, and they have all gone about their business long ago.

MALCOLM COWLEY   JANUARY 28, 1931

Connecticut Valley

Zebulon Trumbull at sixty-five is like a cider barrel set on two short legs. His girth is tremendous; so is his strength. He can lift the rear axle of a Buick unaided. He can lift a fifty-gallon barrel full of cider, but he won't take a drink of it afterwards, not even to slake his thirst. Years ago his only brother died of drinking cider.

Zebulon Trumbull has no children. The money he inherited year by year, as branch by branch the Trumbull family died out, will eventually go to his wife. If she is no longer alive, it will go to his second cousin in Bridgeport.

On the 400-acre farm that his great-grandfather bought from the Indians, he tried for nearly fifty years to make a fortune. He grew tobacco, good tobacco, too, but fertilizer was expensive and all the help were lazy. He ran a dairy with blooded stock, but half his cows were condemned as tubercular. He raised chickens and sold them off; he raised turkeys and lost them to the foxes. He ran a sawmill for two years; then he became a huckster. He traded horses all over the state, till automobiles drove them off the roads; he still boasts that he never got the worst of a bargain. At present he repairs antique furniture and studies the genealogy of his family, which first settled near Providence in 1652. He pores all evening over his one book, a family history; it cost him $25. His hands are scrubbed, so as not to soil its rag-paper pages, but his nails are black and there is dirt in the deep creases of his fingers, dirt that has stayed there forty years, since the days when he hoed tobacco plants in the August sun.

He is not quite used to the electric lights in his new house, nor to the hum of the electric refrigerator in the kitchen. Last year, for a good price, he sold his four hundred acres and moved to town.

Mr. Denison, who bought the Trumbull place, is generous and hurried. His friends tell you that Jim Denison is a good guy, that he deserves his success: God knows he had to work for it. He works too hard; he drinks too hard when he isn't working. He is the best advertising copywriter in New York City. His hands move nervously; his face is gray, deep lined and flabby. Mr. Denison is a middle-aged man at thirty-five.

It was his wife who convinced him that they should buy a farm. She is a homely woman, low voiced and friendly, who dresses in tweeds and has no trouble keeping servants. She used to own a dog, but she felt so bad when he died that she never would have another. She buys antiques—rarely from Zebulon Trumbull, whose prices, she says, are outrageous. With the help of local labor, and some encouragement from her husband, she has remodeled the Trumbull house, painting it a light cream with Chinese-blue shutters and building a pergola where the outhouse used to stand. Last spring she had the carpenter pull down the barn that closed the long view into the valley.

It is a shame, say the Denisons, that the fields below the house are growing up in sweetfern and sumac. They would like to buy sheep to keep down the weeds—but who would care for the sheep during the winter? It's so hard to find help that you can trust, and there are so few natives here in the valley. But isn't it a comfort to have such nice summer neighbors—artists and writers and all that! Sometimes it seems that all the really intelligent people in New York are moving to the country.

The Denisons are known for their hospitality. Every Saturday night they give a party, to which they invite the writers, the painters, the editors, and the Norwegian musician from North Dakota who bought the Levi Adams place. Their invitations are rarely refused. Mr. Denison can mix an insidious cocktail, and there is a barrel of two-year-old Connecticut applejack in his cellar.

Parties at the Denisons are noisy and good humored. Mr. Denison drinks eight or ten slugs of applejack; he says they rest him after a hard week at the office. He talks about the novel he would write if he weren't held to his desk—if he had plenty of time like you writing chaps. The writers and painters don't laugh at him behind his back; they kid him to his face like the good fellows they are. The Norwegian musician plays jazz, very intelligent jazz to which nobody can dance. The artists and writers play ping pong, or go for a stroll with someone else's wife. There is a good deal of loose talk, a few dirty jokes are told, not in whispers, but there is no real evil. Everybody is tired of Greenwich Village affairs; everybody is over thirty. Sometimes the crowd plays Anagrams, or Murder, or even old-fashioned Hide and Seek, with the lights out and couples darting over the maple-shaded lawn in the moonlight. About one o'clock Mr. Denison, dead drunk, goes to sleep on the couch. There is the sound of motors starting, and the dirt road is swept by headlights.

I usually walk home from the Denisons' parties. After the last car has passed, the road is very quiet. The country loses its ravaged daytime look: the roofless barns seem whole and the fields well tended. The mullein stalks in the moonlight are like tobacco; the goldenrod might be a ripe field of wheat.

The Casey boys lead an easy life. In the summer they work at their trades, and there is always more work than they can do. In the winter they hunt, or chop wood, or sit by the kitchen stove and drink hard cider.

Joe Casey is fifty-four. He was married once, but his wife left him because she couldn't stand his drinking. Tom Casey, the baby of the family, is forty-nine and has never married. The two boys live with their mother, a woman of eighty who remembers her girlhood in Donegal. Their father's sword hangs over the mantelpiece, its scabbard worn away diagonally at the tip from dragging for two years through the Virginia mud.

The Casey boys often speak of their father. An immigrant boy, he enlisted in the Union army; he rose in two years to the rank of second lieutenant. He came to this Connecticut valley with no baggage except his sword. Here the struggle was longer, but at the end of twenty years he had his own house and his own land free from mortgage. In those days there was joy in owning land, with the valley full of rich tobacco farms, stock farms, dairy farms, and among them fields of dark-green potato plants and light-green oats. The Casey boys are proud of their father: maybe that's the reason they cling to his now untilled land when almost all the Yankee farmers around them have moved away.

Yankee names are disappearing from the valley. The Briggses, what are left of them, now live in Waterbury. Theodore Doane, too feeble to keep a herd of cattle, is staying with his one son, Homer, who runs a garage at the forks of the road. Old Zebulon is the last of the Trumbulls. The Penney tribe, once numerous in the countryside, has vanished; even the Penney houses have rotted into black, weed-grown soil. The Whipples, father and son, live by the sale of milk, eggs, chickens, green vegetables and building lots; their women work till long after sunset; they are saving money against the day when they will all settle in California. "It's so hard hereabouts in the wintertime," they say.

But life is easy for the Casey boys. In the spring, as soon as the cider barrels are empty and the frost is out of the ground, Joe Casey sets to work at his trade; his brother Tom goes fishing. Joe is a mason: he builds fireplaces, terraces and old-fashioned well curbs. Tom is a painter and paper hanger, but he never works till after the trout season is ended. All summer they are busy at good wages; then, in the middle of autumn, Joe Casey sets to work at the cider mill, taking his pay in barrels of cider. Tom Casey goes hunting.

In November, the Caseys put on their best clothes and, more or less sober, go to attend town meeting. There used to be as many as two hundred voters in the town hall; now there are never more than sixty; last fall only thirty men and women assembled from a town which covers nearly fifty square miles. They always talk of old times and high taxes and the price of land. They argue the question of whether to hire a teacher for next year, or whether to send the town's twelve children to the neighboring city by motor bus. They choose a man—always the same—to represent them in the state legislature. They elect a board of assessors to reduce their own taxes and to raise the assessment of the farms bought by what they call the summer people. Then, more or less sober, the Casey boys go home to spend the winter hunting and chopping wood and sitting by the fire. The snow seeps down; the roads are closed to automobiles; only the postman passes three times weekly in his sleigh. "The country looks like itself in the wintertime," Tom Casey says. "It's like when Pop was living," Joe answers as he goes to the cellar for another pitcher of cider.

Early in May, when the arbutus buds are opening in the woods and the roads are dry enough for motor traffic, the summer people come trooping back. There is the sound of opened shutters, of carpets beaten in the yard. The first smoke rises from a dozen chimneys, to mingle with the haze that sleeps over Tory Hill. The housewives lay plans for a rock garden here, for a terrace or a second fireplace; they must get Joe Casey if he's sober, and really the new maid is unbearable. . . . Then, pausing to look at the hilltop, where the oak buds are a smoky green, they say, "Isn't all this beautiful! Aren't you glad we live in this lovely valley!"

During July and August, the summer people travel incessantly along the valley roads. They drive to the Whipples' for milk and eggs, to the Denisons' for a highball, to Green Pond for a swim. They have social functions of their own—gin parties, ping-pong parties, barn parties, yes, and musicales—which they attend in force. Over the week end their houses are crowded with guests from the city, who exclaim between two drinks, "Oh, how I envy you this lovely old farmhouse!"—"Yes, isn't the valley beautiful," the summer people agree. Yet there is something purely formal in their agreement, something beyond mere boredom with their guests and irritation at hearing the same statement repeated too often. The summer people are not of this country; their hands are not black with its soil; they do not depend on its seasons or live by its fruits.

In autumn, when the neglected orchards of the valley are heavy with apples, and grapes turn purple on the vines, and the fields are dotted with gentians almost the color of the autumn haze, the summer people prepare to go. They sprinkle mothballs in the closets, they lock the shutters, they store their bright lawn furniture in the empty barns. Their cars, waiting at the front gate, are piled with suitcases, unfinished manuscripts or paintings, vaseline glass, and the two Hitchcock chairs they bought at such a bargain. For a moment they wait before starting the motor. They look at the hills, where the oaks are changing color, at the fields overgrown with wine-colored sumac; they look down at the blazing maples in the swamp. Somewhere in the woods a hound is baying on a cold scent; the sound of Joe Casey's axe drifts down from the hill. "Isn't the valley beautiful in October," the summer people repeat without conviction. "Aren't you glad we live here," they say as they drive off.

EUDORA WELTY   OCTOBER 25, 1943

Pageant of Birds

I have been told that this little account needs a generality of some kind made in the first paragraph to Northern readers. I do not think it does, since any generality could only be the commonplace belief I have that magic-making is often the strange compound of humbleness and pride. It is many times the projection out of humbleness to pride, or in the other direction, out of pride to humbleness, the way the saints, for instance, achieved it. Everywhere, the life in a town that goes mostly unseen, because it does not happen to the spectacular inhabitants, never fails to make its own spectacular events out of what is has to work and play with. It has nothing to do with where we live, that we make our own toys and make meaning or bedazzle ourselves out of what is at hand. These colored people I happened to see had got hold of some bright tissue paper.

One summer evening on a street in my town I saw two Negro women walking along carrying big colored paper wings in their hands and talking and laughing. They proceeded unquestioned, the way angels did in their day possibly, although anywhere else but on such a street the angels might have been looked back at if they had taken their wings off and carried them along over their arms. I followed them to see where they were going and, sure enough, it was to church.

They walked in at the Farish Street Baptist Church, which is one of the respectable churches of Negro-town, brick-veneered, and has no hollering or chanting in the unknown tongue. It stands on a corner in the business section, across the street from the Methodist Church, in a block with the clothing stores, the pool hall, the Booker-T movie house, the doctor's office, the pawnshop with gold in the windows, the café with the fish-sign that says "If They Don't Bite We Catch 'em Anyhow," and the barber shop with the Cuban hair styles drawn on the window.

I looked in at the door of the church and saw that the big frame room was empty of people but ready for something. The lights were shining. The ceiling was painted the color of heaven, bright blue, and with this to start on, decorators had gone ahead to make the place into a scene that could only be prepared to receive birds. Pinned all around the walls were drawings of birds—bluebirds, redbirds, quail, flamingoes, wrens, love-birds—some copied from pictures, and the redbird a familiar cover taken from a school tablet. There was greenery everywhere. Sprigs of snow-on-the-mountain, a bush which grows to the point of complete domination in gardens of the neighborhood this time of year, were tied in neat bunches, with single zinnias stuck in, at regular intervals around the room, on the pews and along the altar rail. Over in the corner the piano appeared to be a large mound of vines, with the keyboard bared rather startlingly, like a row of teeth from ambush. On the platform where the pulpit had been was a big easy chair, draped with a red and blue robe embroidered in fleur-de-lys. Above it, two American flags were crossed over a drawing of an eagle copied straight off the back of a dollar bill.

As soon as people began coming into the church, out came Maude Thompson from the rear, all bustling and starched in the obvious role of church leader. She came straight to welcome us. Yes, indeed, she said, there was to be a Pageant of Birds at seven o'clock sharp. I was welcome and all my friends. As she talked on, I was pleased to learn that she had written the pageant herself and had not got it from some Northern YWCA or missionary society, as might be feared. "I said to myself, 'There have been pageants about everything else—why not about birds?'" she said. She told me proudly that each costume had been made by the bird who would wear it. It seemed to gratify her when I went and brought a few more white people. We were seated, unavoidably, because we were white, in the first row, with our feet turned sidewise by a large can of zinnias, but in the first of the excitement we were forgotten and all proceeded as if we weren't there.

Maude Thompson made an announcement to the audience that everybody had better be patient. "Friends, the reason we are late starting is that several of the birds have to work late and haven't arrived yet. If there are any birds in the audience now, will they *kindly get on back here?*" Necks craned and eyes popped in delight when a girl in a dark-blue tissue-paper dress jumped up from a back pew and skittered out. Maude Thompson clapped her hands for order and told how the collection to be taken up would be used to pay for a piano—"not a new one, but a better one." Her hand was raised solemnly: we were promised, if we were quiet and nice, the sight of even more birds than there were represented on the walls. The audience fanned, patted feet dreamily, and waited.

The pageant, decidely worth waiting for, began with a sudden complete silence in the audience, as if by mass intuition. Every head turned, and all eyes fastened upon the front door of the church.

Then came the entrance of the Eagle Bird. Her wings and tail were of gold and silver tin-foil, and her dress was a black and purple kimona. She began a slow pace down the aisle with that truly majestic dignity which only a vast, firmly matured physique, wholly unselfconscious, can achieve. She had obviously got to be the Eagle because she was the most important. Her hypnotic majesty was almost prostrating to the audience, as she moved, as slowly as possible, down the aisle and finally turned and stood beneath the eagle's picture on the wall, in the exact center of the platform. A little eaglet boy, with propriety her son, about two and a half feet tall, very black, entered from the Sunday-school room and trotted around her with a sprightly tail over his knickers, flipping his hands dutifully from the wrist out. He had bows on each shoulder. No smiles were exchanged— there was not a smile in the house. The eagle then seated herself with a stifled groan in her chair, there was a strangled chord from the piano where a bird now sat, and with the little eaglet to keep time by waving a flag jutting out from each wing, the congregation rose and sang "The Star-Spangled Banner." (This was before everything opened that way.)

Then the procession of lesser birds began, and the music—the pianist watched in a broken piece of mirror hidden in the vines—then went gradually into syncopation.

The birds would enter from the front door of the church, portentously, like members of a bridal party, proceed in absolute and easily distinguishable character down the aisle, cross over and take their places in a growing circle around the audience. All came in with an assurance that sprang from complete absorption in their roles—erect in their bright wings and tails and crests, flapping their elbows, dipping their knees, hopping and turning and preening to the music. It was like a dance only inasmuch as birds might dance under the circumstances. They would, on reaching the platform, bow low, first to the Eagle Bird, who gave them back a stern look, and then to the audience, and take their positions, never ceasing to fly in place and twitter now and then, never showing recognition or saying one word to anyone, even each other. There were many more birds of some varieties than of others; I understood that "you could be what you want to." Maude Thompson, standing in a white uniform beside the piano, made a little evocation of each variety, checking down a list.

"The next group of birds to fly will be the bluebirds," she said, and in they flew, three big ones and one little one, in clashing shades of blue crepe-paper. They were all very pleased and serious with their movements. The oldest wore shell-rimmed glasses. There were redbirds, four of them; two robin redbreasts with diamond-shaped gold speckles on their breasts; five "pink-birds"; two peacocks who simultaneously spread their tails at a point halfway down the aisle;

goldfinches with black tips on their tails, who waltzed slowly and somehow appropriately; canary birds, announced as "the beautiful canaries, for pleasure as well as profit," who whistled vivaciously as they twirled, and a small canary who had a yellow ostrich plume for a crest. There was only one "beautiful blackbird, alone but not lonesome," with red caps on her wings; there was a head-wagging purple finch, who wore gold earrings. There was the parrot-bird, who was a man and caused shouts—everyone's instant favorite; he had a yellow breast, one green trouser-leg, one red; he was in his shirt-sleeves because it was hot, and he had red, green, blue and yellow wings. The woman parrot (his wife) followed after in immutable seriousness—she had noticed parrots well, and she never got out of character: she ruffled her shoulder feathers, she was cross, she pecked at her wings, she moved her head rapidly from side to side and made obscure sounds, not quite words; she was so good she almost called up a parrot. There was loud appreciation of the parrots—I thought at first they would have to go back and come in again. The "red-headed peckerwood" was a little boy alone. The "poor little mourning dove" was called, but proved absent. "And last but not least, the white dove of peace!" cried Maude Thompson. There came two doves, very sanctimonious indeed, with long sleeves, nurse's shoes and white cotton gloves. They flew with restraint, almost sadly.

When they had all come inside out of the night, the birds almost surrounded the congregation. They had a finale. They sang, lifting up their wings and swaying from side to side in time to the enthusiastic music, bending and rolling their hips, all singing. And yet in their own and in everybody's eyes they were still birds. They were certainly birds to me.

> And I want TWO wings
> To veil my face
> And I want TWO wings
> To fly away,
> And I want TWO wings
> To veil my face,
> And the world can't do me no harm.

That was their song, and they circled the church singing and clapping with their wings, and flew away by the back door, where the ragamuffins of the alley yelled "Oooh!" and jumped aside to let them pass.

They were so proud of the pageant that I wanted them to have a picture of the group to keep and offered to take it. Maude Thompson said, "Several of the birds could meet you in front of the church door tomorrow afternoon at four."

As a matter of fact, there turned out to be a number of rendezvous which some of the birds failed to keep; and I never got the eagle, who has some very confining job. Loyal birds were finally photographed, however, Maude Thompson supervising the poses. I did not dare interfere. She instructed them to hold up their necks, and reproached the dove of peace for smiling. "You ever see a bird smile?"

Since our first meeting I have chanced on Maude Thompson several times. Every time I would be getting on a train, I would see her in the station; she would be putting on a coffin, or receiving one, in a church capacity. She would always tell me how the pageant was doing, They were on the point of taking it to Forrest or

Mount Olive or some other town. Also, the birds have now made themselves faces and beaks.

"This is going to be one of those things going to grow," said Maude Thompson.

ERNEST HEMINGWAY   MAY 18, 1927

Italy, 1927

The road of the pass was hard and smooth and not yet dusty in the early morning. Below were the hills with oak and chestnut trees, and far away below was the sea. On the other side were snowy mountains.

We came down from the pass through wooded country. There were bags of charcoal piled beside the road, and through the trees we saw charcoal burners' huts. It was Sunday and the road, rising and falling, but always dropping away from the altitude of the pass, went through the scrub woods and through villages.

Outside the villages there were fields with vines. The fields were brown and the vines coarse and thick. The houses were white, and in the streets the men, in their Sunday clothes, were playing bowls. Against the walls of some of the houses there were pear trees, their branches candelabra'd against the white walls. The pear trees had been sprayed, and the walls of the houses were stained a metallic blue-green by the spray vapor. There were small clearings around the villages where the vines grew and then the woods.

In a village twenty kilometers above Spezia there was a crowd in the square, and a young man carrying a suitcase came up to the car and asked us to take him in to Spezia.

"There are only two places, and they are occupied," I said. We had an old Ford coupé.

"I will ride on the outside."

"You will be uncomfortable."

"That makes nothing. I must go to Spezia."

"Should we take him?" I asked Guy.

"He seems to be going anyway," Guy said. The young man handed in a parcel through the window.

"Look after this," he said. Two men tied his suitcase on the back of the car above our suitcases. He shook hands with everyone, explained that to a Fascist and a man as used to traveling as himself there was no discomfort, and climbed up on the running board on the left-hand side of the car, holding on inside, his right arm through the open window.

"You can start," he said. The crowd waved. He waved with his free hand.

"What did he say?" Guy asked me.

"That we could start."

"Isn't he nice," Guy said.

The road followed a river. Across the river were mountains. The sun was taking the frost out of the grass. It was bright and cold and the air came cold through the open wind-shield.

"How do you think he likes it out there?" Guy was looking up the road. His view out of his side of the car was blocked by our guest. The young man projected from the side of the car like the figurehead of a ship. He had turned his coat collar up and pulled his hat down and his nose looked cold in the wind.

"Maybe he'll get enough of it," Guy said. "That's the side our bum tire's on."

"Oh, he'd leave us if we blew out," I said. "He wouldn't get his traveling clothes dirty."

"Well, I don't mind him," Guy said. "Except the way he leans out on the turns."

The woods were gone; the road had left the river to climb; the radiator was boiling; the young man looked annoyedly and suspiciously at the steam and rusty water; the engine was grinding, with both Guy's feet on the first speed pedal, up and up, back and forth and up, and finally out level. The grinding stopped, and in the new quiet there was a great churning bubbling in the radiator. We were at the top of the last range above Spezia and the sea. The road descended with short, barely rounded turns. Our guest hung out on the turns and nearly pulled the top-heavy car over.

"You can't tell him not to," I said to Guy. "It's his sense of self-preservation."

"The great Italian sense."

"The greatest Italian sense."

We came down around curves, through deep dust, the dust powdering the olive trees. Spezia spread below along the sea. The road flattened outside the town. Our guest put his head in the window.

"I want to stop."

"Stop it," I said to Guy.

We slowed up at the side of the road. The young man got down, went to the back of the car and untied the suitcase.

"I stop here so you won't get into trouble carrying passengers," he said. "My package."

I handed him the package. He reached in his pocket.

"How much do I owe you?"

"Nothing."

"Why not?"

"I don't know," I said.

"Then thanks," the young man said, not "thank you," or "thank you very much," or "thank you a thousand times," all of which you formerly said in Italy to a man when he handed you a time table or explained about a direction. The young man uttered the lowest form of the word thanks and looked after us suspiciously as Guy started the car. I waved my hand at him. He was too dignified to reply. We went on into Spezia.

"Well," said Guy, "he went twenty kilometers with us."

A MEAL IN SPEZIA

We came into Spezia looking for a place to eat. The street was wide and the houses high and yellow. We followed the tram track into the center of town. On the walls of the houses were stenciled eye-bugging portraits of Mussolini, with handpainted "vivas," the double V in black paint with drippings of paint down the wall. Side streets went down to the harbor. It was bright and the people were all out for Sunday. The stone paving had been sprinkled and there were damp stretches in the dust. We went close to the curb to avoid a tram.

"Let's eat somewhere simple," Guy said.

We stopped opposite two restaurant signs. We were standing across the street and I was buying the papers. The two restaurants were side by side. A woman standing in the doorway of one smiled at us and we crossed the street and went in.

It was dark inside and at the back of the room three girls were sitting at a table with an old woman. Across from us at another table sat a sailor. He sat there neither eating nor drinking. Further back a young man in a blue suit was writing at a table. His hair was pomaded and shining and he was very smartly dressed and clean-cut looking.

The light came in through the doorway, and through the window where vegetables, fruit, steaks and chops were arranged in a show case. A girl came and took our order and another girl stood in the doorway. We noticed that she wore nothing under her house dress. The girl who took our order put her arm around Guy's neck while we were looking at the menu. There were three girls in all, and they all took turns going and standing in the doorway. The old woman at the table in the back of the room spoke to them and they sat down again with her.

There was no doorway leading from the room except into the kitchen. A curtain hung over it. The girl who had taken our order came in from the kitchen with spaghetti. She put it on the table and brought a bottle of red wine and sat down at the table.

"Well," I said to Guy, "you wanted to eat someplace simple."

"This isn't simple. This is complicated."

"What do you say?" asked the girl. "Are you Germans?"

"South Germans," I said. "The South Germans are a gentle, lovable people."

"Don't understand," she said.

"What's the mechanics of this place?" Guy asked. "Do I have to let her put her arm around my neck?"

"Certainly," I said. "Mussolini has abolished the brothels. This is a restaurant."

The girl wore a one-piece dress. She leaned forward against the table and put her hands on her breasts and smiled. She smiled better on one side than on the other and turned the good side toward us. The charm of the good side had been enhanced by some event which had smoothed the other side of her nose in as warm wax can be smoothed. Her nose, however, did not look like warm wax. It was very cold and firmed, only smoothed in. "You like me?" she asked Guy.

"He adores you," I said. "But he doesn't speak Italian."

"Ich sprech Deutsch," she said, and stroked Guy's hair.

"Speak to the lady in your native tongue, Guy."

"Where do you come from?" asked the lady.

"Potsdam."

"And you will stay here now for a little while?

"In this so dear Spezia?" I asked.

"Tell her we have to go," said Guy. "Tell her we are very ill, and have no money."

"My friend is a misogynist," I said. "An old German misogynist."

"Tell him I love him."

I told him.

"Will you shut your mouth and get us out of here?" Guy said. The lady had placed another arm around his neck. "Tell him he is mine," she said. I told him.

"Will you get us out of here?"

"You are quarreling," the lady said. "You do not love one another."

"We are Germans," I said proudly. "Old South Germans."

"Tell him he is a beautiful boy," the lady said. Guy is thirty-eight and takes some pride in the fact that he is taken for a traveling salesman in France. "You are a beautiful boy," I said.

"Who says so?" Guy asked, "you or her?"

"She does. I'm just your interpreter. Isn't that what you got me in on this trip for?"

"I'm glad it's her," said Guy. "I didn't want to have to leave you here too."

"I don't know. Spezia's a lovely place."

"Spezia," the lady said. "You are talking about Spezia."

"Lovely place," I said.

"It is my country," she said. "Spezia is my home and Italy is my country."

"She says that Italy is her country."

"Tell her it looks like her country," Guy said.

"What have you for dessert?" I asked.

"Fruit," she said. "We have bananas."

"Bananas are all right," Guy said. "They've got skins on."

"Oh, he takes bananas," the lady said. She embraced Guy.

"What does she say?" he asked, keeping his face out of the way.

"She is pleased because you take bananas."

"Tell her I don't take bananas."

"The Signor does not take bananas."

"Ah," said the lady, crestfallen, "he doesn't take bananas."

"Tell her I take a cold bath every morning," Guy said.

"The Signor takes a cold bath every morning."

"No understand," the lady said.

Across from us the property sailor had not moved. No one in the place paid any attention to him.

"We want the bill," I said.

"Oh, no. You must stay."

"Listen," the clean-cut young man said from the table where he was writing, "let them go. These two are worth nothing."

The lady took my hand. "You won't stay? You won't ask him to stay?"

"We have to go," I said. "We have to get to Pisa, or if possible, Firenze, tonight. We can amuse ourselves in those cities at the end of the day. It is now the day. In the day we must cover distance."

"To stay a little while is nice."

"To travel is necessary during the light of day."

"Listen," the clean-cut young man said. "Don't bother to talk with these two. I tell you they are worth nothing and I know."

"Bring us the bill," I said. She brought the bill from the old woman and went back and sat at the table. Another girl came in from the kitchen. She walked the length of the room and stood in the doorway.

"Don't bother with these two," the clean-cut young man said in a wearied voice. "Come and eat. They are worth nothing."

We paid the bill and stood up. All the girls, the old woman, and the clean-cut young man sat down at table together. The property sailor sat with his head in his hands. No one had spoken to him all the time we were at lunch. The girl brought us our change that the old woman counted out for her and went back to her place at the table. We left a tip on the table and went out. When we were seated in the car ready to start, the girl came out and stood in the door. We started and I waved to her. She did not wave, but stood there looking after us.

AFTER THE RAIN

It was raining hard when we passed through the suburbs of Genoa and even going very slowly behind the tram-cars and the motor trucks liquid mud splashed on to the sidewalks so that people stepped into doorways as they saw us coming. In San Pier d'Arena, the industrial suburb outside of Genoa, there is a wide street with two car tracks and we drove down the center to avoid sending the mud on to the men going home from work. On our left was the Mediterranean. There was a big sea running and waves broke and the wind blew the spray against the car. A river bed, that, when we had passed going into Italy, had been wide, stony and dry, was running brown, and up to the banks. The brown water discolored the sea and as the waves thinned and cleared in breaking, the light came through the yellow water and the crests, detached by the wind, blew across the road.

A big car passed us going fast, and a sheet of muddy water rose up and over our wind-shield and radiator. The automatic wind-shield cleaner moved back and forth, spreading the film over the glass. We stopped and ate lunch at Sestri. There was no heat in the restaurant and we kept our hats and coats on. We could see the car outside through the window. It was covered with mud and was stopped beside some boats that had been pulled up beyond the waves. In the restaurant you could see your breath.

The *pasta asciuta* was good; the wine tasted of alum, and we poured water in it. Afterward the waiter brought beefsteak and fried potatoes. A man and a woman sat at the far end of the restaurant. He was middle-aged and she was young and wore black. All during the meal she would blow out her breath in the cold damp air. The man would look at it and shake his head. They ate without talking and the man held her hand under the table. She was good-looking and they seemed very sad. They had a traveling bag with them.

We had the papers and I read the account of the Shanghai fighting aloud to Guy. After the meal he left with the waiter to search for a place which did not exist in the restaurant, and I cleaned off the wind-shield, the lights and the license plates with a rag. Guy came back and we backed the car out and started. The waiter had taken him across the road and into an old house. The people in the house were suspicious and the waiter had remained with Guy to see nothing was stolen.

"Although I don't know how, me not being a plumber, they expected me to steal anything," Guy said.

As we came up on a headland beyond the town the wind struck the car and nearly tipped it over.

"It's good it blows us away from the sea," Guy said.

"Well," I said, "they drowned Shelley somewhere along here."

"This was down by Viareggio," Guy said. "Do you remember what we came to this country for?"

"Yes," I said. "But we didn't get it."

"We'll be out of it tonight."

"If we can get past Ventimiglia."

"We'll see. I don't like to drive this coast at night." It was early afternoon and the sun was out. Below the sea was blue with whitecaps running toward Savona. Back, beyond the cape, the brown and blue waters joined. Out ahead of us a tramp steamer was going up the coast.

"Can you still see Genoa?" Guy asked.

"Oh, yes."

"The next big cape ought to put it out of sight."

"We'll see it a long time yet. I can still see Portofino Cape way behind it."

Finally we could not see Genoa. I looked back as we came out and there was only the sea, and below in the bay, a line of beach with fishing boats and above, on the side of the hill, a town and then capes far down the coast.

"It's gone now," I said to Guy.

"Oh, it's been gone a long time now."

"But we couldn't be sure till we got way out."

There was a sign with a picture of an S-turn and *Svolta Pericolosa*. The road curved around the headland and the wind blew through the crack in the windshield. Below the cape was a flat stretch beside the sea. The wind had dried the mud and the wheels were beginning to lift dust. On the flat road we passed a Fascist riding a bicycle, a heavy revolver in a holster on his back. He held the middle of the road on his bicycle and we turned out for him. He looked up at us as we passed. Ahead there was a railway crossing, and as we came toward it the gates went down.

As we waited, the Fascist came up on his bicycle. The train went by and Guy started the engine.

"Wait," the bicycle man shouted from behind the car. "Your number's dirty."

I got out with a rag. The number had been cleaned at lunch.

"You can read it," I said.

"You think so?"

"Read it."

"I cannot read it. It is dirty."

I wiped it off with the rag.

How's that?"

"Twenty-five lire."

"What?" I said. "You could have read it. It's only dirty from the state of the roads."

"You don't like Italian roads?"

"They are dirty."

"Fifty lire." He spat in the road. "Your car is dirty and you are dirty, too."

"Good. And give me a receipt with your name."

He took out a receipt book, made in duplicate, and perforated, so one side could be given to the customer, and the other side filled in and kept as a stub. There was no carbon to record what the customer's ticket said.

"Give me fifty lire."

He wrote in indelible pencil, tore out the slip and handed it to me. I read it.

"This is for twenty-five lire."

"A mistake," he said, and changed the twenty-five to fifty.

"And now the other side. Make it fifty in the part you keep."

He smiled a beautiful Italian smile and wrote something on the receipt stub, holding it so I could not see.

"Go on," he said, "before your number gets dirty again."

We drove for two hours after it was dark and slept in Mentone that night. It seemed very cheerful and clean and sane and lovely. We had driven from Ventimiglia to Pisa and Florence, across the Romogna to Rimini, back through Forli, Imola, Bologna, Parma, Piacenza and Genoa to Ventimiglia again. The whole trip had only taken ten days. Naturally, in such a short trip, we had no opportunity to see how things were with the country or the people.

THOMAS WOLFE   MARCH 24, 1937

I Have a Thing to Tell You: III

(Nun Will Ich Ihnen 'Was Sagen)

It is astonishing how short a time it takes to get acquainted on a journey. As we made our way a second time along the corridors of the speeding train I reflected that already Stefanowski and I were as accustomed to each other as if we had been friends for many years. As to the new-found friends in our compartment, we were delighted with them all. In the most extraordinary way, and in the space of fifteen minutes' time, we seemed to have entered into the lives of all these people and they in ours. Now we were not only immensely interested in the information they had given us about themselves: we were as warmly, eagerly concerned with the problems that confronted them as if their troubles were our own.

During a long and sumptuous meal—a meal that began with brandy, proceeded over a fine bottle of Bernkasteler and wound up over coffee and more brandy and a good cigar, a meal on which we were both exuberantly determined to spend the remainder of our German money, we discussed our companions again. The little woman, we agreed, was charming. And the young man, although diffident and shy, was very nice. We even had a word of praise for Fuss-And-Fidget now. After we had cracked his crusty shell the old codger was not bad. He really was quite friendly underneath.

"And it does show," said Stefanowski quietly, "how good people really are, how easy it is to get along with one another in this world, how people really like each other—if only—"

"—if only—" I said, and nodded.

"These damned politicians," Stefanowski said.

At length we called for our bill and paid it. Stefanowski dumped his marks upon the table, counted them: "You'll have to help me out," he said. "How many have you got?"

I dumped mine out. We had enough to pay the bill, to give the waiter something extra. And there was enough left over for a double jolt of brandy and a good cigar.

So, grinning with satisfaction, in which our waiter joined amiably as he read our purpose, we paid the bill, ordered the brandy and cigars, and, full of food, of drink, and of the pleasant knowledge of a job well done, we puffed contentedly on our cigars.

We were now running through the great industrial region of western Germany. The pleasant landscape had been darkened by the grime and smoke of enormous works. Now it was grim with the skeletons of enormous smelting and refining plants, disfigured with great heaps of slag, with mountainous dumps. It was a new portion of the land, one of the few I had not seen before. It was brutal, smoky, dense with life, the grimy warrens of industrial towns. But it had the brutal fascination of these places too, the thrilling power of raw, enormous works.

Stefanowski informed me that we were already almost at the border and that, since our own coach went directly through to Paris, we should have no additional need of money for porter's fees.

This made us remember the difficulties of our fellow travelers, who were Germans. We agreed that the existing law which permitted native citizens to take only ten marks from the country was, for people in the business circumstances of our little blonde companion and old Fuss-And-Fidget, a very trying one.

At this moment Stefanowski had a brilliant inspiration, the result of his own generous impulse. "But why," he said, "why can't we help them?"

"How? In what way can we help them?"

"Why," he said, "I have here a permit that allows me to take twenty-three marks out of the country. You have no permit, but everyone is allowed—"

"To take ten marks," I said and nodded. "So you mean then," I concluded, "that since each of us has spent his German money—"

"But can still take as much as is allowed out of the country—yes," he said. "So we could suggest it to them—" he went on.

"—that they give us some of their marks to keep, you mean?"

He nodded. "Yes. It is not much, of course. But it might help."

No sooner said than seized upon. We were almost jubilantly elated at this opportunity of doing some slight service for these people to whom we had taken such a liking. At this moment, even while we were smiling confirmation at each other, a man in uniform came through the car, paused at our table—which was the only one that was now occupied—and quietly but authoritatively informed us that the Pass-Control had come upon the train and that we must return at once to our compartment to await examination. We rose, knowing now we had no time to lose, hastened back along the coaches of the swaying train, entered our compartment again and immediately told our fellows that the inspection would soon begin and that the officials were on the train.

There was a flurry of excitement. Everyone began to get ready. The blonde lady took out her purse and passport and with a worried look began to count her money. Stefanowski watched her quietly for a moment and then, taking out his own certificate and showing it, remarked that he was officially allowed possession of the sum of twenty-three marks, that he had had the sum in his possession, but now had spent it. I took this as my cue and remarked that I too had spent the ten marks that the law allowed me.

Our little blonde companion looked eagerly at both of us and read the friendship of our meaning.

"Then you mean?" she said, and gleefully—"but it would be wonderful, of course, if you would!"

"Have you as much as twenty-three marks?" said Stefanowski.

"Yes," she nodded quickly, with a worried look, "I have more than that. But if you would take the twenty-three and keep them until we are past the frontier—"

He stretched out his hand. "Give them to me," he said quietly. The transfer was completed, the money in his pocket, in the wink of an eye.

In another moment Fuss-And-Fidget had taken ten marks from his pocket and without a word passed them across to me. I thrust the money in my pocket, and we all sat back, a little flushed, excited but triumphant, trying to look composed.

A few minutes later an official opened the compartment door, saluted and asked for our passports. He inspected Stefanowski's first, found everything in order, took his certificate, saw his twenty-three marks, stamped the passport and returned it to him.

Then he turned to me. I gave him my passport and the various papers certifying my possession of American currency. He thumbed through the pages of the passport, which were now almost completely covered with stamps and entries, and finally smiled quite kindly, and returned my passport to me. Then he inspected the passports of the little blonde lady, her companion and Fuss-And-Fidget. Everything, apparently, was in order, save that the lady had confessed to the possession of more than twenty marks, and the official regretfully informed her that he must take from her anything in excess of ten. It would be held at the frontier and restored to her, of course, when she returned. She smiled ruefully, shrugged her shoulders, and gave the man twelve marks. All other matters were evidently now in order, for the man saluted and withdrew.

So it was over then! We all drew a deep breath of relief, and commiserated our charming lady friend upon her loss. But I think we were all quietly jubilant, too, to know her loss had been no greater, that we had been able in some degree to lessen it. I asked Fuss-And-Fidget if I should return his money now or later on. He told me to wait until we had crossed the frontier into Belgium. At the same time, he made some casual explanation, to which none of us paid any serious attention at the time, to the effect that his ticket was good only to the frontier, and that he would utilize the fifteen minutes of our wait at Aachen, the frontier town, to buy a ticket for the remainder of the trip to Paris.

We were now, in fact, approaching Aachen. The train was slackening speed. We were going through a pleasant countryside, a smiling landscape of green fields and gentle hills, unobtrusively, mildly, somehow unmistakably European. The seared and blasted districts of the mines and factories were behind us. We were entering the outskirts of a pleasant town.

This was Aachen. In another moment the train was slowing to a halt before the station. We had reached the frontier. There was to be a wait of fifteen minutes and a change of engines. All of us got out—Fuss-And-Fidget to get a ticket, the others to stretch their legs and get a breath of air.

My Polish friend and I got out and walked forward along the platform to inspect the locomotive. The German locomotive which would here be supplanted by its Belgian successor was a magnificent machine, almost as big as one of the great American engines. The evidence of high velocity was legible in every line of it. What was most remarkable was the tender, a wonderful affair, the whole of which seemed to be a honeycomb of jetting pipes. One looked in through some slanting bars and saw a fountain-like display, composed of thousands of tiny little jets of steaming water. It was a marvelous machine, which bore in every line the evidence of the tremendous engineering talent that had created it.

Knowing how vivid, swift and fugitive are those poignant first impressions that come at the moment when we change from one country to another, I waited with an almost feverish interest for the approach of the Belgian locomotive. I knew in advance it would not be so good as the German one because the energy, the intelligence, the strength and the integrity which produced it were inferior, but I was eagerly sensitized to observe the exact degree and quality of these differences between the powerful, solid and indomitable race that I was leaving and the little people I would now encounter.

Presently we walked back along the platform, found our little blonde-haired lady and, flanking her on either side, began to stroll up and down beside the train. At length, observing the station clock and seeing that the moment scheduled for departure had already come, we moved quickly back towards our own coach and our own compartment.

As we approached it was evident that something had happened. There were no signs of departure. The conductor and the station guard stood together on the platform. No warning signal had been given. And, moreover, there was now evident a kind of subdued tension, a sense of crisis that made my pulse beat quicker as I approached.

I have often observed this phenomenon in life, its manifestations under certain conditions are nearly always identical. A man has leaped or fallen, for example, from a high building to the pavement of a city street. Or a man has been shot, or beaten. He has been struck by a motor car; or again, a man is dying quietly on the street before the eyes of other men. But always, the manifestation of the crowd is just the same. Even before you see the faces of the people, when you see their backs, their posture, the position of the head and shoulders, you know what has happened.

You do not know, of course, the precise circumstance, but what you sense immediately is the final stage of tragedy. You know that someone has just died or is dying, and in the terrible eloquence of backs and shoulders, the *feeding* silence of the watching men, you sense a tragedy that is even deeper. It is the tragedy of man's cruelty and his lust for pain, the tragic weakness that corrupts him, that he loathes but that he cannot cure.

And always, the manifestation of this tragedy is just the same. Even before one arrives one knows from this silent eloquence of shoulders, backs and heads that something ruinous and horrible has happened. I knew the signs too well. And now, as I hastened along beside the train and saw the people gathered in the corridor in that same feeding posture, waiting, watching, in that deadly fascinated silence, I was sure that once again in life I was about to witness death.

That was the first thing that came to me—and I believe to all of us—that someone had died. And what stunned us, what stopped us short, appalled, was that death had come to our compartment. The shades were tightly drawn, the door closed, the whole place sealed impenetrably. We had started to get on the train when this thing burst upon us. And now we saw our lady's young companion standing at the window in the corridor. He motioned quickly to us, a gesture warning us to remain where we were. And as he did it flashed over all of us that the subject of this tragic visitation was the nervous little man who had been the companion of our voyage since morning.

The stillness of the scene, the shuttered blankness of that closed compartment, were horrible. Even as we stared, appalled and horror-stricken, at that fatal curtained closet, which had so short a time ago housed the lives of all of us, and which had now become the tenement of death, the curtained door of the compartment was opened and closed quickly, and a man came out.

He was an official, a burly-looking fellow, with a visored cap, a jacket of olive green. He was a man of forty-five or more, a Germanic type with high blunt cheekbones, a florid face and tawny mustaches, combed out sprouting, in the Kaiser Wilhelm way. His head was shaven, and there were thick creases at the base of the skull and across his fleshy neck. He came out, climbed down clumsily to the platform, signaled exictedly to another officer and climbed back into the train again.

It was a familiar type, one that I had seen and smiled at often, but one that now became, under these ominous circumstances, sinisterly unpleasant. Even the man's physical weight and clumsiness, the awkward way he got down from the train, the awkward way he climbed up again, the thickness of his waist, the unpleasant width and coarseness of his clumsy buttocks, the way his sprouting mustaches seemed to quiver with passion and authority, the sound of his guttural voice, raised coarsely, somewhat phlegmily, as he shouted to his fellow officer, the sense that he was fairly panting with an inflamed authority—all these symptoms had now become, under the ominous prescience of the moment, loathsome, sinister, repellent.

All of a sudden, without knowing why, I felt myself trembling with a murderous and incomprehensible anger. I wanted to smash that fat neck with the creases in it. I wanted to pound that inflamed and blunted face into a jelly. I wanted to kick square and hard, bury my foot, dead center in the obscene fleshiness of those clumsy buttocks. And I knew that I was helpless, that all of us were. Like all Americans, I had never liked the police or the kind of personal authority that it sanctifies. But this feeling, this intensity, with its murderously helpless rage, was different. I felt impotent, shackled, unabled to stir against the walls of an obscene but unshakable authority.

The official with the sprouting mustaches, accompanied now by his colleagues, opened the curtained doors of the compartment again, and now I saw that they were not alone. Two other officials were in the compartment and our nervous little companion—no, he was not dead!—he sat there *huddled*, facing them. His face was white and pasty. It looked greasy, as if it were covered with a salve of cold fat sweat. Under his long nose his mouth was trembling in a horrible attempt at a smile. In the very posture of the men as they bent over him there was something revolting and unclean.

But the official with the thick creased neck had now filled the door and blotted out the picture. He went in followed by a smaller colleague, the door was closed again behind him, and again there was that vicious and ill omened secrecy.

All of this had happened in a moment while we had looked on with stupefied surprise. Now the people gathered in the corridor began to whisper to one another. In a moment our little blonde lady went over, whispered to the young man at the window and then came back, took Stefanowski and myself by the arm and led us away, out of hearing.

Then, as both of us whispered, "What is it?" she looked around cautiously again and said with lowered voice: "That man—the one in our compartment—was trying to get out of the country and they've caught him."

"But why?—What for?—What has he done?" we asked, bewildered.

Again she glanced back cautiously and then, drawing us toward her till our three heads were almost touching, she said, in an awed and almost frightened tone, "They say he is a Jew. They searched his baggage—he was taking money out."

"How much?" said Stefanowski.

"I don't know," she whispered. "A great deal, I think. Several thousand marks. They found it."

"But how—" I began. "I thought everything was finished. I thought they were done with all of us when they went through the train."

"Yes," she said, "but don't you remember he said something about not having a ticket the whole way. He got off the train to get one. And I think that's when they caught him," she whispered. "I think they had their eye on him. That's why they did not question him when they came through the train"—as indeed, I now remembered, "they" had not—"And they caught him here," she went on. "They asked him where he was going and he said to Paris. They asked him how much money he was taking out; he said ten marks. Then they asked him how long he was going to remain in Paris, and for what purpose, and he said he was going to be there for a week and that he was attending this congress of lawyers that he spoke about. They asked him then how he proposed to stay in Paris for a week and attend this congress if all he had was ten marks. And I think," she whispered, "he got frightened then. He began to lose his head. He said he had forgotten, that he had twenty marks besides, which he had put into another pocket. And then, of course, they had him. They searched him. They searched his baggage, and they found more," she whispered in an awed tone. "Much, much more."

For a moment we all stared at one another, too stunned to say a word. Then the little woman laughed in a low, almost frightened, sort of way, a little uncertain "o-hoh-hoh-hoh-hoh" ending on a note of incredulity.

"This man," she whispered again, "this little Jew—"

"I didn't know he was a Jew," I said, "I should not have thought so."

"But he is," she whispered, and looked stealthily around again to see if we were being overheard. "And he was doing what so many of the others have done—he was trying to get out with his money." And again she laughed, the uncertain little hoh-hoh-hoh that mounted on a note of incredulous amazement. And yet, I saw, her eyes were troubled, too.

All of a sudden I felt sick, empty, nauseated. That money, those accursed ten marks, were beginning to burn a hole in my pocket. I put my hand into my vest pocket and the coins felt greasy, as if they were covered with sweat. I took them out and closed them in my fist and started to cross the platform toward the train.

The woman seized me by the arm. "Where are you going?" she gasped. "What are you going to do?"

"I'm going to give that man his money. I can't keep it now."

Her face went white. "Are you mad?" she whispered. "Don't you know that that will do no good? You'll only get yourself arrested and, as for him—he's in trouble enough already. You'll only make it so much worse for him. And besides," she faltered, as the full consequences came to her, "God knows what he has done, what he has said already. If he has told that we have transferred money to one another—we may all be in for it!"

We had not thought of this. But now we did. And as we saw the possible consequence of our act we just stood there and stared helplessly at one another. We just stood there, three abreast, feeling dazed and weak and hollow. We just stood there and prayed.

And now they were coming out of the compartment. The fellow with the sprouting mustache came out first, carrying the little man's valise. He looked around. It seemed to me he glared at us. We just stood still and prayed. We expected now to see all of our baggage come out. We thought that we were in for it.

But in a moment the other three officials came out of the compartment, with the little man between them. They marched him right along the platform, white as a sheet, greasy looking, protesting volubly, in a voice that had a kind of anguished lilt. He came right by us. I made a movement with my arms. The greasy money sweated in my hand and I did not know what to do. I started to speak to him. And at the same time, I was praying that he would not speak. I tried to look away from him, but I could not look away. He came toward us, still protesting volubly that everything could be explained, that all of it was an absurd mistake. And just for a moment as he passed us, he stopped talking, glanced at us, white-faced, smiling pitiably, his eyes rested on us for a moment, and then, without a sign of further recognition, he went on by.

I heard the little blonde woman at my side sigh faintly and I felt her body slump against me. We all felt pretty weak and hollow. In a moment we went on across the platform and got up into the train. The evil tension had been snapped. People were now talking feverishly, still in a low tone but with obvious released excitement. Our little blonde companion leaned from the window of the corridor and spoke to the fellow with the sprouting mustache who was still standing there. "Are—are you going to keep him here?" she said in a low tone. "You're not going to let him go?"

He looked at her stolidly for a moment. Then an intolerable smile broke deliberately across his brutal features. He nodded his head, slowly, with the finality of a gluttonous satisfaction: *"Nein,"* he said, *"Er bleibt."* And, shaking his heavy head ever so slightly from side to side, *"Geht nicht!"*

They had him. Far down the platform we heard the sudden fifing shrill of the engine whistle. The guard cried warning; all up and down the platform doors were slammed. Slowly the train moved from the station. We rolled right past him, very slowly. They had him. They surrounded him. He stood among them, protesting volubly, talking with his hands now, insisting all could be explained. And they said nothing. They had him. They just stood and watched him, each with the faint suggestion of that intolerable slow smile upon his face. They raised their eyes, unspeaking, looked at us as we rolled past, with the obscene communication of their glance and of their smile.

And he—he too paused once from his voluble and feverish discourse as we passed him. He lifted his eyes to us, his pasty face, and he was silent for a moment. And we looked at him for the last time, and he at us—this time, more direct and steadfastly. And in that glance there was all the silence of man's mortal anguish. And we were all somehow naked and ashamed, and somehow guilty. We all felt somehow that we were saying farewell, not to a man but to humanity; not to some nameless little cipher out of life, but to the fading image of a brother's face. We lost him then. The train swept out and gathered speed—and so farewell.

I turned and looked at Stefanowski. He, too, was silent for a moment. Then he spoke.

"Well, then," he said, "I think that this is a sad ending to our trip."

And we? We went back in and took our former seats in our compartment. But it seemed strange and empty now. The ghost of absence sat there ruinously. He had left his coat and hat; in his anguish he had forgotten them. Stefanowski rose and took them, and would have given them to the conductor. But the woman said: "You'd better look into the pockets first. Perhaps there's something in them. Perhaps"—quickly, eagerly, as the idea took her—"perhaps he has left money there."

Stefanowski searched the pockets. There was nothing there. He shook his head. The woman began to search the cushions of the seats, thrusting her hands down around the sides. "It might just be, you know," she said, "that he hid money here." She laughed excitedly, almost gleefully. "Perhaps we'll all be rich."

The young Pole shook his head. "I think they would have found it if he had," he said—and here he paused suddenly, peered out the window, and thrust his hand into his pocket, "I suppose we're in Belgium now. Here's your money." And he returned to her the money she had given him.

She took it and put it in her purse. I still had the ten marks in my hand and was looking at them. The woman looked up, saw my face, then said quickly, warmly, "But you're upset about this thing! You look so troubled."

I put the money back and in a moment said: *"Ich fühle gerade als ob ich Blutgeld in meiner Tasche hätte."*

She leaned over, smiling, and put her hand reassuringly upon my arm: *"Nein. Nicht Blutgeld—Judgeld!"* she whispered. "Don't worry about it. He had plenty more!"

My eyes met those of Stefanowski for a moment and his too were grave. "This is a sad ending to our trip," he said again.

And she—our little blonde companion—she tried to laugh and joke, but her eyes were also full of trouble. She tried to talk us out of it, to talk herself into forgetfulness.

"These Jews!" she cried. "These things would never happen if it were not for them! They make all the trouble. Germany has had to protect herself. The Jews were taking all the money from the country—thousands of them escaped, taking millions of marks with them. And now, when it is too late, we wake up to it! It is too bad that foreigners must see these things, that they've got to go through these painful experiences—it makes a bad impression. They do not understand the reason. But it is the Jews!" she whispered.

We said nothing and the woman went on talking, eagerly, excitedly, earnestly, persuasively, but really as if she were trying to convince herself, as if every instinct of race and loyalty was now being used in an effort to justify something that had filled her with a sense of shame and sorrow. But even as she talked her clear blue eyes were full of trouble. And at length she stopped. There was silence for a moment. Then gravely, quietly, the woman said: "He must have wanted very badly to escape."

We remembered then all he had said and done throughout the journey. And now every act and gesture, every word became invested with a new and terrible meaning. We recalled how nervous he had been, how he kept opening and shutting the door, kept getting up to pace up and down along the corridor. We recalled how he kept peering around at us suspicously, how eagerly he had asked Stefanowski if he would change places with him when the Pole had got up to go in to the dining-car with me. We recalled his explanations about having to buy passage from the frontier to Paris, the explanations he had given to the conductor. And all these things, which at the time we had dismissed as irascible ill temper or trivial explanation, now were revealed in a sequence of terrible significance.

"But the ten marks!" the woman cried at length. "In God's name, since he had all this other money, why did he give ten marks to you? It is so stupid!"

And we could find no reason, except that he had done it because he thought it might alleviate any suspicion in our minds about his true intent; or, what was even likelier, I thought, that he was in such an inner state of nervous frenzy that he had acted blindly, wildly, on the impulse of the moment.

We did not know. We never would find out the answer now. We discussed the money he had given me. The young Pole remarked that I had given the man my name and my address and that if he was later on allowed to complete his journey, he could write to me. But we all knew I would never hear from him again.

Late afternoon had come. The country had closed in, the train was winding though a pleasant, romantic landscape of hills and woods. There was a sense of forest dusk, cool darkling waters, the slant of evening and the wane of light. We knew somehow that we had entered another land. Our little blonde companion peered anxiously out the window and then asked if we were really now in Belgium. The conductor assured us that we were. We gave the man our late companion's hat and coat and explained the reason for them. He nodded, took them, and departed.

The woman had her hand upon her breast, and now when the man had gone I heard her sigh slowly with relief.

In a moment she said quietly and simply: "Do not misunderstand. I am a German and I love my country. But—I feel as if a weight has lifted from me *here*" —she put her hand upon her breast again. "You cannot understand perhaps just how it feels to us but—" and for a moment she was silent as if painfully meditating what she wished to say. Then quickly, quietly: "We are so happy to be—*out!*"

Out? I too was "out." And suddenly I knew just how she felt. I too was "out," who was a stranger to her land, who never yet had been a stranger in it. I too was "out" of that great land whose image had been engraved upon my spirit in my childhood and my youth, before I had ever seen it. I too was "out" from that land which had been so much more to me than land, which had been for me so much more than place. It was a geography of heart's desire. It was a soul's dark wonder, the haunting beauty of the magic land. It had been burning there forever, like the dark Helen burning in man's blood. And now, like the dark Helen, it was lost to me. I had spoken the language of its spirit before I ever came to it. I had spoken the accents of its speech most brokenly from the hour when I first entered it, yet never with a moment's strangeness. I had been at home in it and it in me. It seemed I had been born in it and it in me. I had known wonder in it, truth and magic in it, sorrow, loneliness and pain in it. I had known love in it, and for the first time in my life I had tasted there the bright delusive sacraments of fame.

Therefore, it was no foreign land to me. It was the other half of my heart's home. It was the dark lost Helen I had found, it was the dark found Helen I had lost—and now I knew, as I had never known before, the countless measure of my loss—the countless measure of my gain—the way that now would be forever closed to me—the way of exile and of no return—and another way that I had found. For I knew that I was "out." And that I had now found my way.

To that old master, now, to wizard Faust, old father of the ancient and swarm-haunted mind of man, to that old German land with all the measure of its truth, its glory, beauty, magic and its ruin—to that dark land, to that old ancient earth that I had loved so long—I said farewell.

I have a thing to tell you:

Something has spoken to me in the night, burning the tapers of the waning year; something has spoken in the night; and told me I shall die, I know not where. Losing the earth we know for greater knowing, losing the life we have for greater life, and leaving friends we loved for greater loving, men find a land more kind than home, more large than earth.

Whereon the pillars of this earth are founded, toward which the spirits of the nations draw, toward which the conscience of the world is tending—a wind is rising, and the rivers flow.

Factory Town

Sherwood Anderson Looks at Southern Industry

INSIDE THE FACTORY

Here at least is something going forward. Steel is brought in here. It becomes something man will use.

It becomes a coffee-grinder, a plow, a knife to cut bread, an automobile. The wheels fly, the grinding machines grind. There are a thousand fabricating machines. They fabricate steel, cotton, silk.

The silk mill is a thing of glory. Once you enter it, give yourself to it, you will never forget the experience.

I went into a cotton mill. The looms were weaving ugly cloth. The machines worked with faultless precision. In a corner of a room were four women harnessing a loom.

The various colored threads were being passed through the complex machine. This was done slowly, painfully, by hand.

There, before the workers, was the design of the cloth to be made. Someone had designed the cloth.

Let us say it was to be used for the covers of the seats of automobiles.

There was this slow painful patient harnessing of the loom to make this cloth. Once the loom was harnessed it would go on and on, repeating the design over and over. Harnessing the loom was like laying out the telephone system of a city. It was as complex as that.

Now you start the loom. The wheels turn. All the little steel fingers run back and forth. The shuttles fly. The eyes cannot follow them, so swiftly they fly.

There is this cloth being made, a thousand yards, a hundred thousand yards, a million yards.

Automobiles by the thousands with this cloth covering the seats.

Who designed it? Why is it so ugly?

Suppose an artist were to come into this mill, to design cloth. Let him accept the limitations of the machine as the poet accepts the limitations of the sonnet form.

Here is something gay that might be done, something joyous.

The automobiles, with this cloth covering the seats, will travel on a thousand roads. Lovers will ride out of towns in the automobiles, middle-aged people, clerks, small merchants, lawyers in country towns, doctors, will take their wives and families out to the woods on Sunday.

The cloth being made here, in this factory, will go with them. The design is ugly. It is commonplace. The colors are without gaiety. There is no joy in this cloth being woven here in these looms.

The looms themselves are marvels of perfection. Every year the machines grow more and more complex. They run swiftly. There is a clatter, a whirl, a dance, going on in the factories.

There is more going on in the factories of America than anyone dreams of. All of those who make our laws, who write our books, who sing our songs, stay outside the factories.

I have met labor leaders who have never been inside factories or have merely passed through. There are no factory workers in the halls of Congress. The factory workers do not write for newspapers. They do not edit magazines.

Before day, through the long winter months, these men and women get up out of their beds . . . most of them in ugly houses . . . they eat hurriedly and stumble through dark streets to the gate in the factory yard.

The factories, in which so many millions of Americans work, become every year more and more like prisons. You must have permission to go in. You are escorted.

I would like to see the factories thrown open to all. Let all of us, who buy and sell, who write books, who argue cases in law courts, go in and stay in. Let us wander from machine to machine, seeing the wonder of the machines. Let us talk to the workers who are becoming every year more and more a part of the machines.

Modern industry is a Mississippi. It is a Mississippi in flood. No one understands it. It is controlled by a few men who are cunning in finance. They do not understand it. The factories have become as much a part of our lives as the forests, the fields, the rivers, but they are sealed up. We, on the outside, know little or nothing of them.

We know little or nothing of the lives of the workers. Their lives are lived in the factories. There, behind these walls, are these thousands of people. Within the factory walls they grow a little to know each other. Brief conversations are held. Glance meets glance. Loves come. Whole lives are lived inside the walls of the factories. The workers, coming out at the mill gate at night, or in the morning if they are on the night shift, are tired. They eat, sleep and return into the factories.

In every industrial center miles and miles of little ugly houses in grim streets. The factory workers are buried away in these streets. They are without social standing. Every year the factory workers fall lower and lower in the American social scale. Those who buy and sell, those who make nothing, feel themselves above the workers. They have succeeded in making the workers feel socially inferior. There is an odd humbleness in them.

The humbleness in the workers often results in an amazing kind of quality.

A man who had got rich writing books visited a mill town. Times were hard. There were many people out of work. The man went home and later sent them two barrels of apples. They were as pleased as children, not because they had received the apples but because a man, high up in the social scale, a successful man, a man whose name was on the front pages of newspapers, had noticed them, had remembered and had a kindly thought of them.

The lives of all the factory workers are precarious, and every year become more precarious. Every year the machines in the factories are improved, and with every improvement more and more men and women are thrown out of work. No man knows how long his job will last. There are unemployed men standing at the factory gate. When the job is lost everything is lost. The factory worker, who is strong and willing to work, becomes an object of charity.

SOUP KITCHEN

Have you ever visited a soup kitchen? I saw one recently in a Southern industrial town. Some seven hundred people were fed on the day I was there.

They were Americans, such people as you and I. I stood watching them. I was ashamed of my warm overcoat, my stout shoes.

I made men ashamed standing there.

There was one man approached the soup kitchen three times. Each time his eyes met mine. He was a man of perhaps forty. No doubt he had a wife and family at home. By an odd chance he looked exactly like pictures I have seen of the vice-president of the Southern Confederacy, Mr. Alexander Stephens. The man was ashamed that I, a strong, prosperous-looking man should see him thus defeated, reduced to going to a soup kitchen for food. He stopped beside me. He lied. I had said nothing about his wanting hot soup. "I am not here for soup," he said defiantly. "I came here to meet a friend."

I moved away, went into a corner grocery where I bought a package of cigarettes. I stood by the door looking out. The man dashed into the soup kitchen—it was in the basement of a small church—ladies of the town, their automobiles standing in the street, were down inside there serving the soup.

Presently the man who looked like Alexander Stephens came out. He had consumed his soup and had been given a loaf of bread which he put under his coat. He came hurrying past the corner grocery inside which I stood. I drew back and he did not see me again.

Young girls came to the soup kitchen; children came; men and women came. There was an industry in a depressed state. The factories of the town were running on part time. Thousands of people were out of work.

A woman saw me standing before the store and asked about the soup kitchen. "Where is it?" she asked.

"I do not want any soup," she said quickly. She lied. I saw the hungry look in her eyes. She said she wanted to talk to some of the ladies who were serving the soup. "They are friends of mine," she said proudly.

There was an old workman who came to stand with me and who began to brag. He pointed to the line of people going in and out of the soup kitchen. "I am out of work," he said, "but thank God I am not like that.

"I save every cent when I work," he said, "and I never take a drink.

"It's so," he said. He said that too many workmen, when they had been working all week, felt they had to have a bottle of moon when Saturday night came.

"They blow in their money like that," he said, "but I don't do it.

"I save mine," he said, "every cent of it.

"And now. You see," he said, "now I am out of work but I do not have to go there. I have got me a little money saved. Not much, but a little. I can stand here. I can watch the others go in. I can get me a few slices of pork to fry and some slices of bread," he said, putting his hands into his pockets and walking proudly away.

There is something broken and distraught about factory workers, out of work, shut out of the factories. They stand idly on street corners. There is a queer air of being disconnected with life. They are like hurt creatures standing there.

Automobiles whirl past them in the streets. The life of the city goes on. They have nothing to do, nowhere to go.

In the factories the wheels keep turning. The machines are there, the complex marvelous machines. Every year they become more marvelous, more complex.

They are ready to do their part. Man made them. These men and women, standing in the streets now, so distraught looking and feeling so baffled, so out of place, are willing and ready to serve with the machines.

WILLIAM SAROYAN   APRIL 1, 1936

The Good Year

Juan Cabral was a tall Mexican who worked for my uncle, pruning vines. He was a poor man with a number of possessions: his wife Consuela, his sons Pablo and Pancho, his three daughters, his lame cousin Federico, four dogs, a cat, a guitar, a shotgun, an old horse, an old wagon and lots of pots and pans.

I was in the farmyard talking to my uncle the morning Juan came up the road in his wagon to ask for work.

What's this? my uncle said.

Mexicans, I said.

How can you tell? he said.

The dogs, I said. The Mexicans are a noble and simple people. They are never so poor they cannot keep a pack of hounds. They are Indians, mixed with other noble races.

What do they want? he said.

Work, I said. It will break their hearts to admit it, but that's what they want.

I don't need any help, my uncle said.

They won't care, I said. They'll just turn around and go on to the next vineyard.

The wagon came slowly into the farmyard and Juan Cabral said good morning in Mexican. *Buenos dias, amigos.* In bad English he said, Is there work on this vineyard for a strong Mexican?

Who? said my uncle. (For instance, he said to me.)

Me, said Juan Cabral. Juan Cabral.

Juan Cabral, my uncle said. No, there is no work.

How much is the pay? Juan said.

What'd he say? my uncle said. He lit a cigarette to help him through his bewilderment.

He wants to know how much the pay is, I said.

Who said anything about pay? my uncle said. I'm not hiring anybody.

He wants to know anyway, I said. He knows you're not hiring anybody.

My uncle was amazed.

Well, he said, I'm paying the Japanese thirty cents an hour. Most farmers are paying twenty and twenty-five.

The pay is thirty cents an hour, I said to Juan.

That is not enough, the Mexican said. There are many mouths to feed this winter.

What's he say? my uncle said.

My uncle was pretty sore and wouldn't understand anything Juan said until I said it over again.

He says thirty cents an hour isn't enough to feed all the mouths he's got to feed this winter, I said.

Who's he got to feed? my uncle said.

All them people in the wagon, I said.

Where they going to live? my uncle said.

I don't know, I said. They'll find a place somewhere, I suppose.

Juan Cabral did not speak. One of his dogs came over to my uncle and licked my uncle's hand. My uncle jumped and looked around fearfully. What's this? he said.

It's one of the Mexican's dogs, I said.

Well, get it away from me, my uncle said.

I told the dog to go back to the wagon and it did.

My uncle watched it go back. He not only watched the dog go back, he studied the dog going back.

That's an ordinary dog, he said. You see hundreds of them in the streets.

That's right, I said.

That dog ain't worth a penny, my uncle said.

It ain't even worth a lot less than a penny, I said. You couldn't give that dog away with two dollars.

I wouldn't take that dog for three dollars, my uncle said. What can it do? Can it catch a jackrabbit or anything like that?

No, I said.

Can it scare robbers away? my uncle said.

No, I said. It would go out and lick the hands of robbers.

Well, what good is it? my uncle said.

No good at all, I said.

What do they want to keep a lot of dogs like that for? my uncle said.

They're Mexicans, I said. They're simple Mexican people.

I hear Mexicans do a lot of stealing, my uncle said.

They'll take anything that ain't got roots in the earth, I said.

I got thirteen mouths to feed, not counting my own, said Juan. Thirty cents an hour isn't enough.

Thirteen mouths? said my uncle.

He's counting the animals, I said.

I don't suppose he knows how to prune a vine, my uncle said.

Do you know how to prune a grapevine? I said to Juan.

No, señor, he said. I am a soldier.

What'd he say? said my uncle.

He says he's a soldier, I said.

The war's over, my uncle said.

The Mexican brought out his shotgun and was lifting it to his shoulder by way of demonstrating his being a soldier when my uncle noticed what he was fooling with. My uncle jumped behind me.

Tell him to put that gun away, he said. I don't want any Mexican shooting me accidentally. I believe him. I believe he's a soldier. Tell him to put that God damn gun away. He'll shoot me just to prove he's a soldier.

No he won't, I said.

I don't need any help, my uncle said to Juan Cabral.

Thirty cents an hour is not enough to feed thirteen mouths, not counting my own, said the Mexican.

He put the gun away, and the first thing my uncle knew five young Mexican faces were looking up at him. He almost lost his balance.

Who are these people? he said.

These are the children, I said. Two boys and three girls.

What do they want? my uncle said.

Beans and flour and salt, I said. They don't want much.

Tell them to go away, my uncle said. He don't know how to prune a vine.

Anybody can learn how to prune a vine, I said.

He'll ruin my vineyard, my uncle said.

And steal everything that ain't got roots in the earth, I said.

I'm paying ten cents an hour more than most farmers are paying, my uncle said.

He says it ain't enough, I said.

Well, my uncle said, ask him how much *is* enough.

Señor Cabral, I said to the Mexican, will you work for thirty-five cents an hour? My uncle does not need any help, but he likes you.

Have you a dwelling for my family and the animals? said the Mexican.

Yes, I said. It is modest but comfortable.

Is there much work to do? said the Mexican.

Very little, I said.

What is the nature of the work? said the Mexican.

It is pleasant and healthful, I said. Attending grapevines.

Juan Cabral stepped down from the wagon and came over to my uncle. My uncle was pretty scared. The dogs walked behind the Mexican, and his children were already surrounding my uncle.

Señor, said the Mexican to my uncle, I will work in your vineyard.

I am honored, said my uncle.

He was all mixed up. It was the dogs mostly, but it was also the five Mexican children, and the Mexican's magnificent manners.

It was certainly not the gun. My uncle wouldn't let any power in the world intimidate him.

By three o'clock in the afternoon the Mexicans were established in their little house, and I took Juan Cabral, followed by Pablo and Pancho and his lame cousin Federico, to a vine to teach him to prune. I explained the reasons for each clip of the shears. To keep the shape of the vine. To keep it strong. To let its fresh branches grow upward toward the sun. And so forth. I moved down the row of vines to the next vine. I handed him the pruning shears and asked if he wouldn't enjoy trying to prune the vine. He was very polite and said it would be a pleasure. He worked thoughtfully and slowly, explaining to his children and his lame cousin, as I had explained to him, the reasons for each clip of the shears. His lame cousin Federico, who was a man of sixty or so, was very much impressed.

I suggested that he go on pruning vines until dark and returned to my uncle who was sitting at the wheel of the Ford, dreaming.

How does it look? he said.

Excellent, I said.

We drove back to the city sixty-six miles an hour, as if my uncle wanted to get away from something frightening, and all the way he didn't speak. When we were coming into Ventura Avenue near the Fair Grounds he said, All four of them dogs ain't worth a penny put together.

It ain't the dogs, I said. Mexicans just look at it that way.

I thought that dog was going to bite me, my uncle said.

No, I said. He wouldn't think of it. Not even if you kicked him. His heart is full of love. The same as the Mexicans. The stealing they do never amounts to anything.

Them kids looked pretty healthy, my uncle said.

They don't come any healthier, I said.

What do they eat? my uncle said.

Beans and Mexican bread, I said. Stuff that ain't supposed to be good for you.

Do you think he'll ever learn to prune a vine? my uncle said.

Sure, I said.

I don't suppose he'll go away with the tractor, will he? my uncle said.

No, I said. It's much too heavy.

I lost money on that vineyard last year, my uncle said.

I know, I said. You lost money on it the year before too.

I've been losing money on that vineyard ever since I bought it, my uncle said. Who wants grapes? Who wants raisins?

It may be different this year, I said.

Do you think so? my uncle said.

I think this Mexican is going to do the trick, I said.

That's funny, my uncle said. I've been thinking the same thing. If he feeds them thirteen mouths this winter, not counting his own, it won't be so bad this year.

You can't lose more than you lost last year, I said.

The Japanese are all right, my uncle said, only they don't look at things the way the Mexicans do.

The Japanese wouldn't think of keeping four ordinary dogs, I said.

They'd drive the dogs away, my uncle said.

They'd throw rocks at the dogs, I said.

I think I'm going to have a good year this year, my uncle said.

We didn't say anything more all the way into town.

Me and the Babe

A Story

It is late at night and I am walking on Broadway, but on account of Broadway being the Great White Way it does not seem as late as it is. The lights are all burning and the streets are jammed with taxis and the sidewalks flow with people. I see one sign that has more electric lights in it than a lot of towns I know and the taxis are honking their horns and the show girls are going home with the make-up still on their faces and I am surprised to find out they are not all blondes. It is not unusual for me to be walking on Broadway because I am new to New York and want to find out what the town is like and Broadway is a good place to begin.

One of the things I notice on Broadway is that it is hard to get into conversations with people. I am not the sort of person who goes around trying to get into conversations with people, but night after night I see the same guys standing before the cigar stores and dance halls and I get the idea I would like to know what kind of guys they are. They look different from any guys I have known, they have different kinds of faces, and I would like to know where they were born and what they do in the daytime and w y it is they spend every night in the same place. One or two I know are in the fig t racket, which I can tell by the shape their noses are in, but the others I can't igure out at all.

That is why it is that after I have seen them five or six times running I begin to say hello. I am very friendly when I say hello, but I find out it does not go over. They do not turn out to be what you would call the friendly type, and since they look at me like I had just jumped over the wall of some asylum I soon learn to keep what I have heard referred to as my peace. I begin to think they are underworld characters that the cops are after, but it does not sound convincing even to me because if they were on the limb they would not be sitting out where it could be sawed off from under them. So I give it up as a bad job and conclude they are too busy to say hello to everybody that passes. I am disappointed but I do not stay away from Broadway on that account.

Now on this night I am telling about, when I have gotten to know better than to go around saying hello, I am standing on the curb reading the news flashes that crawl arond the Times Building. I am reading that the Babe has left for Boston when I feel a tap on my shoulder. I look around and there is one of the guys. I have not seen him before but I know he is one of the guys because he has that kind of face and the same kind of clothes. He has on a double-breasted gray suit and a pearl-gray hat and his blue tie matches the handkerchief in his coat. He looks like he has not been up long because he has just shaved himself and you can see the nicks the razor made on his chin.

"Howrya," he says, telescoping the three words into a single sound, and working his mouth into what I take as a smile. I have just gotten used to the idea that Broadway is not a friendly street and so I can think of nothing to say to him. We stand there looking at each other and I notice some gold fillings in his teeth and then he says "Howrya" again. When he says it I catch a whiff of his breath and then I understand why he is so friendly.

"I'm O.K.," I say, not forgetting to talk like I am on Broadway. "How are you?"

"I'm at the top," he says. "Haven't I seen you somewheres before?"

"Maybe," I answer. "I spend a lot of time walking up and down."

"Oh." He looks at me hard. "I guess I have made a mistake. I thought I had seen you somewhere else except just walking up and down. I would have sworn you were the man who said he was going to buy my watch off of me."

"No," I say. "You are mistaken. I have not promised to buy a watch off of no one."

"That is too bad for you," he answers. "It is a very fine watch."

He takes it out of one of the pockets in his vest and holds it out on the palm of his hand.

"You will not have another chance to buy a watch like this at the price I am going to offer it to you."

"I am not in the market for a watch," I say to him. "How is the Babe going to do with Boston?"

"The Babe is a great guy," he replies. "It is a pity his legs got old before the rest of him. I will sell you this watch for twenty-five dollars. It is a real bargain. I would not sacrifice it at such a price except that I have had a lot of bad luck and I need the money. It is yours for twenty-five."

I am not interested in the watch because I have already lost two of them, but I cannot explain this to the guy though. More letters crawl around the Times Building and I see that Boston is getting ready to give the Babe a big reception.

"I hope the Babe comes through with Boston," I say.

"The Babe is a great guy. He is a prince of a fellow. I know him personal. It is too bad his legs went and folded up on him. If you do not buy this watch you are missing the chance of a lifetime. It is worth seventy-five dollars at least."

"I can tell that by looking at it," I answer, even though it looks like an ordinary watch to me and I am no judge of watches anyway. "It looks like a very fine watch."

"I am glad you appreciate a good watch when you see it. You will never have a chance to make a bargain like this. If I did not have so much bad luck I would not be selling it at such a sacrifice. It is worth seventy-five dollars any day of the week but I will sell it to you for twenty-five. Is that a bargain or is it a bargain?"

"It is a bargain," I reply.

"You have said it. It is a pleasure to meet up with a man who knows a bargain when he sees one. This watch is a watch you can be proud of. I am proud of it myself and I would not be selling it except for the hard luck I have had lately. If I don't get twenty-five dollars by morning I will be thrown out of my rooms."

"That is too bad," I say, watching the news flashes again. "I am very sorry to hear that indeed. Tell me more about the Babe. I have always wanted to meet up with a friend of his."

"The Babe is a great guy. He is a prince. If his legs had not gone back on him he would still be at the top. The next time he is in town I will arrange for you and him to meet. I know the Babe like I know my own brother. Are you going to buy this watch?"

"How long have you known the Babe? Do you and he come from the same town."

"I do not know what town the Babe is from and I am not from that town anyway."

"What town are you from?"

"The town I am from is so small it is not even on the map. Even if I told you its name you would not know it. I am waiting to hear if you are going to buy this watch. I have to get hold of twenty-five dollars or I am going to get thrown out of my rooms."

"I have been around this country a lot," I answer, "and I think that maybe I might know the town you are from. What is the name of the town? My town is Franklin, Louisiana. What is yours?"

"I ran away from my town when I was a small boy and I do not like to talk about it. I do not like to even think about it. Why are you so anxious to know where I come from? I did not ask you any questions about where you come from. I only asked you if you wanted to buy a watch. You will never have another chance to buy a fine watch like this for twenty-five dollars."

"I do not have twenty-five dollars," I answer. "I do not even have five dollars. All I have is two dollars and forty cents. It is near the end of the month. Do you think the Babe will come back?"

"I know the Babe personal and he is a great guy but I don't have time to spend all night talking about him. I am sorry you only have two dollars and forty cents. I can't sell this watch for that because it would be too big a sacrifice. I am willing to make a sacrifice but not as big a sacrifice as that. Maybe you can get the twenty-five and meet me later."

"I could not get the twenty-five even if I was going to be thrown out of my rooms."

"That is too bad. You are missing a real bargain. This is a very fine watch."

We have both run out of conversation and then I notice an old fellow standing a few yards down the curb. He has on a pair of rimless spectacles and his hat sits up on the top of his head and in his hand he holds an umbrella even though it is a fine evening and there is no sign of rain. The guy I am talking with sees him the same time I do.

"I have to go," he says. "There is the man who said he would buy the watch off of me."

I look at the man and then I look at him.

"Didn't you say you thought I was the man who said he would buy your watch? Does that old grandpa and me look like each other?"

"I see you think you are a smart guy," he answers. "I do not like smart guys. I do not like guys who go around trying to find out the name of my town neither. The name of my town is my own business."

He walks off and goes up to the old fellow with the umbrella and starts a conversation with him. They talk for a little while and then the guy takes hold of the old fellow's arm and they walk off and are lost in the crowd. I look at the news flashes and they say that the Babe has sent a farewell message to New York and Broadway. The Babe is very sad to have to leave New York, but the day of parting has come. I hope the Babe makes out all right with Boston. I hear he is a great guy.

DOROTHY PARKER JULY 13, 1927

The Sexes

The young man with the scenic cravat glanced nervously down the sofa at the girl in the fringed dress. She was examining her handkerchief; it might have been the first one of its kind she had seen, so deep was her interest in its material, form, and possibilities. The young man cleared his throat, without necessity or success, producing a small, syncopated noise.

"Want a cigarette?" he said.

"No, thank you," she said. "Thank you ever so much just the same."

"Sorry I've only got these kind," he said. "You got any of your own?"

"I really don't know," she said. "I probably have, thank you."

"Because if you haven't," he said, "it wouldn't take me a minute to go up to the corner and get you some."

"Oh, thank you, but I wouldn't have you go to all that trouble for anything," she said. "It's awfully sweet of you to think of it. Thank you ever so much."

"Will you for God's sakes stop thanking me?" he said.

"Really," she said, "I didn't know I was saying anything out of the way. I'm awfully sorry if I hurt your feelings. I know what it feels like to get your feelings hurt. I'm sure I didn't realize it was an insult to say 'thank you' to a person. I'm not exactly in the habit of having people swear at me because I say 'thank you' to them."

"I did not swear at you!" he said.

"Oh, you didn't?" she said. "I see."

"My God," he said, "all I said, I simply asked you if I couldn't go out and get you some cigarettes. Is there anything in that to get up in the air about?"

"Who's up in the air?" she said. "I'm sure I didn't know it was a criminal offense to say I wouldn't dream of giving you all that trouble. I'm afraid I must be awfully stupid, or something."

"Do you want me to go out and get you some cigarettes; or don't you?" he said.

"Goodness," she said, "if you want to go so much, please don't feel you have to stay here. I wouldn't have you feel you had to stay for anything."

"Ah, don't be that way, will you?" he said.

"Be what way?" she said. "I'm not being any way."

"What's the matter?" he said.

"Why, nothing," she said. "Why?"

"You've been funny all evening," he said. "Hardly said a word to me, ever since I came in."

"I'm terribly sorry you haven't been having a good time," she said. "For goodness' sakes, don't feel you have to stay here and be bored. I'm sure there are millions of places you could be having a lot more fun. The only thing, I'm a little bit sorry I didn't know before, that's all. When you said you were coming over tonight, I broke a lot of dates to go to the theater and everything. But it doesn't make a bit of difference. I'd much rather have you go and have a good time. It isn't very pleasant to sit here and feel you're boring a person to death."

"I'm not bored!" he said. "I don't want to go any place! Ah, honey, won't you tell me what's the matter? Ah, please."

"I haven't the faintest idea what you're talking about," she said. "There isn't a thing on earth the matter. I don't know what you mean."

"Yes, you do," he said. "There's something the trouble. Is it anything I've done, or anything?"

"Goodness," she said, "I'm sure it isn't any of my business, anything you do. I certainly wouldn't feel I had any right to criticize."

"Will you stop talking like that?" he said. "Will you, please?"

"Talking like what?" she said.

"You know," he said. "That's the way you were talking over the telephone today, too. You were so snotty when I called you up, I was afraid to talk to you."

"I beg your pardon," she said. "What did you say I was?"

"Well, I'm sorry," he said. "I didn't mean to say that. You get me so balled up."

"You see," she said. "I'm really not in the habit of hearing language like that. I've never had a thing like that said to me in my life."

"I told you I was sorry, didn't I?" he said. "Honest, honey, I didn't mean it. I don't know how I came to say a thing like that. Will you excuse me? Please?"

"Oh, certainly," she said. "Goodness, don't feel you have to apologize to me. It doesn't make any difference at all. It just seems a little bit funny to have somebody you were in the habit of thinking was a gentleman come to your home and use language like that to you, that's all. But it doesn't make the slightest bit of difference."

"I guess nothing I say makes any difference to you," he said. "You seem to be so sore at me."

"I'm sore at you?" she said. "I can't understand what put that idea in your head. Why should I be sore at you?"

"That's what I'm asking you," he said. "Won't you tell me what I've done? Have I done something to hurt your feelings, honey? The way you were over the phone, you had me worried all day. I couldn't do a lick of work."

"I certainly wouldn't like to feel," she said, "that I was interfering with your work. I know there are lots of girls that don't think anything of doing things like that, but I think it's terrible. It certainly isn't very nice to sit here and have some one tell you you interfere with his business."

"I didn't say that!" he said. "I didn't say it!"

"Oh, didn't you?" she said. "Well, that was the impression I got. It must be my stupidity."

"I guess maybe I better go," he said. "I can't get right. Everything I say seems to make you sorer and sorer. Would you rather I'd go?"

"Please do just exactly whatever you like," she said. "I'm sure the last thing I want to do is have you stay here when you'd rather be some place else. Why don't you go some place where you won't be bored? Why don't you go up to Florence Leaming's? I know she'd love to have you."

"I don't want to go up to Florence Leaming's!" he said. "What would I want to go up to Florence Leaming's for? She gives me a pain."

"Oh, really?" she said. "She didn't seem to be giving you so much of a pain at Elsie's party last night, I notice. I notice you couldn't even talk to anybody else, that's how much of a pain she gave you."

"Yeah, and you know why I was talking to her?" he said.

"Why, I suppose you think she's attractive," she said. "I suppose some people do. It's perfectly natural. Some people think she's quite pretty."

"I don't know whether she's pretty or not," he said. "I wouldn't know her if I saw her again. Why I was talking to her was you wouldn't even give me a tumble, last night. I came up and tried to talk to you, and you just said, 'Oh, how do you do'—just like that, 'Oh, how do you do'—and you turned right away and wouldn't look at me."

"I wouldn't look at you?" she said. "Oh, that's awfully funny. Oh, that's marvelous. You don't mind if I laugh, do you?"

"Go ahead and laugh your head off," he said. "But you wouldn't."

"Well, the minute you came in the room," she said, "you started making such a fuss over Florence Leaming I thought you never wanted to see anybody else. You two seemed to be having such a wonderful time together, goodness knows I wouldn't have butted in for anything."

"My God," he said, "this what's-her-name girl came up and began talking to me before I even saw anybody else, and what could I do? I couldn't sock her in the nose, could I?"

"I certainly didn't see you try," she said.

"You saw me try to talk to you, didn't you?" he said. "And what did you do? 'Oh how do you do.' Then this what's-her-name came up again, and there I was, stuck. Florence Leaming! I think she's terrible. Know what I think of her? I think she's a damn little fool. That's what I think of her."

"Well, of course," she said, "that's the impression she always gave me, but I don't know. I've heard people say she's pretty. Honestly I have."

"Why, she can't be pretty in the same room with you," he said.

"She has got an awfully funny nose," she said. "I really feel sorry for a girl with a nose like that."

"She's got a terrible nose," he said. "You've got a beautiful nose. Gee, you've got a pretty nose."

"Oh, I have not," she said. "You're crazy."

"And beautiful eyes," he said, "and beautiful hair and a beautiful mouth. And beautiful hands. Let me have one of the little hands. Ah, look atta little hand! Who's got the prettiest hands in the world? Who's the sweetest girl in the world?"

"I don't know," she said. "Who?"

"You don't know!" he said. "You do so, too, know."

"I do not," she said. "Who? Florence Leaming?"

"Oh, Florence Leaming, my eye!" he said. "Getting sore about Florence Leaming! And me not sleeping all last night and not doing a stroke of work all day because you wouldn't speak to me! A girl like you getting sore about a girl like Florence Leaming!"

"I think you're just perfectly crazy," she said. "I was not sore! What on earth ever made you think I was? You're simply crazy. Ow, my hair-net! Wait a second till I take it off. There!"

WOODY ALLEN   AUGUST 31, 1974

The Scrolls

Scholars will recall that several years ago a shepherd, wandering in the Gulf of Aqaba, stumbled upon a cave containing several large clay jars and also two tickets to the ice show. Inside the jars were discovered six parchment scrolls with ancient incomprehensible writing which the shepherd, in his ignorance, sold to the museum for $750,000 apiece. Two years later the jars turned up in pawn shop in Philadephia. One year later the shepherd turned up in a pawn shop in Philadelphia and neither was claimed.

Archeologists originally set the date of the scrolls at 4000 BC, or just after the massacre of the Israelites by their benefactors. The writing is a mixture of Sumerian, Aramaic and Babylonian and seems to have been done by either one man over a long period of time, or several men who shared the same suit. The authenticity of the scrolls is currently in great doubt, particularly since the word Oldsmobile appears several times in the text, and the few fragments that have finally been translated deal with familiar religious themes in a more than dubious way. Still, excavationist A. H. Bauer has noted that even though the fragments seem totally fraudulent, this is probably the greatest archeological find in history with the exception of the recovery of his cufflinks from a tomb in Jerusalem. The following are the translated fragments.

One . . . And the Lord made an bet with Satan to test Job's loyalty and the Lord, for no apparent reason to Job, smote him on the head and again on the ear and pushed him into a thick sauce so as to make Job sticky and vile and then He slew a 10th part of Job's kine and Job calleth out: "Why doth thou sly my kine? Kine are hard to come by. Now I am short kine and I'm not even sure what kine are." And the Lord produced two stone tablets and snapped them closed on Job's nose. And when Job's wife saw this she wept and the Lord sent an angel of mercy who anointed her head with a polo mallet and of the 10 plagues, the Lord sent one through six, inclusive, and Job was sore and his wife angry and she rent her garment and then raised the rent but refused to paint.

And soon Job's pastures dried up and his tongue cleaved to the roof of his mouth so he could not pronounce the word "frankincense" without getting big laughs.

And once the Lord, while wreaking havoc upon his faithful servant, came too close and Job grabbed him around the neck and said, "Aha! Now I got you! Why art thou giving Job a hard time, eh? Eh? Speak up!"

And the Lord said, "Er, look—that's my neck you have . . . could you let me go?"

But Job showed no mercy and said, "I was doing very well till you came along. I had myrrh and fig trees in abundance and a coat of many colors with two pairs of pants of many colors. Now look."

And the Lord spake and his voice thundered: "Must I who created heaven and earth explain my ways to thee? What hath thou created that thou doth dare question me?"

"That's no answer," Job said. "And for someone who's supposed to be omnipotent, let me tell you, 'tabernacle' has only one 'L.'" Then Job fell to his knees and cried to the Lord. "Thine is the kingdom and the power and glory. Thou hast a good job. Don't blow it."

Two . . . And Abraham awoke in the middle of the night and said to his only son, Isaac, "I have had an dream where the voice of the Lord sayeth that I must sacrifice my only son, so put your pants on." And Isaac trembled and said, "So what did you say? I mean when He brought this whole thing up?"

"What am I going to say?" Abraham said. "I'm standing there at two a.m. in my underwear with the Creator of the Universe. Should I argue?"

"Well, did he say why he wants me sacrificed?" Isaac asked his father.

But Abraham said, "The faithful do not question. Now let's go because I have a heavy day tomorrow."

And Sarah who heard Abraham's plan grew vexed and said, "How doth thou know it was the Lord and not, say, thy friend who loveth practical jokes, for the Lord hateth practical jokes and whosoever shall pull one shall be delivered into the hands of his enemies whether they can pay the delivery charge or not." And Abraham answered, "Because I know it was the Lord. It was a deep, resonant voice, well modulated, and nobody in the desert can get a rumble in it like that."

And Sarah said, "And thou art willing to carry out this senseless act?" But Abraham told her, "Frankly yes, for to question the Lord's word is one of the worst things a person can do, particularly with the economy in the state it's in."

And so he took Isaac to a certain place and prepared to sacrifice him but at the last minute the Lord stayed Abraham's hand and said, "How could thou doest such a thing?" And Abraham said, "But thou said. . . ."

"Never mind what I said," the Lord spake. "Doth thou listen to every crazy idea that comes thy way?" And Abraham grew ashamed. "Er—not really . . . no. . . ."

"I jokingly suggest thou sacrifice Isaac and thou immediately runs out to do it."

And Abraham fell to his knees, "See, I never know when you're kidding."

And the Lord thundered, "No sense of humor. I can't believe it."

"But doth this not prove I love thee, that I was willing to donate mine only son on thy whim?"

And the Lord said, "It proves that some men will follow any order no matter how asinine as long as it comes from a resonant, well modulated voice."

And with that, the Lord bid Abraham get some rest and check with him tomorrow

Three . . . And it came to pass that a man who sold shirts was smitten by hard times. Neither did any of his merchandise move nor did he prosper. And he prayed and said, "Lord, why hast thou left me to suffer thus? All mine enemies sell their goods except I. And it's the height of the season. My shirts are good shirts. Take a look at this rayon. I got button-downs, flare collars, nothing sells. Yet, I have kept thy commandments. Why can I not earn a living when mine younger brother cleans up in children's ready-to-wear?"

And the Lord heard the man and said, "About thy shirts. . . ."

"Yes, Lord," the man said, falling to his knees.

"Put an alligator over the pocket."

"Pardon me, Lord?"

"Just do what I'm telling you. You won't be sorry."

And the man sewed on to all his shirts a small alligator symbol and lo and behold, suddenly his merchandise moved like gangbusters and there was much rejoicing while amongst his enemies there was wailing and gnashing of teeth and one said, "The Lord is merciful. He maketh me to lie down in green pastures. The problem is, I can't get up."

LAWS AND PROVERBS:

Doing abominations is against the law, particularly if the abominations are done while wearing a lobster bib.

The lion and the calf shall lie down together but the calf won't get much sleep.

Whosoever shall not fall by the sword or by famine, shall fall by pestilence, so why bother shaving?

The wicked at heart probably know something.

Whosoever loveth wisdom is righteous but he that keepeth company with fowl is weird.

My Lord, my Lord! What hast thou done, lately?

Dinner Bridge

CHARACTERS
Crowley, *the Foreman*
Amorosi, *an Italian Laborer*
Taylor, *a Negro Laborer*
Chamales, *a Greek Laborer*
Hansen, *a Scandinavian Laborer*
Llanuza, *a Mexican Laborer*
The Inquisitive Waiter
The Dumb Waiter

Scene: An area under repair on the Fifty-ninth Street Bridge. Part of the surface has been torn up, and, at the curtain's rise, three of the men are tearing up the rest of it with picks. Shovels, axes and other tools are scattered around the scene. Two men are fussing with a concrete mixer. Crowley is bossing the job. Crowley and the laborers are dressed in dirty working clothes. In the foreground is a flat-topped truck or wagon. The two waiters, dressed in waiters' jackets, dickies, etc., enter the scene, one of them carrying a tray with cocktails and the other a tray with caviar, etc. The laborers cease their work and consume these appetizers. The noon whistle blows. The waiters bring in a white table cloth and spread it over the truck or wagon. They also distribute six place cards and six chairs, or camp stools, around the truck, but the "table" is left bare of eating implements.

PROGRAM NOTE

This playlet is an adaptation from the Wallachian of Willie Stevens. For a great many years, Long Islanders and Manhattanites have been wondering why the Fifty-ninth Street Bridge was always torn up at one or more points. Mr. Stevens heard the following legend: that Alexander Woollcott, chief engineer in charge of the construction of the bridge, was something of a practical joker; that on the day preceding the completion of the bridge, he was invited to dinner by his wife's brother; that he bought a loaded cigar to give his brother-in-law after the meal, and that the cigar dropped out of his pocket and rolled under the unfinished surface planking. Ever since, gangs of men have been ripping up the surface of the bridge in search of the cigar, but an article the shape of a cigar is apt to roll in any and all directions. This is what has made it so difficult to find the lost article, and the (so far) vain search is the theme of Mr. Stevens' playlet.—*Adapter.*

First Waiter, *to* Crowley: Dinner is served.
(Crowley *and the laborers move toward the table.*)
Taylor, *to* Amorosi: I believe I am to take you in.

Amorosi *gives* Taylor *his arm and* Taylor *escorts him to the table. The laborers all pick up the place cards to find out where they are to sit.)*

Crowley, *to* Amorosi: Here is your place, Mr. Amorosi. And Taylor is right beside you.

(Note to producer: Inasmuch as Taylor *and* Amorosi *do most of the talking, they ought to face the audience. In spite of their nationalities, the laborers are to talk in correct, Crowninshield dinner English, except that occasionally, say every fourth or fifth speech, whoever is talking suddenly bursts into dialect, either his own or Jewish or Chinese or what you will.*

All find their places and sit down. The two waiters now re-enter, each carrying one dinner pail. One serves Crowley *and the other serves* Amorosi. *The serving is done by the waiters' removing the cover of the pail and holding it in front of the diner. The latter looks into the pail and takes out some viand with his fingers. First he takes out, say, a sandwich. The waiter then replaces the cover on the pail and exits with it. All the laborers are served in this manner, two at a time, from their own dinner pails. As soon as one of them has completed the sandwich course, the waiter brings him the pail again and he helps himself to a piece of pie or an apple or orange. But the contents of all the pails should be different, according to the diner's taste. The serving goes on all through the scene, toward the end of which everyone is served with coffee from the cups on top of the pails.)*

Crowley, *to* Amorosi: Well, Mr. Amorosi, welcome to the Fifty-ninth Street Bridge.

Amorosi: Thank you, I really feel as if this was where I belonged.

Hansen, *politely*: How is that?

Amorosi: On account of my father. He was among the pioneer Fifty-ninth Street Bridge destroyers. He had the sobriquet of Giacomo "Rip-Up-the-Bridge" Amorosi.

Taylor, *sotto voce, aside to* Hansen: This fellow seems to be quite a card!

Llanuza: I wonder if you could tell me the approximate date when your father worked here.

Amorosi: Why, yes. The bridge was completed on the fifth day of August, 1909. So that would make it the sixth day of August, 1909, when father started ripping it up.

Taylor, *aside to* Hansen, *in marked Negro dialect:* I repeats my assertation that this baby is quite a card!

Amorosi, *in Jewish dialect:* But I guess it must be a lot more fun nowadays, with so much motor traffic to pester.

Taylor: And all the funerals. I sure does have fun with the funerals.

Crowley, *in Irish brogue:* Taylor has a great time with funerals.

Hansen, Chamales and Llanuza, *in unison:* Taylor has a great time with the funerals.

Amorosi, *to* Taylor: How do you do it?

Taylor, *in dialect:* Well, you see, I'm flagman for this outfit. When I get out and wave my flag, whatever is coming, it's got to stop. When I see a funeral coming, I let the hearse go by and stop the rest of the parade. Then when I see another funeral coming, I stop their hearse and let the rest of *their* procession go on. I keep doing this all morning to different funerals and by the time they get to Forest Hills, the wrong set of mourners is following the wrong hearse. It generally always winds up with the friends and relatives of the late Mr. Cohen attending the final obsequies of Mrs. Levinsky.

Crowley, Hansen, Chamales and Llanuza, *in unison*: Taylor has a great time with the funerals.

Amorosi: I'm a *trumpet* medium myself.

Taylor, *aside to* Hansen: This boy will turn out to be quite a card!

Llanuza: Why do you always have to keep repairing it?

Crowley: What do you mean, what's the matter?

Llanuza: Why do they always have to keep repairing it?

Amorosi: Perhaps Mr. Crowley has the repairian rights.

Taylor, *guffawing and slapping* Hansen *or* Chamales *on the back*: What did I tell you?

Llanuza, *in dialect*: But down in Mexico, where I come from, they don't keep repairing the same bridge.

Amorosi, *to* Llanuza: If you'll pardon a newcomer, Mr. ———, I don't believe I got your name.

Llanuza: Llanuza.

Amorosi: If you'll pardon a newcomer, Mr. Keeler, I want to say that if the United States isn't good enough for you, I'd be glad to start a subscription to send you back to where you came from.

Llanuza: I was beginning to like you, Mr. Amorosi.

Amorosi: You get that right out of your mind, Mr. Barrows. I'm married; been married twice. My first wife died.

Hansen: How long were you married to her?

Amorosi: Right up to the time she died.

Chamales, *interrupting*: Mr. Amorosi, you said you had been married twice.

Amorosi: Yes, sir. My second wife is a Swiss girl.

Hansen: Is she here with you?

Amorosi: No, she's in Switzerland, in jail. She turned out to be a murderer.

Crowley: When it's a woman, you call her a murderess.

Taylor: And when it's a Swiss woman, you call her a Swiss-ess.

(One of the waiters is now engaged in serving Amorosi *with his dinner pail.)*

Waiter, *to* Amorosi: Whom did she murder?

(Waiter exits hurriedly without seeming to care to hear the answer.)

Amorosi, *after looking wonderingly at the disappearing* Waiter: What's the matter with him?

Taylor: He's been that way for years—a born questioner but he hates answers.

Crowley: Just the same, the rest of us would like to know whom your wife murdered.

Taylor, Hansen, Chamales and Llanuza, *to* Crowley: Speak for yourself. We don't want to know.

Crowley: Remember, boys, I'm foreman of this outfit. *(Aside to* Amorosi): Who was it?

Amorosi: *(Whispers name in his ear.)*

Crowley: I don't believe I knew him.

Amorosi: Neither did my wife.

Crowley: Why did she kill him?

Amorosi: Well, you see, over in Italy and Switzerland, it's different from, say, Chicago. When they find a man murdered over in those places, they generally try to learn who it is and put his name in the papers. So my wife was curious about this fellow's identity and she figured that the easiest way to get the information was to pop him.

Taylor: I'm a *trumpet* medium myself.

(Waiter *enters and serves one of the laborers from his dinner pail.*)

Waiter: How long is she in for?

(Waiter *exits hurriedly without waiting for the answer.* Amorosi *again looks after him wonderingly.*)

Hansen, *to* Amorosi: Did you quarrel much?

Amorosi: Only when we were together.

Taylor: I was a newspaper man once myself.

Llanuza, *skeptically*: You! What paper did you work on?

Taylor: It was a tabloid—The Porno-graphic.

(Waiter *enters to serve somebody.*)

Waiter, *to* Taylor: Newspaper men must have lots of interesting experiences. (*Exits without waiting for a response.*)

Amorosi: I suppose you've all heard this story—

The Other Laborers, *in unison*: Is it a golf story?

Amorosi: No.

The others, *resignedly*: Tell it.

Amorosi, *in dialect*: It seems there was a woman went into a photographer's and asked the photographer if he took pictures of children.

(Waiter *enters to serve somebody.*)

Waiter: How does it end? (Waiter *exits hurriedly.*)

Amorosi: She asked the photographer if he took pictures of children. "Why, yes, madam," replied the photographer—

Taylor: He called her "madam."

Amorosi: The photographer told her yes, that he did take pictures of children. "And how much do you charge?" inquired the madam, and the photographer replied, "Three dollars a dozen." "Well," said the woman, "I guess I'll have to come back later. I've only got eleven."

(*The other laborers act just as if no story had been told.*)

Llanuza: Down in Mexico, where I come from, they don't keep repairing the same bridge.

Taylor, *to* Hansen: Can you imitate birds?

Hansen: No.

Taylor, *to* Chamales: Can you imitate birds?

Chamales: No.

Taylor: Can anybody here imitate birds?

The Other Laborers, *in unison*: No.

Taylor: *I* can do it. Long before I got a job on this bridge, while I was helping tear up the crosstown streets, I used to entertain the boys all day, imitating birds.

Amorosi: What kind of birds can you imitate?

Taylor: All kinds.

Amorosi: Well, what do you say we play some other game?

Crowley, *rising:* Gentlemen, we are drawing near to the end of this dinner and I feel we should not leave the table until some one has spoken a few words of welcome to our newcomer, Mr. Amorosi. Myself, I am not much of a talker. (*Pauses for a denial.*)

Taylor: You said a full quart.

Crowley: Therefore, I will call on the man who is second to me in length of service on the Fifty-ninth Street Bridge, Mr. Harvey Taylor. *(Sits down.)*

Taylor, *rising amid a dead silence:* Mr. Foreman, Mr. Amorosi and gentlemen: Welcoming Mr. Amorosi to our little group recalls vividly to my mind an experience of my own on the levee at New Orleans before Prohibition. *(He bursts suddenly into Negro dialect, mingled with Jewish.)* In those days my job was to load and unload those great big bales of cotton and my old mammy used to always be there at the dock to take me in her lap and croon me to sleep.

(Waiter enters, serves somebody with coffee.)

Waiter: What was the experience you was going to tell? *(Exits hurriedly.)*

Taylor: It was in those days that I studied bird life and learned to imitate the different bird calls. *(Before they can stop him, he gives a bird call.)* The finch. *(The others pay no attention. He gives another call.)* A Dowager. (Taylor *is pushed forcibly into his seat.)*

Amorosi, *rising to respond:* Mr. Foreman and gentlemen: I judge from Mr. Taylor's performance that the practice of imitating birds is quite popular in America. Over where I come from, we often engage in the pastime of mimicking public buildings. For example *(he gives a cry.)* The American Express Company's office at Rome. *(He gives another cry.)* The Vatican. *(He gives another cry.)* Hotel McAlpin. *(A whistle blows, denoting that the dinner hour is over.)*

Crowley, *rising:* Shall we join the ladies?

(All rise and resume the work of tearing up the bridge. The waiters enter to remove the table cloth and chairs.)

Waiter *(the more talkative one):* How many Mack trucks would you guess had crossed this bridge in the last half hour? *(He exits without waiting for a reply.)*

(Curtain)

EDMUND WILSON   MARCH 23, 1921

Landscape

The suburb centres about a great disreputable common, upon which the presence of human life seems to have fallen like a disease. The soil is sterile and pale; the grass is dirty and thin; and there are bald spots, as if the earth were eaten by a kind of mange. The instinct for cleanliness and order seems never to have been felt here at all: the common is littered with refuse and waste in sprawling filthy heaps,—tin cans and broken crockery and papers, all plastered down together by the rain. And among the piles old women are picking in garments like the rain-rotted papers and children are playing with lean dogs as mangy as the common. These children, in their rags and dirty shifts, find the first romantic landscape of their games in the muddy stagnant lakes of the hollows and the sodden mountain ranges of the junk.

Along one side of the common and facing directly upon it, stands a row of shabby frame houses which at first seem mere rubbish, like the cans,—old worn-out things thrown away and defaced and disintegrated by the weather out of all recognition as objects which have once served the uses of life. But, as one studies them, they take on the aspect of horrific rectangular masks, glaring, ferocious and gleeful, but not with the expressions of life; their fixed stare is more like the faces of men who have died in delirium or by violence,—the upper windows like wide-open eyes, with half-lowered shades for the lids; the porches like gaping jaws, with the railings for long narrow teeth.

They might almost be totem-pole figures, the gods of some savage tribe; but they are not so solid and bright as the images of barbarous peoples: they are flimsy, half-heartedly built; they are entirely without dignity or pride; the yellow and browns of their sides are smeared and discolored now. They are helplessly down and out; they are beaten and insulted by the elements. But they do not protest against their fall, nor wish to be decent and sound. They are dead creatures rotting and grinning, in an ecstasy of humiliation, with the derision of the eternal spirit of cheapness and indifference and decay for the effort that builds and makes strong and the long labor of beauty.

JOHN GALSWORTHY   APRIL 26, 1919

The Muffled Ship

It was cold and gray, but the band on shore was playing, and the flags on shore fluttering, and the long double-tiered wharf crowded with welcomers in each of its open gaps, when our great strong ship slowly drew alongside, packed with its cheering chattering crowds of khaki figures, letting go all the pent-up excitement of getting home from the war. The songs and the laughter, the cheers, and the shouted questions, the hooting of the launches' sirens, the flutter of flags and hands and handkerchiefs; the faces of old women, of girls, intent, expectant; and behind us the white gulls floating against the gray sky—all made an impression ineffaceable, while our great ship, listed slightly by those thousands of figures straining towards the land which had bred them, gently slurred up against the long, high wharf, and was made fast.

The landing went on till night had long fallen, and the band was gone. At last the chatter, the words of command, the snatches of song, and that most favorite chorus: "Me! Me! Me and my girl!" died away, and the wharf was silent and the great ship silent, and a wonderful clear dark beauty usurped the gray spaces of the sky. By the light of the stars and a half moon the far harbor shores were just visible, and the huddled dark buildings of the near shore, and all the inspiring masts and feathery appanage of ropes on the moored ships, and a bright red light, casting its blood-red gleam on the black water. All the night had that breathless beauty which steeps the soul in quivering quiet rapture. . . .

Then it was that, clearly, as if I had been a welcomer standing on land in one of the wharf gaps, I saw her come—slow, slow, creeping up the narrow channel, in beside the wharf, a great gray silent ship. At first I thought her utterly empty, deserted, possessed only by the huge coiled cables forward, the great rusty anchors, the gray piled-up machinery of structure and funnel and mast, weird in the blue darkness. A lantern on the wharf cast a bobbing golden gleam deep into the oily water at her side. Gun-gray, perfectly mute, she ceased to move, coming to rest against the wharf, and then I saw with a shiver that something clung round her, a sort of gray film of emanation, which shifted and hovered, like the invisible wings of birds in a thick mist. Gradually to my straining eyes that gray filmy emanation granulated, and became faces attached to gray filmy forms, thousands upon thousands, and every face bent towards the shore, staring as it seemed, through me, at all that was behind. Slowly, very slowly I made out those faces of soldiers, helmeted, bulky with the gear of battle, their arms outstretched—and in every face the lips opened, so that one expected to hear the sound of cheering; but there came no sound. And now I could see their eyes. How wonderful they were! They seemed to ask, like the eyes of a little eager boy who asks his mother something that she cannot tell him; and their outstretched hands seemed to be trying to reach her, how lovingly, how desperately they seemed to be trying to reach her! And how terribly their opened lips seemed trying to speak! Yet from all the great gray muffled ship there came not one whisper of sound! "Mother! Mother Canada!" As if I had heard it, I knew they were saying—those opened lips that could speak no more! "Mother! Mother Canada! Home! Home!"

And then away down the wharf there jingled out the chanted words: "Me! Me! Me and my girl!" And, silent as she had come, the great gun-gray muffled ship vanished in all her length, and with her those forms and those mute faces; and I was standing again in the bows beside a coiled hawser, below me the golden gleam bobbing deep in the oily water, and above me the cold stars in beauty shining.

I. TURGENIEFF   FEBRUARY 8, 1922

The Threshold

TRANSLATED BY LEON SAUNDERS

I see an enormous building; in the front wall a narrow door is open wide; dismal darkness is behind the door.

A girl stands in front of the high threshold, a Russian girl. The thick darkness breathes with frost, and with the freezing stream a lingering dull voice comes out of the depth.

"Oh, you desiring to step over this threshold, do you know what awaits you?"

—I do, the girl answers.

"Cold, hunger, hatred, mockery, defiance, jail, sickness, death itself."

—I know.

"Solitude, isolation."

—I know, I am ready. I am willing to bear all the blows.

"Not only from the enemies but also from relatives, from friends?"

—Yes, even from them.

"All right. Are you ready for sacrifice?"

—I am.

"For nameless sacrifice? You will perish, and nobody, nobody will ever know whose memory to honor."

—I do not seek any gratitude, nor compassion. I do not need any name.

—"Are you ready . . . for crime?"

—The girl bowed her head. "Also for crime . . . I am ready." The voice paused, and in a while resumed the questions.

"Know you," it finally spoke, "that you may disbelieve everything you do believe now, you may realize that you have erred and you have ruined your young life in vain?"

—And *that* I know, and still I wish to enter.

"Enter!"

The girl stepped over the threshold and the heavy curtain fell behind her.

—Fool! a voice was heard to exclaim with a gnashing of the teeth.

—Saint! was heard from somewhere.

POETRY

Sic Semper

Now let the old kings lift
　　Their faces, keen in the wind;
We have set their pinnace adrift
　　Laden with men that sinned
Where the sea is gray, and the weeds are long, and the
　　tide is swift.

Let them lift their arms to a sky
　　That is hard and grey like the sea;
Having doomed many to die,
　　Knowing death, and white death's decree,
Let them lift their voices to hopeless clouds in a dolorous
　　cry.

We have had enough of kings
　　And of fools that stutter and creep,
Of courts and of courtly things,
　　While the bodies of men are cheap
And the noses of men are fitted, like those of their swine,
　　with rings.

Wet blood is on their hands
　　That were black with blood before;
They have fouled us with their commands;
　　They have drilled us, a demon corps,
They have sullied the earth with lusts and seared men's
　　souls with brands.

Their eyes to the under-dark!
　　Salt drink to their cynic's lips!
Let them rot in state and stark
　　In the sunken holds of ships,
Let the heavy waters fold like lead about them and leave
　　no mark.

And not for the kings alone
　　Is our fury loosed like hail;
Let the devil look to his own
　　In the day of the flashing flail
Or we strike the invisible kings whose hearts are of gold
　　and stone.

We shall drive forth with goads
    The money changers of earth;
Over the broken roads
    They have trampled on from their birth
They shall plod with burdens who held their hands from
    the bearing of loads.

We asked but a rood to tend,
    We asked them but bread to eat,
Commerce of friend with friend,
    Brief leisure, and little sweet;
They were drunken, and had no mercy; we take what is
    ours in the end.

In the days when all light kings fly
    As the Russian chaff has flown
These, too, will cringe and cry
    By a broken altar-stone;
For the storm has risen; the night of tyrants is seen in the
    thickening sky.

D.H. LAWRENCE   1921

The Revolutionary

Look at them standing there in authority,
The pale-faces.
As if it could have any effect anymore.

Pale-face authority.
Caryatids.
Pillars of white bronze standing rigid, lest the skies fall.

What a job they've got to keep it up.
Their poor, idealist foreheads naked capitals
To the entablature of clouded heaven.

I wish the skies would fall.
I wish the high and super-gothic heavens would come down,
The temple of holy light, the infinite of the spirit.

For I, like a blinded Samson, am imprisoned in it.
Yes, I am not afraid to say I am a Samson
Chained to you, slaves, pale-faces, pillars of humanity, caryatids, you metallic-stunned
    with the weight of your responsibility.

I have every sympathy with you.
The weight of your responsibility, holding up this ideal civilization,
Must be excruciating, unless you stiffen into metal, when you find it easier to stand than to
            move.

That's why I tug at you, individually, with my arm 'round your waist.
And you feel pretty rocky, you pillars.
The house sways.

I shall be glad when it comes down.
I am so tired of the prison of the infinite.
I am so tired of the limitations of the spirit.
I am so tired of pale-face, moral authority.

Am I not gone blind to it all!
What is their sky to me, their effulgence of spirit, their sun of righteousness?
Their pale faces!

To me, now, all faces are dark
All lips negroid.

Save your lips, oh palefaces,
Which are slips of metal
Like the slit in a pillar-box, you columns of divine correspondence.

To me the earth rolls ponderously, superbly
Interrupted by no breath of the pale ghost.
To me, men's footfalls fall with a dull, soft rumble, ominous and lovely.

But not your footfalls, pale-faces.
They are a clicketting of bits of disjointed metal
Working in motion.

To me, men are invisible, palpable presences in the dark
Sending out vibrations of warning, pitch-dark invitation.

But you, pale-faces,
You are painful irregular pillars which give off nothing except rigidity
And I bump against you if I try to move, for you are legion
And I am ensnared among you,
Sightless among all your visuality,
You staring caryatids of humanity.

But see if I don't bring you down, and all your high opinion
And all your ponderous roofed-in infinite of the spirit,
With a smash.

See if I am not lord of the dark and moving host
Before I die.

Invocation to the Social Muse

Señora it is true the Greeks are dead:

It is true also that we here are Americans:
That we use the machines: that a sight of the god is unusual:
That more people have more thoughts: that there are

Progress and science and tractors and revolutions and
Marx and the wars more antiseptic and murderous
And music in every home: there is also Hoover:

Does the lady suggest we should write it out in The Word?
Does Madame recall our responsibilities? We are
Whores Fräulein: poets Fräulein are persons of

Known vocation following troops: they must sleep with
Stragglers from either prince and of both views:
The rules permit them to further the business of neither:

It is also strictly forbidden to mix in maneuvers:
Those that infringe are inflated with praise on the plazas—
Their bones are resultantly afterwards found under newspapers:

Preferring life with the sons to death with the fathers
We also doubt on the record whether the sons
Will still be shouting around with the old huzzas—

For we hope Lady to live to lie with the youngest:
There are only a handful of things a man likes
Generation to generation hungry or

Well fed: the earth's one: life's
One: Mister J.P. Morgan is not one:

There is nothing worse for our trade than to be in style:

He that goes naked goes farther at last than another:
Wrap the bard in a flag or a school and they'll jimmy his
Door down and be thick in his bed—for a month:

(Who recalls the address now of the Imagists?)
But the naked man has always his own nakedness:
People remember forever his live limbs:

They may drive him out of the camps but one will take him:
They may stop his tongue on his teeth with a rope's argument—
He will lie in a house and be warm when they are shaking:

Besides Tovarishch how to embrace an army?
How to take to one's chamber a million souls?
How to conceive in the name of a column of marchers?

The things of the poet are done to a man alone
As the things of love are done—or of death when he hears the
Step withdraw on the stair and the clock tick only:

Neither his class nor his kind nor his trade may come near him
There where he lies on his left arm and will die:
Nor his class nor his kind nor his trade when the blood is jeering

And his knee's in the soft of the bed where his love lies:

I remind you Barinya the life of the poet is hard—
A hardy life with a boot as quick as a fiver:

Is it just to demand of us also to bear arms?

LANGSTON HUGHES   1934

Ballad of Roosevelt

The poet was empty,
The cupboard was bare.
I said, Papa,
What's the matter here?
　　I'm waitin' on Roosevelt, son,
　　Roosevelt, Roosevelt,
　　Waitin' on Roosevelt, son.

The rent was due,
And the lights was out.
I said, Tell me, Mama,
What's it all about?
　　We're waitin' on Roosevelt, son,
　　Roosevelt, Roosevelt,
　　Just waitin' on Roosevelt

Sister got sick
And the doctor wouldn't come
Cause we couldn't pay him
The proper sum—
　　A-waitin' on Roosevelt,
　　Roosevelt, Roosevelt,
　　A-waitin' on Roosevelt.

Then one day
They put us out o' the house.
Ma and Pa was
Meek as a mouse
　　Still waitin' on Roosevelt,
　　Roosevelt, Roosevelt.

But when they felt those
Cold winds blow
And didn't have no
Place to go
　　Pa said, I'm tired
　　O' waitin' on Roosevelt,
　　Roosevelt, Roosevelt.
　　Damn tired o' waitin' on Roosevelt.

I can't git a job
And I can't git no grub.
Backbone and navel's
Doin' the belly-rub—
　　A-waitin' on Roosevelt,
　　Roosevelt, Roosevelt.

And a lot o' other folks
What's hungry and cold
Done stopped believin'
What they been told
    By Roosevelt,
     Roosevelt, Roosevelt—

Cause the pot's still empty,
And the cupboard's still bare,
And you can't build a bungalow
Out o' air—
    Mr. Roosevelt, listen!
    What's the matter here?

MAX ENDICOFF   1927

The Excavation

Clusters of electric bulbs
Like giant chrysanthemums
Paint the black cavern
With streaks and blots
Of faded yellow.
In grotesque mimicry
The monstrous shadows
Ape each movement of the toiling men.
The stale, pungent odor of unpacked earth
Tickles the nostrils.
Through the wood-plank roof
The dull-booming rumble
Of scampering traffic
Trickles in—
But is swallowed up
By the harsh purr of the drill
As it bites frenziedly
Into the dogged rock.

And overhead, unseen,
A mountain of stone is kept upright
By a slender steel beam
And a theory.

Ode for School Convocation

Mechanically, the academic file
Winds to the platform spreading doctoral hoods
And tassels toward the moderate breeze.
The rows and rows of parents on the lawn
Are starched and honorable with ceremony.
Even the students are serious and hushed
While the hymn flourishes from the electric organ.
And then the final doctor finds his chair.
And then the final stop. The President
Welcomes, remembers, hopes, somewhat despairs—
The world being stranger than it was—finally
Declares determination and a firm belief.
Starched and honorable with ceremony
The rows and rows of parents on the lawn
Welcome determination and a firm belief,
Shift more securely in the moderate breeze.
Even the students are serious and deep
With historic intentions in the moderate breeze.

Now are the years again. Suddenly all the years
Of intention. These faces rapt with occasion
Stir unanimously serious. Surely a glance can tell
The President's reticent rationed dodging,
The paraded faculty's slight foolishness,
The parents' bluff at understanding, the boys' real bewilderment.
Still their faces stir with intention. The wish
Crosses confused under them, but the wish is real.

As Emerson lifts in quotes above the platform
And dies of distortion halfway to the gate.

Where the real wish died, conforming to its shadow
Under the glare of phosphore towers by day
And neon signs by night. A world's trade.
Discussed more tangibly in hotel rooms
By traveling salesmen. Attempted none the less
By the concluding President and the warm applause.

Between the pliant hedges at the public tea,
The faculty meets the parents, bows,
Suggests the frosted cakes, and prefers lemon.

Two Poems

I

worshipping Same
they squirm and they spawn
and a world is for them, them; whose
death's to be born)

his birth is their fear is their blind fear
—haunts all unsleep
this cry of one fiend
a thousand dreams thick

(cringing they brood
breeding they wince)
his laugh is a million griefs wide (it
shall bury much stench)

and a hundred joys high are such shoulders
as cowards will scheme
to harness: let all
unfools of unbeing

set traps for his heart,
lay snares for his feet
(who wanders through only white darkness
who moves in black light

dancing isn'ts on why, digging bridges with mirrors
from whispers to stars;
climbing silence for ifs
diving under because)

only who'll say
"and this be my fame,
the harder the wind blows the
taller i am"

II

conceive a man, should he have anything
would give a little more than it away

(his autumn's winter being summer's spring
who moved by standing in november's may)
from whose (if loud most howish time derange

the silent whys of such a deathlessness)

remembrance might no patient mind unstrange
learn (nor could all earth's rotting scholars guess
that life shall not for living find the rule)

and dark beginnings are his luminous ends
who far less lonely than a fire is cool
took bedfellows for moons mountains for friends

—open your thighs to fate and (if you can
withholding nothing) World, conceive a man

ELIZABETH BISHOP   1941

Roosters

At four o'clock
in the gun-metal blue dark
we hear the first crow of the first cock

just below
the gun-metal blue window
and immediately there is an echo

off in the distance,
then one from the back-yard fence,
then one, with horrible insistence,

grates like a wet match
from the broccoli patch,
flares, and all over town begins to catch.

Cries galore
come from the water-closet door,
from the dropping-plastered hen-house floor,

where in the blue blur
their rustling wives admire,
the roosters brace their cruel feet and glare

with stupid eyes
while from their beaks there rise
the uncontrolled, traditional cries.

Deep from protruding chests
in green-gold medals dressed,
planned to command and terrorize the rest,

the many wives
who lead hens' lives
of being courted and despised;

deep from raw throats
a senseless order floats
all over town. A rooster gloats

over our beds
from rusty iron sheds
and fences made from old bedsteads,

over our churches
where the tin rooster perches,
over our little wooden northern houses,

making sallies
from all the muddy alleys,
marking out maps like Rand McNally's:

glass-headed pins,
oil-golds and copper-greens,
anthracite blues, alizarins,

each one an active
displacement in perspective;
each screaming, "This is where I live!"

Each screaming
"Get up! Stop dreaming!"
Roosters, what are you projecting?

You, whom the Greeks elected
to shoot at on a post, who struggled
when sacrificed, you whom they labeled

"Very combative . . ."
what right have you to give
commands, and tell us how to live,

cry "Here!" and "Here!"
and wake us here where are
unwanted love, conceit and war?

The crown of red
set on your little head
is charged with all your fighting-blood.

Yes, that excrescence
makes a most virile presence,
plus all that vulgar beauty of iridescence.

Now in mid-air
by twos they fight each other.
Down comes a first flame-feather,

and one is flying,
with raging heroism defying
even the sensation of dying

And one has fallen,
but still above the town

his torn-out, bloodied feathers drift down;

and what he sung
no matter. He is flung
on the gray ash-heap, lies in dung

with his dead wives
with open, bloody eyes,
while those metallic feathers oxidize.

St. Peter's sin
was worse than that of Magdalen
whose sin was of the flesh alone;

of spirit, Peter's,
falling, beneath the flares,
among the "servants and officers."

JOHN CROWE RANSOM   1934

Painted Head

By dark severance the apparition head
Smiles from the air a capital on no
Column or a Platonic perhaps head
On a canvas sky depending from nothing;

Stirs up an old illusion of grandeur
By tickling the instinct of heads to be
Absolute and to try decapitation
And to play truant from the body bush;

But too happy and beautiful for those sorts
Of head (homekeeping heads are happiest)
Discovers maybe thirty unwidowed years
Of not dishonoring the faithful stem;

Is nameless and has authored for the evil
Historian headhunters neither book
Nor state and is therefore distinct from tart
Heads with crowns and guilty gallery heads;

So that the extravagant device of art
Unhousing by abstraction this once head
Was capital irony by a loving hand
That knew the no treason of a head like this;

Makes repentance in an unlovely head
For vinegar disparagement of flesh

Till, the hurt flesh recusing, the hard egg
Is shrunken to its own deathlike surface;

And an image thus: the body bears the head
(So hardly one they terribly are two)
Feeds and obeys and unto please what end?
Not to the glory of tyrant head but to

The increase of body. Beauty is of body.
The flesh contouring shallowly on a head
Is a rock-garden needing body's love
And best bodiness to colorify

The big blue birds sitting and sea-shell flats
And caves and on the iron acropolis
To spread the hyacinthine hair and rear
The olive garden for the nightingales.

W.H. AUDEN   1939

In Memory of
W.B. Yeats

I

He disappeared in the dead of winter.
The brooks were frozen, the airports almost deserted,
And snow disfigured the public statues;
The mercury sank in the mouth of the dying day.
O all the instruments agree
The day of his death was a dark cold day.

Far from his illness,
The wolves ran on through the evergreen forests,
The peasant river was untempted by the fashionable quays;
By mourning tongues
The death of the poet was kept from his poems.

But for him it was his last afternoon as himself,
An afternoon of nurses and rumors;
The provinces of his body revolted,
The squares of his mind were empty,
Silence invaded the suburbs,
The current of his feeling failed. He became his admirers.

Now he is scattered among a hundred cities,

And wholly given over to unfamiliar affections;
To find his happiness in another kind of wood,
And be punished under a foreign code of conscience;
The words of a dead man
Are modified in the guts of the living.

But in the importance and noise of tomorrow,
When the brokers are roaring like beasts on the floor of the Bourse,
And the poor have the sufferings to which they are fairly accustomed,
And each in the cell himself is almost convinced of his freedom,
A few thousand will think of this day,
As one thinks of a day when one did something slightly unusual.
He was silly like us: His gift survived it all.

O all the instruments agree
The day of his death was a dark cold day.

II

Earth, receive an honored guest;
William Yeats is laid to rest:
Let Irish vessel lie
Emptied of its poetry.

Time that is intolerant
Of the brave and innocent,
And indifferent in a week
To a beautiful physique,

Worships language and forgives
Everyone by whom it lives,
Pardons cowardice, conceit,
Lays its honors at their feet.

Time that with this strange excuse
Pardoned Kipling and his views,
And will pardon Paul Claudel,
Pardons him for writing well.

In the nightmare of the dark
All the dogs of Europe bark,
And the living nations wait,
Each sequestered in its hate.

Intellectual disgrace
Stares from every human face,
And the seas of pity lie
Locked and frozen in each eye.

Follow, poet, follow right
To the bottom of the night,

With your unconstraining voice
Still persuade us to rejoice.

With the farming of a verse
Make a vineyard of the curse,
Sing of human unsuccess
In a rapture of distress.

In the deserts of the heart
Let the healing fountains start,
In the prison of his days
Teach the free man how to praise.

KENNETH REXROTH   1937

Requiem for the Dead in Spain

The great geometrical winter constellations
Lift up over the Sierra Nevada,
I walk under the stars, my feet on the known round earth,
My eyes following the lights of an airplane,
Red and green, growling deep into the Hyades.
The note of the engine rises, shrill, faint,
Finally inaudible, and the lights go out
In the southwest haze beneath the feet of Orion.

As the sound departs I am chilled and grow sick
With the thought that has come over me. I see Spain
Under the black windy sky, the snow stirring faintly,
Glittering and moving over the pallid upland,
And men waiting, clutched with cold and huddled together,
As an unknown plane goes over them. It flies southwest
Into the haze above the lines of the enemy,
Sparks appear near the horizon under it.
After they have gone out the earth quivers
And the sound comes faintly. The men relax for a moment
And grow tense again as their own thoughts return.

I see the unwritten books, the unrecorded experiments
The unpainted pictures, the interrupted lives,
Lowered into the graves with the red flags over them.
I see the quick gray brains broken and clotted with blood,
Lowered each in its own darkness, useless in the earth.
Alone on a hilltop in San Francisco suddenly

I am caught in a nightmare, the dead flesh
Mounting over half the world presses against me.

Then quietly at first and then rich and full bodied,
I hear the voice of a young woman singing.
The emigrants on the corner are holding
A wake for their oldest child, a driverless truck
Broke away on the steep street and killed him,
Voice after voice adds itself to the singing.
Orion moves westward across the meridian,
Rigel, Bellatrix, Betelgeuse, marching in order,
The great nebula glimmering in his loins.

ROBERT PENN WARREN   1934

For a Friend Parting

Endure friend-parting yet, old soldier,
Scarred the heart, and wry; the wild plum,
Rock-rent, ax-bit, has known with the year bloom,
And tides, the neap and spring, bear faithfully.
Much you have done in honor, though wrathfully:
That, we supposed, was your doom.

O you who by the grove and shore walked
With us, the heart unbraced, yet unbetrayed,
Recall: the said, unsaid, though chaff the said
And backward blown. We saw above the lake
Tower the hawk, his wings the light take!
What answer to our dread?

Follow the defiles down. Forget not,
When journey-bated the nag, rusted the steel,
The horny clasp of hands your hands now seal;
And prayers of friends, ere this, kept powder dry.
Rough country of no birds, the tracks sly:
Thus faith has lived, we feel.

Troop Train

It stops the town we come through. Workers raise
Their oily arms in good salute and grin.
Kids scream as at a circus. Business men
Glance hopefully and go their measured way.
And women standing at their dumbstruck door
More slowly wave and seem to warn us back,
As if a tear blinding the course of war
Might once dissolve our iron in their sweet wish.

Fruit of the world, O clustered on ourselves
We hang as from a cornucopia
In total friendliness, with faces bunched
To spray the streets with catcalls and with leers.
A bottle smashes on the moving ties
And eyes fixed on a lady smiling pink
Stretch like a rubber-band and snap and sting
The mouth that wants the drink-of-water kiss.

And on through crummy continents and days;
Deliberate, grimy, slightly drunk we crawl,
The good-bad boys of circumstance and chance,
Whose bucket-helmets bang the empty wall
Where twist the murdered bodies of our packs
Next to the guns that only seem themselves.
And distance like a strap adjusted shrinks,
Tightens across the shoulder and holds firm.

Here is a deck of cards; out of this hand
Dealer, deal me my luck, a pair of bulls,
The right draw to a flush, the one-eyed jack.
Diamonds and hearts are red but spades are black,
And spades are spades and clubs are clovers—black.
But deal me winners, souvenirs of peace.
This stands to reason and arithmetic,
Luck also travels and not all come back.

Trains lead to ships and ships to death or trains,
And trains to death or trucks, and trucks to death,
Or trucks lead to the march, the march to death,
Or that survival which is all our hope;
And death leads back to trucks and trains and ships,
But life leads to the march, O flag! at last
The place of life found after trains and death
—Nightfall of nations brilliant after war.

The Waltz of the Twenty-Year-Olds

Good for the wind, good for the night, good for the cold
Good for the march and the bullets and the mud
Good for legends, good for the stations of the cross
Good for absence and long evenings. Funny ball
At which I danced and, children, you will dance
To the same dehumanized orchestral score
Good for fear, good for machine guns, good for rats
Good as good bread and good as simple salad

But here is the rising of the conscript sun
The waltz of the twenty-year-olds sweeps over Paris
Good for a shot of brandy at dawn and the anguish before the attack
Good for the waiting, the storm and the patrols
Good for night silence under rocket flares
Good for youth passing and the rusting heart
Good for love and death, good to be forgotten
In the rain and shadow cloaking the battlefields
Child soldiers trundled in no other bed
But the ditch already tailored to their measure

The twenty-year-old waltz sweeps through the bistros
And breaks like a laugh at the entrance to the Métro

Army classes of yesterday, vanished dreams
Fourteen, Fifteen, Sixteen: listen. They hum
Like us the trite refrain, like us believe it
And like us in those days, may God forgive them
Value more than their lives at a single moment
Of drunkenness or folly or delight
What do they know of the world? Does living mean
Quite simply, Mother, to die very young?

Soldier (T.P.)

When the runner's whistle lights the last miles of darkness
And the soldier stumbles into the hard green clothes
(From the night where his earth is the dream of a stranger
And the years are stripped from his heart like a sigh;
Where death and life and their child are—civilian)
And stands for his hour there in the cold green lines
That are always waiting for something, or waiting;
There wakes in the cropped dusty head, one supposes,
In the blistered hands, in the soft uneasy eyes,
The smell of the ages where no one is dying
And the old dog stirs in his sleep in the sun:
The world where they marry and live in houses.

But his house and his wife are—pending; and the life
That was his to starve in, to waste as he chose,
Has no option now: the iron unchanging
Chance that had governed his price like a plate's
Is smashed for an instant, as the atoms' wills
Are fused in the grim solicitude of State.
Yet it is not You the sergeants hoarsely
Curse at there where the traveling sand
Obscures the relief map of the parade ground.
That You may be, perhaps—as Justice
May be, may be; *this* world's justice
Is here, is now—as you too are, soldier.

What have you learned here? To bear, and be silent.
To do what I must, as I must: that is, to die.
What are the soldier's answers? Yes, sir;
No, sir; no excuse, sir . . . *But (sir) there is no room there, to die—*

To die or to live . . . Hush, no one is listening.
Ask as you please, there is no one here to reply.
Here what they teach is—other people's deaths;
Who needs to learn why another man should die?
Who has taught you, soldier, why you yourself are dying?
And there is no time, each war, to learn.
You must live or die as the dice are thrown on a blanket;
As the leaf chars or is kindled; as the bough burns.

The Roman Soldier

Wearing some kind of iron hat, armed to the teeth with
whatever weapons are latest, he has stood in some square from
occupied Troy to now: seen from outside, monolithic:

dreaming inside of Vermont, or the Abruzzi, or Yorkshire,
or his father's boats tied to the jetty, or his girl in the grass,
or he's some slab without dreams, how do we know? Still less does he

know whether he's an angel with a sword or a fiend with a fork.
Somebody stuck him where he is, mostly among enthusiasts
who would hang him by the heels and spit on his head if they could.

If you up-end the poor doll, its eyes will roll.
                                        Statuary
these figures are stationed across the colored countries and the years,
all much alike, but there has been no intercommunication.

Promise of Peace

The heads of strong old age are beautiful
Beyond all grace of youth. They have strange quiet,
Integrity, health, soundness, to the full
They've dealt with life and been attempered by it.
A young man must not sleep, his years are war
Civil and foreign but the former's worse,
But the old can breathe in safety now that they are
Forgetting what youth means, the being perverse,
Running the fool's gauntlet and getting cut
By the whips of the five senses. As for me
If I should wish to live long it were but
To trade those fevers for tranquillity,
Thinking, though that's entire and sweet in the grave,
How shall the dead taste the deep treasure they have?

Assignment

Luna Nine, mission accomplished, swivel your eyes
downward to Vietnam and see if you could
land softly there and send us signals of what
goes on.

      Or is the layer of dust too thick, the weather of lies
too dense for landing? Luna Nine, you should
pierce the haze, find in the cover of leaves
what our soldiers never reach - the Vietcong hiding,
crouching and crawling in the burnt-up rice -
                        all those thin

little men no bigger than boys who elude
our bigger boys. See if you can
send pictures of their small stomachs, their dogged minds
and the empty ones of their southern brothers dulled,
by incessant war, to will or choice.

             Luna Nine,
transmit the cortex of Ky and let us see
the brain of Ho. Show us the wombs
of village mothers, seeded to replace
the small lives spindled, folded, stapled, mutilated
by this war.

             We have
pictures enough of shattered bodies, theirs and ours, we need
a special vision: the computer eye, freed
from the warping and wavering of mortal sight, the words
of victory, right, prestige, and all that fogs
the lens. Quick, Luna Nine -
land - transmit -
reveal.

THOMAS HARDY 1921

The Haunting Fingers

A fantasy in a Museum of Musical Instruments

"Are you awake,
  Comrades, this silent night?
Well 'twere if all of our glossy gluey make
Lay in the damp without, and fell to fragments quite!"

"O viol, my friend,
  I sleep not, though dawn nears,
And I fain would drowse away to its utter end
This dumb dark stowage after our loud melodious years!"

And they felt past handlers clutch them,
    Though none was in the room,
Old players' dead fingers touch them,
    Shrunk in the tomb.

"'Cello, good mate,
  You speak my mind as yours:
Doomed to this voiceless, crippled, corpselike state,
What vibrant frame so trapped and taken long endures?"

"Once I could thrill
  The populace through and through,
Wake them to passioned pulsings past their will" . . . .
(A contrabasso spoke so, and the rest sighed anew.)

And they felt dead touches travel
    Over their tense contours,
And with old skill unravel
    Cunningest scores.

"The tender pat
  Of her airy finger-tips
Upon me daily—I rejoiced thereat!"—
Thuswise a harpsichord, as from dampered lips.

"My keys' white shine,
  Now sallow, met a hand
Even whiter . . . Tones of hers fell forth with mine
In sowings of sound so sweet no lover could withstand!"

And its clavier was filmed with fingers
    Like weak wan flames in the air,
Or a phosphorus gleam that lingers
    In mould laid bare.

"Gayer than most
  Was I," reverbed a drum;
"The regiments, marchings, throngs, hurrahs! What
    a host
I stirred—even when crape mufflings gagged me well-nigh
    dumb!"

Thrilled an aged viol:
  "Much tune have I set free
To spur the dance, since my first timid trial
Where I had birth—far hence, in sun-swept Italy!"

And he feels the dead fingers on him
    Of those who pressed him then;
  Who seem with their glance to con him,
    Saying, "Not again!"

"A holy calm,"
  Mourned a shawm's voice subdued,
"Would steep my rhythms when Sabbath hymn and
    psalm
Poured from devout souls met in weekly sanctitude."

"I faced the sock
  Nightly," (twanged a sick lyre,)
"Over ranked lights! O charm of life in mock,
O scenes that fed love, hope, wit, rapture, mirth, desire!"

Thus they, till each dead player
    Stroked thinner and more thin,
  And the morning sky grew grayer,
    And day looked in.

BABETTE DEUTSCH   1941

About Hell

Those who have spent a week or a day in hell
Watch native streets take on a foreign air;
Interiors grow strange, table and chair
And even the uncut book harbors a scorching smell.
No walk is ever the same, no room, no face,
But nether heat plays blackly over it,
Shadowing with furrows of the pit
A child's clear brow. Such bear from place to place

Hell's landscape: cliffs of silence closing in
Upon them, gulfs of rage opening before;
The idiot waste stretches beside the door;
Then in their ears resuming fires begin.
Let them jump on a bus or a boat or push into a train.
They are loaded down with the endured, the known.
On everything they touch that ash is blown.
Hell stares back from every mirror and pane.
It travels with the traveler everywhere
Like no other country visited.
He retains the citizenship of the dead,
And returns home to find that hell is there.

DYLAN THOMAS   1945

The Conversation of Prayers

The conversation of prayers about to be said
By the child going to bed and the man on the stairs
Who climbs to his dying love in her high room,
The one not caring to whom in his sleep he will move
And the other full of tears that she will be dead,

Turns in the dark on the sound they know will arise
Into the answering skies from the green ground,
From the man on the stairs and the child by his bed.
The sound about to be said in the two prayers
For the sleep in a safe land and the love who dies

Will be the same grief flying. Whom shall they calm?
Shall the child sleep unharmed or the man be crying?
The conversation of prayers about to be said
Turns on the quick and the dead, and the man on the stairs
Tonight shall find no dying but alive and warm

In the fire of his care his love in the high room.
And the child not caring to whom he climbs his prayer
Shall drown in a grief as deep as his made grave,
And mark the dark-eyed wave, through the eyes of sleep,
Dragging him up the stairs to one who lies dead.

The Lost Wife

In the daytime, maybe, your heart's not breaking,
For there's the sun and the sky and working
And the neighbors to give you a word or hear you,
But, ah, the long nights when the winds come shaking
The cold black curtain, pulling and jerking,
And no one there in the bed to be near you.

And worse than the clods on the coffin falling
Are the clothes in the closet that no one wears now
And the things like hairpins you're always finding.
And you wouldn't mind the ghost of her calling
As much as knowing that no one cares now
If the carpet fades when the sun gets blinding.

I look in the houses, when twilight narrows,
And in each a man comes back to a woman.
The thought of that coming has spurs to ride me.
—Death, you have taken the great like sparrows,
But she was so slight, so small, so human.
You might have left her to lie beside me.

The Death of the Hired Man

Mary sat musing on the lamp-flame at the table,
·Waiting for Warren. When she heard his step,
She ran on tiptoe down the darkened passage
To meet him in the doorway with the news
And put him on his guard. "Silas is back."
She pushed him outward with her through the door
And shut it after her. "Be kind," she said.
She took the market things from Warren's arms

And set them on the porch, then drew him down
To sit beside her on the wooden steps.

"When was I ever anything but kind to him?
But I'll not have the fellow back," he said.
"I told him so last haying, didn't I?
If he left then, I said, that ended it.
What good is he? Who else will harbor him
At his age for the little he can do?
What help he is there's no depending on.
Off he goes always when I need him most.
He thinks he ought to earn a little pay
Enough at least to buy tobacco with,
So he won't have to beg and be beholden.
'All right,' I say, 'I can't afford to pay
Any fixed wages, though I wish I could.'
'Someone else can.' 'Then someone else will have to.'
I shouldn't mind his bettering himself
If that was what it was. You can be certain,
When he begins like that, there's someone at him
Trying to coax him off with pocket money—
In haying time, when any help is scarce.
In winter he comes back to us. I'm done."

"Sh! not so loud: he'll hear you," Mary said.

"I want him to: he'll have to soon or late."

"He's worn out. He's asleep beside the stove.
When I came up from Rowe's I found him here,
Huddled against the barn door fast asleep,
A miserable sight, and frightening, too—
You needn't smile—I didn't recognize him—
I wasn't looking for him—and he's changed.
Wait till you see."

                    "Where did you say he'd been?"

"He didn't say. I dragged him to the house,
And gave him tea and tried to make him smoke.
I tried to make him talk about his travels.
Nothing would do: he just kept nodding off."

"What did he say? Did he say anything?"

"But little."

                    "Anything? Mary, confess
He said he'd come to ditch the meadow for me."

"Warren!"

                    "But did he? I just want to know."

"Of course he did. What would you have him say?
Surely you wouldn't grudge the poor old man
Some humble way to save his self-respect.
He added, if you really care to know,
He meant to clear the upper pasture, too.

That sounds like something you have heard before?
Warren, I wish you could have heard the way
He jumbled everything. I stopped to look
Two or three times—he made me feel so queer—
To see if he was talking in his sleep.
He ran on Harold Wilson—you remember—
The boy you had in haying four years since.
He's finished school, and teaching in his college.
Silas declares you'll have to get him back.
He says they two will make a team for work:
Between them they will lay this farm as smooth!
The way he mixed that in with other things.
He thinks young Wilson a likely lad, though daft
On education—you know how they fought
All through July under the blazing sun,
Silas up on the cart to build the load,
Harold along beside to pitch it on."

"Yes, I took care to keep well out of earshot."
"Well, those days trouble Silas like a dream.
You wouldn't think they would. How some things linger!
Harold's young college-boy's assurance piqued him.
After so many years he still keeps finding
Good arguments he sees he might have used.
I sympathize. I know just how it feels
To think of the right thing to say too late.
Harold's associated in his mind with Latin.
He asked me what I thought of Harold's saying
He studied Latin, like the violin
Because he liked it—that an argument!
He said he couldn't make the boy believe
He could find water with a hazel prong—
Which showed how much good school had ever done him.
He wanted to go over that. But most of all
He thinks if he could have another chance
To teach him how to build a load of hay——"

"I know, that's Silas' one accomplishment.
He bundles every forkful in its place,
And tags and numbers it for future reference,
So he can find and easily dislodge it
In the unloading. Silas does that well.
He takes it out in bunches like big birds' nests.
You never see him standing on the hay
He's trying to lift, straining to lift himself."

"He thinks if he could teach him that, he'd be
Some good perhaps to someone in the world.
He hates to see a boy the fool of books.
Poor Silas, so concerned for other folk,
And nothing to look backward to with pride,
And nothing to look forward to with hope,
So now and never any different."

Part of a moon was falling down the west,
Dragging the whole sky with it to the hills.
Its light poured softly in her lap. She saw it
And spread her apron to it. She put out her hand
Among the harplike morning-glory strings,
Taut with the dew from garden bed to eaves,
As if she played unheard some tenderness
That wrought on him beside her in the night.
"Warren," she said, "he has come home to die:
You needn't be afraid he'll leave you this time."

"Home," he mocked gently.

                  "Yes, what else but home?
It all depends on what you mean by home.
Of course he's nothing to us, any more
Than was the hound that came a stranger to us
Out of the woods, worn out upon the trail."

"Home is the place where, when you have to go there,
They have to take you in."

                 "I should have called it
Something you somehow haven't to deserve."

Warren leaned out and took a step or two,
Picked up a little stick, and brought it back
And broke it in his hand and tossed it by.
"Silas has better claim on us you think
Than on his brother? Thirteen little miles
As the road winds would bring him to his door.
Silas has walked that far no doubt today.
Why doesn't he go there? His brother's rich,
A somebody—director in the bank."

"He never told us that."

               "We know it, though."

"I think his brother ought to help, of course.
I'll see to that if there is need. He ought of right
To take him in, and might be willing to—
He may be better than appearances.
But have some pity on Silas. Do you think
If he had any pride in claiming kin
Or anything he looked for from his brother,
He'd keep so still about him all this time?"

"I wonder what's between them."

                    "I can tell you.
Silas is what he is—we wouldn't mind him—
But just the kind that kinsfolk can't abide.
He never did a thing so very bad.
He don't know why he isn't quite as good
As anybody. Worthless though he is,
He won't be made ashamed to please his brother."
"I can't think Si ever hurt anyone."

"No, but he hurt my heart the way he lay
And rolled his old head on that sharp-edged chair-back.
He wouldn't let me put him on the lounge.
You must go in and see what you can do.
I made the bed up for him there tonight.
You'll be surprised at him—how much he's broken.
His working days are done; I'm sure of it."

"I'd not be in a hurry to say that."

"I haven't been. Go, look, see for yourself.
But, Warren, please remember how it is:
He's come to help you ditch the meadow.
He has a plan. You mustn't laugh at him.
He may not speak of it, and then he may.
I'll sit and see if that small sailing cloud
Will hit or miss the moon."

                              It hit the moon.
Then there were three there, making a dim row,
The moon, the little silver cloud, and she.

Warren returned—too soon, it seemed to her,
Slipped to her side, caught up her hand and waited.

"Warren," she questioned:

                    "Dead," was all he answered.

EDWIN ARLINGTON ROBINSON   1919

The Mill

The miller's wife had waited long,
    The tea was cold, the fire was dead;
And there might yet be nothing wrong
    In how he went and what he said:
"There are no millers any more,"
    Was all that she had heard him say;
And he had lingered at the door
    So long that it seemed yesterday.

Sick with a fear that had no form
    She knew that she was there at last;
And in the mill there was a warm
    And mealy fragrance of the past.
What else there was would only seem
    To say again what he had meant;
And what was hanging from a beam
    Would not have heeded where she went.

And if she thought it followed her,
  She may have reasoned in the dark
That one way of the few there were
  Would hide her and would leave no mark:
Black water, smooth above the weir
  Like starry velvet in the night,
Though ruffled once, would soon appear
  The same as ever to the sight.

ROBERT GRAVES   1957

The Second-Fated

My stutter, my cough, my unfinished sentences,
Denote an inveterate physical reluctance
To use the metaphysical idiom.
Forgive me: what I am saying is, perhaps this:—

  Your accepted universe, by Jove's naked hand
Or Esmun's, or Odomankoma's, or Marduk's—
Choose which name jibes—formed scientifically
From whatever there was before Time was,
And begging the question of perfect consequence,
May satisfy the general run of men
(If 'run' be an apt term for patent paralytics)
That blueprints destine all they suffer here,
But does not satisfy certain few else.

  Fortune enrolled me among the second-fated
Who have read their own obituaries in *The Times*,
Have heard 'Where, death, thy sting? Where, grave, thy victory?'
Intoned with unction over their still clay,
Have seen two parallel red-ink lines drawn
Under their manic-depressive bank accounts,
And are therefore strictly forbidden to walk in grave-yards
Lest they scandalize the sexton and his bride.

  We, to be plain with you, taking advantage
Of a brief demise, visited first the Pit,
A library of shades, completed characters;
And next the silver-bright Hyperborean Queendom,
Basking under the sceptre of Guess Whom?,
Where pure souls matrilineally foregather.
We were then shot through by merciful lunar shafts
Until hearts tingled, heads sang, and praises flowed;
And learned to scorn your factitious universe
Ruled by the death which we had flouted;

Acknowledging only that from the Dove's egg hatched
Before aught was, but wind—unpredictable
As our second birth would be, or our second love:
A moon-warmed world of discontinuance.

EDNA ST. VINCENT MILLAY   1921

Sonnet

What's this of death, from you who never will die?
Think you the wrist that fashioned you in clay,
The thumb that set the hollow just that way
In your full throat and lidded the long eye
So roundly from the forehead, will let lie
Broken, forgotten, under foot, some day
Your unimpeachable body, and so slay
The work he most had been remembered by?

I tell you this: whatever of dust to dust—
Goes down, whatever of ashes may return
To its essential self in its own season,
Loveliness such as you will not be lost,—
But, cast in bronze, upon his urn
Make known him master, and for what good reason.

JAMES JOYCE   1932

Ecce Puer

Of the dark past
A child is born.
With joy and grief
My heart is torn.

Calm in his cradle
The living lies.
May love and mercy
Unclose his eyes!

Young life is breathed
On the glass;
The world that was not
Comes to pass.

A child is sleeping:
An old man gone.
O, father forsaken,
Forgive your son!

CONRAD AIKEN   1935

Prelude

In heavenly stillness when the evening stands
deep as a world above your lifted hands—
deep as a world above your lifted face
the profound ocean of unspoken space—

look, as the darkness deepens, your arms reach farther
godlike and fisherlike the world to gather;
but still the streaming waters elude your meshes,
weeds and flotsam outnumbering the fishes.

Nothing is there? But again the stillness comes;
once more against the dark your godhead looms;
the vaster net of a vaster self you fling,
and draw toward you the innumerable Thing.

What god with angry face would you find there?
or what immortal food or end of care?
Greatly your own greatness the net brings back;
or, weakly dared and flung, your own soul's lack.

HART CRANE   1932

The Broken Tower

The bell-rope that gathers God at dawn
Dispatches me as though I dropped down the knell
Of a spent day—to wander the cathedral lawn
From pit to crucifix, feet chill on steps from hell.

Have you not heard, have you not seen that corps
Of shadows in the town, whose shoulders sway
Antiphonal carillons launched before
The stars are caught and hived in the sun's ray?

The bells, I say, the bells break down their tower;
And swing I know not where. Their tongues engrave
Membrane through marrow, my long-scattered score
Of broken intervals. . . . And I, their sexton slave!

Oval encyclicals in canyons heaping
The impasse high with choir. Banked voices slain!
Pagodas, campaniles with reveilles outleaping—
O terraced echoes prostrate on the plain! . . .

And so it was I entered the broken world
To trace the visionary company of love, its voice
An instant in the wind (I know not whither hurled)
But not for long to hold each desperate choice.

My word I poured. But was it cognate, scored
Of that tribunal monarch of the air
Whose thigh embronzes earth, strikes crystal Word
In wounds pledged once to hope—cleft to despair?

The steep encroachments of my blood left me
No answer (could blood hold such a lofty tower
As flings the question true?)—or is it she
Whose sweet mortality stirs latent power?—

And through whose pulse I hear, counting the strokes
My veins recall and add, revived and sure
The angelus of wars my chest evokes:
What I hold healed, original now, and pure . . .

And builds, within, a tower that is not stone
(Not stone can jacket heaven)—but slip
Of pebbles—visible wings of silence sown
In azure circles, widening as they dip

The matrix of the heart, lift down the eye
That shrines the quiet lake and swells a tower . . .
The commodious, tall decorum of that sky
Unseals her earth, and lifts love in its shower.

DELMORE SCHWARTZ   1959

Gold Morning, Sweet Prince

What the sad and passionate gay player of Avon avowed
With vivid exactness, eloquent variety is as immense
As the sea is. The sea which neither the humble nor the proud
Can dam, control, nor master. No matter what our sense
Of existence, or whence we came or where we hope and seek,
He knew us all before we were, he knew the strong, the weak,

The silly, the reticent, the pious, the powerful, the experience
Of fortune, sudden fame, extremes reversed, inevitable loss
Whether on land or sea. He knew mortality's immortality
And essential uncertainty as he knew the land and the sea.

And knew the reality of nobility,
And saw the cowering, towering power of treachery:
He hated the flakes and butterflies of lechery.

And he believed, at times, in truth, hope, loyalty and charity.

See: he saw what was and what is and what has yet to come
to be:

A gentle monarch murdered in helpless sleep.
A girl by Regent Hypocrisy seduced.
A child by Archduke Ambition jailed and killed.
A loving, loyal wife by a husband loving and brave
Falsely suspected, accused—of handkerchiefs!
Stabbed by his love, his innocence, his trust
In the glib cleverness of a self-abating knave.
Look: Ophelia lolls and babbles in the river named Forever,
Never never never never never.
Cordelia is out of breath and Lear
Has learned at last that flattery is clever:
That words are free, sentiments inexpensive, vows
And declarations worthless and priceless: at last he knows
How true love is sometimes speechless, always sincere;
He knows—and knows too late—at last—how love was very
near and dear.

Are all hearts and all girls always betrayed?
Is love never beyond lust, disgust and distrust?
See: it is clear: Duncan is in his grave
And Desdemona weeps beneath the willow tree,
Having been granted little time to weep, pray or rave:
Is this the truth? the truth which is one, eternal, and whole?
Surely the noble, the innocent, the gifted and the brave
Sometimes—surely, at times—prevail. If one living soul
Is caught by cruelty and killed by trust
Whence is our consolation before or above the grave?

Ripeness is all: the rest is silence. Love
Is all. We are such stuff as love has made us
And our little life, green, ripe or rotten and rotted, is what
it is
Because of love accepted, rejected, refused and jilted, wilted,
faded or raided, neglected or betrayed.
Some are defeated, some are mistreated, some are fulfilled,
and some come to flower and succeed,
Knowing the patience of energy from the black root to the
rounding fruit:
And if this were not true, if love were not kind and cruel,
Generous and unjust, heartless and irresistible, painful to the
savant and gentle to the fool,

Fecund and various, wasteful and precarious, lavish, savage,
    and tender, begetting the lion and the lamb,
The peacock, the spaniel, the tiger, the lizard, the chicken
    hawk and the dove,
All would be nothing much, all would be trivial, nothing
    would be enough, love would not be love:
For as there is no game and no victory when no one loses,
So there is no choice but the choice of love unless one chooses
Never to love, seeking immunity, discovering nothingness.

This is the only sanctuary, this is the only asylum unless
We hide in a dark ark, and deny or refuse to believe,
And refuse to hope, that there descends in the unknown
    hidden night and loss the ultimate dove,
Crying forever with all the others who are damned and hope-
    less that *love is not love.*

Gold morning, sweet prince, black night has always descend-
    ed and has always ended:
Gold morning, prince of Avon, sovereign and king
Of reality, hope and speech: may all the angels sing
With all the sweetness and all the truth with which you sang
    of any thing and every thing.

W.B. YEATS   1930

Cracked Mary and the Bishop

Bring me to the blasted oak
That I, midnight upon the stroke,
All find safety in the tomb,
May call a curse out of the sky
Ere the one or t'other die,
None so old as he and I:
The solid man and the coxcomb.

Nor was he bishop when his ban
Banished Jack the Journeyman,
All find safety in the tomb,
Nor so much as parish priest,
Yet he, an old book in his fist,
Cried that we lived like beast and beast:
The solid man and the coxcomb.

The bishop has a skin, God knows,
Wrinkled like the foot of a goose,
All find safety in the tomb,
Nor can he hide in holy black
The heron's hunch upon his back,
But a birch tree stood my Jack:
The solid man and the coxcomb.

Set me by that oak, for he
That had my virginity
All find safety in the tomb
Wanders out into the night
And there is shelter under it,
But should that other come, I spit:
The solid man and the coxcomb.

Cracked Mary Reproved

I

I care not what the sailors say;
All those dreadful thunderstones,
All that storm that blots the day
Can but show that heaven yawns;
Great Europa played the fool
That changed a lover for a bull.
Fol de rol, fol de rol.

II

To round that shell's elaborate whorl,
Adorning every secret track
With the delicate mother-of-pearl,
Made the joints of heaven crack;
So never hang your heart upon
A roaring, ranting journeyman.
Fol de rol, fol de rol.

JOHN BERRYMAN   1963

Another Dream Song

Filling her compact and delicious body
with chicken páprika, she glanced at me
twice.
Fainting with interest, I hungered back
and only the fact of her husband and four other people
kept me from springing on her

or falling at her little feet and crying
"You are the hottest one for years of night
Henry's dazed eyes
have enjoyed, Brilliance." I advanced upon
(despairing) my spumoni.—Sir Bones: is stuffed,
de world, wif feeding girls.

—Black hair, complexion latin, jewelled eyes
downcast . . . The slob beside her feasts . . . What wonders is
she sitting on, over there?
The restaurant buzzes. She might as well be on Mars.
Where did it all go wrong? There ought to be a law against Henry.
—Mr. Bones: there is.

Dilemma

There are two wives that you can be,
And either one remains the worse:
The blind, whose hands are both for me,
Or the wide-eyed and the perverse.

In never a finger strays to flesh
That is not mine, shall I be glad?
When it returned it might refresh
Me with a touch it never had.

I would not feel your palms grow pale
Because I held them from the light.
Go . . . And yet I shall bewail
Your absent eyes when they are bright

With treacherous thought that tries my blood,
With some intent I would pluck out—
Were it not that while I stood
The other wife awoke the doubt.

The Monstrous Marriage

She who with innocent and tender hands
reached up to take the wounded pigeon
from the branch found it turn

into a fury as it bled. Maddened she clung
to it stabbed by its pain and the blood
of her hands and the bird's

blood mingled while she stilled it for
the moment and wrapped it in her thought's
clean white handkerchief. After that

she adopted a hawk's life as her own.
For it looked up and said, You are
my wife for this. Then she released it.

But he came back shortly. Certainly,
since we are married, she said to him, no
one will accept it. Time passed.

I try to imitate you, he said while she
cried a little in smiling. Mostly,
he confided, my head is clouded

except for hunting. But for parts of
a day it's clear as any man's—by
your love. No, she would

answer him pitifully, what clearer than
a hawk's eye and reasonably the
mind also must be so. He turned his

head and seeing his profile in her
mirror ruffled his feathers and gave
a hawk's cry, desolately.

Nestling upon her as was his wont he
hid his talons from her soft flesh
fluttering his wings against her sides

until her mind, always astonished at
his assumptions, agonized, heard
footsteps and hurried him

to the open window whence he flew. After
that she had a leather belt made upon
which he perched to enjoy her.

ANNE SEXTON   1972

Angel of Little Neck Clams

Angel of little neck clams, do you know famine?
The babies blow up like bubbles; they have swallowed
their teddy bears whole. The fathers are not merely thin.
The fathers are houses of bones; they slump by the road
and sleep all day. They dig for grubs and roots
and garbage; they eat leaves and sour grass soup.
They dream of menus. They dream of Mama's breast.

They dream of loaves of fresh baked bread,
of a roasted goat rolling in blood and all the rest.
They have sometimes baked rats until they are dead.
There is no nobility in it or anything like that.
We of Le Cote Basque, we of the automat

know nothing. It is our souls we keep on a diet.
They bloat like old fish. And then they are quiet.

Angel of Clean Sheets

Angel of clean sheets do you know bed bugs?
Once in a madhouse they came like specks of cinnamon
as I lay in a chloral cave of drugs,
as old as a dog, as quiet as a skeleton.
Little bits of dried blood. One hundred marks
upon the sheet. One hundred kisses in the dark.

White sheets smelling of soap and Chlorox
have nothing to do with this night of soil,
nothing to do with barred windows and multiple locks
and all the webbing in the bed, the ultimate recoil.
I have slept in silk and in red and in black.
I have slept on sand and one fall night, a haystack.

I have known a crib. I have known the tuck-in of a child
but inside my hair waits the night I was defiled.

JOHN UPDIKE   1967

Subway Love

Negress serene though underground,
what weddings in northward Harlem
impressed upon you this cameo
stamp of stoic repose?
Beauty should never be bored
with being beautiful.

Bright lights shatter at our speed.
Couplings cluck, the darkness yells.
The child beside you sidles in
and out of sleep, and I,

poor sooty white man scarcely visible,
try not to stare.

O loveliness blind to itself:
sockets thumbed from clay wherein
eyelids are petals of shadow,
cheekbones and jawbone whose carriage
is of a proud rider in velvet,
lips where eleven curves live.

Eurydice, come follow me,
my song is silent, listen:
I'll hold your name in love so high
oceans of years will leave it dry;
mountains of time will not begin
to move a moment of your skin.

The doors gape wide at Fifty-ninth.
The Kiosk steps are black with blood.
I turn and find,
rebuked by light,
you gone, Negress serene,
tugged northward into night.

OSCAR WILLIAMS   1944

Subway

Under the church's lawn, in the land of electric clocks,
The subway train is plunging into the lungs of the rocks:
And as the bald Negro with the glasses reads his True Story
And the old woman is quivering behind her morning glory,
The inconceivable girl with the timetable, feather and leer,
A mammoth dumpling of sex, is ensconced on the atmosphere.

Beneath the tons of complacence the subway deftly delves
With people sitting satisfied with their disconsolate selves:
A child across the way is dangling out of a fairy-tale book,
Dipping in the advertisements the divining rod of her look:
The dismal fans are languidly stroking the beard of the wind:
Behind the newspaper fronts the sins of thought are sinned.

This is the skin of death and every pore is a face
Pulsating against tomorrow, the vacuum thighs of space:
This is life the story-teller, telling endless tales
To keep himself alive as the iron eyelid falls:
This is the explosion chamber, the secret room of the spark
Where the populations whirl with the poured breath of the dark.

A jungle of prongs is scraping the tough hide of the present:
The huge centipede of station leaps at the vein imprisoned:
The subway's galvanized throat is torn into craters of speed:
The sullen meanwhile is bulging with the ingots of greed:
And what is true is in conspiracy with the things that seems
And steel continues to scream, so long as man screams.

JOHN HOLLANDER   1959

A Lion Named Passion

*". . . the girl had walked past several cages occupied by
other lions before she was seized by a lion named Passion.
It was from his cage that keepers recovered the body."*

—*The New York Times*, May 16, 1958

Hungering on the gray plain of its birth
For the completion of the sunny cages
To hold all its unruly, stretching forth
Its longest streets and narrowest passages,
The growing city paws the yielding earth,
And rears its controlling stones. Its snarl damages
The dull, unruffled fabric of silences
In which the world is wrapped. The day advances
And shadows lengthen as their substances
Grow more erect and rigid, as low hearth
And high, stark tower rise beneath the glances
Of anxious, ordered Supervision. North
Bastion and eastern walls are joined, and fences
Are finished between the areas of Mirth
And the long swards of Mourning. Growth manages
At once vigor of spurts, and the rigor of stages.

If not the Just City, then the Safe one: sea
And mountain torrent warded off, and all
The wildest monsters caged, that running free,
The most exposed and open children shall
Fear no consuming grasp. Thus the polity
Preserves its fast peace by the burial
Of these hot barbarous sparks whose fiery, bright
Eruption might disturb blackness of night
And temperateness of civil love. The light
Of day is light enough, calm, gray, cozy
And agreeable. And beasts? The lion might
Be said to dwell here, but so tamed is he,
Set working in the streets, say, with no fright
Incurred by these huge paws which turn with glee

A hydrant valve, while playing children sprawl
And splash to the bright spray, dribbling a shiny ball—

So innocent he is, his huge head, high
And chinny, pointed over his shoulder, more
A lion rampant, blazoned on the sky,
Than monster romping through the streets, with gore
Reddening his jaws; so kind of eye
And clear of gaze is that sweet beast, that door
Need never shut, nor window bar on him.
But look! Look there! One morning damp and dim
In thick, grey fog, or even while the slim
And gaily tigering shadows creep on by
The porch furniture on hot noons, see him
Advancing through the streets, with monstrous cry,
Half plea, half threat, dying in huff of flame!
This must be some new beast! As parents spy,
Safe, from behind parked cars, he damps his roar—
It is the little children he is making for!

When elders, not looking at each other, creep
Out of their hiding places, little men,
Little women, stare back, resentment deep
Inside their throats at what had always been
A Great Place for the Kids: infants asleep
And growing, boys and girls, all, all eaten,
Burned by the prickly heat of baby throbbing,
Already urging scratching hands; the sobbing
After certain hot hurts in childhood; stabbing
Pulses and flashing floods of summer that leap
Out, in the dusk of childhood, at youth, dabbing
At the old wounds from which fresh feelings seep.
"O help me! I am being done!" the bobbing
Hip and awakened leg, one day, from heap
Of melting body call. Done? No, undone!
Robbing the grave of first fruits, the beast feeds again.

Burning is being consumed by flaming beasts,
Rebellious and unappeasable. The wind
Of very early morning, finally, casts
A cool sweet quenching draught on hunger's end,
Those ashes and whitened bones. Each day, to lists
Of dead and sorely wounded are assigned
The tasks of memory. Mute crowds push by
The useless cages and restraining, high,
(But not retaining) walls. Against the sky
Only these ruins show at dawn, like masts,
Useless in ships becalmed, but hung with dry
Corpses, or like unheeded fruit that blasts
High in trees, wasted. Menacing, wild of eye,
The city, having missed its spring, now feasts,
Nastily, on itself. Jackals attend
The offal. And new cities raven and distend.

The Windy City

The lean hands of wagon men
put out pointing fingers here,
picked this crossway, put it on a map,
set up their sawbucks, fixed their shotguns,
found a hitching place for the pony express,
made a hitching place for the iron horse,
the one-eye horse with the fire-spit head,
found a homelike spot and said, 'Make a home,'
saw this corner with a mesh of rails, shuttling
    people, shunting cars, shaping the junk of
    the earth to a new city.

The hands of men took hold and tugged
And the breaths of men went into the junk
And the junk stood up into skyscrapers and asked:
Who am I? Am I a city? And if I am what is my name?
And once while the whistles blew and blew again
The men answered: Long ago we gave you a name,
Long ago we laughed and said: You? Your name is
    Chicago.

Early the red men gave a name to a river,
    the place of the skunk,
    the river of the wild onion smell,
    Shee-caw-go.

Out of the payday songs of steam shovels,
Out of the wages of structural iron rivets,
The living lighted skyscrapers tell it now as a name,
Tell it across miles of sea blue water, gray blue land:
I am Chicago, I am a name given out by the breaths of
    working men, laughing men, a child, a belonging.

So between the Great Lakes,
The Grand De Tour, and the Grand Prairie,
The living lighted skyscrapers stand,
Spotting the blue dusk with checkers of yellow,
    streamers of smoke and silver,
    parallelograms of night-gray watchmen,
Singing a soft moaning song: I am a child, a belonging.

How should the wind songs of a windy city go?
Singing in a high wind the dirty chatter gets blown
    away on the wind—the clean shovel,

the clean pickax,
lasts.

It is easy for a child to eat breakfast and pack off
    to school with a pair of roller skates,
    buns for lunch, and a geography,
Riding through a tunnel under a river running backward,
    to school to listen . . how the Pottawattamies . .
    . . and the Blackhawks . . ran on moccasins . .
    between Kaskaskia, Peoria, Kankakee, and Chicago.
It is easy to sit listening to a boy babbling
    of the Pottawattamie moccasins in Illinois,
    how now the roofs and smokestacks cover miles
    where the deerfoot left its writing
    and the fox paw put its initials
    in the snow . . for the early moccasins . . to read.

It is easy for the respectable taxpayers to sit in the
    street cars and study the faces of burglars,
    the prison escapes, the hunger strikes, the cost of
    living, the price of dying, the shop gate battles of
    strikers and strikebreakers, the strikers killing
    scabs and the police killing strikers—the strongest,
    the strongest, always the strongest.

It is easy to listen to the haberdasher customers hand
    each other their easy chatter—it is easy to die
    alive—to register a living thumbprint and be dead
    from the neck up.
And there are sidewalks polished with the footfalls of
    undertakers' stiffs, greased mannikins, wearing up-to-
    the-minute sox, lifting heels across doorsills,
    shoving their faces ahead of them—dead from the
    neck up—proud of their sox—their sox are the last
    word—dead from the neck up—it is easy.

Lash yourself to the bastion of a bridge
and listen while the black cataracts of people go by,
    baggage, bundles, balloons,
    listen while they jazz the classics:

        "Since when did you kiss yourself in
        And who do you think you are?
        Come across, kick in, loosen up.
        Where do you get that chatter?"

        "Beat up the short change artists.
        They never did nothin' for you.
        How do you get that way?
        Tell me and I'll tell the world.
        I'll say so, I'll say it is."

"You're trying to crab my act.
You poor fish, you mackerel,
You ain't got the sense God
Gave an oyster—it's raining—
What you want is an umbrella."

"Hush baby—
I don't know a thing.
I don't know a thing.
　Hush baby."

"Hush baby—
It ain't how old you are,
It's how old you look.
It ain't what you got,
It's what you can get away with."

"Bring home the bacon.
Put it over, shoot it across.
Send 'em to the cleaners.
What we want is results, re-sults
And damn the consequences.
　　　　Sh . . . . sh . . . .
You can fix anything
If you got the right fixers."

"Kid each other, you cheap skates.
Tell each other you're all to the mustard—
You're the gravy."

"Tell 'em honey.
Ain't it the truth, sweetheart?
　Watch your step.
　You said it,
　You said a mouthful.
We're all a lot of damn fourflushers."

"Hush baby!
Shoot it,
Shoot it all!
Coo coo, coo coo"—
This is one song of Chicago.

It is easy to come here a stranger and show the whole
　works, write a book, fix it all up—it is easy to come
　and go away a muddle-headed pig, a bum and a bag
　of wind.

Go to it and remember this city fished from its
　depths a text: "independent as a hog on ice."
Venice is a dream of soft waters, Vienna and Bagdad
　recollections of dark spears and wild turbans;

Paris is a thought in Monet gray on scabbards,
fabrics, façades; London is a fact in a fog
filled with the moaning of transatlantic
whistles; Berlin sits amid white scrubbed quad-
rangles and torn arithmetics and testaments;
Moscow brandishes a flag and repeats a dance
figure of a man who walks like a bear.
Chicago fished from its depths a text: Independent
as a hog on ice.

Forgive us if the monotonous houses go mile on mile
Along monotonous streets out to the prairies—
If the faces of the houses mumble hard words
At the streets—and the street voices only say:
"Dust and a bitter wind shall come."

Forgive us if the lumber porches and doorsteps
Snarl at each other—
And the brick chimneys cough in a close-up of
Each other's faces—
And the ramshackle stairways watch each other
As thieves watch—
And dooryard lilacs near a malleable iron works
Long ago languished
In a short whispering purple.

And if the alley ash cans
Tell the garbage wagon drivers
The children play the alley is Heaven
And the streets of Heaven shine
With a grand dazzle of stones of gold
And there are no policemen in Heaven—
Let the rag-tags have it their way.

And if the geraniums
In the tin cans of the window sills
Ask questions not worth answering—
And if a boy and a girl hunt the sun
With a sieve for sifting smoke—
Let it pass—let the answer be—
"Dust and a bitter wind shall come."

Forgive us if the jazz timebeats
Of these clumsy shadows
Moan in saxophone undertones,
And the footsteps of the jungle,
The fang cry, the rip claw hiss,
The sneak-up and the still watch,
The slant of the slit eyes waiting—
If these bother respectable people

with the right crimp in their napkins
reading breakfast menu cards—
forgive us—let it pass—let be.

If cripples sit on their stumps
And joke with the newsies bawling,
"Many lives lost! many lives lost!
Terrible accident! many lives lost!"—
If again twelve men let a woman go,
"He done me wrong; I shot him"—
Or the blood of a child's head
Spatters on the hub of a motor truck—
Or a 44-gat cracks and lets the skylights
Into one more bank messenger—
Or if boys steal coal in a railroad yard
And run with humped gunnysacks
While a bull picks off one of the kids
And the kid wriggles with an ear in cinders
And a mother comes to carry home
A bundle, a limp bundle,
To have his face washed, for the last time,
Forgive us if it happens—and happens again—
    And happens again.

    Forgive the jazz timebeat
    of clumsy mass shadows,
    footsteps of the jungle,
    the fang cry, the rip claw hiss,
    the slant of the slit eyes waiting.

Forgive us if we work so hard
And the muscles bunch clumsy on us
And we never know why we work so hard—
If the big houses with little families
And the little houses with big families
Sneer at each other's bars of misunderstanding;
Pity us when we shackle and kill each other
And believe at first we understand
And later say we wonder why.

Take home the monotonous patter
Of the elevated railroad guard in the rush hours:
"Watch your step. Watch your step. Watch your step."
Or write on a pocket pad what a pauper said
To a patch of purple asters at a whitewashed wall:
"Let every man be his own Jesus—that's enough."

The wheelbarrows grin, the shovels and the mortar
    hoist and exploit.
The stone shanks of the Monadnock, the Transportation,
    the People's Gas Building, stand up and scrape

at the sky.
The wheelbarrows sing, the bevels and the blue prints
    whisper.
The library building named after John Crerar, naked
    as a stock farm silo, light as a single eagle
    feather, stripped like an airplane propeller,
    takes a path up.
Two cool new rivets say, "Maybe it is morning,"
    "God knows."

Put the city up; tear the city down;
    put it up again; let us find a city.
Let us remember the little violet-eyed
    man who gave all, praying, "Dig and
    dream, dream and hammer, till your
    city comes."

Every day the people sleep and the city dies;
    every day the people shake loose, awake and
    build the city again.

The city is a tool chest opened every day,
    a time clock punched every morning,
    a shop door, bunkers and overalls
    counting every day.

The city is a balloon and a bubble plaything
    shot to the sky every evening, whistled in
    a ragtime jig down the sunset.

The city is made, forgotten, and made again,
    trucks hauling it away haul it back
    steered by drivers whistling ragtime
    against the sunsets.

Every day the people get up and carry the city,
    carry the bunkers and balloons of the city,
    lift it and put it down.

    "I will die as many times
    as you make me over again,"
    says the city to the people,
"I am the woman, the home, the family,
I get breakfast and pay the rent;
I telephone the doctor, the milkman, the undertaker;
    I fix the streets
    for your first and your last ride—
Come clean with me, come clean or dirty,
I am stone and steel of your sleeping numbers;
    I remember all you forget.
    I will die as many times . .
    as you make me over again."

Under the foundations,

Over the roofs,
The bevels and the blue prints talk it over.
The wind of the lake shore waits and wanders.
The heave of the shore wind hunches the sand piles.
The winkers of the morning stars count out cities
And forget the numbers.

At the white clock-tower
lighted in night purples
over the boulevard link bridge
only the blind get by without acknowledgements.

The passers-by, factory punch-clock numbers,
        hotel girls out for the air, teameoes,
        coal passers, taxi drivers, window washers,
        paperhangers, floorwalkers, bill collectors,
        burglar alarm salesmen, massage students,
        manicure girls, chiropodists, bath rubbers,
        booze runners, hat cleaners, armhole basters,
        delicatessen clerks, shovel stiffs, work plugs—
They all pass over the bridge, they all look up
        at the white clock tower
        lighted in night purples
        over the boulevard link bridge—
And sometimes one says, "Well, we hand it to 'em."

Mention proud things, catalogue them,
The jack-knife bridge opening, the ore boats,
        the wheat barges passing through.
Three overland trains arriving the same hour,
        one from Memphis and the cotton belt,
        one from Omaha and the corn belt,
        one from Duluth, the lumberjack and the iron range.
Mention a carload of shorthorns taken off the valleys
        of Wyoming last week, arriving yesterday, knocked on
        the head, stripped, quartered, hung in ice boxes today
        mention the daily melodrama of this humdrum,
        rhythms of heads, hides, heels, hoofs hung up.

It is wisdom to think the people are the city.
It is wisdom to think the city would fall to pieces
        and die and be dust in the wind
If the people of the city all move away and leave no
        people at all to watch and keep the city.
It is wisdom to think no city stood here at all until
        the working men, the laughing men, came.
It is wisdom to think tomorrow new working men, new
        laughing men, may come and put up a new city—
Living lighted skyscrapers and a night lingo of lanterns
        testify tomorrow shall have its own say-so.

Night gathers itself into a ball of dark yarn.
Night loosens the ball and it spreads.
The lookouts from the shores of Lake Michigan
        find night follows day, and ping! ping! across
        sheet gray the boat lights put their signals.
Night lets the dark yarn unravel, Night speaks and
        the yarns change to fog and blue strands.

The lookouts turn to the city.
The canyons swarm with red sand lights
        of the sunset.
The atoms drop and sift, blues cross over,
        yellows plunge.
Mixed light shafts stack their bayonets,
        pledge with crossed handles.
So, when the canyons swarm, it is then the
        lookouts speak
Of the high spots over a street . . . mountain language
Of skyscrapers in dusk, the Railway Exchange,
The People's Gas, the Monadnock, the Transportation,
Gone to the gloaming.

The river turns in a half circle.
The Milwaukee Avenue bridge curves
        over the river curve.
        Then the river panorama
        performs for the bridge,
        dots . . . lights . . . dots . . . lights,
        sixes and sevens of dots and lights,
a lingo of lanterns and searchlights,
circling sprays of gray and yellow.

A man came as a witness saying:
"I listened to the Great Lakes
And I listened to the Grand Prairie,
And they had little to say to each other,
A whisper or so in a thousand years.
'Some of the cities are big,' said one.
'And some not so big,' said another.
'And sometimes the cities are all gone,'
Said a black knob bluff to a light green sea."

Winds of the Windy City, come out of the prairie,
        all the way from Medicine Hat.
Come out of the inland sea blue water, come where
        they nickname a city for you.

Corn wind in the fall, come off the black lands,
        come off the whisper of the silk hangers,
        the lap of the flat spear leaves.

Blue water wind in summer, come off the blue miles

of lake, carry your inland sea blue fingers,
carry us cool, carry your blue to our home.

White spring winds, come off the bag wool clouds,
come off the running melted snow, come white
as the arms of snow-born children.

Gray fighting winter winds, come along on the tearing
blizzard tails, the snouts of the hungry
hunting storms, come fighting gray in winter.

Winds of the Windy City,
Winds of corn and sea blue,
Spring wind white and fighting winter gray,
Come home here—they nickname a city for you.

The wind of the lake shore waits and wanders.
The heave of the shore wind hunches the sand piles
The winkers of the morning stars count out cities
And forget the numbers.

VACHEL LINDSAY　　　　　　　　　　　　　　　　1922

Billboards and Galleons

Inscribed to Stephen Graham

I.

Each day is Biloxi's birthday party
Splendid with many a sun-kissed wonder,
Splendid with many a swimming girl.
Oh there is melted the heart of stone,
Fantasy, rhyme and rhapsody ring,
From street-car and Ford and yellow taxi,
Argosies crowded to shrieking capacity—
With moon-struck boy, and sun-struck girl.
Tourists, residents, what you please—
From the whirling south, from the whirling north.
Bees near the hive, or far from home,
Dreaming of love like honeycomb.
Barney Google is what they sing,
Mister Sheehan, Mister Gallagher,
Black Joe, and Old Kentucky Home,
Swing Low Sweet Chariot, Maryland, Dixie,
Sometimes I Feel Like a Mourning Dove,
The Pullman Porters on Parade,
Or Hear now my Song of Love.

But storms come down from the soul of the universe,
Put the long coast in imminent jeopardy,
Despoiling felicity, quenching the ecstacy,
Hide my fantastical town from me,—
Where every street is a valentine,
The kind we gave to love in youth
Where the lace is deep, three layers deep.
In, and in, and in, you look:—gossamer book! fairy book!

Once when such a storm was on,
When every spiritual hope seemed gone,
I was burning the world like a bridge, behind me,
I was walking in water so no one could find me—
In the edges of the waves, where the waves meet the beach:—
Forest, and sea waves, both, within reach.
Far from my prairie home,
Far from the old hive, far from my home
Dreaming of love like honeycomb!
Twisted winds, coming down, from Heaven knows where,
Blistered feet were mine, sea-weed was my hair.
Dream sea birds flew down on fanatical wings,
Flew down through tremendous red-rainbow-rimmed rings.
They were speaking of glory, speaking of death,
Were shrieking creepy, fanatical things.
Many unwritten songs of mine, long forgotten,
And dim resolves, and loves forgotten,
Swept in with the driftwood and foamy flakes.
Yet I said: "I will march 'til my soul re-awakes,"
Yet I said: "My brain with marveling sings
That 'courage and sleep, courage and sleep are the principal things,

March on, sleep-walkers, till courage comes,
March, while the sad heart breaks,
Whirl on, like a leaf, then fight again—
Sleep and courage! sleep and courage! the fate of men!"

It was there, on the proud Spanish trail I was walking,
And I thought of Don Ivan, my Spanish ancestor,
Friend of Columbus, and Isabel's guest.
From the stormy right came the green sea talking.
I was walking the old Spanish trail toward Biloxi,
So famous for legends of Spanish chivalry!
City of feathers, balloons and confetti,
City of hearties, of birthday parties!
Oh streets of valentines in long lines,
Great garden of mocking bird melody!
Oh filigree city of fogs and mystery!
Far from the old hive, far from my home,
I was dreaming of love like honeycomb.
And, startling pathways, starry-white
Were revealed by the lightning and street light,
Revealed,
Revealed by the lightning and street light.

II.

Buzzing autos, like black bees
Hurried through the magnolia trees,
Then billboards, to make nations stare
Came into the vision, flashy, and vain,
Washed by the midnight sea-born rain.
Washed by the midnight sea-born rain,
They went like cliffs up to the sky,
America's glories flaming high,
Festooned cartoons, an amazing mixture,
Shabby, shoddy, perverse and twistical,
Shamefully boastful, shyly mystical.
Politics, with all its tricks, both old parties in a fix!
Donkey and elephant short of breath
La Follette scaring them half to death.

The snappy Saturday Evening Post
Displaying, and advertising most
The noisiest things from coast to coast.
Exaggerated Sunday papers,
Comic sheets like scrambled eggs
And Andy Gump's first-reader capers;—
All on those billboards to the sky.
Who put them there, in the way, and why?
Pictured skyscrapers of the night,
Marble-topped, tremendous, white!
There were Arrow-collar heroes proud,
Holding their heads above the crowd,
Looking for love like honeycomb.
There was many an ice cream soda vendor.
There were business kings in a daisy chain,
Then movie queens in a daisy chain,
Sugar faced, unlaced, and slender:—dreaming of love like honeycomb.

Then all the rascals of the land,
All the damned for the last ten years,
Rising from their doom with tears,
Skeletons, skeletons, leather and bone,
Each dead soul chained to a saxophone—
Watching the roaring storm above,
Looking for honey-dreams, and love.
All on those billboards to the sky!
Who put them there, in the way, and why?

Then a railroad map of the U.S.A.,
Then a soul-road map of the U.S.A.,
Showing all the flowers of the land,
But nowhere, love like honeycomb.
Only signboards, only billboards,
Washed by the midnight sea-born rain,
Washed by the midnight sea-born rain.

There were open boxes of fine cigars,

As big and bold as Pullman cars.
And on the brass-bound lids of these
Old Spain was pictured as you please.
But why were these billboards to the sky—
Who put them there, in the way, and why?

      III.

And then I thought all the splendor had gone—
I was in darkness—plunging on.
On the left were summer resort and lawn,
And the flash of the car of the midnight train.
On the right—little waves, then great waves
Then masts and shafts, then the wrecks of rafts—
Then the wrecks of the galleons of Spain.

Red coins, then jewels, drowned parrots, drowned peacocks,
Then a tolling sound, a tolling sound,
Then the wrecks of the galleons of Spain,
Rolling by, rolling on in the rain.
Love-calls, death-cries; drowned pirates, drowned beauties—
Drowned Incas, then drowned Montezumas;
First friars of Quetzal, then nuns of Quetzal,
First friars of Christendom, then nuns of Christendom,
Lost faces, sweet as the honeycomb.
Rolling by, rolling on in the rain,
Rolling by, rolling on in the foam.

And I said: "I will march 'til my soul re-awakes,"
And I said: "My mind with marveling sings
That 'courage and sleep, courage and sleep are the principal things,'"

For there came dead eagles, then dead panthers,
Then, millions of men to the edge of the sky:—
Dead Spanish legions, from the deep sea regions—
While increasing rain whipped the sea and the air.
Then there came a noise like a vulture crying.
Then there came a cheering, cheering sound—
Bullrings slowly whirling around,
Bullrings, bullrings, round and round.
Then waves like Seminoles, waves like Negroes,
Dragging up their chains from the deep,
Singing of love like honeycomb.
Then waves like tobacco fields, waves like corn fields,
Waves like wheat fields, turning to battlefields.
Then round table crusaders, then world-paraders,
Tall kings in shining silver line
As though for a miracle and a sign,
Singing songs like Spanish wine!

Then I saw the bad Pizarro,
Then hours of dewy jungle-glow—
Dim Peru and Mexico.

Then the wild seeker, Coronado singing of love like honeycomb,
With all his furious train foaming by in the rain,
Singing in eternal sleep,
Lifted, singing from the deep.
Then the tall town of Eldorado,
Passing by, like a fog and a shadow.
And then I saw a girl more pale
Than any fairy ever shone—
A white light in the southern night.
As cold as the north Auroral light
Reigning over the sea alone!
My heart was like a burning world,
I saw it flame above the dawn,
Her robe, her footstool and her throne!
And she was like a moon and pearl
And like an alabaster stone!
So far away in the utmost sky!
Her beauty like the honeycomb
The secret love, Glory and Fate—
Her wings from the earth to Heaven's gate,
A pillar in the dawn apart.
Then she was gone. The dawn was gone.
Black storm, black storm! And I plunged on!
Then lightning bolts across the sky,
Then a great bubble like a dome,
In whirling, whirling, whirling splendor,
Then Sancho Panza! Then Don Quixote,
He, who could not know surrender,
Glory's ultimate contender,
Singing in eternal sleep,
Lifted, singing from the deep,
Singing of love like honeycomb!
Then windmills, windmills, round and round,
Then a great storm, a fearful cry, a bell of doom—
A tolling sound, a tolling sound, a tolling sound
Then the wrecks of the galleons of Spain—
Rolling by, rolling on in the rain
Rolling by, rolling on in the foam.

By these ships, on the right were the red waves cleft.
Then, again, on the left, stood the billboards there,
Queerly fine to the zenith line,
Overhead to the zenith line—
Washed by the midnight sea-born rain,
Washed by the midnight sea-born rain,
Gleaming down, as the wrecks went by,
Looking at fair, lost Spain!

Between these visions I plunged on,
And straight ahead came the wonder of dawn,
In that foggy dawn:—storm-washed Biloxi!
The piers were wrecks, street-cars were wrecks, side-walks were wrecks.

Yet straight ahead arose from the dead
The valentine, filigree, towers of mystery,
The snow-white skyscrapers of new history.

Oh fantasy, sugar, and mockery!
Oh mocking birds in their whimsy!
Oh pretty, lazy Biloxi,
City haughty and fair, knowing not why:—
And—looking high at the mast-filled sky—
Haughtily, patronizingly there,
Looking up at the ghost-filled sky,
Looking at fair, lost Spain.

ALLEN TATE   1932

Elegy

Jefferson Davis: 1808-1889

No more the white refulgent streets
Never the dry hollows of the mind
Shall he in fine courtesy walk
Again, for death is not unkind.

A civil war cast on his fame
The four years' odium of strife
Unbodies his dust; love cannot warm
His tall corpuscles to this life.

What did we gain? What did we lose?
Be still; grief for the pious dead
Suspires from bosoms of kind souls
Lavender-wise, propped-up in bed.

Our loss put six feet under ground
Is measured by the magnolia's root;
Our gain's the intellectual sound
Of death's feet round a weedy tomb.

In the back chambers of the State
(Just preterition for his crimes)
We curse him to our busy sky
Who's busy in hell a hundred times

A day, though profitless his task,
Careless what Belial may say,
He who wore out the perfect mask
Orestes fled in night and day.

Dunbarton

When Uncle Devereux died,
Daddy was still on sea-duty in the Pacific;
it seemed spontaneous and proper
for Mr. MacDonald, the farmer,
Karl, the chauffeur, and even my Grandmother
to say, "your Father." They meant my Grandfather.
He was my Father. I was his son.
On our yearly autumn get-aways from Boston
to the family graveyard in Dunbarton,
he took the wheel himself—
like an admiral at the helm.
Freed from Karl and chuckling over the gas he was saving,
he let his motor roller-coaster
out of control down each hill.
We stopped at the *Priscilla* in Nashua
for brownies and root beer,
and later "pumped ship" together in the Indian summer. . . .
At the graveyard, an original modern Christ
gave a sheepdog's nursing patience
to Grandfather's Aunt Lottie,
his Mother, the stone but not the bones
of his Father Francis.
Failing as when Francis Winslow could count
them on his fingers,
the clump of virgin pine still stretched patchy ostrich necks
over the disused millpond's fragrantly woodstained water,
a reddish blur,
like the ever blackening wine-dark coat
in our portrait of Edward Winslow
once sheriff for George the Second
the sire of bankrupt Tories.
Grandfather and I
raked leaves from our dead forebears,
defied the dank weather
with "dragon" bonfires.
Our helper, Mr. Burroughs,
had stood with Sherman at Shiloh—
his thermos of shockless coffee
was milk and grounds;

his illegal home-made claret
was as sugary as grape jelly
in a tumbler capped with paraffin.
I borrowed Grandfather's cane
carved with the names and altitudes
of Norwegian mountains he had scaled—
more a weapon than a crutch.
I lanced it in the fauve ooze for newts.
In a tobacco tin after capture,
the umber yellow mature newts
lost their leopard spots,
lay grounded as numb
as scrolls of candied grapefruit peel.
I saw myself as a young newt,
neurasthenic, scarlet
and wild in the wild coffee-colored water.
In the mornings I cuddled like a paramour
in my Grandfather's bed,
while he scouted about the chattering greenwood stove.
Grandfather found
his grandchild's fogbound solitudes
sweeter than human society.

CRITICISM

The Duty of Harsh Criticism

Today in England we think as little of art as though we had been caught up from earth and set in some windy side street of the universe among the stars. Disgust at the daily deathbed which is Europe has made us hunger and thirst for the kindly ways of righteousness, and we want to save our souls. And the immediate result of this desire will probably be a devastating reaction towards conservatism of thought and intellectual stagnation. Not unnaturally we shall scuttle for safety towards militarism and orthodoxy. Life will be lived as it might be in some white village among English elms; while the boys are drilling on the green we shall look up at the church spire and take it as proven that it is pointing to God with final accuracy.

And so we might go on very placidly, just as we were doing three months ago, until the undrained marshes of human thought stirred again and emitted some other monstrous beast, ugly with primal slime and belligerent with obscene greeds. Decidedly we shall not be safe if we forget the things of the mind. Indeed, if we want to save our souls, the mind must lead a more athletic life than it has ever done before, and must more passionately than ever practise and rejoice in art. For only through art can we cultivate annoyance with inessentials, powerful and exasperated reactions against ugliness, a ravenous appetite for beauty; and these are the true guardians of the soul.

So it is the duty of writers to deliberate in this hour of enforced silence how they can make art a more effective and obviously unnecessary thing than it has been of late years. A little grave reflection shows us that our first duty is to establish a new and abusive school of criticism. There is now no criticism in England. There is merely a chorus of weak cheers, a piping note of appreciation that is not stilled unless a book is suppressed by the police, a mild kindliness that neither heats to enthusiasm nor reverses to anger. We reviewers combine the gentleness of early Christians with a promiscuous polytheism; we reject not even the most barbarous nor most fatuous gods. So great is our amiability that it might proceed from the weakness of malnutrition, were it not that it is almost impossible not to make a living as a journalist. Nor is it due to compulsion from above, for it is not worth an editor's while to veil the bright rage of an entertaining writer for the sake of publishers' advertisements. No economic force compels this vice of amiability. It springs from a faintness of the spirit, from a convention of pleasantness, which, when attacked for the monstrous things it permits to enter the mind of the world, excuses itself by protesting that it is a pity to waste fierceness on things that do not matter.

153

But they do matter. The mind can think of a hundred twisted traditions and ignorances that lie across the path of letters like a barbed wire entanglement and bar the mind from an important advance. For instance, there is the tradition of unreadability which the governing classes have imposed on the more learned departments of literature, such as biography and history. We must rebel against the formidable army of Englishmen who have achieved the difficult task of becoming men of letters without having written anything. They throw up platitudinous inaugural addresses like wormcasts, they edit the letters of the unprotected dead, and chew once more the more masticated portions of history; and every line they write perpetuates the pompous tradition of eighteenth century "book English" and dissociates more thoroughly the ideas of history and originality of thought. We must dispel this unlawful assembly of peers and privy councillors round the wellhead of scholarship with kindly but abusive, and, in cases of extreme academic refinement, coarse criticism.

That is one duty which lies before us. Others will be plain to any active mind; for instance, the settlement of our uncertainty as to what it is permissible to write about. One hoped, when all the literary world of London gave a dinner to M. Anatole France last year, that some writer would rise to his feet and say: "Ladies and gentlemen, we are here in honor of an author who has delighted us with a series of works which, had he been an Englishman, would have landed him in gaol for the term of his natural life." That would have shown that the fetters of the English artist are not light and may weigh down the gestures of genius. It is not liberty to describe love that he needs, for he has as much of that as any reasonable person could want, so much as the liberty to describe this and any other passion with laughter and irony.

There is a more serious duty than these before us, the duty of listening to our geniuses in a disrespectful manner. Criticism matters as it never did in the past, because of the present pride of great writers. They take all life as their province to-day. Formerly they sat in their studies, and thinking only of the emotional life of mankind—thinking therefore with comparative ease, of the color of life and not of its form—devised a score or so of stories before death came. Now, their pride telling them that if time would but stand still they could explain all life, they start on a breakneck journey across the world. They are tormented by the thought of time; they halt by no event, but look down upon it as they pass, cry out their impressions, and gallop on. Often it happens that because of their haste they receive a blurred impression or transmit it to their readers roughly and without precision. And just as it was the duty of the students of Kelvin the mathematician to correct his errors in arithmetic, so it is the duty of critics to rebuke these hastinesses of great writers, lest the blurred impressions weaken the surrounding mental fabric and their rough transmissions frustrate the mission of genius on earth.

There are two great writers of to-day who greatly need correction. Both are misleading in external things. When Mr. Shaw advances, rattling his long lance to wit, and Mr. Wells follows, plump and oiled with the fun of things, they seem Don Quixote and Sancho Panza. Not till one has read much does one discover that Mr. Shaw loves the world as tenderly as Sancho Panza loved his ass, and that Mr. Wells wants to drive false knights from the earth and cut the stupidity and injustice out of the spiritual stuff of mankind. And both have to struggle with their temperaments. Mr. Shaw believes too blindly in his own mental activity; he imagines that if he continues to secrete thought he must be getting on. Mr. Wells dreams into the extravagant ecstasies of the fanatic, and broods over old hated things or the future peace and wisdom of the world, while his story falls in ruins about his ears.

Yet no effective criticism has come to help them. Although in the pages of Mr. Shaw enthusiasm glows like sunsets and the heart of man is seen flowering in a hundred generous and lovely passions, no one has ever insisted that he was a poet. We have even killed his poetry with silence. A year ago he lightened the English stage, which has been permanently fogged by Mr. Pinero's gloomy anecdotes about stockbrokers' wives and their passions, with "Androcles and the Lion," which was a miracle play and an exposition of the Christian mysteries. It taught that the simple man is the son of God, and that if men love the world it will be kind to them. Because this message was delivered with laughter, as became its optimism, English criticism accused Mr. Shaw of pertness and irreverence, and never permitted the nation to know that a spiritual teacher had addressed it. Instead, it advised Mr. Shaw to return to the discussion of social and philosophical problems, in which his talent could perhaps hope to be funny without being vulgar.

Mr. Wells' mind works more steadily than Mr. Shaw's, but it suffers from an unawareness of the reader; an unawareness, too, of his material; an unawareness of everything except the problem on which it happens to be brooding. His stories become more and more absent-minded. From "The Passionate Friends" we deduced that Mr. Wells lived on the branch line of a not too well organized railway system and wrote his books while waiting for trains at the main line junction. The novel appeared to be a year book of Indian affairs; but there were also some interesting hints on the publishing business, and once or twice one came on sections of a sympathetic study of moral imbecility in the person of a lady called Mary, who married for money and impudently deceived her owner. And what was even more amazing than its inchoateness was Mr. Wells' announcement on the last page that the book had been a discussion of jealousy. That was tragic, for it is possible that he had something to say on the subject, and what it was no one will ever know. Yet this boat of wisdom which had sprung so disastrous a leak received not one word of abuse from English criticism. No one lamented over the waste of the mind, the spilling of the idea.

That is what we must prevent. Now, when every day the souls of men go up from France like smoke, we feel that humanity is the flimsiest thing, easily divided into nothingness and rotting flesh. We must lash down humanity to the world with thongs of wisdom. We must give her an unsurprisable mind. And that will never be done while affairs of art and learning are decided without passion, and individual dulnesses allowed to dim the brightness of the collective mind. We must weepingly leave the library if we are stupid, just as in the middle ages we left the home if we were lepers. If we can offer the mind of the world nothing else we can offer it our silence.

The Motive of the Critic

Nearly all discussions of criticism, it seems to me, start off with a false assumption, to wit, the assumption that the primary motive of the critic, the impulse which makes a critic of him and not a politician or a stockbroker, is pedagogical—that he writes because he is possessed by a yearning to disseminate some specific doctrine, epistemological, psychological, historical, or aesthetic. This is true, I believe, only of bad critics, and its degree of truth increases in direct ratio to their badness. The motive of the critic who is really worth reading—the only critic of whom, indeed, it may be said truthfully that it is at all *possible* to read him—is something quite different. That motive is not the motive of the pedagogue, but the motive of the artist. It is simply a desire for self-expression, a thirst to function more broadly and brilliantly than the general, obscure in origin but irresistible in force. His choice of criticism rather than creative writing is chiefly a matter of temperament—perhaps, more accurately, a matter of hormones and intestinal flora—with accidents of education and environment to help. The feelings that happen to be dominant in him at the moment the scribbling frenzy seizes him and that move him powerfully to seek expression for them in words, are feelings inspired, not by life itself, but by books, pictures, music, sculpture, architecture, religion, philosophy—in brief by some other man's feelings about life. They are thus second-hand, and are rightly regarded by creative artists as inferior to their own first-hand reactions.

If a critic continues on this plane, if he lacks the intellectual agility and enterprise needed to make the leap from the work of art to the vast and mysterious complex of phenomena behind it, then he remains a mere reviewer of and valet to the ideas of his betters, and is of little more importance to the world than a schoolmaster, a newsmonger, or an auctioneer. But if a genuine artist is concealed within him—if his feelings are really profound and original, and his capacity for self-expression is above the average of educated men—then he moves inevitably from the work of art to life itself, and begins to take on a dignity that he formerly lacked. It is impossible to think of a man of any actual force and originality, universally recognized as having those qualities, who spent his whole life appraising and describing the work of other men. Did Goethe, or Carlyle, or Matthew Arnold, or Sainte-Beuve, or Macaulay, or even, to come down a few pegs, Lewes, or Lowell, or Hazlitt? Certainly not. The thing that becomes most obvious about the writings of all such men, once they are examined carefully, is that the critic is always being swallowed up by the creative artist—that what starts out as the review of a book, or a play, or other work of art, usually develops very quickly into an independent essay upon the theme of that work of art, or upon some theme that it suggests—in a word, that it becomes a fresh work of art, and only indirectly related to the one that suggested it. This fact, indeed, is so plain that it scarcely needs statement. What the pedagogues always object to in, say, the Quarterly reviewers is that they forgot the books they were supposed to review, and wrote long papers—often, in fact, small books—expounding ideas of their own, many of them vastly removed from the ideas in the books under review. Every critic who is really worth reading falls into this habit. He cannot stick to his task: what is before him is always infinitely less interesting to him than what is within him. If he is genuinely first-rate—if what is within him stands the test of type, and wins an audience, and produces the reactions that every artist craves—then he usually ends by abandoning the criticism of specific works of art altogether, and setting up shop as a general merchant in general ideas, i.e., as an artist working in the materials of life itself.

Mere reviewing, however conscientiously and competently it is done, is plainly a much inferior business. Like writing poetry, it is chiefly a function of intellectual immaturity. The young literatus just out of the university, having as yet no capacity for grappling with the fundamental mysteries of existence, is put to writing reviews of books, or plays, or music, or painting. Very often he does it extremely well; it is, in fact, not hard to do well, for even decayed pedagogues often do it, as such graveyards of the intellect as the *New York Times* bear witness. But if he continues to do it, whether well or ill, it is a sign to all the world that his growth ceased when they made him Artium Baccalaureus. Gradually he becomes, whether in or out of the academic grove, a pedagogue, which is to say, an artisan devoted to diluting and retailing the ideas of his superiors—not an artist, not even a bad artist, but almost the antithesis of an artist. He is learned, he is sober, he is painstaking and accurate—but he is as hollow as a jug. Nothing is in him save the ghostly echoes of other men's thoughts and feelings. If he were a genuine artist he would have thoughts and feelings of his own, and the impulse to give them objective form would be irresistible. An artist can no more withstand that impulse than a politician can withstand the temptations of a job. There are no mute, inglorious Miltons, save in the hallucinations of poets. The one sound test of a Milton is that he functions as a Milton. His difference from other men lies precisely in the superior vigor of his impulse to self-expression, not in the superior beauty and loftiness of his ideas. Other men, in point of fact, often have the same ideas, or perhaps even loftier ones, but they are able to suppress them, usually on grounds of decorum, and so they escape being artists, and are respected by right-thinking persons, and die with money in the bank, and are forgotten in two weeks.

Obviously, the critic whose performance we are commonly called upon to investigate is a man standing somewhere along the path leading from the beginning that I have described to the goal. He has got beyond being a mere cataloguer and valuer of other men's ideas, but he has not yet become an autonomous artist—he is not yet ready to challenge attention with his own ideas alone. But it must be plain that his motion, in so far as he is moving at all, must be in the direction of that autonomy—that is, unless one imagines him sliding backward into senile infantilism: a spectacle not unknown to literary pathology, but too pathetic to be discussed here. Bear this motion in mind, and the true nature of his aims and purposes becomes clear; more, the incurable falsity of the aims and purposes usually credited to him becomes equally clear. He is not actually trying to perform an impossible act of arctic justice upon the artist whose work gives him a text. He is not trying, with mathematical passion, to find out exactly what was in that artist's mind at the moment of creation, and to display it precisely and in an ecstacy of appreciation. He is not trying to bring the work discussed into accord with some gaudy theory of aesthetics, or ethics, or truth, or to determine its degree of departure from that theory. He is not trying to lift up the fine arts, or to defend democracy against sense, or to promote happiness at the domestic hearth, or to convert sophomores into right-thinkers, or to serve God. He is not trying to fit a group of novel phenomena into the orderly process of history. He is not even trying to discharge the catalytic office that I myself, in a romantic moment, once sought to force upon him. He is, first and last, simply trying to express himself. He is trying (a) to arrest and challenge a sufficient body of readers, to make them pay attention to him, to impress them with the charm and novelty of his ideas, to provoke them into an enchanted awareness of him, and (b) to achieve thereby for his own inner ego that agreeable feeling of a function performed, a tension relieved, a katharsis attained which Beethoven achieved when he wrote the Fifth Symphony, and a hen achieves every time she lays an egg.

It is, in brief, the "obscure, inner necessity" of Joseph Conrad that moves him: everything else is an afterthought. Conrad is moved by that necessity to write romances; Beethoven was moved to write music; poets are moved to write poetry; critics are moved to write criticism. The form is nothing; the only important thing is the motive power—and it is the same in all cases. It is the hot yearning of every man who has ideas to empty them upon the world, to hammer them into plausible and ingratiating shapes, to compel the attention and respect of his equals, to lord it over his inferiors. So seen, the critic becomes a far more transparent and agreeable fellow than ever he was in the discourses of the psychologists who sought to make him a mere appraiser in an intellectual customs house, a gauger in a distillery of the spirit, a just and infallible judge upon the cosmic bench. Such offices, in point of fact, never fit him. He always bulges over their confines. So labelled and estimated, it always turns out that the specific critic under examination is a very bad one, or no critic at all. But when he is thought of, not as pedagogue, but as artist, then he begins to take on reality, and, what is more, dignity. Carlyle was surely no just and infallible judge; on the contrary, he was full of prejudices, biles, naïvetés, humors. Yet he is read, consulted, attended to. Macaulay was unfair, inaccurate, fanciful, lyrical—yet his essays live. Arnold had his faults too, and so did Sainte-Beuve, and so did Goethe, and so did many another of that line—and yet they are remembered today, and all the learned and conscientious critics of their time, laboriously concerned with the precise intent of the artists under review, and passionately determined to set it forth with god-like care and to relate it exactly to this or that great stream of ideas—all these pedants are forgotten. What saved Carlyle, Macaulay and company is as plain as day: They were first-rate artists. They could make the thing charming, and that is always a million times more important than making it true.

Truth, indeed, is something that is believed in only by persons who have never tried personally to pursue it to its fastnesses and grab it by the tail. It is the adoration of second-rate men—men who always receive it at second hand. Pedagogues believe in immutable truths and spend their lives trying to determine them and propagate them; the intellectual progress of man consists largely of a concerted effort to block and destroy their enterprise. In the department of aesthetics, wherein critics mainly disport themselves, it is almost impossible to think of a so-called truth that shows any sign of being permanently true. The most profound of principles begins to fade and quiver almost as soon as it is stated. But the work of art, as opposed to the theory behind it, has a longer life, particularly if that theory is obscure and questionable, and so cannot be determined accurately. Hamlet, the Mona Lisa, Faust, Dixie, Parsifal, Mother Goose, Annabel Lee, Huckleberry Finn—these things, so baffling to pedagogy, so contumacious to the categories, so mysterious in purpose and utility—these things live. And why? Because there is in them the delightful flavor of odd and attractive personality, because the quality that shines from them is not that of correct demeanor but that of creative passion, because they pulse and breathe and speak, because they are genuine works of art. So with criticism. Let us forget all the heavy effort to make a science of it; it is a fine art, or nothing. If the critic, retiring to his cell to concoct his treatise upon a book or play or what-not, produces a piece of writing that shows sound structure, and brilliant color, and the flash of novel and persuasive ideas, and civilized manners, and the charm of an uncommon personality in free function, then he has given something to the world that is worth having, and sufficiently justified his existence. Let him leave the exact truth to professors of aesthetics, who can no more determine it than he can, and will infallibly make it idiotic. He is an artist, not a schoolmaster.

What I preach will be labelled at once and thrust into its pigeon-hole: it is impressionism. True. But it is impressionism that is not to be monkeyed with: it depends too much upon the impressionist.

ROBERT BRUSTEIN   NOVEMBER 7, 1964

The Curse of Official Culture

What has been the most characteristic pattern of American history? The commission of some crime, paid for with a hundred years of remorse. Whether it be the extermination of the Indian, the enslavement and repression of the Negro, the despoliation of natural resources and the ugly rape of virgin land by industry, the exploitation of immigrant laborers, the uglification of our cities and the demoralization of the young, or the dropping of the first atomic bomb on a civilian population, the initial wickedness has always been followed by elaborate contrition—and sometimes even by an attempt at rectification, as when, for example, the plunder of such rascals as Ford, Rockefeller and Carnegie is partially returned through altruistic foundation grants. American remorse is currently being directed toward the arts and the artist—victims of omission rather than of commission, since for years the objects of Philistine neglect. But the question arises whether the recent development of an expiatory cultural conscience simply isn't making matters worse.

Certainly, the arts have never before been the object of so much patronage and goodwill; but just as certainly, they have rarely been surrounded by so much cant, pretension and deadness of spirit. There is, to be sure, a good deal of energy coursing through contemporary American fiction, poetry and sculpture—even through recent painting, though much of this energy seems to me misdirected. But these are private arts, conceived in solitude, their execution less affected by external demands. When the arts are collaborative, like our movies and plays, or institutional, like our TV, radio and much of our architecture—or when the artist himself becomes a public man, politician or performer—there is always a corresponding loss in spontaneity and conviction, and a corresponding gain in hollowness, swank and phony glitter. How is the "cultural revolution" debasing our public arts and artists, and can this sorry situation be reversed?

Perhaps I can define the difficulty better by stating my premise that what is *public* in this country is always in danger of becoming *official;* and this itself results from an irrepressible native desire to apply political criteria to the realm of culture. Although the most lasting modern art has been the product of a uniquely gifted individual, creating out of a lonely and independent consciousness, our democratic temper demands an art which is communal, social and generic. Thus, the artist is expected to be as representative of the whole people as a Senator, and his art as reflective of majority desires as a bill passed through Congress. This has certainly been the view of the government, ever since it discovered that American culture could be an effective weapon in the Cold War. Thinking to improve our "image" abroad, the State Department prefers to export works that are as American as apple pie, increasing the sugar and starch content for overseas consumption. But it was not the official production of *The Skin of Our Teeth* that impressed discerning European audiences, it was the unofficial tour of the now-defunct Living Theater, even though that trip received not a penny of aid from the US government, and was supported through money raised at a public auction.

RUNNING FOR RECOGNITION

On the other hand, the problem is not that we sponsor the wrong things to represent us abroad; it is that we would use the artist and his art for political purposes in the first place. Certainly, something very odd happens to even the most-idiosyncratic individuals when they are forced to act in an official capacity—look at Edward Albee and John Steinbeck in Soviet Russia, discoursing on the American Way of Life. Or look at what has happened to Norman Mailer and James Baldwin, both of whom are now neglecting their proper business as writer-intellectuals in order to function as official spokesmen for a group. Literature and politics, never very comfortable bedfellows, are beginning to nuzzle up to each other again, and the writer is running for office, both literally and figuratively, flexing a set of muscles that have long remained unused. Still, as in the 'thirties, this is accompanied by a falling off in honesty, truth and complexity. Of course, there are many who believe that this is an advance, and that the artist who develops in "silence, exile and cunning" is less to be valued than the one who involves himself with his time in a practical way. But these are generally people who have little interest in art, though they obviously have a fervent faith in the artist. As for myself, I have long believed that the greatest threat to the writer today is the temptation to power and influence, and I have no faith whatever in the artist-politician. For while the artist may bring a sense of style to politics, he brings, I am afraid, no superior wisdom. Quite the contrary, his politics is often a frightening blend of lunacy and demagoguery, while his art—and this is worse— becomes an instrument of his power drive rather than of his imagination.

The desire for power by the contemporary American artist is easily understood; it is linked to his desire for fame and prestige. These rewards have been denied him for so long in his own country that, now that they are at last possible, he stands, as Yeats said of Keats, like a little boy with his face pressed against a sweet shop window, ready to gorge. Resisting these sweets undoubtedly takes an heroic effort of the moral will—but some have made the effort successfully, and survived. Edmund Wilson is an exemplary figure in this respect. Although not an artist, he suffers from similar assaults upon his privacy by those who are anxious to exploit his personality. His answer always takes the same form—a printed card, mailed to every would-be promoter, declining all lectures, testimonials, interviews, tintypes and television appearances. Then there is J.D. Salinger, about whose work it is possible to have many opinions, but who has certainly carried on an admirable struggle to protect himself against press agents, prying reporters and *papparazzi*.

GORGING ON SWEETS

To reject the sweets that the United States is ready to offer is to appear to some observers like a demented malcontent or an outdated eccentric, and it certainly encourages alienated behavior—Salinger lives like a hermit, barricaded in Vermont, and Wilson has often declared that he feels in modern America like a stranger in a foreign land. To gorge on such sweets, however, is to risk such a severe case of ego-indigestion that the very salivary sources of art begin to dry up.

That these sources are in danger now of drying up is evident enough in the various cultural complexes mushrooming around the country—most evident, I think, at New York's Lincoln Center for the Performing Arts. Here one can see how, for all its good intentions, public art turns official, and how official art soon degenerates into mere fashion and ostentation. Even the architecture at the Center seems to suggest this, since both the New York State Theater and Philharmonic Hall have the appearance of modernistic fishbowls, functioning less to house good music and ballet than for people to be *seen*. That Philharmonic Hall has poor acoustics, in fact, has always struck me as symbolic—to listen to Mozart there is less important than to get a good view of Lenny Bernstein, and of the other members of the audience. The interior of the New York State Theater (also plagued by bad acoustics) actually *looks* like a member of the audience—a rich, middle-aged matron, all gussied up for opening night: the lights are shaped like massive diamonds, the chandelier like a great jeweled pendant, and the tiers like chased gold bracelets. Naturally, this wealthy display is reflected in the price of the tickets which have been hiked so high that the single artistic force in the entire complex, the New York City Ballet, is now threatening to withdraw from Lincoln Center because of its powerlessness to maintain its traditional $4.50 top.

The directors of the ballet believe that culture should be a matter of genuine desire and not of padded pocketbooks, and that a company should be permitted to lead its audience, instead of following the audience's style and taste. This does not seem to be the conviction of the directors of Lincoln Center. For it is an axiom of official culture that it be shaped to the demands of an existing audience, generally a high-paying one, and that profit and protocol should never be neglected. It would hardly be unfair, in fact, to define official culture as the pursuit of power, fame and money under the guise of disinterestedness—self-interest masquerading as altruism.

COMMERCIAL COMMODITY

This, of course, is the pattern of American business as well, and you may ask how the performing arts can be expected to escape the restrictions of private enterprise. The answer is, they must. It is true that a successful collaborative unit is extremely difficult to maintain in a competitive society: that the task is not impossible has been proved by the New York City Ballet under the reign of George Balanchine. But compare this dedicated and faithful company with the Lincoln Center Repertory Theater, under the reign of Elia Kazan and Robert Whitehead. Coming from Broadway with little experience in any other than a commercial theater system, these men could not help but bring with them the standards of their native environment, despite their ringing declarations of high ideals. As a result, their first season was a scandal—not because the plays "failed" or because the productions were poorly prepared or because the actors were clumsy and uncoordinated. These are problems that can be improved with time and training. The season was a scandal because the company failed so signally to live up to its own policy statements. The plays were indistinguishable from Broadway commodities; the actors began to defect; one of the directors accepted a movie offer; and, worst of all, after all the cant about the virtues of the repertory system, the program was limited, when the other works failed at the box office, to one best-selling *succés de scandale*.

The author of this work, by the way, is the perfect playwright for the company because he has become the official American dramatist *par excellence.* It was not simply that Arthur Miller, who frequently criticizes other playwrights for being too private and too personal, produced a thinly disguised confessional autobiography of his own, but rather that he tried to pass off this personal history as a universal insight into evil, as if his own peculiar domestic embroilments were directly related to the Nazi extermination centers. When Arthur Miller develops a cavity, he thinks the whole world has the toothache. Much the same kind of confused motives were attached to the commercial aspects of his *After the Fall.*

When Mr. Miller gave this play to Lincoln Center, he did so—as he repeated frequently in an article for *The New York Times*—at considerable financial sacrifice because he believed in the aims of the company. But the play had already been sold, reputedly for a staggering sum, to that highbrow cultural organ, the *Saturday Evening Post;* it later enjoyed a whopping movie sale; and it is now being prepared for a road tour by a commercial producing unit having no connection with Lincoln Center. If this is what Mr. Miller calls self-sacrifice, what would he call self-interest?

OFFICIAL EMOTIONS

Let us conclude this exploration of official culture with a brief examination of its official organ of perpetuation, dissemination and publicity: the review pages of *The New York Times.* Now I yield to none in my admiration for the care and expertise with which this good grey presence reports the news, but I can no longer withhold my conviction that its major reviewers have become a very serious obstacle to the existence of a genuine culture. Although it is usually difficult to generalize about anything so personal as the tastes of a reviewer, it is nonetheless almost inevitable that the theater, movie, book and television reporters for the *Times* will dislike whatever is authentic, daring and original, while applauding the pompous, the phony and the pretentious. The only way to account for such monolithic consistency is to assume that the *Times* reviews are not guided by personal taste at all—they are guided by *official* emotions, which is to say, by what the reviewers think they *ought* to feel. To take some quick examples, the two most important movie and play reviews of the year, I suppose, were those of *Dr. Strangelove* and *After the Fall.* Needless to say, Bosley Crowther attacked Stanley Kubrick's superb film breakthrough because it maligned the character of those who rule our country, later praising as a "major American picture" an inferior piece of melodramatic trash called *Fail Safe* because it "does not make its characters out to be maniacs and monsters and morons." If art followed such standards, it would quickly give a polite cough and expire. And Howard Taubman, composing his usual high school theme on the virtues of "enchantment" in the theater, wrote a glowing notice of *After the Fall* which will no doubt be anthologized some day (along with Brooks Atkinson's review of *J.B.*) as an example of the intimate link between highmindedness and wrongheadedness. As for Orville Prescott, who always claims to be bored when he is really offended (remember how "dull, dull, dull" he thought *Lolita?*) and Jack Gould, whose activity as guardian of everybody's hurt feelings has helped to banish genuine comedy from television, these men are interchangeable, as are most of the reviewers on the paper. *The New York Times,* having become a self-enclosed organism, tries desperately to keep its reviews in line with its editorial policy; but nothing better demonstrates the essential antagonism between the subversive world of art and the official world of liberal democracy.

The lesson, if we are thinking seriously about a Great Society, is that these worlds must be kept apart, if either is to find health. Liberalism has traditionally been responsible for a great many social advances; but there is a debased liberalism which functions as the sentiment of those who want to make a lot of money and feel good about it. It is this form of liberalism that is now in control of much of the official culture, marketing fashion under the device of advancing the arts. Official culture is also controlled by many who are sincerely well-intentioned, and wish to expiate for America's Philistine past—but even these good intentions are paving a lot of infernal boulevards. For the sad fact is that, despite all the attention being paid to the arts—despite all the gleaming buildings being dedicated to culture—we are worse off now in many ways than in Babbitt's time.

SQUEAK, NOT THUNDER

The only way to improve the situation, I think, is to revise our attitudes radically toward the whole question of culture, and we must begin by developing some interest in the essence of art, and not just its external appearance. This means we must no longer pretend that every squeak heard on the avenue is the thunder of a major American talent, or that what the official critic praises and damns has anything to do with real success and failure, or that the size and eminence of an audience measure the value and importance of a work, or that theater architecture has very much relation to theater art, or that opulent surroundings are in any way conducive to serious creativity. We must stop constructing cultural complexes, and start building cultural complexity; we must stop responding to what is comfortable and safe, and start attending to what is radical and audacious; we must stop exploiting the artist's personality, and start probing his vision; and, above all, we must stop trying to assimilate our more dangerous artists, blunting their dissent with a bland and thoughtless acceptance that evades the issues of their work.

THE THIRD ACT

This probably sounds like a large order, and it is, for it means nothing less than a cultural *counter*-revolution which pushes hard against the present tide. It means relaxing our attitude toward the arts, treating them neither as political weapons, social events nor official functions but rather as something important in themselves, aspects of our contemplation, relaxation and spiritual growth. And it means letting the artist develop in peace and quiet, with nothing to distract him except the demands of his work. That something like this is necessary can be seen from a quick glance at the battlefield of the "cultural revolution" which is now strewn with the discarded corpses of those who might possibly have been great. Naturally, there are still a number of gifted men and women in America, creating in seclusion, impervious to the pull of politics or the pressure of fashion; but there are many more whose development has been cut off by premature acclaim, and who now may never realize their full potential. It was F. Scott Fitzgerald, another fine writer felled by fashion, who once complained there were no second acts in American lives.

Well, we have now reached the second act, and it is a stinker. It is up to those who really care about art whether the curtain will ever rise on a third.

The Word Became Flesh

The Greeks made dancing the core of their drama because dancing was both natural and necessary to them. Their gods were gods who danced. Their children were trained to dance as part of their public education; their young men and girls danced; they all danced at weddings and festivals, just as they dance today in village taverns or on the islands on the first of May. Greek youths learned through the war dance the various postures of attack and defense, and the military formations of an army. Good dancers and good fighters were called by the same name, *prylés*, while those whose lack of skill kept them in the back rows of the chorus, or in the rear of the army, were alike referred to as *psilés*, unequipped. The public square in Sparta was used so commonly for meetings in which the population offered thanks to the gods by singing and dancing that the place itself was called *choros*. Dancing was potent not only to entertain, but to worship, to petition, to narrate, to celebrate, to teach, to bring down vengeance. "If this behavior is to go unpunished," cries the chorus in Sophocles' "Oedipus," "what's the use of my dancing?" Because music and dancing were essential parts of the religious, political and military organization of the Dorian states, the chorus was a life form before it was an art form. When it became a part of drama it had behind it maturity of experience, and before it a critical audience unwilling to tolerate mediocrity in an art with which it was thoroughly conversant.

What was it like, this dancing for which the tribes assembled from all of Greece, for which prizes were given and statues erected? What was the hidden strength of the Greek drama that led one of our contemporary economists to remark, "If the dramatist could go back to the Greek and really understand it, he would give us that something new that the theatre today needs"?

It is probable that Madame Sikelianos, thoroughly familiar as she is with the tradition of the Greek dance, gave, in the plays which she directed at Delphi in 1927 and 1930, the best conception in modern times of what choral dancing may have been. For those of us not fortunate enough to have seen those Greek plays in a Greek theatre with Greek actors and a Greek audience, the question becomes not so much what choral dancing must have been, but rather, what a modern equivalent of such dancing might be. Which of the great dancers we have seen, for example, might be imagined leading a chorus in that exposed arc encircled by stone and by myriad watching eyes?

Pavlova, attaining perfection in one sort of dance, cannot be imagined in an arena. She would soar delicately above it, above the horrors, the fears, the flayings of flesh and fortune. Isadora Duncan, with her magnificent body, bare feet and unbound hair, could encompass the heroic space, drawing strength from the stones which Pavlova's delicate feet in their satin shoes would scarcely touch. Perhaps in the moment when she twisted a red flag around her body to the battle cry of the "Marseillaise," or in the majesty of mourning for her children, Isadora Duncan may have danced something akin to the terror and pity of the ancient choruses; but for the most part no matter what she named her dances, she was always primarily a beautiful woman dancing, a grace surrounded by lesser graces, moving sensuously to music, flinging flowers into the air. By very virtue of its opulent beauty the dancing of Isadora Duncan lacked the fierce impersonality that must have been one element of the Greek chorus.

The dance mimes of Mei Lan-fang afford a consummate example of another type of dancing, dancing based on age-old sophistication, strict discipline of body and voice, and a jealously guarded tradition going back seven hundred years before Christ. Here are many elements that move us as Greek dancing must have moved its audience; the undercurrent of music, felt in the action of the dancer even when no music is heard; the accentuation of gesture and step by the sound of instrument; the voices rising, at moments of climax, into a chant. Yet the technique is distinctly an indoor technique demanding a close view. The precise notation of reality, never copying, but arranging in a brilliant pattern, results in perfection, but not a perfection suited to the portrayal of elemental forces, or to the demands of an elemental playing space.

It is, perhaps, in the powerfully energized dancing of Mary Wigman that we gain a conception, not of what Greek choral dancing may have been, for it would be presumption to say that, but of what a modern equivalent of such dancing might be. For the dancing of Mary Wigman is elemental, having its springs in the dark places of the earth and the dark places of the spirit. In "Dance to the Earth" or "Witch Dance," Wigman might be the priestess of Apollo at Delphi, maddened by mantic vapors, drawing her strength from the very navel of the earth. The terrific thud of those powerful feet might be the Bacchae; with some such hard exultance of racing and leaping the Furies must have pursued their victim; and in how many plays, at the breathless moment waiting for the disclosure from within the house—the emergence of Oedipus with blood streaming down his face, the procession of maidens bearing Phaedra's body cut down from the rafters—how often at such a moment one longs for some such hypnotic, sinister movement as that of Wigman's whirling dance in which she starts with a great sweep and closes in on herself and on you in a series of concentric circles that gradually fill space and shatter time.

Movement alone, however, was not enough. What sounds that were suitable to the struggles of gods and giants echoed along Parnassus or Kynortion? Or again, since that question may never be answered, what parallel have we today of speech rhythmic, sustained, varied, powerful enough to unite actors and spectators in common supplication or celebration?

Voices chanting in unison alternating with single voices rising in flexible, strongly accented beats produce a form of speech associated through the ages with the act of worship, and still used in our own country, with various modifications, in Roman, Greek, Jewish and Protestant churches. Subdued for the interior setting and conventionalized for expediency, the ardor and the urgency of this form of choral speech usually dies, though the Negro services in the South and revival meetings elsewhere often attain a frenzy suggesting the Dionysiac. Watch sixty thousand people under the hot stars of a California night, swaying rhythmically to the singing of a white-robed chorus marching with palm branches around a sepulcher, their choral chant, punctuated by the hoarse, curiously erotic cries of the woman evangelist, and you gain some conception of the emphatic response of an audience to waves of sound and movement.

In mass recitations such as those in workers' theatres, emotion is internal, springing from intense belief in the words uttered and in a further belief that uttering these words may actually help the condition described. The technique, differing of course with the degree of experience and the quality of the direction of the group, is, at its best, the most effective use of mass voices heard in modern times. These workers' groups regard the theatre as a weapon which they are learning to use with power. Sometimes it is a concerted chant, ending with words fired like bullets, as in "Miners on Strike":

18,000 miners in Kentucky, Tennessee down
in the mines night of mines airless mines
mining money and not getting any
18,000 miners in Kentucky, Tennessee
            are on strike!

The alternate use of full chorus and single voices is used in "We Demand," in which only the theme and the repetitions are emphasized by the full chorus, while individual voices make the demand:

We demand
    Demand
        The society of the future . . .
We demand
    Demand
        A society in which there shall be
        No race prejudice
        No exploitation of labor
        No inherited wealth
We demand
    Demand
        A society in which the liberated egotism of
        man shall be directed wholly
                Wholly
        To the understanding, the education and
        the betterment of mankind.

Was it with some such belief in the power of the word that the word became flesh when the chorus of children in "The Suppliants" longed to avenge their fathers, or when the chorus in "The Bacchanals" unloosed the hounds of madness?

In the intervals between choral dances it is probable that the Greek chorus did not relapse into the state of coma usual between dances upon later stages. Sit in Constitution Square and watch a group of present-day Athenians listening to a story: study the constantly changing flow of expression, the sympathetic gestures, shrugs, movements of the torso, watch the subtle response of the whole body, and you have some idea of how eloquently the chorus must have listened to the play, of how the reactions of the chorus quickened the reactions of the audience. It was the business of the chorus to know the play thoroughly, and to communicate that knowledge to the audience.

The dark knowledge of the chorus could not be used, however, to alter the train of events upon the stage. It was because the Greeks believed, at least in the greatest period of drama, that those events were set in motion by the gods, that they felt in their theatre a certain emotion which we seldom experience in ours, namely, terror. The very words "pity" and "terror" have become stencils to us, and it is hard to make them mean anything. But they meant something to the Greeks. On at least one occasion during a dramatic festival, a child died of fright and a woman suffered a miscarriage.

Our modern plays often arouse pity, in that we are united sympathetically with the human sufferer. They seldom inspire terror, because we have no sense of, or belief in—or at least no acknowledged belief in—a hidden cause or fate. The tragedies in our plays are usually coincidental. For example, when you see, in "Street Scene," the woman in the room with her lover and the husband coming down the street, you have an impulse to warn them. You feel that the husband just happened to arrive at this moment and that the tragedy may still be averted. In a Greek drama you would never think of warning the participants, of telling Agamemnon not to enter the house or Deianeira not to give the shirt to Herakles. Through the principals, caught in the toils, the men and women of the Greek audience were united with the human sufferer, but it was the chorus that united them with the secret forces that brought him low.

Just so long as the knowledge of secret forces energized the chorus, investing dancing, chanting and listening with the impersonal seal of inevitability, just so long the Greeks had a theatre. When they let the chorus become an interlude, a pleasant interruption, a *divertissement,* they drew the teeth of tragedy and reduced the bawdy splendors of Aristophanes to the level of high comedy. It is a fact that should give pause to anyone considering the twelve thousand theatre people on relief in America today, as well as those pondering the decline of community playhouses or the parlous state of Broadway's economic health, that the first European theatre, the one that for twenty-five centuries has potently influenced life and art, was a theatre based on the belief that drama, through rhythmic speech, dynamic movement and contagious listening, can influence human thought and lead to human action.

Irrational Elements
in Art and Politics

Today we live in a world that, for the last 30 years, has been less and less governed by reason and love. The meaning of this nightmarish world, its whole intention and direction, was first grasped, I believe, by a group of modern artists who translated it into visible symbols, long before any but a few solitary observers like Henry Adams understood the facts of our time by historic and philosophic analysis. For this reason, one cannot understand the politics of our time, or the general state of our civilization, without interpreting the art of the last fifty years: for it is in painting and sculpture, sometimes decades before the event, that the facts of our life have been brought within an observable frame. At the same time, one cannot understand the latest developments in art, during the last decade particularly, without reference to the politics of our time, for the two are in a far closer relationship than either the politician or the artist has yet perceived.

Before I discuss the irrational elements in art and politics, it is important to make a fundamental discrimination, which applies to all the forces at work in our civilization. Those of us who came to modern art in our youth, with an almost crusading enthusiasm, often defended it against the pained criticisms of the traditionalists by saying that this new art, post-impressionism, cubism, futurism, vorticism, or what not, was an "expression of our age"; and in that very fact we saw the proof of its validity and importance. But this judgment was formed on the basis of the great hope and confidence promoted by the previous century of progress, as it called itself, when we were sure that every new institution was better than the old, just because it came later, and we had not yet lived long enough to see that slavery, torture, the random extermination of civilian populations, might also be hailed, in the name of progress, as the wave of the future. Painfully we have at last learned that if art was an expression of our civilization, it might express these evils, in symbolic form, quite as readily as it expresses the positive and formative forces that had, in fact, a great contribution to make to man's development. We must distinguish, then, two processes at work in our civilization, one upbuilding, life-bestowing, life-regarding, the other de-building, destructive, life-betraying or life-denying, leading to ultimate extermination and annihilation. Modern art, departing from the traditional forms that had held sway since the Renaissance, responded to both sides of our existence; and the first step toward defining the irrational elements in art is to recognize and set apart those that arose, on the whole, out of the positive energies and vitalities in our civilization.

The radical transformation in art that dates from the death of Cézanne has accompanied and in part interpreted the radical transformations of space, time, and energy in engineering and medicine, that have taken place within the last fifty years. No close correspondence between the symbols of art and the conceptions of science should be looked for: indeed the attempt to justify the appearance of a few erratic spots on a modern canvas by reference to a photographic plate dealing with the path of an atomic particle, is specious, not to say pathetic, for if true it would reduce the mission of the modern painter to mere illustration. If one recalls Renaissance painting, which was contemporary with the great age of exploration, one is astonished to find so few images of the new world that disclosed itself to the traveler and the adventurer: but if one looks closer, both the sea-captain and the painter employed the same method of locating objects in space, by drawing fixed co-ordinates, by means of which the ship's course or the object's boundaries could be accurately plotted.

So with modern art during the last half century: by its very detachment from the Renaissance world of ordered objects, viewed from a fixed position in space, it has disclosed the new multi-dimensional world revealed by science and carried into our daily life by invention. This is a world in which fixed relations between objects are altered by speed, and in which both rapid travel and long distance communications superimpose upon the environment in which we familiarly operate, one or more other vivid environments that warp the photographic image. Marcel Duchamps' famous "Nude Descending a Staircase" was a startlingly realistic anticipation of the results of the dissection of motion by the stroboscopic camera, as disclosed a few decades later by Gjon Mili. So, too, though the Renaissance painter, to perfect his mastery of surface form and volume, took the lead in the dissection of the human body, it is only in our time, with the advance of scientific analysis, and the revelations of the X-ray, that the subcutaneous reality of organs, tissues, and cells, has become part of our daily consciousness.

For us, today, reality no longer can be represented fully by surface images: the invisible is as real, as present, as operative as that which is open to our immediate gaze. I would not say that this multi-dimensional world has often been adequately represented or symbolized in any public form, except perhaps in the terrifying abstraction of three-dimensional chess; still less that many artists have succeeded in translating it into intelligible and orderly symbols of art; but the sculptures of the Constructivists, particularly of Naum Gabo, come close to revealing and interpreting the new world of space, time, energy, motion, and constructing equivalent forms that captivate the spirit. On the whole this art has been a healthy influence; and the same can be said, with certain reservations, for the effort, led by the cubists more than a generation ago, to do justice to machines and machine forms as objects of perception. This was a task in which photographers, beginning with Stieglitz, painters beginning with Duchamp-Villon and Léger, sculptors beginning with Brancusi, and architects, beginning afresh with LeCorbusier, have united to acclimate the mind and spirit of man to the new machine-conditioned, machine-made world that he was creating. By contemplating these new forms, by extracting from them new values, quickened sensuous perceptions, often perceptions of great fineness and delicacy, as in the paintings of Loren MacIver, modern man made himself at home in the very world from which the antiseptic, dehumanized procedures of science had excluded him. That too was a gain in values: likewise a gain in spiritual balance, provided the machine was not conceived as a demiurge that ruled all other human needs.

One more aspect of modern art, on the positive and affirmative side, must be mentioned—though it is an ambivalent contribution and from the first showed disturbing openness to the forces of disintegration. This has to do with the multi-dimensional nature of the human personality, with all the interrelations that exist between the inner and the outer, from the autonomic nervous system and the pre-conscious processes to the subtlest manifestations of thought and feeling: with all the layers of self from the id to the super-ego. Thanks to Sigmund Freud, our age has re-discovered and re-established the inner world: the world of fantasy and dreams, that spontaneous fountain of free creativity, in which nothing is probable because everything is possible, a world in which the demonic and angelic are forever at war. A generation ago, the expressionists and the surrealists began to interpret this world for us, often retaining some of its most endearing qualities; its humor, as in the delicate fantasies of Klee and Chagall, in the droll contraptions of Pierre Roy, even occasionally in the deliberately paranoid art of Dali, as in the painting of the half melted watches depending limply from a tree. Aesthetically, these images were often fragmentary: symbolically they existed in a self-enclosed void. But many of the surrealists, whose work seems to rise out of the blackest depths of the unconscious, also turned out to be much closer to the increasingly grim realities of the outer world. I recall my own premonitory uneasiness at seeing the blasted landscapes and dismantled factories in Lurçat's paintings of the early thirties: they prepared one for the destruction of the coming war, as the mutilated human forms that appeared in surrealist art prepared one for the nauseating horrors of Hitler's extermination camps. The exacerbating sensations, the emotional violence, the actual tortures and butcheries, of the period of victorious Fascism—the period dominated by Hitler and Stalin—could be interpreted only in distorted forms and sadistic images, forms close to the productions of madness, in a picture like Picasso's famous Guernica Mural. The human content of those pictures was sometimes so unbearable that they raised the question as to whether the artist himself was merely portraying the evil and madness of our age, or actually, by his very images, participating in it and extending its influence—just as our comic books and our gangster motion pictures and radio plays actually do on the lowest everyday level.

At the first try many of these manifestations of modern art might seem as difficult for a layman to interpret as the latest equation of nuclear physics. But in time the more positive productions, associated with the more formative processes in our civilization, became individually more intelligible, though anything like a synthesis between the various aspects of life and reality that have been symbolized in art during the last fifty years has so far proved unattainable: indeed, just the opposite has happened, because with the further development of painting, particularly in America, the split between the integrating and the disintegrating tendencies has become deeper. That split has become as deep, in fact, as the difference between the deeply human life-furthering purposes of UNRRA and the Marshall Plan (in its original form) and the anti-human and life-threatening purposes associated all over the world—and above all in our own country—with the development of agents of atomic and bacterial extermination.

One part of our art has responded to the formative and rational elements in our civilization and has sought to interpret and translate them: the other part has responded to, has recorded, has intensified the horror and misery and madness of our age, with its code of unrestricted violence and its scientifically contrived technics of demoralization, disintegration, and extermination. As one looks back over the art of the last forty years, these two facts are increasingly plain, and the ways which seemed to run parallel at first have parted further and further. Plainly, the narrow path, the path of discipline, order, rationality, discrimination, the path of mature and loving emotional development, fruitful and creative in every occasion it embraces, has become ever narrower, and the effort to follow its upward course has become lonelier and lonelier. Those artists who are committed to this way have fallen out of fashion; and sometimes, for lack of response, have ceased actively to create. While, on the other hand, the broad path, the path that leads to destruction—to the corruption of the human, to the denial of love, to systematized disorder, to non-communicativeness and non-intercourse at any level, has become wider and wider. So it is in art; so it is in politics. The glorification of brutality characterizes all the arts today: both highbrow and lowbrow have become connoisseurs of violence. The enemies of the human race are no longer isolated tyrants, like Hitler and Stalin: in the very act of opposing their programs of revolutionary enslavement by the same means these dictators employed, we ourselves have increasingly taken on their inhuman or irrational characteristics.

As if the cult of violence were not a sufficient threat to our rationality, indeed to our very humanity, the painting of our time discloses still another danger: the surrender to the accidental and the denial of the possibility of coherence and intelligibility: what one might call the devaluation of all values and the emptying out of all meanings. This ultimate expression of meaningless began in an almost innocent, because still humorous, form, at the end of the first World War, in the cult of Da-daism: an irreverent commentary on the inflated platitudes of politicians. But by now the cult of the meaningless is a grimly humorless one: the negative responses that its empty splotches and scrawls at first provoke in a perceptive mind will be met, on the part of the devotees, with a fanatic gleam of reproach. Cracks, erosions, smudges, denials of all order or intelligibility, with not even as much capacity for evocative association as a Rorschach ink-blot—this is the ultimate form and content of the fashionable art of the last decade. To gaze piously into this ultimate emptiness has become the last word in art appreciation today. The artists who produce these paintings, or the sculptures that correspond to them, are often people of serious talent: sometimes their early work discloses the fact that they were people of original ability, perfectly able as far as technical command of the means goes, to express whatever human thought or feeling the artist of any age might express. But now all their talent, all their energy, is concentrated on only one end: a retreat, not only from the surface world of visible buildings and bodies, but a retreat from any kind of symbol that could, by its very organization, be interpreted as having a connection with organized form: a retreat into the formless, the life-less, he disorganized, the dehumanized: the world of non-significance, as close as possible to blank non-existence.

In these final images the modern artists who seem, however patiently we behold them, to say nothing to us, are in fact saying a great deal. Paintings that we must, in all critical honesty, reject as aesthetic expressions, we must yet accept as despairing confessions of the soul, or as savage political commentary on our present condition arising from the depths of the unconscious. For there is one special quality in these paintings that lowers their standing as works of art: they are too factual, too realistic, they are too faithful reflections of the world we actually live in, the world we are so energetically preparing to suffer death in. These symbols of nothingness, true revelations of our purposeless mechanisms and our mechanized purposes, this constant fixation on what is violent, dehumanized, infernal—all this is not pure aesthetic invention, the work of men who have no contacts with the life around them. Just the contrary: their ultimate negation of form and meaning should remind us of the goal of all our irrational plans and mechanisms. What they say should awaken us as no fuller and saner images might. These men, these paintings, these symbols have a terrible message to communicate: their visual nihilism is truer to reality than all the conventional paintings that assure us so smoothly that our familiar world is still there—and will always be there.

Let us not reproach the artist for telling us this message, which we have not the sensitivity to record or the courage to tell to ourselves: the message that the future, on the terms that it presents itself to us now, has become formless, valueless, meaningless: that in this irrational age, governed by absolute violence and pathological hate, our whole country, our whole civilization, might vanish from the face of the earth as completely as images of any sort have vanished from these pictures: as dismayingly as that little isle in the Pacific vanished from the surface of the ocean under the explosion of the hydrogen bomb. This is the new apocalypse, haunted by more terrible spectres than the traditional Four Horsemen, as they appeared to the innocent eyes of John of Patmos—a revelation that promises neither a new heaven nor a new earth but an end that would nullify and make meaningless the whole long process of human history. Let the painters who have faced this ultimate nothingness, who have found a symbol for it, be understood if not honored: what they tell us is what we are all hiding from ourselves. . .

And this brings me, finally, back to the artist, whose last message I have tried to interpret. If he is not to betray his art as well as his humanity, he must not think that nausea and vomit are the ultimate realities of our time. Those obscenities are indeed a part of the actual world we are conditioned to; but they do not belong to the possible world of the creator and the transvaluer, who brings forth out of his own depths new forms and values that point to new destinations. The artist, too, has the responsibility to be sane, the duty to be whole and balanced, the obligation to overcome or transform the demonic and to release the more human and divine elements in his own soul: in short, the artist has the task of nourishing and developing every intuition of love and of finding images through which they become visible. If all he can say in his pictures is, "This is the end"—let it be the end and let him say no more about it. Let him be silent until he has recovered to the capacity to conjure up once more, however timidly at first, a world of fine perceptions and rich feeling, of values that sustain life and coherent forms that re-enforce the sense of human mastery.

No one has fully taken in all the new dimensions of our world; no one effectively commands all the forces that are now at humanity's disposal. But we know that mankind today, thanks to the pooling of reserves and treasures from every culture and historic epoch, including our own, is in possession of energies, vitalities, humanities, and divinities now only feebly and fitfully used, which are capable of redeeming our civilization. Catastrophe is perhaps nearer to us than salvation, as a war of unrestricted extermination is perhaps nearer to us than the foundation of universal peace, based on justice and loving co-operation: but the destructive nightmare, in whose grip mankind is now so helplessly tossing and turning, is no more real than the benign dream.

We need the help of the artist to rally, by his example and effective demonstration, the forces of life, the passionate commitments of love, to recall to us all the qualities we have violated this last century in the untrammelled pursuit of power. Henry Adams' Prayer to the Virgin, as the only possible answer to those cosmic forces he—almost alone—had the insight to anticipate and foretell, must be re-written and re-painted in a thousand expressive ways. Every word of the final invocation of the last few stanzas has meaning for us today. And first of all: "Help [us] to see," for it is our unseeingness that has permitted us to stumble so close to the edge of the abyss. "Help us to know," for the withholding of knowledge and the reluctance to draw conclusions from the knowledge we do possess, add willful ignorance to willful blindness. But above all we must recover that which we have lost through the very techniques of scientific knowledge and invention: the power to feel, which is at the basis of all truly human relationships, for once sympathy, pity, and love are withdrawn, intelligence will likewise fail us, and we shall treat other men as if they were mere things or objects. Let us remember, then, those final words of Henry Adams' invocation to the Virgin: "Help us to *feel*, not with our insect sense, with yours that felt all life alive in you: infinite passion, breathing the breath you drew." Yes: help us to *feel*. Our numbness is our death. Whatever our immediate fate may be, as individuals or as a nation, we must, as a condition of survival, recover our humanity again: the capacity for rational conduct, free from compulsive fears and pathological hatreds: the capacity for love and confidence and co-operation, for humorous self-criticism and disarming humility, in our dealings with each other, and in our dealings with the rest of the human race, including, it goes without saying, our enemies. Even should we meet disaster or death through the attempt to replace the politics of dehumanized and absolute power by the politics of love, that defeat would only be a temporary one. For the God in us would remain alive—to quicken the spirit of those that follow us.

The New Realism

The roller-coaster dips and turns of American art have finally brought us around again to familiar ground. We are back to realism. Whether this is just another diverting change of fashion, or whether it marks a significant event, like the demise of the Academy of the New, or is evidence of a deep cultural weariness with abstractions in general, remains to be seen. At any rate, a changing of the vanguard is with us, and while we are waiting for the stragglers from various abandoned outposts to dump their picks and shovels, laser beams, moire patterns, graph paper, masking tape, and other passé paraphernalia, we have time to consider the nature and possibilities of this new phenomenon.

The subject is inseparably linked with the use of the camera. In our culture, where machine-produced patterns and images are pervasive, the traditional visual arts are bound to be affected, one way or another, by the omnipresent picture-making machines. In current practice, artists who derive their imagery from the external world may either use photography as a primary source, combine direct observation with photographic references, or renounce the camera altogether and depend on direct observation, knowledge, and visual memory for the creation of images. Of these processes, the first is chic, the second conventional, and the third radical. Which of them prevails will determine the character and quality of the new realist painting.

The camera dominates the school of "Sharp-Focus Realism" recently seen at a Sidney Janis exhibition in New York. Either photographic processes are directly employed, photographs are copied, or artists function as humanoid cameras. In this style, the glittering and shiny images of our chrome civilization are rendered with merciless accuracy. The banalities of advertising, picture post cards, newspaper images, and other artifacts of pop culture are reproduced with cool assurance. These artists use their human skills to ape the camera and even attempt to surpass its slick perfection and impartiality. That anyone would want to do such a thing and then laboriously do it, does provoke some kind of shock. As an impudent nihilist gesture of self-abasement, this mechanical art does make a comment on our dehumanized condition, and although that strange combination of emotional emptiness and deadly competence may have impact as a titillating absurdity, to my eye, most sharp-focus realism seems little more than an obsessive tour de force. However, it will undoubtedly be the next fad of the New York novelty market and will probably be solemnly discussed in Instant Art History books.

Whereas sharp-focus realists baldly proclaim their alliance with the camera, those artists who combine direct observation with photographic assistance, or those whose way of seeing has been unconsciously conditioned by the camera, are

175

not so simple. Inter-reaction between photographic and traditional image-making processes has been going on since the 19th century. Artists as disparate as Degas and Eakins have recognized the possibilities of photography. Degas was attracted by the perversity of camera angles and employed them in the creation of daring new pictorial structures. Eakins used photographs for practical information and thereby narrowed his vision of color and form. Realists like Hopper and Wyeth both reveal the weak draftsmanship that goes with camera-conditioned vision, though they redeem that failing by their subtle control of abstract elements and their evocations of mood and light.

Camera involvement in realism is ambiguous, to say the least. One popular realist hero of the moment, Philip Pearlstein, works in a slavishly photographic manner, with mindless delineation of cast shadows and painstaking rendition of misunderstood surface lumps and bumps. He relies heavily on cameralike cropping, yet denounces the use of photographs, and even has the presumption to suggest that Ingres, whose work is intensely selective, learned, and abstract (light years removed from Pearlstein), depended on the camera. A superior contemporary painter like Pederson-Krag generally works directly from nature, but occasionally uses photographs, which she hides when visitors appear. This minor transgression in no way interferes with the serene and mysterious power of her painting. Use or nonuse of the camera is evidently not a clear-cut esthetic or moral issue. Yet, in general, I sense that those artists who employ photographs or camera-oriented vision (as distinct from photographers who use cameras) tend to be limited by the machine's limits. Their work is frequently compromised by an obligation to produce paintings that can match the camera's vulgar verisimilitude.

Finally, there are those realist painters, young and old, who depend entirely on their human vision to discover the rhythms of the external world. They contemplate the creatures, places, and things of the earthly domain as they exist in space and light, observe the relationships that occur, and record their response by a direct physical process of mark-making. They are the latter-day American offspring of those painters, from Manet to Morandi, who have paid ardent attention to the forms of nature. They also care more about an artist's work and what it reveals of his methods than they care about his assigned role in art history. For them, Cezanne is significant because he devoted a lifetime to recording an intense visual exploration of his immediate surroundings, not because he incidentally discovered new ways of seeing that led to cubism. Van Gogh appeals to them because he was passionately engaged in a process of revealing the movement, structure, color and light of the visual world, not because the emotional aspect of his work was later linked to the gross neurotic effusions of expressionism.

For the artists who have returned to the external world for their imagery, the accepted doctrines of Clement Greenberg's chauvinist abstract academy are simply ignored. They are not committed to the impenetrable sacred flatness of the picture plane. They don't care about inventing private iconography or finding clever new ways to tickle overblown areas of canvas into acceptable decorative form. They are tired of the conventional ambiguities of Modern Art. They are not bound to a trivial artistic tradition defined by the likes of Jackson Pollack on one hand, and Jack Bush on the other. They are engaged in the expression of immediate experiences of the big world, rather than the creation of egocentric abstractions. These artists use the process of direct observation and creative action as a mode of existence, as a means of establishing a link with the world. For them the process is more important than the product. Most of them are completely indifferent to the novelty-seeking, marketing ploys of the New York art game. Some of them live like mystics or hermits. Learning to see is their lifetime vocation. For them, the age-old facts of painting and drawing are only means for discovering the shape and mystery of the forms about them.

This return to a primal condition of direct experience and action seems to me the most vital aspect of the new realism. It is one mode of contemporary creative activity where purely human responses and gestures are employed. Insofar as it engages both artists and viewers in a renewed awareness of this changing vulnerable world, it has both esthetic and educational promise. Out of it may come a body of original work.

No great prophetic vision is needed to perceive that abstract painting is reaching a dead end. Those monotonous nonobjective paintings that numerically dominated the recent Whitney annual in New York or Philip Johnson's latest sterile donations to the Museum of Modern Art in that city are just samples of a generally exhausted style. By now, the prevailing conventions of post-war abstract painting have become academic, restrictive, and intolerably boring. The move toward realism is not only an act of rebellion against those limits, it is also a return to an old American painting tradition and a new approach to the objective world.

STEPHEN KOCH APRIL 26, 1969

Warhol

"I never wanted to be a painter. I wanted to be a tap dancer."

A party is in progress, and lots of sleek-looking people stand artfully around; glasses clink, there's the genteel rumble of talk, people are circulating a little faster than they ought. The faces seem vaguely famous; the memory squints, unsuccessfully trying to bring into focus who or what they are. But it doesn't work, they aren't famous enough. This is an art-world party, the art world being a subculture where fame (I don't mean merit) is a somewhat superior brand of chic. But suddenly—the moment seems timed by a master of the inevitable but unexpected entrance—a man arrives with an entourage. Like an automatic transmission shifting silently upward, the whole room responds to that *really* famous silvered hair, the dark glasses, and leather jacket. Around him orbit, say, a couple of rather battered guys dressed in next week's super-clothes and two or three ostentatiously depraved girls with hair that looks like it was yanked out of a Brillo box. Without letting anybody notice, everybody takes a quick glance toward what is now the center. The rumble of voices remains unchanged, but the environment of the party has been made to cohere. Glasses clink. A scene has been made.

I have no intention of arguing that any of Andy Warhol's paintings or graphic works—or for that matter, any of his films, with the thoroughly ambivalent exception of *"The Chelsea Girls"*—has much intrinsic artistic value; they are merely objects on the scene. On the contrary, what Warhol *does*—the acts and artifacts considered in themselves—is finally not very interesting at all. Everything he does depends on its context, wherein an insignificant action may suddenly be made to *signify,* point to its environment, and thus become astonishingly transformed. For the past eight years, Warhol has been radiating (rather than creating or acting out) a weirdly passive "existential"—ontological—drama with its vital artistic interest. The drama in some ways reached its climax last summer, when this man who makes a point of utter passivity and renunciation of the masculine principle was shot down by a manhating woman who had apparently become—what else?—entirely dependent on him. "I feel different now," Warhol said after recuperating. "I used to think everybody was always kidding."

Warhol is a sweet, silent, pathologically mild-mannered guy with an intuitive genius for stepping into the mainstream of philosophy, art, aesthetic history, and the sociology of both media and the image in our time, and simply standing there, as if he were in a chic living room, at their exact point of convergence. For somebody who has written and talked about so much, Warhol has received very little intelligent criticism; though as an artist for whom the work is almost nothing and its context almost everything, he ought to be especially interesting to intellectuals, whose job after all can virtually be defined as the articulation of contexts. Most writers agree that Warhol's gift is not fundamentally plastic but theatrical; that he has a cool uncanny knack for locating objects and himself within the environments proper to them, simultaneously defining that environment and "creating" the object's status within it. Fewer writers remark that this gift is not fundamentally "creative" in the Promethean sense, but rather a species of preternaturally good taste ("People are so fantastic," he once said. "You can't take a bad picture"); or that this good taste is closer to the "art" of the interior decorator or scene designer than it is to Cézanne. But almost nobody notices that Warhol's art has a remarkable relevance to certain traditions and metaphors about art and the artist that have dominated important aspects of Western cultural life at least since Baudelaire, or that Warhol's style speaks to and through those traditions with an ultra-naive and often staggering economy of means.

The first big Warholvian *coup de théâtre* imitated Marcel Duchamp by inducing people to look at Coke bottles, Campbell's soup cans, and Brillo boxes through that special "aesthetic" modality of perception reserved for looking at things which are functionless. Look at, say a telephone, physically effacing its function. It will become something new. Ever since Duchamp's dadaist jokes with the urinal and the bottle rack, we've known that scrutiny can aestheticize any object in this way; all that's required is a simple shift of gears in consciousness.

The Duchampian game in which objects are aestheticized merely by turning to them with a certain glint in your eye does have continuing value, though not as the comical "anti-art" polemic so often ascribed to it. Nothing is deader than a dead joke, and the chic giggles over Duchamp's bottle-rack died out half a century ago. But like its companion movement, surrealism, the Duchampian dimensions of dada left behind something more important: new possibilities of metaphor. If you look at any object through the aestheticizing Duchampian prism, you are likely to be made peculiarly aware of the process of looking itself, conscious not merely of the object but also of the *feel*, the nature, the very matrix and interplay of your perceptions. The object thus will refer you again to yourself and your own personal capacity to transform objects and their environment.

It is possible to understand this rather specialized aesthetic experience as a metaphor, in consciousness, for the perception of things at large, in which the unlike things compared and fused are the self and the world. This is a process which found its great bard in Wallace Stevens, and it has enormous importance not only for Stevens' poetry, but for significant sectors of modern painting, sculpture, music—as well as film, where the aesthetic shades (or rather, leaps) into the kinesthetic, gripping the sensorium from Eisenstein to Kubrick's "2001" to the wonderful stomach-flipping automobile chase in "Bullitt." It is a major modernist procedure for creating metaphors, and an anti-romantic one, since it locates the world of art's richness not in Baudelaire's Elsewhere but in the here and now. At least almost.

Warhol goes further. He wants to be transformed into an object himself, quite explicitly wants to remove himself from the dangerous, anxiety-ridden world of human action and interaction, to wrap himself in the serene fullness of the functionless aesthetic sphere. Desiring the glamorous peace of existing only in the eye of the beholder, he tries to become a celebrity, a star, making no bones at all about his preference for objecthood over being human. "Machines have less problems," he once told an interviewer. "I'd like to be a machine, wouldn't you?" Another time: "The reason I'm painting this way is I want to be a machine. I think it would be terrific if everybody was alike." Another time: "I love Los Angeles . . . I love Hollywood . . . Everybody's plastic—but I love plastic. I want to be plastic." And again: "I still care about people but it would be easier not to care. . . . It's too hard to care . . . I don't want to get too close . . . I don't like to touch things. . . . That's why my work is so distant from myself."

Warhol's self-transformation into an object—into that plastic machine which is the sixties' ultimate, exemplary celebrity—is possible only because of his extreme fame. Being famous is one of the things his career is all about—fame and passivity are the two themes that dominate everything he does. "In the future," he once remarked in an almost spectacularly brilliant aphorism, "everybody will be world-famous for at least fifteen minutes." Just as the bottle rack became art by being placed in the context of art (a context created above all by the media) Warhol *is* Pop Art. And just as the bottle rack has no intrinsic interest, the famous man has done nothing to deserve his fame except to become famous and then rest passive within it. This is by no means easy to do, but nonetheless the coveted prize is won not by action but a kind of framed inaction. In fact, Warhol's career is part of—is the culmination of—that continuing critique of the man of action, which has played its dual role in the history of art and masculinity since Baudelaire. Warhol always succeeds because he never tries. As with the tycoon, failure is not in his vocabulary. He is the last dandy.

Baudelaire wrote:

> "The character of the dandy's beauty consists above all in the cold appearance which comes from the unshakable resolution not to be moved; one might say the latent fire which makes itself felt, and which might, but does not wish to, shine forth."

The remark suggests what might be called a style of latency, an art of the immanent underlying both the soup cans and those meek, blank stares from behind the dark glasses. Transforming himself into the object-celebrity, Warhol has made a commitment to the Baudelairian "resolution not to be moved"—an effort to ensconce himself in the aesthetic realm's transparent placenta, removed from the violence and emotions of the world's time and space. So Warhol turns out to be a romantic, after all. But the world's violence and emotions are also located within the aestheticized human-object himself, just as they are immanent within the "eye of the beholder," who half-sees, half-imagines them swarming there just beneath the quiet surface: ("we have cops coming up here all the time," he says. "They think we are doing awful things and we aren't"). The pale cold light Baudelaire saw repressed within the dandy is the fire of life itself—whose latency, in this context, brings the category of art into being.

And so, as a super-celebrity, Warhol lives out the metaphoric distinction between life and art in the eyes of the Beautiful People, his beholders. Famous for being famous, he is a pure image. This, too, is part of that ontological drama I mentioned. Ever since Pirandello at least, a metaphor for questions of being and authenticity of identity has been working its way through modern consciousness, in the form of the idea of the theater and in images of theatricalism. The theatrical distinction between actor and audience is analogous to the metaphoric distinction between life and art, and between the object and the beholder. Turning the theatrical metaphor into the life of a celebrity, Warhol becomes its last embodiment. Nobody turns to the theater for his dream box anymore, but millions dream of celebrity, celebrity for anything. The scramble for it is like a fight for a life raft among a throng drowning in the sea of nonexistence. But Warhol doesn't fight. He floats.

Some final words about the relevance of all this to Warhol's interest in movies. Until recently, his movies have remained pretty consistently within the limited social and intellectual ambience of the plastic arts, where his shift from painting to films (around 1966) has been taken very seriously as a commentary on the future of the object and of easel painting as art. But his early films, *Eat, Sleep, Star,* etc., were of objects, or nearly so. They were absolutely nontheatrical and eventless. When shown, their single effect was to make Warhol more of a celebrity and more of an object. He himself never appears in these films; the "stars" are humble anonymities stared at forever by a camera eye, which has, as opposed to most cinematography, ceased to mimic the lightness and curiosity and life of human looking, and is instead an object's eye. In these movies, the camera eye—Warhol's own—fulfills itself as machine, just as Warhol's public desire to be a machine is fulfilled while his painter's eye grinds on forever, endlessly recording an "objective" dead reality. The Duchampian situation is compounded and made reflexive.

But at a certain point Warhol's movies came alive, to become a kind of sexualized *cinéma verité*. Rather than "act" (since in any sense of the word, he never allows himself to act) Warhol retained his passivity by being the "director," which consists of letting the camera run while members of his vast, ever-changing entourage pile up on or near a bed and play at being themselves, which they sometimes do with marvelous pyrotechnic grace. It is a mindless cinematic transformation of Pirandello, in which the author for whom the characters are searching stands off-camera, utterly inert, letting the film run on and on, never opening the possibility of failure by attempting to act himself. In his few walk-ons, Warhol is always the only figure on the screen who seems out of place. "Acting" is something left to mere subordinates, and through that quiescence, Warhol remains the superstar who outshines them all.

Passivity above all. Immobility is action. The loser wins. In one of his most famous films, *Star*, Warhol simply let the camera run for eight hours on the Empire State Building. Somewhere along the line he is reported to have exclaimed, "The Empire State Building is a star!" making a metaphor of his own for a change. This person who has made himself into an object, turned the building into a person, while the eye of the beholder idiotically ran on and on. The camera and the big building stood there together, serving as a final metaphor for the relation between object and perceiver in Baudelairian aesthetic during this strange, glamorous gasp of its decadence. But of course, the Empire State Building was already a metaphor in most people's minds, Warhol's undoubtedly included. The great phallus of the torn urban pastoral landscape rises up to penetrate—what? To penetrate most of the electronic media channels of the United States, and the empty evening sky.

CLIVE BELL   MAY 19, 1920

Matisse and Picasso

The names go together as do those of Shelley and Keats or Fortnum and Mason. Even to people who seldom or never look seriously at a picture they have stood, these ten years, as symbols of modernity. They are preeminent: and for this there is reason. Matisse and Picasso are the two immediate heirs to Cézanne. They are in the direct line: and through one of them a great part of the younger generation comes at its share of the patrimony. To their contemporaries they owe nothing: they came into the legacy and had to make what they could of it. They are the elder brothers of the movement, a fact which the movement occasionally resents by treating them as though they were its elder sisters.

Even to each other they owe nothing. Matisse, to be sure, swept for one moment out of his course by the overwhelming significance of Picasso's early abstract work, himself made a move in that direction. But this adventure he quickly, and wisely, abandoned; the problems of cubism could have helped him nothing to materialize his peculiar sensibility. And this sensibility—this peculiar emotional reaction to what he sees—is his great gift. No one ever felt for the visible universe just what Matisse feels; or, if one did, he could not create an equivalent. Because, in addition to this magic power of creation, Matisse has been blest with extraordinary sensibility both of reaction and touch, he is a great artist; because he trusts to it entirely he is not what for a moment apparently he wished to be—a chef d'école.

Picasso, on the other hand, who never tried to be anything of the sort, is the paramount influence in modern painting—subject, of course, to the supreme influence of Cézanne. All the world over are students and young painters to whom his mere name is thrilling; to whom Picasso is the liberator. His influence is ubiquitous: even in England it is immense. Not only those who for all their denials—denials that spring rather from ignorance than bad faith—are mere apes of the inventor of cubism, but artists who float so far out of the main stream as the Spensers and the Nashes, Mr. Lamb and Mr. John, would all have painted differently had Picasso never existed.

Picasso is a born chef d'école. His is one of the most inventive minds in Europe. Invention is as clearly his supreme gift as sensibility is that of Matisse. His career has been a series of discoveries, each of which he has rapidly developed. A highly original and extremely happy conception enters his head, suggested, probably, by some odd thing he has seen. Forthwith he sets himself to analyze it and disentangle those principles that account for its peculiar happiness. He proceeds by experiment, applying his hypotheses in the most unlikely places. The significant elements of Negro sculpture are found to repeat their success in the drawing of a lemon. Before long he has established what looks like an infallible method for producing an effect of which, a few months earlier, no one had so much as dreamed. This is one reason why Picasso is a born chef d'école. And this is why of each new phase in his art the earlier examples are apt to be the more vital and well nourished. At the end he is approaching that formula towards which his intellectual effort tends inevitably. It is time for a new discovery.

Meanwhile a pack of hungry followers has been eyeing the young master as he made clearer and ever clearer the nature of his last. To this pack he throws hint after hint. And still the wolves pursue. You see them in knots and clusters all along the road he has travelled, gnawing, tugging at some unpicked ideas. Worry! Worry! Worry! Here is a crowd of old laggards still lingering and snuffling over "the blue period." A vaster concourse is scattered about the spot where the nigger's head fell; and of these the strongest have carried off scraps for themselves, which they assimilate at leisure, lying apart. While, round the trunk of cubism, is a veritable sea of swaying, struggling, ravenous creatures. The howling is terrific. But Picasso, himself, is already far away, elaborating an idea that came to him one day as he contemplated a drawing by Ingres.

And, besides being extraordinarily inventive, Picasso is what they call "an intellectual artist." Those who suppose that an intellectual artist is one who spends his time on his head mistake. Milton and Mantegna were intellectual artists: it may be doubted whether Caravaggio and Rostand were artists at all. An intellectual artist is one who feels first—a peculiar state of emotion being the point of departure for all works of art—and goes on to think. Obviously Picasso has a passionate sense of the significance of form; also, he can stand away from his passion and consider it; apparently in this detached mood it is that he works. In art the motive power is heat always: some drive their engines by means of boiling emotion, others by the incandescence of intellectual passion. These go forward by intense concentration on the problem; those swing with breathless precision from feeling to feeling. Sophocles, Masaccio and Bach are intellectuals in this sense, while Shakespeare, Correggio and Mozart trust their sensibility almost as a bird trusts its instinct. It never entered the head of a swallow to criticize its own methods; and if Mozart could not write a tune wrong that was not because he had first tested his idea at every point, but because he was Mozart. Yet no one ever thought of going to a swallow for lessons in aviation: or, rather, Daedalus did, and we all know what came of it.

That is my point. I do not presume to judge between one method of creation and another; I shall not judge between Matisse and Picasso; but I do say that, as a rule, it is the intellectual artist who becomes, in spite of himself, schoolmaster to the rest. And there is a reason for this. By expressing themselves, intellectual artists appeal to us aesthetically; but, in addition, by making, or seeming to make, some statement about the nature of the artistic problem, they set us thinking. We feel sure they have something to say about the very stuff of art which we, clumsily enough, can grasp intellectually. With purely aesthetic qualities the intellect can do nothing; but here, it seems, is something the brain can get hold of. Therefore we study them and they become our leaders; which does not make them our greatest artists. Matisse may yet be a better painter than Picasso.

Be that as it may, from Matisse there is little or nothing to be learnt, since Matisse relies on his peculiar sensibility to bring him through. If you want to paint like him, feel what he feels, conduct it to the tips of your fingers, thence onto your canvas, and there you are. The counsel is not encouraging. These airy creatures try us too high. Indeed, it sometimes strikes me that even to appreciate them you must have a touch of their sensibility. A critic who is apt to be sensible was complaining the other day that Matisse had only one instrument in his orchestra. There are orchestras in which fifty instruments sound as one. Only it takes a musician to appreciate them. Also, one hears the others talking about "the pretty, tinkley stuff" of Mozart. Those who call the art of Matisse slight must either be insensitive or know little of it. Certainly Matisse is capable of recording, with an exquisite gesture and not much more, just the smell of something that looked as though it would be good to eat. These are notes. Notes are often slight—I make the critics a present of that. Also of this: it takes a more intense effort of the creative imagination to leave out what Tchekov leaves out of his short stories than to say what Meredith put into his long ones.

In the Plutarchian method there was ever a snare, and I have come near treading in it. The difference between Matisse and Picasso is not to be stated in those sharp antitheses that every journalist loves. Nothing could be more obtuse than to represent one as all feeling and the other all thought. The art of Picasso, as a matter of fact, is perhaps more personal even than that of Matisse, just because his sensibility is perhaps even more curious. Look at a cubist picture by him amongst other cubists. Here, if anywhere, amongst these abstractions, you would have supposed that there was small room for idiosyncrasy. Yet at M. Léonce Rosenberg's gallery no amateur fails to spot the Picassos. His choice of colors, the appropriateness of his most astonishing audacities, the disconcerting yet delightful perfection of his taste, the unlooked for yet positive beauty of his harmonies, make Picasso one of the most personal artists alive.

And if Picasso is anything but a dry doctrinaire, Matisse is no singing bird with one little jet of spontaneous melody. I wish his sculpture were better known in England, for it disposes finely of the ridiculous notion that Matisse is a temperament without a head. Amongst his bronze and plaster figures you will find sometimes a series consisting of several versions of the same subject, in which the original superabundant conception has been reduced to bare essentials by a process which implies the severest intellectual effort. Nothing that Matisse has done gives a stronger sense of his genius, and, at the same time, makes one so sharply aware of a brilliant intelligence and of erudition even.

Amongst the hundred differences between Matisse and Picasso perhaps, after all, there is but one on which a critic can usefully insist. Even about that he can say little that is definite. Only, it does appear to be true that whereas Matisse is a pure artist, Picasso is an artist and something more—an involuntary preacher if you like. Neither, of course, falls into the habit of puffing out his pictures with literary stuff, though Picasso has, on occasions, allowed to filter into his art a, to me most distasteful, dash of sentimentality. That is not the point, however. The point is that, whereas both create without commenting on life, Picasso, by some inexplicable quality in his statement, does, unmistakably, comment on art. That is why he, and not Matisse, is master of the modern movement.

VIRGINIA WOOLF   MAY 13, 1925

Pictures

Probably some professor has written a book on the subject, but it has not come our way. The Loves of the Arts—that is more or less the title it would bear, and it would be concerned with the flirtations between music, letters, sculpture, and architecture, and the effects that the arts have had upon each other throughout the ages. Pending his inquiry, it would seem on the face of it that literature has always been the most sociable and the most impressionable of them all; that sculpture influenced Greek literature, music Elizabethan, architecture the English of the eighteenth century, and now, undoubtedly, we are under the dominion of painting. Were all modern paintings to be destroyed, a critic of the twenty-fifth century would be able to deduce from the works of Proust alone the existence of Matisse, Cézanne, Derain, and Picasso; he would be able to say with those books before him that painters of the highest originality and power must be covering canvas after canvas, squeezing tube after tube, in the room next door.

Yet it is extremely difficult to put one's finger on the precise spot where paint makes itself felt in the work of so complete a writer. In the partial and incomplete writers it is much easier to detect. The world is full of cripples at the moment, victims of the art of painting, who paint apples, roses, china, pomegranates, tamarinds, and glass jars as well as words can paint them, which is, of course, not very well. We can say for certain that a writer whose writing appeals mainly to the eye is a bad writer; that if, in describing, say, a meeting in a garden, he describes roses, lilies, carnations, and shadows on the grass, so that we can see them, but allows to be inferred from them ideas, motives, impulses, and emotions, it is that he is incapable of using his medium for the purposes for which it was created and is, as a writer, a man without legs.

But it is impossible to bring that charge against Proust, Hardy, Flaubert, or Conrad. They are using their eyes without in the least impeding their pens, and they are using them as novelists have never used them before. Moors and woods, tropical seas, ships, harbors, streets, drawing-rooms, flowers, clothes, attitudes, effects of light and shade—all this they have given us with an accuracy and a subtlety that make us exclaim that now at last writers have begun to use their eyes. Not, indeed, that any of these great writers stops for a moment to describe a crystal jar as if that were an end in itself; the jars on their mantelpieces are always seen through the eyes of women in the room. The whole scene, however solidly and pictorially built up, is always dominated by an emotion which has nothing to do with the eye. But it is the eye that has fertilized their thought; it is the eye, in Proust above all, that has come to the help of the other senses, combined with them, and produced effects of extreme beauty and of a subtlety hitherto unknown.

Here is a scene in a theatre, for example. We have to understand the emotions of a young man for a lady in a box below. With an abundance of images and comparisons we are made to appreciate the forms, the colors, the very fibre and texture of the plush seats and the ladies' dresses and the dullness or glow, sparkle or color, of the light. At the same time that our senses drink in all this our minds are tunnelling, logically and intellectually, into the obscurity of the young man's emotions which, as they ramify and modulate and stretch further and further, at last penetrate so far, peter out into space, a shred of meaning, that we can scarcely follow. But more, were it not that suddenly, in flash after flash, metaphor after metaphor, the eye lights up that cave of darkness, and we are shown the hard, tangible, material shapes of bodiless thoughts hanging like bats in the primeval darkness where light has never visited them before.

A writer thus has need of a third eye whose function it is to help out the other senses when they flag. But it is extremely doubtful whether he learns anything directly from painting. Indeed, it would seem to be true that writers are of all critics of painting the worst—the most prejudiced, the most distorted in their judgments; if we accost them in picture galleries, disarm their suspicions, and get them to tell us honestly what it is that pleases them in pictures, they will confess that it is not the art of painting in the least. They are not there to understand the problems of the painter's art. They are after something that may be helpful to themselves. It is only thus that they can turn these long galleries from torture chambers of boredom and despair into smiling avenues, pleasant places filled with birds, sanctuaries where silence reigns supreme. Free to go their own way, to pick and choose at their will, they find modern pictures, they say, very helpful, very stimulating. Cézanne, for example—no painter is more provocative to the literary sense, because his pictures are so audaciously and provocatively content to be paint and not words that the very pigment, they say, seems to challenge us, to press on some nerve, to stimulate, to excite. That picture, for example, they explain (standing before a rocky landscape, all cleft in ridges of opal color as if by a giant's hammer, silent, solid, serene), stirs words in us where we had not thought words to exist; suggests forms where we have never seen anything but thin air. As we gaze, words begin to raise their feeble limbs in the pale border-land of no man's language, to sink down again in despair. We fling them like nets upon a rocky and inhospitable shore; they fade and disappear. It is vain, it is futile; but we can never resist the temptation. The silent painters, Cézanne and Mr. Sickert, make fools of us as often as they choose.

But painters lose their power directly they attempt to speak. They must say what they have to say by shading greens into blues, posing block upon block. They must weave their spells like mackerel behind the glass at the aquarium, mutely, mysteriously. Once let them raise the glass and begin to speak and the spell is broken. A storytelling picture is as pathetic and ludicrous as a trick played by a dog; and we applaud it only because we know that it is as hard for a painter to tell a story with his brush as it is for a sheep dog to balance a biscuit on its nose. Doctor Johnson at the Mitre is much better told by Boswell; in paint Keats's nightingale is dumb; with half a sheet of notepaper we can tell all the stories of all the pictures in the world.

Nevertheless, they admit, moving round the gallery, even when they do not tempt us to the heroic efforts which have produced so many abortive monsters, pictures are very pleasant things. There is a great deal to be learnt from them. That picture of a wet marsh on a blowing day shows us much more clearly than we could see for ourselves the green and silvers, the sliding streams, the gusty willows shivering in the wind, and sets us trying to find phrases for them, suggests even a figure lying there among the bulrushes, or coming out at the farmyard gate in top boots and mackintosh. That still life, they proceed, pointing to a jar of red-hot pokers, is to us what a beefsteak is to an invalid—an orgy of blood and nourishment, so starved we are on our diet of thin black print. We nestle into its color, feed and fill ourselves with yellow and red and gold, till we drop off, nourished and content. Our sense of color seems miraculously sharpened. We carry those roses and red-hot pokers about with us for days, working them over again in words. From a portrait, too, we get almost always something worth having—somebody's room, nose, or hands, some little effect of character or circumstance, some knick-knack to put in our pockets and take away. But again, the portrait painter must not attempt to speak; he must not say, "This is maternity; that intellect"; the utmost he must do is to tap on the wall of the room, or the glass of the aquarium; he must come very close, but something must always separate us from him.

There are artists, indeed, who are born tappers; no sooner do we see a picture of a dancer tying up her shoe by Degas than we exclaim, "How witty!" exactly as if we had read a speech by Congreve. Degas detaches a scene and comments upon it exactly as a great comic writer detaches and comments, but silently, without for a moment infringing the reticence of paint. We laugh, but not with the muscles that laugh in reading. Mlle. Lessore has the same rare and curious power. How witty her circus horses are, or her groups standing with field-glasses gazing, or her fiddlers in the pit of the orchestra! How she quickens our sense of the point and gaiety of life by tapping on the other side of the wall! Matisse taps; Derain taps; Mr. Grant taps; Picasso, Sickert, Mrs. Bell, on the other hand, are all mute as mackerel.

But the writers have said enough. Their consciences are uneasy. No one knows better than they do, they murmur, that this is not the way to look at pictures; that they are irresponsible dragon-flies, mere insects, children wantonly destroying works of art by pulling petal from petal. In short, they had better be off, for here, oaring his way through the waters, mooning, abstract, contemplative, comes a painter, and, stuffing their pilferings into their pockets, out they bolt, lest they should be caught at their mischief and made to suffer the most extreme of penalties, the most exquisite of tortures—to be made to look at pictures with a painter.

LEO STEIN   MARCH 30, 1918

Renoir and the Impressionists

The group of painters known as the Impressionists have been at the centre of the stage or near it for almost a generation. Theirs had been the dominating influence in most radical enterprises during that time until the moment when the cubist experiments in pictorial absolutism turned painting entirely aside from its traditional aims. But though the impressionists had been for so long first in contemporary influence, there had been changes in the prominence of the individuals of the group. The emergence as of primary importance of Manet, Monet and Degas in the earlier period, and of Cézanne and Renoir in the later, is significant of changes in pictorial purpose and interest.

Before their coming, the immensely robust Courbet had broken with the romantic tradition in its current forms and was busily presenting to the eyes of his shocked fellow-men the substance of actual things. He showed the volume and weight of solid flesh, the density and mass of green foliage, the heavy roll of waters, and the juicy fulness of red apples. He was a wonderful master of the painter's craft who saturated his canvases with the amplitude of objects realized as valid in their own right. But like all the greater realists he was a romantic at heart, that is he strove to project a world of his own which should be the proof of his creative impulse, of his feeling that the artist did not paint merely what he saw, but that in satisfying his own spiritual demand he saw the truth of things. His buoyant arrogance proclaimed the spiritual Jehovah, proud in the consciousness of his creative temper and will.

All the impressionists were deeply influenced by Courbet, some more and some less directly. In the case of Manet, where Spanish influence—especially that of Goya—was added, there was the purpose to reduce Courbet to terms of simpler pictorial means. Courbet had modelled very elaborately with all the nuance in his forms that studio light would give. Manet tried for greater simplification in the masses by adding to the silhouette so much of modelling only as was necessary for giving essential character to the form. In view of what has since been done the modeling of Manet seems elaborate enough, but in comparison with Courbet and the others of his time, its flatness was conspicuous. His broad masses of color fitted together with subtly adapted edges, broke with the traditional, enveloped figure and the atmospheric bath of the older art. There lay in it fresh possibilities of a painting that should have the clarity of definition of the early mosaics and frescos, with the least sacrifice of realistic rendering. Manet was furthermore the least romantic of his group, the one most simply a realist and most easily content with setting forth the things as he saw them. Of course there was an individual vision which every artist has, but Manet's was to an unusual extent impersonal. His transcriptions were colored more by his technical than by his emotional qualities.

While Manet was building up his masterly constructions, Pissaro and Monet were exploring the possibilities of color in the open air. In this apparently Pissaro was the leader, though the more energetic and assertive Monet is in general regarded as the greater man. He is indeed the greater force, but as unquestionably he is the lesser artist. Pissaro's gentle serviceableness, his modest readiness to learn new things even from much younger men, and the restraint always to be found in his expression, have lessened in some measure his reputation. His work is quite uneven and at his best his line and color are fine and pure rather than powerful. His most successful pictures establish a rarely sympathetic contact with their subjects, but like Manet, Pissaro is lacking in profound conception. He also is quite limitedly a realist, though in his case the realism is soberly refined.

Monet on the other hand is vigorous and emphatic. Gifted with great power of optical discrimination and analysis, inexhaustible in industry, sturdily honest and unalterably convinced, he got something more than a fair share of credit for his moderate creative gifts. He too was a romantic, but of the shallow kind, in whom romantic magniloquence disguises the flabbiness of line, the lack of tang in color, and the essential commonplace of composition. He profited by the fact that his subject was almost exclusively landscape, which is so readily evocative of feeling, so near to music in its capacity to move, that it serves favorably to cover over an artist's vital limitations. A comparison of Monet's landscapes with his still life and his few figure things, will make evident the spiritual and imaginative poverty of a very capable painter.

The time had come in the course of the eighties and the early nineties when the influence of Manet, Monet, and of Degas also, had been quite fully absorbed, and when the need of other things than these men had to offer, was felt by many. Both Manet and Monet were superficial, with little sense of deeper fact or feeling. Pissaro was too slight. In Degas there was more profundity, but it was largely critical in temper. He influenced mostly the satirists in art but did not lead far in the direction of the general heart of man. Those young men therefore who were seeking for a creative inspiration, turned to Cézanne, that strange man secluded in the south, at Aix in Provence, who with eager passion sought to make reality more real, to make into a picture the very substance of God's word. Cézanne's eye was not turned to nature in admiration of the world of things; there was no simple joy in things; there was no taking anything for granted. Here was again the romantic temper at its deepest, the wish to recreate a world near to the heart's desire, a world that should be the symbol of a forth-reaching passion, of the will for a profounder emotional and intellectual life. But to Cézanne, unlike Courbet, the world was a means and a means only. He had much affection but very little sympathy for men and things. His eyes indeed looked outward, but his soul's vision turned within and he sought with endless, passionately impatient insistence, to make the outer world the carrier of his inner need. He did not paint most of his pictures for the picture's sake but rather from a desire for the mastery that would permit of adequate self-expression. The only picture that for Cézanne really counted was the picture that he would paint when, like a god, knowing and compelling to the uttermost, he would fling forth his definitive creation. Cézanne was a kind of Faust who never knew despair, but strove indomitably to be master of the moment when he could say to that which he had made, "O still delay, thou art so fair." In the meantime he was almost indifferent to the stuff that he actually succeeded in producing, for it was so hopelessly unlike that which he longed to see. Although he never lost his faith, he recognized that he himself would not in the flesh enter the holy valleys of the promised land. "I shall die," he said, "the primitive of the way that I have discovered."

No greater contrast to Cézanne could be found than Renoir, the last of this illustrious group to come to recognition, and in whom the blend of the romantic with the realist is almost perfect. Whereas Cézanne was always painting on tomorrow's picture with passionate aspiration, Renoir with equally passionate joy was busy with today's. Whereas Cézanne despised even his best, Renoir enjoyed all that he did when he was in the right mood, and he was almost always in the right mood. Although a lifelong student, constantly occupied with the problems of the painter's art, he did not let those problems stand between him and his pictures. His every canvas was an experiment, not because he treated it as such, but because his mind was open to what was growing under his brush. At times he worked hard at particular problems, but even in the pictures that were most definitely records of such hard work the joy in the thing overcame and crowned the product with the crown of sympathetic pleasure. Cézanne cared for nothing but his soul's purpose and his soul's salvation, while Renoir finds his soul wherever he looks abroad, in the fair faces and the warm bodies of women, in the delight of children, in the light and life of field and sky and water, and in the freshness and glow of fruit and flowers. Never has there been a more outward turning mind, a more cheerful and joyous devotion to the visible world. Nor is this visibility a superficial one. With few exceptions every picture of Renoir's is an individual thing, even when there are a score of almost exact replicas. His endless buoyancy thrills through the products of his brush in the flood of an indivisible life. Therefore his pictures so wonderfully supplement and sustain each other, and Renoir lovers are insatiable. Collectors of his pictures have them by the scores and find that each accession adds not itself alone but gives addition also to the life of all the others. To Renoir so richly endowed, fulness has been given in the way of achievement, and despite retarded recognition, the hideous pain of a prolonged and afflicting illness and a crippled state of many years' duration, his artist's life has been one of quite singular fortune.

Renoir is so far the fullest synthesis that has appeared of the various strivings of Courbet, Manet, Pissaro and Monet. His modelling is full and rich and yet translated so perfectly into terms of color, that it functions as a flat decoration. Year by year, decade after decade, his progress in the mastery of these characters has continued till in the first twelve or thirteen years of this century he reached supreme achievement. Since then with failing strength there is some falling off in completeness, although there is in some respects progress even in the latest. But his joy has never waned. He is, in theological language, a man once-born, one who has never trafficked with sin but who came to birth in the full light of grace. A greater than he may come when one with equal gifts shall plunge to deeper spiritual levels and make manifest the more inclusive drama of life, the victory of the powers of life over the powers of death. But the shadow of death has never clouded the art of Renoir and if he has a limitation it is the very simplicity, the serene graciousness of his pure and noble joy.

MICHAEL GOLD   OCTOBER 22, 1930

Wilder: Prophet of the Genteel Christ

THE CABALA by Thornton Wilder. New York: Albert and Charles Boni.
THE BRIDGE OF SAN LUIS REY by Thornton Wilder. New York: Albert and Charles Boni.
THE WOMAN OF ANDROS by Thornton Wilder. New York: Albert and Charles Boni.
THE ANGEL THAT TROUBLED THE WATERS by Thornton Wilder. New York: Coward-McCann.

Here's a group of people losing sleep over a host of notions that the rest of the world has outgrown several centuries ago: one duchess's right to enter a door before another; the word order in a dogma of the Church; the divine right of Kings, especially of Bourbons."

In these words Thornton Wilder describes the people in his first book, "The Cabala." They are some eccentric old aristocrats in Rome, seen through the eyes of a typical American art "pansy" who is there as a student.

Marcantonio is the sixteen-year-old son of one of the group; he is burned out with sex and idleness, and sexualizes with his sister, and then commits suicide. Another character is a beautiful, mad Princess, who hates her dull Italian husband, falls in love with many Nordics and is regularly rejected by them. Others are a moldy old aristocrat woman who "believes," and a moldy old Cardinal who doesn't, and some other fine worm-eaten authentic specimens of the rare old Italian antique.

Wilder views these people with tender irony. He makes no claim as to their usefulness to the world that feeds them; yet he hints that their palace mustiness is a most important fact in the world of today. He writes with a brooding seriousness of them as if all the gods were watching their little lavender tragedies. The style is a diluted Henry James.

Wilder's second novel was "The Bridge of San Luis Rey." This famous and vastly popular yarn made a bold leap backward in time. Mr. Wilder, by then, had evidently completed his appraisal of our own age. The scene is laid in Lima, Peru; the time is Friday noon, July 20, 1714. In this volume Wilder perfected the style which is now probably permanent with him; the diluted and veritable Anatole France.

Among the characters of San Luis Rey are: (1) A sweet old duchess who loves her grown daughter to madness, but is not loved in return; (2) A beautiful unfortunate genius of an actress who after much sexualizing turns nun; (3) Her tutor, a jolly old rogue, but a true worshipper of literature; (4) Two strange brothers who love each other with a passion and delicacy that again brings the homosexual bouquet into a Wilder book, and a few other minor sufferers.

Some of the characters in this novel die in the fall of a Bridge. Our author points out the spiritual lessons imbedded in this Accident; viz: that God is Love.

The third novel is the recent "The Woman of Andros." This marks a still further masterly retreat into time and space. The scene is one of the lesser Greek islands, the hour somewhere in B. C.

The fable: a group of young Greeks spend their evenings in alternate sexual bouts and lofty Attic conversations with the last of the Aspasias. One young man falls in love with her sister, who is "pure." His father objects. Fortunately, the Aspasia dies. The father relents. But then the sister dies, too. Wistful futility and sweet soft sadness of Life. Hints of the coming of Christ: "and in the East the stars shone tranquilly down upon the land that was soon to be called Holy and that even then was preparing its precious burden." (Palestine.)

Then Mr. Wilder has published some pretty, tinkling, little three-minute playlets. These are on the most erudite and esoteric themes one could ever imagine; all about Angels, and Mozart, and King Louis, and Fairies, and a Girl of the Renaissance, and a whimsical old Actress (1780) and her old Lover; Childe Harold to the Dark Tower Came; Proserpina and the Devil; The Flight into Egypt; a Venetian Prince and a Mermaid; Shelley, Judgment Day, Centaurs, God, The Woman in the Chlamys, Christ; Brigomeide, Leviathan, Ibsen; every waxwork in Wells's Outline, in fact, except Buffalo Bill.

And this, to date, is the garden cultivated by Mr. Thornton Wilder. It is a museum, it is not a world. In this devitalized air move the wan ghosts he has called up, each in "romantic" costume. It is an historic junkshop over which our author presides.

Here one will not find the heroic archaeology of a Walter Scott or Eugene Sue. Those men had social passions, and used the past as a weapon to affect the present and future. Scott was the poet of feudalism. The past was a glorious myth he created to influence the bourgeois anti-feudal present. Eugene Sue was the poet of the proletariat. On every page of history he traced the bitter, neglected facts of the working-class martyrdom. He wove these into an epic melodrama to strengthen the heart and hand of the revolutionary workers, to inspire them with a proud consciousness of their historic mission.

That is how the past should be used; as a rich manure, as a springboard, as a battle cry, as a deepening, clarifying and sublimation of the struggles in the too-immediate present. But Mr. Wilder is the poet of the genteel bourgeoisie. They fear any such disturbing lessons out of the past. Their goal is comfort and status quo. Hence, the vapidity of these little readings in history.

Mr. Wilder, in a foreword to his book of little plays, tells himself and us the object of his esthetic striving:

"I hope," he says, "through many mistakes, to discover that spirit that is not unequal to the elevation of the great religious themes, yet which does not fall into a repellent didacticism. Didacticism is an attempt at the coercion of another's free mind, even though one knows that in these matters beyond logic, beauty is the only persuasion. Here the schoolmaster enters again. He sees all that is fairest in the Christian tradition made repugnant to the new generations by reason of the diction in which it is expressed. . . . So that the revival of religion is almost a matter of rhetoric. The work is difficult, perhaps impossible (perhaps all religions die out with the exhaustion of the language), but it at least reminds us that Our Lord asked us in His work to be not only gentle as doves, but as wise as serpents."

Mr. Wilder wishes to restore, he says, through Beauty and Rhetoric, the Spirit of Religion in American Literature. One can respect any writer in America who sets himself a goal higher than the usual racketeering. But what is this religious spirit Mr. Wilder aims to restore? Is it the crude self-torture of the Holy Rollers, or the brimstone howls and fears of the Baptists, or even the mad, titanic sincerities and delusions of a Tolstoy or Dostoievsky?

No, it is that newly fashionable literary religion that centers around Jesus Christ, the First British Gentleman. It is a pastel, pastiche, dilettante religion, without the true neurotic blood and fire, a daydream of homosexual figures in graceful gowns moving archaically among the lilies. It is Anglo-Catholicism, that last refuge of the American literary snob.

This genteel spirit of the new parlor-Christianity pervades every phrase of Mr. Wilder's rhetoric. What gentle theatrical sighs! what lovely, well composed deaths and martyrdoms! what languishings and flutterings of God's sinning doves! what little jewels of Sunday-school wisdom, distributed modestly here and there through the softly flowing narrative like delicate pearls, diamonds and rubies on the costume of a meek, wronged Princess gracefully drowning herself for love (if my image is clear).

Wilder has concocted a synthesis of all the chambermaid literature, Sunday-school tracts and boulevard piety there ever were. He has added a dash of the prep-school teacher's erudition, then embalmed all this in the speciously glamorous style of the late Anatole France. He talks much of art, of himself as Artist, of style. He is a very conscious craftsman. But his is the most irritating and pretentious style pattern I have read in years. It has the slick, smug finality of the lesser Latins; that shallow clarity and tight little good taste that remind one of nothing so much as the conversation and practice of a veteran cocotte.

Mr. Wilder strains to be spiritual; but who could reveal any real agonies and exaltations of spirit in this neat, tailor-made rhetoric? It is a great lie. It is Death. Its serenity is that of the corpse. Prick it, and it will bleed violet ink and *apéritif*. It is false to the great stormy music of Anglo-Saxon speech. Shakespeare is crude and disorderly beside Mr. Wilder. Neither Milton, Fielding, Burns, Blake, Byron, Chaucer nor Hardy could ever receive a passing mark in Mr. Wilder's classroom of style.

And this is the style with which to express America? Is this the speech of a pioneer continent? Will this discreet French drawing-room hold all the blood, horror and hope of the world's new empire? Is this the language of the intoxicated Emerson? Or the clean, rugged Thoreau, or vast Whitman? Where are the modern streets of New York, Chicago and New Orleans in these little novels? Where are the cotton mills, and the murder of Ella May and her songs? Where are the child slaves of the beet fields? Where are the stockbroker suicides, the labor racketeers or passion and death of the coal miners? Where are Babbitt, Jimmy Higgins and Anita Loos's Blonde? Is Mr. Wilder a Swede or a Greek, or is he an American? No stranger would know from these books he has written.

But is it right to demand this "nativism" of him? Yes, for Mr. Wilder has offered himself as a spiritual teacher; therefore one may say: Father, what are your lessons? How will your teaching help the "spirit" trapped in American capitalism? But Wilder takes refuge in the rootless cosmopolitanism which marks every *emigré* trying to flee the problems of his community. Internationalism is a totally different spirit. It begins at home. Mr. Wilder speaks much of the "human heart" and its eternal problems. It is with these, he would have us believe, that he concerns himself; and they are the same in any time and geography, he says. Another banal evasion. For the human heart, as he probes it in Greece, Peru, Italy and other remote places, is only the "heart" of a small futile group with whom few Americans have the faintest kinship.

For to repeat, Mr. Wilder remains the poet of a small sophisticated class that has recently arisen in America—our genteel bourgeoisie. His style is their style; it is the new fashion. Their women have taken to wearing his Greek chlamys and faintly indulge themselves in his smart Victorian pieties. Their men are at ease in his Paris and Rome.

America won the War. The world's wealth flowed into it like a red Mississippi. The newest and greatest of all leisure classes was created. Luxury-hotels, golf, old furniture and Vanity Fair sophistication were some of their expressions.

Thorstein Veblen foretold all this in 1899, in an epoch-making book that every American critic ought to study like a Bible. In "The Theory of the Leisure Class" he painted the hopeless course of most American culture for the next three decades. The grim, ironic prophet has been justified. Thornton Wilder is the perfect flower of the new prosperity. He has all the virtues Veblen said this leisure class would demand; the air of good breeding, the decorum, priestliness, glossy high finish as against intrinsic qualities, conspicuous inutility, caste feeling, love of the archaic, etc. . . .

All this is needed to help the parvenu class forget its lowly origins in American industrialism. It yields them a short cut to the aristocratic emotions. It disguises the barbaric sources of their income, the billions wrung from American workers and foreign peasants and coolies. It lets them feel spiritually worthy of that income.

Babbitt made them ashamed of being crude American climbers. Mr. Wilder, "gentle as the dove and wise as the serpent," is a more constructive teacher. Taking them patiently by the hand, he leads them into castles, palaces and far-off Greek islands, where they may study the human heart when it is nourished by blue blood. This Emily Post of culture will never reproach them; or remind them of Pittsburgh or the breadlines. He is always in perfect taste; he is the personal friend of Gene Tunney.

"For there is a land of the living and a land of the dead, and the bridge is love, the only survival, the only meaning." And nobody works in a Ford plant, and nobody starves looking for work, and there is nothing but Love in God's ancient Peru, Italy, Greece, if not in God's capitalist America 1930!

Let Mr. Wilder write a book about modern America. We predict it will reveal all his fundamental silliness and superficiality, now hidden under a Greek chlamys.

EDMUND WILSON   MAY 4, 1932

The Literary Class War

I

In the fall of 1930, a year after the stockmarket crash, there appeared in The New Republic an attack by Michael Gold on Thornton Wilder. Michael Gold is, of course, a Communist and his article was an attempt to arraign Wilder at the bar of the Communist ideology. He declared that Wilder's writings were the poetry "of a small sophisticated class that has recently arisen in America—our genteel bourgeoisie" and on a plane with "luxury-hotels, golf, old furniture and Vanity Fair sophistication." "The Bridge of San Luis Rey" and "The Cabala" were among the things which enabled this "parvenu class to forget its lowly origins in American industrialism"—providing them with "a short cut to the aristocratic emotions" and disguising "the barbaric sources of their income, the billions wrung from American workers and foreign peasants and coolies," letting them "feel spiritually worthy of that income." Wilder's Christianity was merely "that newly fashionable literary religion that centers around Jesus Christ, the First British Gentleman"; and his style a "neat, tailor-made rhetoric" whose serenity was "that of a corpse" and which, when pricked, would "bleed violet ink and *aperitif*." How, he asked, could "this discreet French drawing-room hold all the blood, horror and hope of the world's new empire? . . . Where are the modern streets of New York, Chicago and New Orleans? . . . Where are the cotton mills, and the murder of Ella May and her songs? Where are the child slaves of the beet fields? Where are the stockbroker suicides, the labor racketeers or the passion and death of the coal miners?"

This assault provoked one of the most violent controversies which the literary world has lately known. The writer of the present article, at that time on the staff of The New Republic, had felt when he first read Gold's article that the latter had overshot his mark and given to Wilder's popularity more Marxist importance than it deserved. But as the letters began to shower in and kept on for months without abatement, he was finally forced to the conclusion that there *was* a class issue involved in the dispute. For equally severe attacks on other equally popular authors had never brought forth anything like this. The people who applauded Gold seemed to be moved by a savage animus; those who defended Wilder pleaded or protested in the tone of persons who had seen a dearly beloved thing desecrated. Strange cries from the depths arose, illiterate and hardly articulate.

The editors of The New Republic finally decided that the controversy had reached a point where some sort of official comment ought to be made on it. And the present writer composed an editorial in which he justified Gold's attack— pointing out that Thornton Wilder obviously owed a good deal to Proust; that the pinings and dissatisfactions which were the dominant emotions in Proust represented the illness of the cultivated classes in a capitalistic society which neither the modern luxuries of the Ritz nor the collector's recapturing of the past could do more than deaden a little; and that Wilder, without intending it and though a writer of genuine merit, had popularized Proust for American readers, tapping the main of his intoxicating sentimentality and bringing a pipe-line to every American home. It was a sedative for sick Americans; and both the sedative and the demand for it were the results of the same situation: a race of people disposed to idealism but deprived of their original ideals and now making themselves neurotic in the attempt to introduce idealism into the activities of a precarious economic system—manufacturing, salesmanship, advertising—the condition for whose success was that they must swindle the working class and each other.

The present writer was not in a position to take other writers to task too severely for coming under the influence of Proust, as he had himself not very long before written for the same magazine a long and sympathetic essay on "A la Recherche du Temps Perdu" and had also published a novel not unflavored by the fumes of the cork-lined chamber. And his editorial on the Wilder-Gold controversy was written from the bourgeois point of view, as Gold's article had been from the proletarian. Yet it was too Marxist for many New Republic readers, who at once in a revival of the controversy transferred their indignation from Michael Gold to myself. The letters kept coming in till The New Republic was obliged to shut down on publishing them for fear the discussion would go on forever.

The situation was made more complicated by the fact that Gold himself on his side was under criticism from his own Marxist camp. He had just published and had had considerable success with his autobiographical book about the New York East Side, "Jews Without Money," and Communist critics were censoring him for having made it center around an individual: the theory was that there should be no protagonist in a real Communist work of art, that the subject should always be the group. Melvin Levy, in an otherwise appreciative review—appearing also in The New Republic—had insisted that "Jews Without Money" was "written without reference to the mass"; that "labor organizations and strikes" were "not mentioned," though they were "probably more a part of the life of this group than any other in America"—that the big shirtwaist makers' strike and the Triangle Fire, for example, though they had taken place during the period with which "Jews Without Money" dealt, got no attention in it; and that the characters were not proletarians at all, but "merely poor people" whose failures and desires were not inevitable, but merely individual accidents: if they had not happened to have hard luck, they might have turned into contented petty bourgeois. Yet it was evident that Levy himself had not always been so clear as to the duty of the revolutionary writer: he had himself not long before published a novel about Greenwich Village, which, I believe, did not deal at all with the struggles of the proletariat; and in a review of an earlier book of Gold's he had complained that some of the stories had been "tailored to meet a pattern of 'proletarian literature' and propaganda. . . . It is not merely that they sacrifice artistic excellence for propaganda: if they did that successfully, they would be justified. But they have not the veracity and conviction that make good propaganda. They are distant and unreal: unmoving."

To the first of these reviews Michael Gold made a very eloquent reply:

> I think Comrade Levy [he wrote] is too dogmatic in his application of the proletarian canon. There is nothing finished or dogmatic in proletarian thought and literature. We cannot afford it. We are pioneers. . . . It would be fatal for us to have fixed minds. Proletarian literature is taking many forms. There is not a standard model which all writers must imitate, or even a standard set of thoughts. There are no precedents. Each writer has to find his own way. All that unites us, and all we have for a guide, is the revolutionary spirit. . . .
>
> To my mind, it is the task of each proletarian writer to describe that portion of proletarian life with which he is most saturated. . . . Comrade Levy is disappointed because I . . . did not include the triangle fire and the great garment strikes. Yet I could do nothing else honestly and emotionally at the time. I could only describe what I had seen with my own eyes. I did not want to falsify the emotional value and bring in material that I did not feel. I do not believe any good writing can come out of this mechanical application of the spirit of proletarian literature. In America, where everything is confused, we must begin humbly with the things we know best.

He then went on to make an interesting plea:

> It is difficult to write proletarian literature in the country, because all the critics are bourgeois. If a Thornton Wilder writes books in praise of the Catholic theology, or if a Robinson Jeffers preaches universal pessimism and mass-suicide, that is art. But if a revolutionary writer, even by implication, hows the social ideals that are stirring in the

heart of the working class, he is called a propagandist. This taunt which one meets on every side creates a powerful psychic force which proletarian writers will have to ignore. I will admit it had set up inhibitions in my own mind that I have not yet overcome. Perhaps Levy has perceived this in "Jews Without Money," but I assure him that it is hard to overcome in a first book. It will take other books; it will take a group literature and collective experimentation before we can feel as easy in our proletarian world as every bourgeois writer feels in his. Meanwhile, let us not fear to be crude or propagandistic. We are going somewhere; the rest of literature is sinking into the arms of Catholicism, and death.

In short, the whole episode took place in an atmosphere of intellectual confusion—an atmosphere which has not yet cleared up. The result seems to have been that Michael Gold has taken to writing for The New Masses little Communist Sunday-school stories in which the role of a proletarian hero is subordinated with effort and with imperfect artistic success to the drama of a social group; while Thornton Wilder, apparently not unmoved by the outcry in The New Republic, has brought out a series of little plays several of which—and they are quite good—deal with American subjects—one of them transferring the Christian motif so obnoxious to his Marxist critics from the Greek island of "The Woman of Andros" to Trenton, New Jersey, and another presenting an American Pullman car with a technique based, as Wilder explains, on the Japanese Noh plays but with an effect faintly reminiscent of Dos Passos and John Howard Lawson in their New Playwrights' Theatre days. And he has been reported to have made the statement that he believed every very popular book must have some kind of sentimentality concealed in it.

Yet there is no question that the Gold-Wilder row marked definitely the eruption of the Marxist issues out of the literary circles of the radicals into the field of general criticism. After that, it became very plain that the economic crisis was to be accompanid by a literary one.

II

But what does a revolutionary literature really mean in America? What is bourgeois art? what is proletarian art? What are the relations between the literature and the art and the dominant social class of a period?

Michael Gold has thrown some light on the subject in his reply to Levy quoted above. But the bourgeois critics sometimes talk as if the Marxists contemplated the destruction of all human art and literature up to date and the immediate creation of a proletarian culture as something completely different and new—and the Marxists, or pseudo-Marxists, sometimes seem to lend color to this idea.

The truth is, however, that art has given rise through the changes of history to a class which cuts across the social classes. The artists, like the scientists, like the engineers, constitute a kind of guild, and this guild is always tending to be independent of class, international and interracial. The artist's tradition, his craft, has been evolved through a variety of societies by individuals from a variety of classes. And the minds of the greatest artists, like those of the greatest scientists, are always reaching out beyond the limits of their time and place. "But we to whom the world is fatherland as the sea is to fishes," said Dante, "though they drank the Arno before they had teeth and though they love Florence so much that they suffer unjust exile for having loved her—"

Yet the art of each period is bound up with the interests of the dominating classes: it is a part of that Marxist superstructure which rests on the methods of production. The writer nine times out of ten gets his principal characters from that class; and even if he steps outside it, his point of view will still be colored by the point of view of the class. His images, his rhythms, his technique, will all be affected by its habits. The artist belongs to two worlds: a classless supernational one which does not exist yet, but which the mind can partially apprehend, and a real one of which he is part.

Which elements in a writer's writings belong to which of these worlds? How much are his literary instruments, the very language in which he conveys his ideas and feelings, fashioned only for a special use so that they are doomed automatically to be scrapped with the outgrowing of certain social relations?

It is important as well as absorbing to speculate about these questions; but we can never answer them precisely till social relations have actually changed, until the dominating class has lost its power.

In this connection, Trotsky's book on Russian literature after 1917, "Literature and Revolution," is a work of unique interest. Here we are able to study for the first time the effects on a national literature of the dispossession of a dominant class. As Trotsky says, the French Revolution does not present an analogy, because the culture of the rising bourgeoisie had already come to maturity before the revolution occurred; whereas in Russia the proletariat had not produced a culture of its own. And as we are made to see the unexpected ways in which the visions of the novelists, the emotions and images of the poets, the standards of the critics, turned out to be determined by their attitudes toward the social-economic crisis, we are given seriously to think about many features in our own contemporary literature which may previously have seemed to us of the pure essence of high abstracted intellect and art.

Yet the political line-up in Russian literature was not the whole story. Trotsky could see—being himself a brilliant writer—that there were elements of the old culture which would carry through and help to make the new. He never makes the mistake which the stupider type of Marxist makes of supposing that the attitude is everything, that social-economic ideology is the whole of art. He gives their due as artists—as persons specially gifted for writing and with specially developed expertness at it—even to the White émigrés for whom he has politically the most scorn. And in any case he does not look forward to a proletarian culture which will be the antithesis of bourgeois culture. "It is fundamentally incorrect," he says, "to contrast bourgeois culture and bourgeois art with proletarian culture and proletarian art. The latter will never exist, because the proletarian regime is temporary and transient. The historic significance and the moral grandeur of the proletarian revolution consist in the fact that it is laying the foundations of a culture which is above classes and which will be the first culture that is truly human." There would not be time during this transition period for the proletariat to create a distinctive culture—the new socialist culture would grow out of the bourgeois culture behind it.

I do not know whether Trotsky's political eclipse has had the effect of bringing his literary views into disrepute among orthodox Communists. In any case, it is true, of course, that quite different views have been put forward. One hears, for example, of Russian writers who, in their effort to eliminate from their writings every trace of the bourgeois ideology, have reduced syntax and language to what they regard as an ABC of essentials and turn out to be as unintelligible to the proletarians at whom they are aiming as if they were symbolist poets. But after all proletarian children will have to learn in their schools the old syntax and the old vocabulary until socialism shall have evolved naturally its own new kind of speech to go with its new way of thinking.

> The study of literary technique alone [writes Trotsky] is a necessary stage and it is not a brief one. Technique is noticed most markedly in the case of those who have not mastered it. . . . They who refuse to master technique will come to look "unnatural," imitative and even buffoonlike. It would be monstrous to conclude from this that the technique of bourgeois art is not necessary to the workers. Yet there are many who fall into this error. "Give us," they say, "something even pockmarked, but our own." This is false and untrue. A pockmarked art is no art and is therefore not necessary to the working masses. . . . Proletarian art should not be second-rate art. One has to learn regardless of the fact that learning carries within itself certain dangers because out of necessity one has to learn from one's enemies. One has to learn and the importance of such organizations as the Proletcult cannot be measured by the rapidity with which they create a new literature, but by the extent to which they help elevate the literary level of the working class, beginning with its upper strata.
> Such terms as "proletarian literature" and "proletarian culture" are dangerous, because they erroneously compress the culture of the future into the narrow limits of the present day. They falsify perspectives, they violate proportions, they distort standards and they cultivate the arrogance of small circles, which is most dangerous.

And if this was the case in Russia after the bourgeoisie had been expropriated, how much more difficult in America to get away from the bourgeois culture which is still that of the dominating class! Yet Communist criticism in America has often been harsh in the cases of just those writers who have mastered the bourgeois technique and tried to use it to show us the world from the proletarian point of view. I have already mentioned the strictures made on Michael Gold's "Jews Without Money"; and in the case of Edward Dahlberg, the author of "Bottom Dogs," I understand that his writings have been rejected by The New Masses on the ground that they were "a libel on the proletariat." As a matter of fact, Michael Gold and Dahlberg are surely the creators of some of the only specimens of original proletarian literature which we have yet had in this country. The conclusion of "Jews Without Money," in which the East Side boy who has seen and shared the miserable sinking of his family in the slums of the American city to which they had come in the hope of a new life, lonely, unhappy, neurotic, driven almost to suicide by a boyhood spent in sweatshops, hears for the first time a soap-box orator preaching the revolution and realizes for the first time that there may yet be a way out for his people, that the degraded human spirit may prevail against the slums yet—this scene is more moving and convincing than much Communist propaganda. And Dahlberg's sour and sensitive pictures of the back-yard life of the American cities, if they do not flatter the proletariat, are certainly not calculated to please the bourgeoisie. Dahlberg seems to me significant for the revolutionary movement because he is writing of his bottom dogs from and for a point of view which, however little Marxist, is quite outside the bourgeois picture, and because in doing this, he has found a new literary language based on the common speech.

Part of the rather discouraging attitude of the Marxist camp toward some of those who ought to be its principal poets is due, I believe, to a family situation. Marxism, like other things, has academic see: it has its pedantry and its pretentious charlatanism. As in other fields, the people who are doing the original new work never seem quite right to the scholars; and there is always an opportunity for a mediocre writer with a turn for argumentation to make out an impressive case against a gifted writer without one. And sometimes it is the latter who is himself impressed. What one feels about some Marxist criticism is that it is the work of people, who however competent they may be as Marxist theoreticians, have themselves no artistic ability and little appreciation of art and are consequently not equipped to deal with artistic questions. Trotsky is very clear on this point: "It is very true," he writes, "that one cannot always go by the principles of Marxism in deciding whether to accept or reject a work of art. A work of art should, in the first place, be judged by its own law, that is, by the law of art."

The worst Marxist criticism has, therefore, a good deal in common with Humanism. Communist criticism has behind it a powerful living movement whereas Humanism is feeble and effete; but Marxism at its worst is like Humanism in that both are in the position of trying to gauge the value of works of art on the basis of their literal conformity to a body of fixed moral dogma. The question is, does the work of art contribute toward a certain social end? The question itself is a proper one, but this does not mean that everybody who asks it is fitted to give an answer. What happens in the case of the Humanist or the academic type of Marxist is that he elaborates in a void, a sphere of sheer abstraction, a set of ideal specifications for advancing the end proposed. It is as if a businessman, intent on the promotion of his business, who had never had any experience of either the materials or the tools of carpentry and who had never done any sitting, were to draw up careful designs for the construction of chairs for his office. The only difference is that the Humanist locates in the past, where as a matter of fact it never existed, his ideal theoretical chair, whereas the Marxist locates it in the future, where it has never existed yet. They cannot understand that art is something that has to grow out of the actual present substance of life to meet life's immediate needs. The artist, as I have said above, may see into his own future; but the Humanist or the non-artistic Marxist has no credentials whatever which should convince us that he can see into the future of art.

Thus Marxism at its most academic misjudges, it seems to me, the true roles of many of the elements of present bourgeois culture. In the case, for example, of all that department of contemporary literature which stems from French symbolism and of which the chief representative is Joyce, the Marxist assumes too easily that expressing, as to a great extent it does, the morbidity and introversion of bourgeois culture in its decline, it must be completely valueless to the future. This takes no account of its psychological or of its technical discoveries. Bound up as these unquestionably are with the sickness of bourgeois society, Joyce like Freud and Dostoevsky will probably continue to have something to teach us about understanding the mind of man even under communism, and hence in remolding it. And the literary devices of the neo-Symbolists may well turn out to be among the technological improvements made under capitalism which communism will be glad to take over. "The last word of capitalism, the Taylor Plan," wrote Lenin, "combined the refined cruelty of bourgeois exploitation with a certain number of scientific gains which are extremely valuable for the analysis of the mechanical movements necessary in working. . . . The Soviet Republic should take over every technical advance which is scientific in character and offers some advantage." It should be possible to convince Marxist critics of the importance of a work like "Ulysses" by telling them that it is a great piece of engineering—as it is. Henry Ford bought the Johannson gauges because they were true to the millionth of an inch, and the Soviets would be glad to have them. The Joyces and the Eliots and the Cummingses possess the Johannson gauges of consciousness. One of the principal achievements of these writers, furthermore, has been the invention of a literary shorthand which syncopates the syntax of the old literary language, and this shorthand is likely, I should say, to play its role in the creation of the language of the future.

The question of the difficulty of these works seems to me far less serious than it is sometimes assumed to be. Most working-class people at present would never be able to read Joyce; but then, not very many bourgeois do either. Yet his influence has filtered through the whole body of bourgeois literature, from the more popular serious novelists and dramatists who imitate him to the sketches in the barbership weeklies. It is a question of technical education. Every Marxist assumes that proletarians will prove themselves equal—they do today—to mastering the mechanical techniques. Why should they not master the artistic ones as well? The difficulties of literary and artistic works are always being overadvertised by the mandarins who have an interest in keeping a monopoly of them and who usually don't understand them themselves. Art, like everything else, requires study and practice; but there is no reason why proletarians, given the opportunities, should not learn all there is to be learnt about it and bring its benefits to the rest of society just as the chemist or the electrical engineer does. The tendency to reject works of art on the ground of their outlandishness or difficulty suggests on the part of the Marxist critic as it does on the part of the academic bourgeois a simple lack of competence in his calling.

It is true that the artists I speak of are occupied to a considerable extent in giving voice to the gaga state of mind of the contemporary cultivated bourgeois and that these developments of method and style are closely bound up with this. But a really first-rate book by an agonizing bourgeois may have more human value, more revolutionary power, than second-rate Marxists who attack it. A really great spirit does not lie even though its letter killeth. Personally I can testify that the writer who has made me feel most overwhelmingly that bourgeois society was ripe for burial was none of our American Marxist journalists but Proust.

I should add that all these mistaken views which unintelligent Marxists derive from Marxism are attributed to it even more frequently by bourgeois critics who want to discredit it by saddling it with absurdities.

To a Revolutionary Critic

THE GREAT TRADITION by Granville Hicks. New York: The Macmillan Company.

Dear Granville Hicks: I feel too strongly about your book, "The Great Tradition," to write an impersonal review of it; the author and the critic have too much in common. Both of us believe that the central feature of modern life is a struggle between classes which is also a struggle of the working class against all forms of exploitation. Both of us believe that the battle extends to every front, even the literary front. We don't regard literature as a mere department of politics: that would be silly. But both of us are convinced that literature and politics, art, science and education, all are departments of life, and that no artist or writer can divest himself of his role in life. He takes, or eventually will be forced to take, one side or the other, and both of us have made the same choice.

This doesn't at all mean that we agree on every subject. There is room on our side for many shades of belief, and it seems to me that your own shade is too sanguine. You face the future with entire confidence, saying that "even in the days of stress, revolutionary writers will have a kind of courage that others cannot share. . . . They will know that they are participating in a battle that, in the long run, is for civilization itself, and they will have no doubt of the outcome." A football coach might talk like this at a pep-rally on the evening before a big game—"We can't lose, we simply can't lose." To me it seems wiser to acknowledge that the other side may win, even though their triumph would destroy living forces in our present civilization. That civilization itself may disappear in the next great series of imperialist wars.

It is because the stakes are so high and the outcome is undecided that I cannot write impersonally about "The Great Tradition." Inevitably your book will serve as a weapon in the struggle. It will perform this service less by direct argument than by the cogency of its interpretations, less by precept than by example. If the weapon is bad, it is sure to be used against us. That is why I demand that it be nothing less than superb. I am delighted by its virtues, saddened by its faults, and I want to speak bluntly about one and the other.

"The Great Tradition" is possibly the first book in which the history of American literature since the Civil War is arranged into a simple and intelligible pattern. This in itself is a rare virtue, and it becomes still rarer when one considers that you have achieved it without sacrificing your sense of literary values to your political admirations or antagonisms, and without ever lapsing into the multihorrendous style adopted by most of those who try to be Marxian critics.

The book is full of good critical writing, sound judgments and illuminating phrases. In large part, moreover, it fulfills its chief purpose—which was, I take it, to show that revolutionary writing, instead of being alien to the American tradition, was always at the heart of it.

These are considerable achievements, and you will forgive me for treating them more briefly than your faults, which are harder to define. Chief among them is a certain harshness and literalness of approach, which becomes most obvious in your discussion of Henry James. You say of his novels that for the most part they seem "completely remote from the lives of the vast majority of men." You say that his characters exist in a world "of almost complete abstractions," and with such a world you have no patience whatever. Defending the tradition of exact, class-conscious realism, you seem to ask that every novel should present a world as round and unmistakable as the lid of a garbage can. And you completely disregard the realism that Henry James achieved by virtue of his very abstractions.

You cannot forgive him for living in exile. As for Robert Herrick, Upton Sinclair, Frank Norris, the muckraking novelists who stayed at home, you cannot forgive them for remaining middle-class in the midst of their revolt. You judge them, not in relation to the society they tried to express, but rather from the standpoint of a revolutionary critic of the year 1933. With a better sense of historical perspective, your judgments might remain essentially the same, but would lose their dogmatic tone, would become a shade more lenient and persuasive.

In general you ask entirely too much of novelists, and at the same time too little. You ask too much sociological knowledge—as, for example, when you say that "to describe the contemporary scene regional writers would have had to record the breakdown of sectional lines, the growth of extra-regional alliances, the increasing industrialization of agriculture, the steady march of the factory across the continent. They would have had to show how machinery reduced the labor time spent in producing a bushel of wheat from three hours to ten minutes . . . how the shrinkage of the public domain killed the optimism that had thrived while the westward pilgrimage went on." It doesn't seem to occur to you that they might have described and demonstrated all these things, might have thoroughly displayed their sociological insight, and still might have remained inferior novelists for want of other qualities which you do not demand of them—warmth, vigor, imagination, an eye for human oddities, an ear for the good music of words.

Moreover, just as your demands on authors are one-sided, so your explanation of their motives is simplified to the point of distortion. People are poor and do this; people are rich and do that—so runs the easy formula. Thus, speaking of writers in my own college generation, you say that they ignored society and cultivated art in the abstract because, "if a privileged group feels in no danger of losing its privileges, it comes in time to take them for granted." You say that they decided "to make the most of the advantages with which they were blessed. . . .It was the natural response of the members of a privileged group." But later, you continue, after the Wall Street crash, these esthetes in large part become radicals, because, "in the first place, many of these complacent youths were directly affected by the depression, as their incomes or their fathers' incomes declined."

Now I happen to belong, with many of my friends, among these writers whose motives you are trying to set forth, and I can assure you that under Harding and Coolidge they weren't privileged in the least. They were miserably paid white-collar workers who lived in garrets or basements, ate somewhat irregularly and wrote for magazines that were careless about paying for contributions. So far from being an expression of their privileged position in society, their literary opinions were essentially a protest against society—in those days it seemed quite useless to protest by political action. It happens, moreover, that since the depression several writers of this category have lived rather better than they did before, being older and better established in their profession. They had nothing to lose during prosperity; now they have something; yet this has not prevented them from becoming radicalized. Here is a paradox which cannot be explained by the dry formula of economic determinism—which, incidentally, is not the method proper to Marxian critics.

Not at this point, but sometimes at others, you overstep the thin line which separates unfavorable judgment from abuse. Thus, granting the truth of everything you say about James Branch Cabell's books, I can see no justification for your ascribing a "fundamental venality" to their author; phrases like this belong elsewhere than in a history of literature. As for Thornton Wilder, it is simply untrue that "his work merely reflects the cowardice and dishonesty of his spirit." People can disagree with us without being dishonest and fight for the existing order without being cowards.

Faults like harshness, narrowness, dogmatism, are not at all inherent in our position. It is our business, I think, to leave them to our opponents. Let them, lacking sounder arguments, heap abuse on people with whom they disagree. Let *them* be stingy of praise. Let *them* burn books and misrepresent the culture of the past and even, if they choose, set out to destroy it lest it threaten their position; it is our own function to interpret and preserve that culture for a living future. Let *them* be harsh, arid, one-sided and dogmatic. Let them, in a word, write propaganda; they need it in order to justify things as they are and make people accept the bleak world toward which they are leading. Generosity and human warmth are fighting on our side. We need simply discharge our responsibility as critics, we need simply find and set down the truth in its human complexity, being confident that the truth is all the propaganda we need.

"The Education of Henry Adams"

Four generations after one member of the Adams family helped compose the Declaration of Independence, another sat down and wrote a book declaring it null and void. So rapidly had events come to pass that it required just a century and a quarter to demolish America's greatest act of faith with her most withering words of denial. Between John Adams and his great-grandson Henry lay the total wreck of a dream. The disaster had robbed Henry Adams not only of his illusions but equally of his usefulness; the thing that had come about was beyond Henry Adams' ability to cope with or fight against or repair; he, who had burned to participate in American life, was reduced to becoming its stern and dissident historian. Hence, to confess his own failure, and to reveal the far greater failure that had brought his own about, and to fail (as he thought) in confessing it, Adams sat down and wrote the "Education."

The "Education" found its most responsive readers in those years following the World War when they too had reason to believe that American life had failed them, and to every American intellectual who still retained inside him vestiges of the American moralist, Adams' grim citation of a century's crimes and blunders helped explain the plight of the modern world. The demonstration seemed Euclidean enough to justify the bitterly ironic tone which overhung it: for here was Henry Adams, supremely well born, talented, eager, thoughtful, industrious, confessing that every ideal he owned had been traduced; insisting that the world of action had been impossible to enter, and the world of thought powerless to give hope. Only chaos, explosion, cataclysm loomed ahead. A sensitive person was better out of life; in it, a Henry Adams could only by turns shudder and grow brutally cynical.

The book which reached these conclusions remains an important document of American intellectual and moral inquiry, if only because not a dozen Americans of any period were intellectually and morally of a stature to produce it. It is predicated of very nearly a first-rate mind and something like a first-rate experience. If the mind fails us, it is chiefly from not being purposeful enough; if the experience, it is from being largely of one kind. Adams came to know everything within the reach of the cultivated man of the world, everything to be had of drawing-rooms and libraries, colleges and clubs, churches and ruins, senates and courts; but, though such contact was capable of a thousand variations, its bounds were immovably fixed. Henry Adams was an aristocrat, and a peculiarly modern aristocrat: the tame and squeamish product of London or Boston, quite unlike his spacious Renaissance ancestor for whom privilege meant an extension, not a curtailment, of adventures.

This is palpable everywhere through the "Education"; but something else about Henry Adams is palpable in its very title. Adams self-consciously sought to channel his experiences and to convert them into education. The attitude is praiseworthy enough, but at the outset it is interesting to note what produced it. What first of all produced it, we may suppose, was his Puritan background, quivering with moral earnestness: a background which, moreover, if it served as a spur to education, served equally as a backstop; and which, if it accounts during four generations for the Adams strength, accounts no less for its want of suppleness. But the Puritan impulse coincided perfectly with something else which caused Adams to treat life as education: the nineteenth-century crusade for progress and enlightenment. The nineteenth century seemed to think that if man only knew enough, and remained a "moral" animal, he could reform and stabilize the world. The belief was hardly one which Adams, as he grew older, was encouraged to share; but the atmosphere that produced it was one he never outgrew. It was a moral as well as an intellectual impulse that caused him to plunge headlong into the flood of science and philosophy that engulfed his age; it was some desperate faith in pure knowledge, which even a highly ironic temperament could not extinguish, that turned Henry Adams into a lifelong student. True enough, it was difficult for him to make something systematic and cosmic of all he studied. The result, in that line, was never much more than brilliant dilettantism; but it saved Adams, if not from disillusionment, then from disintegration.

If the "Education" were no more than a worldling's reminiscences and a student's recapitulations, all tied together with philosophical ribbons, we might praise its prose and wit and acknowledge its intellectual expressiveness of an era; but we should put it among the memorials, and not the text books, of American experience. But the "Education" is a grand-scale study of maladjustment, of the failure of an exceptional personality to mesh with a prodigious civilization; posing, with one gesture, the problem of the man and his times. The problem of each, by the time Adams' autobiography was made public, had grown greater and more acute; so that in the decade following Adams' death the "Education" had a significance it only partly had in his lifetime and that there is small likelihood it will ever have again.

Like most serious autobiographies, the "Education" is an attempt, not to record a man's life, but to explain it. It is the work, at bottom, of one who set out both to judge and to justify himself. This dual intention is significant, even though what Adams attempted to justify was failure. We may take the liberty of supposing that this dual intention was embodied very simply: Adams judged himself by asking a question, and justified himself by returning an answer. Why—he asks in effect—should someone who started off with every opportunity, and with faith and eagerness, have ended up with so little achieved, dissentient and in utter flight? Because, he answers, the world he had set out to serve had been seized by forces he would not accept for master; and nothing better remained than to try to understand those forces and inveigh against them.

The "Education" is, then, a perfectly *conscious* study of frustration and deflected purpose; of the failure of a superior man to find the right place, or any tolerable place, in a civilization growing ever more corrupt, rapacious and vulgar. No one ever wrote a more deliberate apologia of his life than Henry Adams. I shall have much to say later concerning the make-up of the particular man, concerning his blunders and prejudices; his distaste for enduring his situation, his predisposition to abandon it. But all that has a psychological importance, not a philosophical one; it delimits, but does not destroy, the real meaning of his book. What gives the "Education" its lasting value, what made a generation of futilitarians clasp it to their breasts, is the validity of the predicament regardless of the shortcomings of the man. For if not Henry Adams, then another, or many others, were paralyzed by the terms of that struggle in which he was so centrally engaged. Confronted by the greed of a banking civilization, the crookedness of boss-rule politics, the vulgarity of a parvenu culture, the cynicism of an exploitative ruling class, the middle-class intellectual was pretty well doomed either to suffer or succumb or escape. At the best, if his convictions had real fiber, he might die fighting the reformer's luckless battle; more likely he would accept the situation, as John Hay did, and wax fat off the spoils; or flee it and accept its more graceful counterpart elsewhere, as did Henry James; or take to excoriating it, aware that his mockery was the sign of his weakness, as Adams felt driven to do.

There appeared, in any case, to be no lasting adjustment that could be called an honest one. The superior man might, by the world's standards, succeed or fail; it hardly mattered, since he could not remain whole. No doubt he best avoided contamination by going into retirement; but then he was not fully alive, and then he had abandoned his responsibilities. If he remained in action, he might deceive himself into thinking that he was fighting the good fight by opposing specific men, by championing specific measures; but if he remained in action and refused to deceive himself, he knew he had for enemy the whole huge mass of things. And unless one was an incorrigible idealist or a convinced revolutionary, that was a task leading to dislocation and despair. Henry Adams, very early, became too pessimistic and cynical to go on being a participant. He chose, instead, a place on the sidelines, and from there set about recording the minutes of all the unsavory transactions of America's public life. The picture of such proceedings which Adams drew, or at least suggested, in the "Education" is a final one. For not only were its revelations damning, but its sources were unimpeachable. It was the indictment of a supremely placed worldling who had listened at the most private keyholes, who had been told—or allowed to guess—the secrets of those who worked behind the scenes. Scarcely anyone else who did so little knew so much. Adams' indictment stands: the great documentary merit of the "Education" is its demonstration of what nineteenth-century America had become, and by what process, and on what terms.

The philosopical merit, which once seemed a merit so much greater, is by no means so great. For the intellectuals of the twenties, the "Education" was an epic after their own hearts. *Epic* is no idly used word; the scale and severity of the book are important. In one sense, the most misleading thing about it is its impressiveness. Written with much of the formality that Gibbon used in his "Memoirs," and in the same third person, it comes at the reader with so magisterial an air that halfway through it he grants it the confidence reserved for an attested masterpiece. The Adams manner confers on the Adams apologia a definite extrinsic weight. There is the sense of a large mind and an imposing personality; there is the sense—unimpaired by the irony of the book—of deep purpose and high seriousness. Henry Adams, who lived his life in a minor key, took every precaution to write about it in a major one. The "Education" is a completely full-dress performance.

The 1920's could use such an authoritative approach. The 1920's could bend the knee before a master who celebrated their own misgivings and disappointments. He enobled their dilemma. He gave dignity to their frustration. For theirs was the individualist's dilemma and for them the idea of integrity involved the idea of withdrawal; environment, to them, defeated the arts as participation corrupted the thinker. Their dilemma too, sprang from personal weakness no less than from social disorder. The "Education" gave to the 1920's, not the signal to fight but the leave to withdraw, by revealing how a better man had got waylaid and misplaced, had been passed up and slurred over and left to go unsung; for surely there is something in the tone of the "Education" that suggests, as not the least of the nineteenth century's blunders, its failure to recognize the worth of Henry Adams. On its lowest level, there is an immense amount of self-pity in Adams' book. On their lowest level, there was an immense amount of self-pity in the futilitarians of the twenties. Deep called unto deep.

But at another level there was something in the "Education" to make it one of the justly pivotal books of its era. It may express futility, but its tone is not wholly negative; there is something affirmative in it. And what it affirms is a toughness of mind, a quality of searching, weighing, testing, of coming to clear-eyed conclusions about the nature of things. Above all, it sets forth a mind and morality that spurned the optimistic and opportunistic formulas, from Emerson's down, that had made of American life such a shallow, shifty, spurious thing. At least the *idea* of education which Adams, solitary and recusant, imposed upon himself, was an exemplary idea. What Adams signifies at his best is unadulterated and grown-up thinking. This was something that his pupils of the twenties, groping backward in American letters—stumbling over the confusions of the Transcendentalists, the rampant Americanism that mars the democratic fervor in Whitman—could not easily find elsewhere. No wonder, then, that they thought they had found more than they actually did.

For impressive as the "Education" is, and definitive as is its mood, it somehow is not profound. It befits very few of us to condescend to Adams on the score of his cultural background, his political knowledge, his cerebral weight; but the fact remains that it is not for his "discoveries," or his clarifications of the human struggle, that we can seek him out. Those celebrated later chapters of the "Education"—The Dynamo and the Virgin, A Dynamic Theory of History*—are superb intellectual exercises, but it is hard to believe that they offer a synthesis which is more than personally brilliant and picturesque. When Adams looked to the past, for example, it was originally in search of perspective. He set about contrasting twelfth-century "unity" with twentieth-century "multiplicity," and the contrast is striking. But to what end? He conceived the earlier age as the better one, but must have known that it was impossible to return to it. The structure of twelfth-century life has no application in ours; the old wheels went

---

*For which he was mainly indebted to his brother Brooks.

round from a social force that had become inoperative and spent. Yet, more and more in the manner of an escapist, Adams tried to go back; there came to be more than an esthete's interest in his medieval studies, in the long twilight mystic spell of Chartres. Coldly judged, does not one pamper one's maladjustment by pining for what one cannot have?

There was nothing shallow about Adams' inquiry into human culture, either in its feeling or its facts; but it failed to produce any profound philosophy of life, even a profound skepticism. Adams knew too much, he knew (or thought he knew) too well whither things were drifting, he had—too arrogantly—a disbelief that any good could come of it, ultimately to profit from his career of "education." The philosophy he did evolve is understandable enough, and one must grant that there was a basis in experience for it. But it comes to no more than the pessimism of one who sees the world being ruined, and the cynicism of one who gives up trying to reclaim it. And in Adams there was also an uglier cynicism, of sitting back and watching the world, with a not unmalign satisfaction, go to Hell. The motif of effort and education which carefully governs Adams' autobiography tends to obscure this uglier cynicism; but from a reading of the "Letters" one knows that it was there, and one sees how, after a time, the moralist in Adams gave up being in any sense a crusader and became a merely captious and querulous censor.

A crusader in the old Adams style Henry never was at any time. In John and John Quincy Adams there was a little of Hamlet and much of Coeur-de-Lion; there was the impulse, scarcely questioned, to act. Henry never had that impulse. At the very outset of his career, he thought rather of being *induced* to enter politics—thought of his dignity as soon as his duty. The silver-platter method failed, and in a way Henry would have no other. It was not simply that he was as proud as he was ambitious, or as squeamish as he was moral; it was that for a lifelong career in opposition the work was too grubby, too dispiriting, too harsh, the odds against winning were too fantastically high. The reformer who would take on so forbidding a task needed to be something of a fanatic; and after all Henry Adams was from the beginning the most sensitive of intellectuals, the most cultivated of worldlings.

It would be absurd to imagine such a man becoming a John Brown, a William Lloyd Garrison, a Debs. But it would surely not be absurd to imagine such a man becoming a Matthew Arnold. Each was born in the shadow of a name outstanding for earnestness, each was by temperament the reverse of a democrat, and each grew up to find a place waiting for him in that world where society and intellect, art and politics, meet. There may have been a decisive difference in the fact that Arnold had a living to earn, and Adams did not. But Arnold was not self-indulgent and Adams was; so that Arnold became the embattled foe of what seemed to him the powers of darkness, and Adams merely their bitter and acidulous historian. (It only counts against Adams the more that he understood the issues in a far wider sense than Arnold understood them.) There was something in Adams which, though it might have borne the arduousness of high public office, balked at the indignities of Arnold's private campaigning. By Adams' strongly developed eighteenth-century standards of worldliness, Arnold was doubtless a little plodding, a little ridiculous. He called Arnold the most honest man he knew, but he was never driven to accept the burdens of such an honesty. It was his Chesterfieldian sensibilities that largely ruined Adams; that turned him into a man who thought one way and lived another.

For he lived, during many years, in elegant and patrician retirement, choosing for his intimates the Hays, Cabot Lodges, Theodore Roosevelts for whom morally he had no respect; traveling *en prince;* entertaining *en connaisseur;* parading in his letters a calculated snobbery that sneered at Stevenson's indigent bohemianism, that instantly seized on Kipling's social second-rateness, that inveighed half to the point of mania against the Jews. He said of himself that he "should have been a Marxist," and knew, overwhelmingly, that he could never have been one. The whole story is told, I think, by Adams' reactions to English upper-class life. With his mind he saw all too well its hypocrisy, insularity, complacence; but temperamentally the sweetest air he ever breathed was that of London dinner-parties and English country houses.

The present moment is not congenial, and not disposed to be fair, to the "Education." The book compels respect for a sense of weight behind, not in, it. It suggests tragedy; but it is not—at least on the terms it set out to be—tragic, because the author chose the less costly form of defeat, and the less noble. Impotence, to Adams, was preferable to mutilation. Psychologically—by which I mean that were Henry Adams the problem of a novelist—his life followed a convincing pattern. But in real life, an ultimate failure of character is not to be excused by being explained; nor does a lifetime of self-analysis compensate for a failure to see things through morally. If a crude capitalist era "crushed" Adams, it was as much from being enervated by the fruits of it as from being poisoned by its roots. Was Adams willing—was he ever willing—to lose just part of the world to gain his own soul? It is just possible to say Yes; but if so, Adams' reason was purely pride.

However great the merits of the "Education," its "method" can already be seen to have failed. Culture and education are of the highest importance—according to some philosophies, the very end of living. But for Henry Adams they were clearly intended to be a means, carrying him forward to a better understanding and fulfilment of his obligations. Instead, they produced in him the indecision of a Hamlet; they became a kind of luxury, a kind of solace, and a kind of escape. It may be that Adams has taught us more in autobiography than he could have in action. It is at least certain that he has warned us more unforgettably. For it is not from confusing the mind by overloading it; it is not from dissent without protest, or opposition without strife, or humanism without humanity, that the beleagured intellectual can save himself, or that the world he views with horror can be saved.

Nearer My Land to Thee

Underlying the imaginative life in America all through the years of panic, depression and the emergence of international civil war was an enormous body of writing describing the American scene that is one of the most remarkable phenomena of the era of crisis. That literature has hardly run its course, and it may even dominate the scene for many years to come; but for all its shapelessness and often mechanical impulse, it is a vast body of writing that is perhaps the fullest expression of the experience of the American consciousness after 1930, and one that illuminates the whole nature of prose literature in those years as nothing else can. For that literature of nationhood, beginning with the documentation of America in the depression and reaching a thunderous climax in an effort to seek out the American tradition, is largely the story of the American people as they came to understand it for themselves in a period of unprecedented crisis. It is the story of that now innocent, now calculating, now purely rhetorical, but always significant experience in national self-discovery which had its origin in the same obsession with society in crisis that led to the social novels of the period, but went on to create original or to reclaim traditional forms in a passionate effort to make a living record of contemporary American experience. It is the story of a vast new literature in itself, some of it fanatical or callow, some of it not writing at all, much of it laboriously solid and curious and humble, whose subject was the American scene and whose drive always was the need, born of the depression and the international crisis, to chart America and to possess it. It is the story of a literature of collective self-consciousness, a people's and a nation's biography; a story of physical and human geography, composed under pressure, often testifying only to the immediacy of that pressure, yet for all its occasional opportunism or naïveté, never without some fundamental joy in the study of America and the pride taken in its aroused self-comprehension.

Whatever form this literature took—the WPA guides to the states and roads; the reaction against the skepticism and now legendary "frivolity" of the twenties; the half-sentimental, half-commercial new folklore that manufactured or inflated comic demigods out of the reclaimed past; the endless documentation of the dispossessed in American life—it testified to so extraordinary a national self-scrutiny, signified so widespread and insistent a need, that all other considerations of it seem secondary. As if it marked a release of energies more thwarted in the past than anyone had suspected, a release of powers of affirmation crying for expression, whole divisions of writers now fell upon the face of America with a devotion that was baffled rather than shrill, and an insistence to know, and to love what it knew, that seemed unprecedented. Never

211

before did a nation seem so hungry for news of itself, and not since those early years of the nineteenth century when the American had been the world's eighth wonder to European observers did America—if only the very texture of the country—seem so magnetic a subject in itself to so many different minds. The question now was no longer posed from afar—*What is an American?* Here the intelligence was native, as the subject was its very self, and by that very token a moving and always astonishing hunger for self-knowledge, since it seemed to express a profoundly innocent unanimity of spirit.

For better or worse this new nationalism was a pervasive force, a new historic consciousness that gave new meaning to contemporary experience and thought, and to appreciate that is to see something in the experience of the times that we are perhaps not now fully prepared to understand. For here, in the revealing—especially revealing because it was so often mechanical—effort of so many American writers to seek out the reality of America in times of crisis, is an authentic and curiously unconscious characterization of a tragic period. Here, in the vast granary of facts on life in America put away by the WPA writers, the documentary reporters, the folklorists preparing an American mythology, the explorers who went hunting through darkest America with notebook and camera, the new army of biographers and historians—here, stocked away like a reserve against bad times, is the raw stuff of that contemporary mass record which so many imaginative spirits tried to depict and failed to master. What we study here is all too often only a sub-literature, significantly a preparation for literature—evidence of a nostalgia too easily content with the trappings of sentimental autobiography and romance; evidence of a need to retreat into the solid comfort of descriptive facts, of a social awareness that found its appropriate expression in photographic details and sociological captions. Yet in that signal literature of empiricism which embodies the failure of so many to discriminate between the need for the past and the comforting surface of that past, is the record of what most deeply interested the contemporary imagination.

Here, in this body of writing, is evidence of how deeply felt was the urge born of the crisis to recover America *as an idea*—and perhaps only thus to build a better society in the shell of the old; only thus to prepare a literature worthy of it. Out of the decade of unrelieved crisis and failure, of fumbling recovery and tension and war; out of the panic and extremism of so many of its finest talents; out of the desire to assess what could be known and to establish a needed security in the American inheritance, came the realization of how little, for all its now world-famous triumphs, American writing had served the people and how little it had come to grips with the subject that lay closest at hand—itself.

There is a profound significance in the fact that this need to search out the land, to compile records, to explain America to itself, found its most abundant expression in a literature of formal social exploration and descriptive journalism. The novel, as Allen Tate said just a little contemptuously, may be an impure literary form because it is so much like history; but in a period when society is changing too rapidly and violently for literature even to command the necessary detachment for imaginative truth, the serious novel will suffer in its effort to dominate what is not yet really known. In times of crisis people prefer to take their history straight, and on the run; and the documentary journalist who writes it on the run will give them history in terms which they are prepared to understand. If we ask why so many documentary journalists did more with their material than the social novelists who seemed to be working with the same material, the fact seems inescapable that because of the very nature of the crisis and the explosive strains it imposed, too many contemporary imaginations were simply not equal to it. Nothing proves that so well, perhaps, as the readiness of so many novelists today to desert the novel altogether, or the palpable fact that so many writers enjoyed a greater certainty and ease when they no longer felt it necessary to impose an imaginative unity upon their work.

The decline of the novel all through the period, a moral and physical decline, tells its own story in this respect. In so curious and difficult a revolutionary period as our own, so peculiarly hazardous a period, no one needs to be told how difficult it is for the imaginative spirit to command a necessary poise. Yet while the preponderance of descriptive non-fiction can be attributed partly to those who can appreciate reality only in terms of public events, there is an advantage the typical social reporter of the period enjoyed that explains why, as it happens, he often did succeed brilliantly within his sphere. For there is a sense in which the reality of our time has been composed of public events—a series of shattering shocks and tremors that has pounded away mercilessly at the mind. In such a period, marked by so pervasive and unexampled a sense of insecurity, the social reporter did not have to affect certainty; he was only a spectator of the passing show, a taker of notes. And because of the very nature of those repeated shocks, the moral and intellectual climate of the time *seemed* to call for nothing more than so passive (at most passively indignant) and even sardonic a spirit as the documentary literature of the thirties provided.

Like the effect Henry James sought in "The Princess Casamassima," the reporting mind that opened the way for this new nationalism might be described as one "of our not knowing, of society's not knowing, but only guessing and suspecting and trying to ignore what goes on irreconcilably, subversively, beneath the vast smug surface." The surface was now anything but smug, and, far from trying to ignore what went on beneath it, the world of contemporary opinion was haunted by its subterranean revolution. Yet that conviction of "our not knowing, of society's not knowing," was the field in which the documentary reporter and traveler now operated with ease and a certain serene humility that in that "not knowing" lay his usefulness as an observer and his ability to satisfy his readers on the same level. In that "not knowing, of society's not knowing," indeed, was the test of his participation in the great contemporary experience, for society, which knew only that it did not know, would respond to and believe in only those writers who pressed it on—not too hard, certainly—to grasp the first facts about itself.

What the documentary literature provided was a register of the learning process, an example of a new social consciousness in America whose greatest distinction was the *fact* of that consciousness in itself, the sense of a grim and steady awareness rather than of great comprehension. In this respect none of the devices the documentary and travel reporters used is so significant as their reliance upon the camera. Ever since the daguerreotype had come into American life, writers had been affected by the photographic standard; but now they became curiously abject before it. Nothing in this new literature, indeed, stands out so clearly as its attempt to use and even to imitate the camera. In a whole succession of books—Erskine Caldwell's and Margaret Bourke-White's "You Have Seen Their Faces" and "Say, Is This the USA"; Dorothea Lange's and Paul S. Taylor's "An American Exodus"; Archibald MacLeish's "Land of the Free" (pictures by courtesy of the Farm Security Administration); James Agee's and Walker Evans' "Let Us Now Praise Famous Men," the new genre developed by Pare Lorenz in "The River," etc.—the words and pictures were not only mutually indispensable, a kind of commentary upon each other, but curiously interchangeable.

Even the non-illustrated books of social "reportage," like Edmund Wilson's "The American Jitters" and "Travels in Two Democracies," James Rorty's "Where Life Is Better," Nathan Asch's "The Road: In Seach of America," Louis Adamic's "My America," showed that their authors were always seeking to *catch* reality on the run, as it were; to identify the object seen by etching it on the mind; to give it a kind of wry objective irony or bitterness. Indeed, the technical and psychological fascination of the camera may be considered even to have given a new character to contemporary prose, a transformation which can be appreciated only in terms of its moral example, since it was the camera's essential passiveness that made for its technical influence over so many writers.

As a few great Americans have proved so well, the camera can be an extraordinary medium for the sensitive imagination; but in the crisis-begotten literature of the documentary school it served to give the general appearance of what Lincoln Kirstein described as the function of the candid camera in our time, to make up "in quantitative shock what it lacks in real testimony. . . . Its only inherent characteristic is the accidental shock that obliterates the essential nature of the event it pretends to discover." The photographs in most of the documentary books were anything but candid-camera shots, of course. Few artists today have created anything so rich and meaningful as the photographs Walker Evans contributed to "Let Us Now Praise Famous Men" and his own volume of "American Photographs," and the photographs in the documentary books by photographers like Ben Shahn, Dorothea Lange, Carl Mydans and others were often of extraordinary merit. But the extent to which the camera *as an idea* affected documentary and travel reporters and served them as a prime symbol of a certain enforced simplicity and passivity of mind, is still little appreciated.

In the vast flood of social reports there were naturally a good many books which merely exploited the camera technique on its lowest level, books as superficial as the average weekly picture-magazine or as loud as a tabloid headline. But while there were necessarily a good many books of this order, books which merely pandered to public excitement, the real significance of the literary use of the camera is that many serious writers were so affected by its use—or symbolism—that they seemed interested only in photographing the country on the run, in giving to the accumulated weight of a thousand different details and impressions of the national texture the solid testimony of their "education." In this respect the camera served to give documentary prose a hard, wry, noncommital character—a character entirely appropriate to its obsession with the surface drama of the times, its stabbed and stablike consciousness, its professed contempt for "illusion." What the fascination of the camera represented, in a word, was a kind of sick pride in its fiercely objective "realism." The camera did not fake or gloss over; it told "the truth of the times"; it was at once so aggressive and uncertain that it highlighted an awakened, ironic, militant, yet fundamentally baffled self-consciousness. Most important, the camera reproduced endless *fractions* of reality. In itself so significant a medium of tension, it fastened upon the atmosphere of tension. And if the accumulation of visual scenes seemed only a collection of "mutually repellent particles," as Emerson said of his sentences, was not that discontinuity, that havoc of pictorial sensations, just the truth of what the documentary mind saw before it in the crisis period?

Revealing in a land so rich in descriptive facts, content with a kind of fever brilliance or anger or wit in the presence of so stupendous and humiliating a disorder as the depression scene provided, the documentary-travel reporter thus had his happiness. America lay all before him, his to choose; and how much there was to see and how little to annotate! The sharecropper, for example, fascinated the writer out to see the country, since he embodied so visual a conception of all that had to be recognized and redeemed in America. He provided an occasion for catharsis; he was a special contemporary phenomenon that fixed the general sense of outrage and quickened the sensibility of fellowship. Yet one had only to look at him (Margaret Bourke-White having taken his picture, imprisoning his agony for all history to gape at) to know how little there was to say. One had only to look at his South to believe that what one saw was the American drama of this day and age, all the pressures of the time brought together at the point of maximum curiosity and rage. Yet having looked, what was there to say that the Farm Security Administration did not have down in its files, the sociologist in his statistics? Here was America, all of it undoubtedly America—but America in a gallery of photographs, an echo of the people's talk, a storehouse of vivid single impressions.

Here was America—the cars on the unending white ribbon of road; the workers in the mills; the faces of farmers' wives and their children in the roadside camp, a thousand miles from nowhere; the farmer's wife with her child sitting on the steps of the old plantation mansion, where the columns were gray and crumbling with age. Here was the child in the grimy bed, the Okies crossing the desert in their jalopies, the pallor of August in the Dust Bowl, the Baptist service in the old Negro church. Here was the greatest creative irony the reportorial mind of the crisis period could establish—a picture of Negro farmers wandering the road, eating their bread under a billboard poster furnished by the National Association of Manufacturers—"America Enjoys the Highest Standard of Living in the World." Here was the migrant family sleeping on sacks in the roadside grass, above them the railroad legend: "Travel While You Sleep." Here was the Negro sitting in the fields near Memphis (more men than jobs at the Bridgehead Labor Market), saying: "They come off the plantations 'cause they ain't got nothin' to do. . . . They come to town and they *still* got nothin' to do." Here was the treeless landscape in southwestern Oklahoma, a country strewn with deserted and crumbling houses, the farmers driven off by the tractors, a picture of land where the tractors now kneaded the earth right "to the very door of the houses of those whom they replace."

Here, indeed, was an America that could only be quoted and photographed, described in pictures or in words that sought to be pictures. "America today is the scene of a mighty drama," Erskine Caldwell wrote in "Say, Is This the USA," "the like of which we have never before experienced." There was no audience; everyone was on the stage playing his part. And if there were doubts as to what the play meant, "in the meantime there is action on top of action, there is action galore. . . . All these people, all this abundance, all these things, is this America we live in; but none of us knows what to do about it. This is us, this is what we have; but nobody knows what to do next." Like Thomas Wolfe, who was reduced to making lists of all those things and scenes in the world he tried vainly to bind together, the documentary reporter, precisely because he was unable or unwilling to bind anything together, was driven to make lists of single impressions, lists of objects and names, above all lists of all those people scattered in the lava flow of the thirties who had stories to tell. America was everywhere, *in* everything; America was people everywhere; people on farms and on relief; people on the road, farmers in town standing before store-windows; the girl on the bus who was going from town to town looking for work; the anonymous sharecropper who told his woes and said sharply, "These things are a pressin' on us in the state of Mississippi"; the migrant farmer in California who said of Oklahoma: "No, I didn't *sell* out back there. I *give* out"; the Negro boy Erskine Caldwell met who built coffins underground because he had served three years on a chain gang in Georgia for owing a white man $11, and had said he would let daylight burn itself out—*he* would never look at it—before he would get caught in such a jam again.

Yes, America lay all before the documentary reporter, his to choose; and what did it matter if the America he saw was often only the America he came prepared to see? He made up his pattern and the country—so rich in patterns for different minds—always lived up to it. Sherwood Anderson, who early in the thirties published a book appropriately entitled "Puzzled America," had one pattern. Theodore Dreiser, who published another on "Tragic America," had his pattern, the Dreiser pattern, always tragic. In "The 'Argonauts,'" a book by five leftist college students who went out to see the country "for themselves"—the rootlessness of young people without jobs had long since made a virtue out of necessity—one saw an America that consisted rather exclusively of CIO organizers, chain-gangs, sharecroppers, ugly native fascists, leftist movie stars. In Edmund Wilson's early book of this type—"The American Jitters," published in the worst year of the depression—all the savagery and inchoate bitterness of 1932 went into coruscating snapshots of police fighting hunger-marchers, Tammany Hall, the Fish Committee investigating the Red Menace, suicides in Brooklyn, and the unhappy depositors of the Bank of United States. In his "Travels in Two Democracies" all the nervous brilliance so latent in the travelogue report went into a portrait of extraordinary density, yet one in which everything in America from Hull House to Radio City looked as if it had been photographed on Inauguration Day, 1933, with all the banks closed and the country running a fever.

From Portland to Portland, from Detroit to the Gulf, from New York to Hollywood, there were patterns for all. In Louis Adamic's "My America," a sprawling book of impressions by a writer whose immigrant past had given him an outsider's curiosity and a vibrant democratic fraternalism, America appeared as a strange but promising land that was essentially "a process—long and endless." Nathan Asch's highly introspective "The Road" bore no relation to the cautious, unpanicky middle-class Indiana of the Lynds' "Middletown in Transition"; Benjamin Appel's studiously leftist "The People Talk" was not the same America that Rollo Brown found in "I Travel by Train"; but it was all America nevertheless. In "Where Life Is Better: An Unsentimental American Journey" (the main title was ironic), James Rorty described an America built on fear and ignorance and hatred, an America "building stockades of fascism with which to protect what was left of its grandiose acquisitive dream." He saw an America, all retching ugliness and class conflict, that moved him to cry in despair: "What profound failure of American life did this drift of human atoms signify and embody, and to what would it lead? The people had not possessed the landscape, nor had the landscape possessed them. The balance was indeed broken." Yet though what he saw seemed only "some profound profanation of the human spirit," in the end he was moved to confess that he did not know what America was. "I suspect that no one knows. Certainly I am in no position to make any categorical pronouncements. . . ."

No. No one knew. The girl in the bus, groping her way in the darkness from job to job; the boy on the road waiting for a lift; the salesman in the store, his baffled eyes belying his professional smile; the hotel clerk who said of the titled refugees from fascism: "I used to think America would always stay the same, but now with all kinds of people coming here it's bound to change." What were they trying to say that only all America could say for them? Did they know? Did anyone know, when the pictures said so much, when one's whole experience on the road was a succession of pictures on the mind?

Exile's Return

After their years in Europe, the exiles of the arts came lingering homewards, came straggling half hopefully, half regretfully from their long vacations in Paris, Rome, Normandy or the Tyrol, at Oxford or on the Riviera. They had gone abroad at a moment of crisis and monetary disorganization when, living cheaply on American currency, they lived like noblemen; at a moment, too, when it seemed that America had qualities of freshness, confidence and vigor to offer the intellectual world of Europe. The humility of earlier exiles like Henry James, the air of patronage toward American letters adopted by Ezra Pound, were attitudes they did not understand. Taking things for granted, they were themselves taken for granted by Europeans of their own professions. They enjoyed themselves, acquired new theories of writing or painting, and wrote enthusiastic letters to their friends, who followed them abroad.

For some years after the War, it seemed that Paris was about to become the intellectual capital of the United States, but those years passed quickly. The exiles, most of them, had no intention of becoming expatriates. Financially they depended on America for the incomes that kept them temporarily in Europe. Intellectually, too, they depended on American life for their subject matter; sooner or later they had to revisit their sources. And so, their minds well stored, their pockets empty, they came sailing in second or third-class cabins, even steerage, toward the city where their future lay.

Their return, the ambitions they carried with them, the defeat of these ambitions, their slow readjustment—all this chapter of literary history is the subject of the five articles that follow.* Having my choice of treatment, I shall write in the first person; after all, I was one of the returning exiles. And I shall describe my own experiences, partly because they seem interesting in themselves, partly because they suggest the adventures of other writers, young men and women of my own age lately returned from their apprentice years abroad. The problems we faced must still be faced by our successors: I hope they arrive at more profitable solutions.

Early in August, 1923, just before my twenty-fifth birthday, I landed in New York, after a sultry night in the Lower Bay, spent drinking the last of the prunelle which Ramon Guthrie had carried with him from his brother-in-law's farm in Lorraine. Nobody met us at the dock; I didn't know even where to send our trunks, and was much too poor to stay at a hotel. While the customs man was hastily glancing through our baggage—it hadn't the look of containing anything subject to duty—I made several telephone calls, as a result of which our problems

*Only the first is reprinted here—Editor's Note.

were solved for the moment. Our two trunks would go to the house of a friend far downtown, almost in the shadow of the Woolworth Building. We ourselves would spend the morning at the apartment of Matthew Josephson, then editor of Broom. We took a taxicab down Fourteenth Street, passing a row of wholesale meat markets, in front of which a few newspapers fluttered in the weak breeze, passing the Elevated station at Ninth Avenue, with its look of being a Chinese pagoda, passing two rows of high brownstone houses, and the Convent of Our Lady of Guadaupe, marked only by a cross, and the Fourteenth Street Armory, and turning south on Sixth Avenue under the El pillars. everything was strange to me: the enervating heat first of all, and the colors of the houses, and the straight vistas, and the girls on the streets in their bright dresses, and the lack of anything green to break the monotony of the square streets, the brick, concrete and iron. The next year—the next three years, in fact—would be spent in readjusting myself to this once familiar environment.

Looking back at the early autumn of my return, I cannot help feeling that most of my decisions, though made for the highest moral reasons, were ill suited to the circumstances and costly in their results. I had, for example, the choice that must be made by almost all apprentice writers, between free-lance authorship and working in an office. In the first case, I should be living by my own profession, yet everything I wrote would inevitably be molded by the need for carrying it to market. In the second case, four-fifths of my time would be wasted, yet the remaining fifth could be devoted to writing for its own sake, to the disinterested practice of the art of letters. This was my justification for taking a job—this and the fact that a job was offered me. Not until two years later did I realize that when one's writing ceases to have a functional relationship to one's life, when it becomes a way of spending otherwise idle evenings, it loses part of its substance. At best it has an unreality which can usually be recognized, an after-hours atmosphere of rhetoric, fantasy and gesture to be explained by the situation which produced it: the writer is seeking compensation for the qualities missing in his business career. More often there are no idle evenings; writing disappears from his life, giving way to the unhealthy feeling that he is better than his vocation, by which he is *frustrated*, from which he must violently *escape* to write a novel, a drama, an epic. But the fear persists that the book would be a failure: isn't it better to be paid each Saturday and talk drunkenly each Saturday night about the unwritten novel? . . .

I avoided this mood by falling into a different error, one almost as fatal: I assumed too many obligations. My job, for the first month at least, meant working nine or ten hours a day under pressure; but this was only the beginning of my duties. In addition to being proofreader, copywriter and general utility man for Sweet's Architectural Catalogue, I also became an associate editor of Broom, a position without pay or honor which involved reading manuscripts and proof, writing letters—and articles, too, when I had an hour to spare—pacifying subscribers, insulting contributors and raising money. With my wife I tried to redecorate our flat in Dominick Street, the most battered and primitive lodging to be found in New York. I attended literary teas that lasted all night. I composed an open letter to the Postmaster General and another to the editor of The Dial, both very insolent in tone. I engaged in more literary controversies than I can now remember. I wrote book reviews for Dr. Canby and poems for nobody in particular. I intrigued for a higher salary. Meanwhile, with Josephson, Guthrie and a few others, I tried to reproduce in New York the conditions which had seemed so congenial to us abroad—while praising in the same breath the picturesque American qualities of the machine age and the New Economic Era.

Reading the letters I wrote that year, and the entries in my notebook, I feel that everything I learned in France, the whole course of my thinking, had prepared me for an uncomfortable season of readjustment. On the fifth of July, in my last letter from Normandy, I told Kenneth Burke: "The famous two years are ending with little accomplished and much learned. Yet it seems to me that their great value was not so much the knowledge of books and writing they helped me to acquire as the aid they gave me in reaching a personal philosophy." I was using a big word. My philosophy was really an attitude, or at best a collection of beliefs, some personal, some borrowed, some definitely proclaimed, some almost unconscious, and all of them together forming a dubious basis for my actions during the months that followed.

I believed, first of all, that the only respectable ambition for a man of letters was to be a man of letters—not exclusively a novelist, an essayist, a dramatist, but rather one who adopts the whole of literature as his province, "who devotes himself to literature," I wrote with fervor, "as one might devote a life to God or the Poor."

I believed that the man of letters, while retaining his particular point of view, which was primarily that of the poet, should concern himself with every department of human activity, including science, sociology and revolution.

I believed that more writers were ruined by early success than by the lack of it, and was therefore willing to make a fool of myself in order to avoid being successful.

I was violently opposed to what I called "the fallacy of contraction." "Writers," I observed in my notebook, often speak of 'saving their energy,' as if each man were given a nickel's worth of it, which he is at liberty to spend—one cent on Love, one cent on Livelihood, two cents on Art or other wasteful activities, and the remainder on a big red apple. . . . To me, the mind of a poet resembles Fortunatus' purse: the more spent, the more it supplies.

"There are many writers who deliberately contract the circle of their interests. They refuse to participate in the public life of their time, or even in the discussion of social questions. They avoid general ideas, are 'bored' by this, 'not concerned' with that. They confine themselves to literary matters—in the end, to literary gossip. And they neglect the work of expanding the human mind to its extremest limits of thought and feeling—which, as I take it, is the aim of literature."

I was grandiloquent in those days; I was also highly moral, but in a fashion acquired from my literary friends in Paris. A writer could steal, murder, drink or be sober, lie to his friends or with their wives: all this, I said, was none of my concern; but my tolerance did not extend to his writing. Here I demanded high courage, absolute integrity, and a sort of intelligence which was in itself a moral quality. Moreover, since art and its subject matter have a curious interaction, I was beginning to extend the same sort of judgments to life itself, praising an artist's career for qualities I admired in books—for being original, arbitrary, surprising, romantic . . .

The last word is revealing. I myself, after a period of admiring classicism, had become in the strictest sense a romantic, one who read and admired the writers of the romantic era from Monk Lewis and Byron to Gérard de Nerval and Pétrus Borel. At the same time I was interested in applying their methods to new material drawn from the age of technology and high-pressure selling. I was determined to be humorless, having developed a furious contempt for "those beaten people who regard their own weakness with a deprecatory smile." And I had catchwords which reappeared in everything I wrote: "disinterestedness," "indiscretion" (I considered it a high virtue), "disdain," "significant" or "arbitrary gestures," "violence," "manifestoes," "courage."

My letters were filled with impractical projects:

"Yesterday, Kenneth," I wrote on June 29, "it struck me with the force of revelation that the time has come for us to write some political manifestoes. We are not critics or short-story writers; we are poets: in other words, we are interested in every form of human activity. To be ticketed and dismissed as such-and-such sort of a writer gives me a pain behind the ears. Also, I am eaten with the desire to do something significant and indiscreet. An Open Letter to President Harding. An Open Letter to the Postmaster General on the Censorship, in which I admit the right to censor, point out how dangerous my opinions are, even in book reviews, and demand why I am not suppressed. And other manifestations: for example, a call to voters to cease voting, an attack on the liberals, an attack on the Socialists and Communists. Imagine all these documents appearing together in a political issue of Broom. What a stink. But the stink would mean something. In a country as hypocritical as the United States, merely to enumerate the number of laws one has broken would be a significant gesture. And if all the literary forces of law and order rose up against us, we could always retire to farming or reading proofs. Think it over. The step is not to be taken tomorrow. And I have the feeling, Kenneth, that some such courageous and indiscreet step is required of us, if we are not going to resign ourselves to petty literary wars with Ezra Pound, Robert McAlmon, even Floyd Dell."

And so I was planning to carry literary ideals into the political world; I was contemplating a crusade and was prepared to be one of the leaders. But I was also a disciple: for the first and last time in my life I admitted to having a master.

"I have been intending to write you a letter about Louis Aragon," I said on June 4, "for his is a character which demands a long explanation. . . . Imagine this elegant young man, from a family whose social position is above reproach: a young man so gifted that the word 'genius' must have been applied to him ever since he was four years old and wrote his first novel. A brilliant career stretches in front of him. He has read everything and mastered it. Suddenly, at a given age, he rejects his family and social connections and, with a splendid disdain acquired from his early successes, begins to tell everybody exactly what he thinks. And he continues to be successful. He has so much charm, when he wishes to use it, that it takes him years to make an enemy; but by force of repeated insults he succeeds in this aim also. He retains all that hatred of compromise which is the attribute of youth—and of a type of youth we never wholly possessed. He disapproves of La Nouvelle Revue Française; therefore he refuses to write for it, although all other channels of publication are closed to him already.

"He lives literature. If I told him that a certain poem of Baudelaire's was badly written, he would be capable of slapping my face. He judges a writer largely by his moral qualities, such as courage, vigor of feeling, the refusal to compromise. He proclaims himself a romantic. In practice this means that his attitude toward women is abominable: he is either reciting poetry, which soon ceases to interest them, or trying to sleep with them, which becomes equally monotonous. He is always seriously in love; he never philanders. Often he is a terrible bore. He is an egoist and vain, but faithful to his friends. . . . I have met other people whose work is interesting, but Aragon is the only one to impose himself by force of character. I ought to add that he has a doglike affection for André Breton.

"My apologies for this long digression, but I think it will explain a good deal . . . for I admit that Aragon has had a great influence on me, which I have tried to keep in the moral sphere." I meant specifically that I was trying to keep him out of my poems. In this attempt I was partially unsuccessful, for his influence was stronger than I recognized at the time—stronger because the ideals he imposed on me were not merely his own, but those of a literary school, which had set itself the task of acting as the conscience of a generation of French writers.

The source of its standards lay, I think, in Rimbaud, but not so much in his works as in his life. At the age of nineteen, after producing some of the most interesting and, from the standpoint of literary history, the most fruitful poems in the French language, he had forsaken writing for adventure. This defection never ceased to worry his admirers—and what young French writer was not his admirer in the years that followed the War? How could they justify themselves for continuing to be men of letters when Rimbaud, with all his genius, had preferred a career of action? An obvious answer was to combine the two elements, by making literature an active and adventurous career, by exploring the possibilities of words and images as Rimbaud had explored the coasts of the Red Sea. . . . Such was the general attitude which, through Breton and Aragon, had reached me at third hand.

Breton and Aragon were rebels by conviction: they had been leaders of the Dadaists, whose movement was dribbling away in quarrels; they were about to become the founders of Super-realism. Their attitude toward the career of letters was too extreme to be popular among French writers, but it was understood and even respected. I was then convinced of its truth; even today I feel that it was a valid reaction to the situation existing in France. It produced exciting careers, and helped to produce many interesting works of art. The question was whether it would bear transplanting to another country.

Gertrude Stein Comes Home

The first glimpse you get of her, as she trudges resolutely up on the lecture platform, is reassuring. This solid elderly woman, dressed in no-nonsense rough-spun clothes, seems at once smaller and more human than her monumental photographs or J. Davidson's squat image of her. As she looks out over the audience and thanks us, with a quick low hoot of laughter, for "controlling yourselves to 500," we laugh too, in appreciative relief, and settle back in our seats to give her the once-over. This Gertrude Stein woman may not be so crazy, after all. Some of our wariness eases off. She has made a good beginning, there's no denying that.

But why are we here? Well, there are two answers to that question. Miss Stein knows one; we know the other. She knows we have come because we are interested—not so much in her as in her writing. We know better. We are here because we are curious—not so much about her writing, which we have never read, and probably never shall, as about herself—an apparently sensible, perhaps really sane woman who has spent most of her life writing absolute balderdash, and then, by gum, a year ago published a book that was perfectly plain sailing, and got her on the best-seller lists. We want to see what this creature looks like, we want to hear what she has to say for herself.

Now that we can get a good look at her face, that too is reassuring. The photographs we have seen didn't show those deep black eyes that make her graven face and its archaic smile come alive. Her short-cropped hair doesn't look queer, it looks as right as a cap on a grandmother. And though this is her first visit home in thirty-one years, her voice is as unmistakably American—she says "Amorrican"—as any of ours. As we listen to her low-pitched, harshly pleasant sound, we realize, with further grateful relief, that we were afraid she might have added, on top of her swami-like incomprehensibility, some of the affected patter of the expatriate. But no, we can see right away that she is too stubborn to have done anything like that. Foreign parts of speech have not affected her at all: she talks in as flatly sensible an American tone as any Middle Western aunt. We also notice with approval that she indulges in no gestures—except the natural, grandmotherly one of taking her pince-nez off and putting them on; and we soon discover, with mixed feelings, that she is not a very good lecturer: she drops her voice at the end of every sentence, and talks more and more to one side of the room, so that a good third of us have to cup our ears and guess at the words we miss.

She is talking about herself, trying to explain what she has been up to all this time, and how she happens to write the way she does. It all sounds very sensible at first. She writes, she says, just the way she talks, and she tries to prove it by reading progressive examples from her books. But immediately, with the very first example, we notice a difference. That tonelessness that helps to lend an idiotic quality to her writing is emphatically absent from her reading. She reads, indeed, with an exaggerated emphasis, putting back all the italics and commas and dashes she has carefully not written. The passages she reads make startlingly good sense. A great light begins to break over us: by knowing what to accent, where to pause, we too might dig some meaning out of Gertrude Stein. It isn't true, then, that all that work of hers is just a lumberyard; there *is* a nigger in the woodpile, after all. A few of us make a mental note to try reading "Tender Buttons," say, aloud—in the strictest privacy. Something might come of it.

Quite soon she says something funny. We laugh, not very loudly, and then look aghast. Was it meant to be funny? But Miss Stein doesn't seem to mind, she is even smiling herself. What a relief! We undo another tender mental button, and laugh whenever we feel like it. Towards the end of the lecture a few of us are shaking hysterically, and at the least excuse. But she doesn't seem to notice, and most of us are still sitting solemnly enough. After the lecture she is surrounded by an apparently reverent semicircle of undergraduates, who want to know still further. Her face a little flushed now from so much talking, she answers their questions with dogmatic directness. Yes, she considers herself a genius. No, self-expression has nothing to do with it. No, it is not her job to make people understand what she writes. Yes, she feels just like everybody else; she has often said to Picasso, who is also a genius: "Do you feel any different from anybody else?" and no, neither does he.

The total impression we carry away is that of a fundamentally serious, not to say megalomaniac writer—are all really serious people megalomaniacs?—who has come back home for a visit in the happy consciousness that she has triumphed at last. Her own country, after thirty years of neglect, is delighting to honor her. Later, when you hear her in a fifteen-minute "interview" on the radio, that impression is further confirmed. Miss Stein is having a swell time, wish young Miss Stein could be here too. She loves the tall buildings, the people on the street, she had a grand time at the football game, America is certainly a wonderful country. Miss Stein is decidedly bullish on America; her enthusiasm is delightful—a delighted visitor's enthusiasm. And she really seems to believe that we have hailed her as a genius, not welcomed her as a freak. She tells her "readers" not to worry so much about understanding her. If you enjoy a thing you understand it, she says; and she wouldn't be read if she weren't enjoyed; therefore her readers understand her. Unfortunately this pretty piece of logic blinks the fact that practically nobody does read her. Some of us may have sat through "Four Saints in Three Acts" (we went either to have a good laugh or to feel snobbish), or we have read what the newspapers have to say about her, or perhaps "The Autobiography of Alice B. Toklas," or we have taken one horrified or amused dip into one of her serious books—but if we did we hardly stayed in a minute; the water was too cold and there were too many queer fish around.

There is certainly some grudging admiration in our welcome to Gertrude

Stein—even Republicans thought more of Upton Sinclair after the scare he gave them in California. We are Greek enough to reverence (or fear) as well as gibe at what we do not understand. Our intolerant, cocksure skepticism always wavers in the face of quiet certainty. But Miss Stein has been away a long time. She thinks we are polite. She is wrong: we are simply timid, unsure of our ground, unsure of hers as well. There are a lot of things in the world we don't know anything about, and she may be one of them. This incommunicable meaning of hers may even be important. Why not?—especially if the meanings we have been able to communicate with have one by one proved unimportant, meaningless or false. And so we totter reverently from her presence, and explode with laughter just outside the door. That doesn't mean, of course, that our reverence is any more fake than our laughter.

What Miss Stein does not seem to have gathered is that our altars to the Unknown God—and they are many—are at the same time sideshows, with the barker-priests always drumming up trade. If she really thinks, as she seems to, that the guarantee of her genius is the popular notice she is receiving here, she would do well to let another thirty years elapse before she tries it again. By that time she may have learned that newsboys don't care what they're shouting about so long as they sell their papers.

GILBERT HARRISON   MARCH 18, 1967

Alice B. Toklas

Alice Toklas had almost reached 90. We had a joke. Last spring on her 89th birthday in Paris, I promised to return with my wife, for a celebration of her 90th on April 30. She said she might not last that long. I said I expected people to keep dates they made. She was by then no longer able to walk. A few years earlier she had become almost totally blind. An operation restored enough sight for her to read with great effort. You entered the room and she would be sitting by the window, holding a large magnifying glass above the page. I had just come from an exhibition of Picasso's recent paintings and I told her I didn't think she needed to see them because they weren't that good. "*You* may not like them," she said, "but you cannot say that *I* would not like them. I'll see them for myself." She was a strong-minded woman. A few years ago, she said to Joe Barry, tapping her head, "*This* will be the last to go."

She thought old age was an indignity, and she didn't know why the Lord let her live so long after Gertrude Stein's death at the end of World War II. To those who saw her in those worst, saddest months, she seemed a shadow; she spoke of herself as "nothing but the memory" of Miss Stein. But she had always been more than that, and the next 20 years were proof. Her own character gathered itself around not only keeping alive the name and work of Gertrude Stein (all the unpublished writings got into print through her persistence), but also around her gardening, dog walking, cooking, and the writing of memoirs, a cookbook and endless letters on any stationery that happened to be at hand. ("This paper is somewhat used, as an American once said of the renaissance furniture his wife was buying.") And from 1947 on, there were the frequent though not constant calls by friends, acquaintances and curio hunters on all of whom her acute judgment was visited. Some were "undesirables whom I once was fond of who now want sympathy, advice or just the address of a good hotel in Istanbul, or the address of a schoolmate, or an autograph of Gertrude's youth." There were others, such as Thornton Wilder, who "called to take me to supper with such gaiety, such Wilder cheer . . . and then breathless but not speechless (that's Wilder too isn't it) proceeded like a magician to produce from a valise more than a valise ever held before, real Kentucky whiskey, tins of lobster, nylon stockings." Here she was writing to Isabel Wilder, to whom she promised that "when Thornton comes back, we'll open [the whiskey] and I'm going to taste it too and then it will be corked and put away in the furthest dark corner of a little hideaway shelf and when you are merry we'll have a nip. It will be a wild moment, won't it." She was 74.

She had come to Paris in 1907, in her middle twenties, had met Miss Stein and been captivated. She later recalled that "Gertrude laughed her wonderful and what she called her distralto laugh. It was the first thing I heard from her that afternoon that I arrived in Paris 40 years ago next September. It came from under her coral brooch—and it was coral color, like the brooch." They were established in the rue de Fleurus, Alice managing, Gertrude writing, for nearly 25 years, after which they moved to 5 rue Christine. There Miss Toklas stayed for most of the two decades of her life alone, caring for the furniture and the pictures and the white poodle they had had together. Then the pictures were taken away by court action brought by the heirs of Gertrude Stein's eldest brother, who, under Miss Stein's will, were to have the paintings after Alice Toklas' death. The court said, in effect, that she couldn't be trusted with those early canvases of Picasso, Matisse, Juan Gris. The rue Christine apartment was finally taken away too. The house had been sold, and the new owner had another tenant in mind. Friends tried to prevent the eviction, without success. It was a nightmare. Alice wrote Donald Gallup of the Yale University Libarary that her maid, Madeleine, thought "that if General de Gaulle is not going to save me I had better go to a hotel at once!" A new apartment was found. The walls were so thin that "a neighbor sneezed the other day and I heard it distinctly." Tenants were not permitted to hang pictures, but "I only have one, a Dora Maar, and that is put on the floor against the wall." She was 86.

The one picture she minded not having, had been gone long since. Gertrude Stein left Picasso's portrait of her to the Metropolitan Museum in New York, and on the day it was picked up to go to its new home, Alice and Picasso bid it farewell. "Picasso came early and stayed a long time with me alone," she wrote. "He was very sweet at his very best, and then when he got up to go he said 'Eh bien, neither you nor I will ever see it again.' And he stood alone in front of it quite a few minutes drinking it in as only his eyes can. And then he saluted it quite seriously, quite simply, and he kissed my hand and said 'Au revoir cherie.' After all, the portrait is their youth, its intensity and theirs are all one. And I missed its going so very much."

Gertrude Stein had read anything and everything in English that came her way. Alice was more selective. She settled, finally, for Henry James and Ivy Compton-Burnett, the latter "witty and amusing beyond words." She would quote with relish Ivy Compton-Burnett's complaint "I don't understand why I am not a best seller, don't I write about the scandalous subjects people love to read— adultery, incest, embezzlement?" But the most exciting books, first and last, were cookbooks. Shortly after returning to Paris with Gertrude Stein from their one and only journey back to the United States in the thirties, Alice wrote a Chicago friend to thank her for a cookbook that "has been a consolation and an inspiration in these busy upsetting interrupted days before moving. When things get too black, I peer into it and am immediately lost to everything outside. That's what a real nice cookbook can do for me. And next month when [Gertrude and I] have moved and finally settled in I'll be using it all the time in my lovely new little kitchen."

The move to which she referred was to the rue Christine and the rest of that letter says something about who did what: "We are so busy running and so running about—and Gertrude blows a fuse at least once a day and I completely lose my temper and succeed in getting what we must have from recalcitrant gas companies or gentle but obstinate carpenters. . . . And now I must fly to it, to say they must not do whatever it is they may be doing." She did more for Miss Stein than type manuscripts, answer mail, cook, polish the furniture, needlepoint small chair coverings for which Picasso made the designs, market, bar the door to intruders—but she did all these things too.

Her judgments of people were shrewd, never mean, rarely mild. She was not easily deceived, unless she wished to be, which she did if the errant or unfaithful friend had been *their* friend in glorious days past. The wily lady art dealer who wanted to exhibit the Stein paintings in New York in the fifties and offered to bring Alice Toklas along with them, as part of the show, got nowhere. Of another enterprising lady, Alice wrote: "What an inexhaustible, restless, disturbing outpouring of unemployable energy. Someone has just told me of a friend's having invented a lovely new word, 'underwhelmed.' Poor—is indeed underwhelming." Her standards of housekeeping never permitted unreserved approval of servants. They came and went, as did her comments: "If no word has come to you from me before," she wrote a friend in America "It is because the very naughty *femme de menage* has not turned up since [a week ago]. She has said it is because a dear cousin died, because her daughter returned from the country and had been unprepared to enter a technical school—she will give me a further choice when she finally comes back in three days." Elsewhere, she noted that Poppy Cannon had written an introduction to the recipes in the *Alice B. Toklas Cookbook*, and "Americanized them, so that they may be intelligible to the US, if not to me."

She never lost her passion for America or her strong American accent. She told of going to the American embassy in Paris in 1960, before a visit to Italy. She had forgotten to bring her old passport, "so I had to go over again with it and they said to bring photographs. Then they gave me a fistful of papers to fill out which took all my spare time for three days ("where are your divorced husbands and nieces and their children by previous marriages'), then I got there with the papers filled and the photographs and the old passport and I fell asleep in a chair and a nice young woman led me to her desk and in a very little while a man came and asked me to swear allegiance and fidelity (which I haven't had to do since 1914)." Italy was an escape from the Paris winter, which she hated. The apartments got colder as she aged. She didn't have colds, though, because "the microbes aren't heated enough to breed."

Her letters were full of teasing fun. To someone who apologized for typewriting a letter, Alice replied: "Can it be said with all possible appreciation of the distinction of your handwriting that it is illegible more frequently than not. Does no one say this cruel thing to you. And do you forgive me for doing so. The old Baronne Pierlot covered pages and pages, she was a great letter writer, with a marvelous calligraphy that absolutely no one could decipher. Gertrude once said to her, its beauty and its illegibility are quite independent, one upon the other, which made our old friend cackle but it was too late to be effective."

Occasionally, in the fifties, friends drove her out to the countryside, or to the south of France. She describes a trip to Antibes, "in full sun, windows open to the sea day and night, full moon and sunlight, no mistral, the Picassos of a splendor, Corbusier's chapel like a bathhouse deluxe—helping the effect, almonds, peaches and mimosa blossoms, a lovely long day with Picasso, a day to Provence to revisit old cities and alas to revive old memories. There are moments each day of a light that only the pure in heart deserve, primitive Greek. It is the most overwhelming rare and precious vision we are likely to have in the unholy days we are in." On one of those trips she discovered a cure for insomnia: "One clove garlic cooked for ten minutes in one portion vegetable, any kind, but the garlic should not cook long. In three hours you are asleep."

Iceland was suddenly a possibility. There had been a suggestion, in 1955, that she come and talk. "I'd go like a shot if they will pay my air passage." But why should they, she wondered, "Should I give a *causerie* in drawing rooms on Picasso or onion soup or both? Oh my dear what a lark—off to Iceland! which will be Gulf-stream comfortable all new new new. To slip out some spring morning in a place one doesn't know has always been my idea of pleasurable excitement."

There was a jaunt to La Begie, where there was a "François premier pavilion, an 11th century chapel, large flowers, vegetable gardens, fruit trees and a vast plantation of tobacco, all this surrounded by walls." Nice she found less pleasant: "We are on a hill but without a view, in an inconceivably commonplace landscape. We are surrounded by small villas of retired functionaries, for the first time in my life I am in the midst of *petit bourgeoisie* and not liking it, depressing if I thought of it which I don't. The rue Christine is working class, which I prefer." Still, the cooking was good. "Herbs and spices," she told Carl Van Vechten, had always been her "Stars and Stripes."

I see her listening, amused, hunched in her chair, the cap of still-dark hair, the sandals and wool skirt and jacket and large glittering brooch and matching ring. I see the breakfast tray in the garden of Bilignin in the happy summer of 1937, with Alice's wild strawberry jam and the warm biscuits, and I recall the walk that day past a pond where a white lily floated and Gertrude Stein saying, "Oh reach for it and bring it to Alice and she will love you the rest of your life." An irresistible request.

Alice Toklas could not cut off the past any more than she could a present which reached into the everlasting. She would be with Gertrude Stein again. It had always been the love "whose service is perfect freedom." In 1957, Alice Toklas was converted to Roman Catholicism. She kept that comfort to herself, but she looked forward to "the peopled Heaven—not only God and Jesus, but the angels and the saints."

IRVING HOWE   SEPTEMBER 25, 1961

In Search of a Moral Style

For the generation of American writers that began publishing shortly after the First World War, the crisis of traditional values was no longer a problem in quite the way it had been for writers in the late 19th Century. By now the crisis of values was an accepted fact, and therefore not so much a painful conclusion toward which their novels and poems might reach as a necessary assumption from which their novels and poems had to begin.

Perhaps the most vivid account of this new generation of writers, a generation that was to reach its finest achievement during the mid-twenties, has come from the poet and critic John Peale Bishop. In his essay "The Missing All"—the title is taken from an Emily Dickinson poem that begins "The missing All prevented me/From missing minor things"—Bishop described how the young literary men returning from the war felt they had been cheated not merely of health and time but more important, of truth and honor. They formed "really the first literary generation in America. There had been groups before, but they were not united by a communion of youth, a sense of experience shared and enemies encountered. . . ." They felt themselves to be cut off from the world of all who had come immediately before them, all who spoke with authority. They were not in rebellion against the political order of Western capitalism, but in revulsion from its moral disorder. As Bishop wrote:

The most tragic thing about the war was not that it made so many dead men, but that it destroyed the tragedy of death. Not only did the young suffer in the war, but every abstraction that would have sustained and given dignity to their suffering. The war made the traditional morality inacceptable; it did not annihilate it; it revealed its immediate inadequacy. So that at its end the survivors were left to face, as they could, a world without values.

For writers like Hemingway, Fitzgerald, Cummings and the early Dos Passos there could no longer be any question of clinging to traditional values. But more important, there could not even be a question of trying to find a new set of values; they were beyond such ambitions or delusions, they knew it was their lot to spend their lives in uncertainty, and the problem that troubled them most was how to do this without violating their feelings about courage and dignity. To be sure, the very desire to find an honorable style of survival in a time of moral confusion indicated a certain strength of moral intent, and the hope of preserving courage and dignity while experiencing a crack-up of values implies the continued hold of certain values. Even these, however, become gravely problematic when they are raised to the level of a troubled self-consciousness.

These writers went through just this kind of crisis. Almost by instinct they backed away from large-scale beliefs or ideals; they had had enough of "idealism," and lived in a magnified fear of platitudes. They had given up, if they had ever had it, the hope of achieving a coherent moral perspective; they were concerned with something more desperate, more fragmentary, more immediate. They were struggling to survive, as men of sensibility who had lost their way and knew it. The best of these writers were in search of what I propose to call a *moral style*. I mean by this improvised phrase: a series of tentative embodiments in conduct of a moral outlook they could not bring to full statement; or a series of gestures and rituals that would be made to serve as a substitute for a moral outlook that could no longer be summoned; or a fragmentary code of behavior by which to survive decently, as if there were—the drama consisting in the fact that there is not—a secure morality behind it. The search for a moral style, which I take to be fundamental to the best American writing between the First World War and the depression years, is a search undertaken by men who have learned that a life constricted to the standard of *faute de mieux* can still be a rigorous, even an exalting obligation. Or to put it in more homely terms, the idea of moral style is a 20th Century equivalent of the New England notion of "making do." How one "makes do," whether with grace or falsity, courage or evasion, is the great problem.

The great problem, above all, is in the work of the most influential American novelist of our time, Ernest Hemingway. Who, by now, is not familiar with the shape and colors of Hemingway's world? His recurrent figures are literary expatriates in the wastes of *nada*, bullfighters who have lost their nerve and skill, rich young men without purpose, wounded soldiers who would sign "a separate peace" in order to withdraw from the world's battles, distraught young women grasping at physical sensation as if it were a mode of salvation, tired gangsters, homeless cafe-sitters, stricken Spaniards: men and women always on the margin, barely able to get by from day to day. There emerges from this gallery of figures the characteristic hero of the Hemingway world: the hero who is wounded but bears his wound in silence, who is sensitive but scorns to devalue his feelings into words, who is defeated but finds a remnant of dignity in an honest confrontation of defeat. In almost all of Hemingway's books there is a tacit assumption that the deracination of our life is so extreme, everyone must find a psychic shelter of his own, a place in which to make a last stand.

But note: to make a last stand—for if defeat is accepted in Hemingway's world, humiliation and rout are not. His fictions present moments of violence, crisis and death, yet these become occasions for a stubborn, quixotic resistance through which the human capacity for satisfying its self-defined obligations is both asserted and tested. "Grace under pressure": this becomes the ideal stance, the hoped-for moral style, of Hemingway's characters. Or as he put it in describing Romero's bullfighting style in *The Sun Also Rises*: "the holding of his purity of line through the maximum of exposure."

It may be true, as Edmund Wilson claims, that Hemingway showed a taste for scenes of killing, but at his best he wished to squeeze from them some precarious assertion—or perhaps more accurately, some credible facsimile—of value. The Hemingway hero turns to his code, a mixture of stylized repression and inarticulate decencies, so that manners become the outer sign of an inexpressible heroism and gestures the substance of a surviving impulse to moral good. And what is this code? The determination to be faithful to one's own experience, not to fake emotions or to pretend to sentiments that are not there; the belief that loyalty to one's few friends matters more than the claims and dogmas of the world; the insistence upon avoiding self-pity and public displays; the assumption that the most precious feelings cannot be articulated and that if the attempt is made they turn "rotten"; the desire to salvage from the collapse of social life a version of stoicism that can make suffering bearable; the hope that in direct physical sensation, the cold water of the creek in which one fishes or the purity of the wine made by Spanish peasants, there will be found an experience that can resist corruption (which is one reason Hemingway approached these sensations with a kind of propitiatory awe, seldom venturing epithets more precise than "fine" and "nice," as if he feared to risk a death through naming). Life now consists in keeping an equilibrium with one's nerves, and that requires a tight control over one's desires, so that finally one learns what one cannot have and then even not to want it, and above all, not to make a fuss while learning. As Jake Barnes says in *The Sun Also Rises*: "I did not care what it was all about. All I wanted was how to live in it."

A code pressing so painfully on the nervous system and so constricted to symbolic gratifications is almost certain to break down—indeed, in his best work Hemingway often shows that it does. After a time, however, his devotion to this code yielded him fewer and fewer psychic returns, since it is in the nature of the quest for a moral style that the very act of approaching or even finding it sets off a series of discoveries as to its radical limitations. As a result the later Hemingway, in his apparent satisfaction with the moral style he had improvised, began to imitate and caricature himself; the manner becomes that of the tight-lipped tough guy, and the once taut and frugal prose turns corpulent.

At first glance, F. Scott Fitzgerald's novels seem closer to the social portraiture of Edith Wharton than to the moral fables of Hemingway. Few American writers have commanded so fine a sense of social gradations, not merely in terms of class relationships but even more in the subtle nuances of status which in our country often replace or disguise class relationships. Fitzgerald is a writer very much of the historical movement, the laureate of the twenties, the *wunderkind* of the jazz age, and his talent, profligacy and tragic personal fate seem symbolic tokens of that historical moment. But in addition to the Fitzgerald who made of his "extreme environmental sense" a foundation of his gift for rendering social manners, there was the Fitzgerald who had been seized and driven by a vision of earthly beatitude which, all through his life, allowed him neither rest nor fulfillment.

Fitzgerald was an eternal adolescent infatuated with the surfaces of material existence. He worshipped money, he worshipped glamor, he worshipped youth, but above all, he worshipped the three together in a totality of false values. Like Keats before the bake shop, he stared with a deep yearning at the blessings of the rich, the ease and security with which they moved through the years, apparently free from the tyranny of work and the burden of circumstances, and thereby enabled to cultivate their own sense of what might be. He thought that in the American dream of money there lay imbedded a possibility of human realization, because money means power and when you have power you can do anything—you can even, as Jay Gatsby supposes, obliterate the past. He felt that youth was the greatest of human possessions, indeed a kind of *accomplishment* for which the young should be praised. His work was a glittering celebration of immaturity, the American fear of aloneness and limitation.

The preceding paragraph condenses the kind of critical attacks to which Fitzgerald was subject during his career: it is true, all of it true, but not the whole truth about his writing.

For the man who composed *The Great Gatsby* and *The Last Tycoon* was a writer who had gone to war against the unexamined convictions of his youth, and at a terrible price in suffering and blood, had triumphed. This writer noted that "all the stories that came into my head had a touch of disaster in them—the lovely young creatures in my novels went to ruin, the diamond mountains of my short stories blew up, my millionaires were as beautiful and damned as Thomas Hardy's peasants." Fitzgerald knew—it was to anchor this knowledge that he put Nick Carraway into *The Great Gatsby* as narrator—that the vitality and ambition of Jay Gatsby were lavished on "a vast, vulgar and meretricious beauty." He knew—it was to release this knowledge that he created the looming figure of Monroe Stahr in *The Last Tycoon*—that "life is essentially a cheat and its conditions are those of defeat, and that the redeeming things are not 'happiness and pleasure' but the deeper satisfactions that come out of struggle." As one of Fitzgerald's critics, Andrews Wanning, has remarked: "his style keeps reminding you . . . of his sense of the enormous beauty of which life, suitably ornamented, is capable; and at the same time of his judgment as to the worthlessness of the ornament and the corruptibility of the beauty."

The preceding paragraph condenses the kind of critical praise with which Fitzgerald was honored in the years after his death; it is true, all of it true, but only if one also remembers how accurate were the attacks against him.

Yet there is more to Fitzgerald than this counterposition of early illusion and later self-discovery. In his best writing—which consists not merely of one or two novels and several stories but also of a succession of extraordinary passages appearing almost anywhere in his books, like sudden flares of beauty and wisdom—Fitzgerald confronted both early illusion and later self-discovery from a certain ironic distance. Supremely American that he was, Fitzgerald tried to preserve something of the sense of human potentiality which had first led him to be enticed by the vulgarity of money and the shallowness of youth. He knew how important, and finally irrelevant, was that depreciation of material values in the name of some moralistic ideal which had become a set attitude in American thought and writing; he sensed that, endlessly rehearsed, this depreciation had actually come to reinforce the power of material values, partly because it could not come to grips with the society that drove men to concern themselves with money and partly because any claim of indifference to such a concern was in America likely to be a mere Sunday pose. As Fitzgerald had worshipped wealth, youth and glamor, they were surely false; as he later turned upon them, his turning was true; but even in his turning he kept some essential part of his earlier worship, and—one is inclined to say—he was right to do so.

Where Hemingway had tried to salvage a code for men at the margin of society, Fitzgerald tried to construct a vision of human possibility at its center. He enjoyed neither doctrinal support in religion nor a buoying social goal nor even a firm awareness of traditional culture that might have helped him sustain and enlarge this vision. Fitzgerald was struggling to achieve something of vast importance for our society, even though he could hardly have named it and we, in turn, can seldom enlarge upon it. He tried to create a moral style out of the sheer urgencies of desire and talent, and finally it came to a search, at the very least, for a mode of gracefulness in outer life and, at the very best, for some token of grace in a world where grace could no longer be provided by anyone but man himself.

William Faulkner, last of the three major American novelists to begin writing in the decade after the First World War, enjoyed a more secure sense of social place and moral tradition than either Hemingway or Fitzgerald. The impact of the fundamentalist Protestantism of the South was still fresh to his imagination, even if more as a discipline than a dogma; the power of a commanding historical myth, the myth of heroic Southern resistance and defeat in the Civil War, was everywhere to be felt in the world of his youth; and the idea of kinship, a deep tacit awareness of the bonds of family and clan, was still a reality in his early experience, as it would later be in the series of novels set in his imaginary Yoknapatawpha County.

In one major respect, however, Faulkner began as a thoroughly "modern" writer, caught up with the same emotions of uprootedness and uncertainties of value which afflicted Hemingway: his early novels *Soldiers' Pay* and *Sartoris* reflect, though not nearly so well as those of Hemingway, the belief of a generation that it is adrift, "lost" in the aftermath of a terrible war. Provincial though the early Faulkner was, he had nevertheless been bruised by troubles of the outer world, and for all his attachment to the Southern homeland he always retained a lively conviction as to the prevasiveness of malaise in modern life. But as a man and writer he had available resources which both Hemingway and Fitzgerald lacked. Where Hemingway turned in his novels and stories to a marginal world he had partly observed and partly imagined, and Fitzgerald tried to impose his vision of human possibility upon such recalcitrant material as the lives of the very rich and very young, Faulkner could still turn back to a living segment of American society—back to the familiar places of the South, the homeland he knew with an intimacy beyond love or hate. Until shortly before he began to write, the South had possessed a compact and homogenous culture, and the exploration of the virtues and guilts of this culture, as well as the testing of its myth, became for him a life-long preoccupation.

Each of Faulkner's novels written during his great creative outburst—from *The Sound and the Fury* in 1929 to *Go Down, Moses* in 1942—represents an increasingly severe and fundamental criticism of the homeland. Not merely of the South alone, to be sure; for when Faulkner composed his despairing estimate of social loss in *The Sound and the Fury* he was also portraying some of the central disabilities of modern civilization. But the foreground subject in the Yoknapatawpha novels is the immediate present and recent past of the South. At every point in these novels Faulkner had available—or wrote as if there were still available—persons, places and principles to which he could look for moral support and standards. He *turned back*, as neither Hemingway nor Fitzgerald could, to the hillsmen, the poor farmers, the Negroes and the children, all of whom seemed to him apart and pure, surviving in the interstices of a decadent society, unable significantly to change its course, yet vital enough to serve him as figures of moral and dramatic contrast.

Now in what is obviously a simplification, one can regard the whole development of Faulkner's Yoknapatawpha saga as a gradual discovery that these figures prove less and less competent as moral guides for the contemporary world. That Faulkner clearly understands as much is suggested by the history of Ratliff, the choric figure in the Snopes trilogy who is so marvellously self-assured in *The Hamlet* but so fumbling in *The Mansion* when he must approach the modern South. Faulkner has been exhausting the psychic and moral resources he had supposed to be present for him in the world of Yoknapatawpha; slowly, he has been emerging to the same needs and bewilderments that other writers now feel. The idea of a return to primitive simplicity retains its strength in Faulkner's book insofar as it is kept by him at a certain distance from the present, or can be recognized as metaphor rather than prescription.

In his later books Faulkner still turns for moral contrast and support to the kinds of characters he had admired in the earlier ones—the back-country saints, the earthy madonnas, the Negroes, the children, the good simple men. But now it is with very little of the old conviction: you need only contrast his use of Nancy in *Requiem for a Nun* with Dilsey in *The Sound and the Fury*. He turns to such figures because he has nowhere else to go, but he turns to them, I would suggest, not with any firm conviction as to their moral power but simply in the hope of imposing on and through them his hopes and standards.

The search for moral style is recurrent in modern writing. It places tremendous burdens upon literature, almost the burden of demanding that literature provide us with norms of value we find impossible to locate in experience. It tends to demand from literature a kind of prophetic gratification which would have seemed decidedly strange to earlier generations of readers. Yet precisely this aspect of the work of such modern figures as Hemingway, Fitzgerald and Faulkner makes them seem so close to us, so very much the spokesmen for our needs and our desires.

A Preface to
Modern Literature

It is my purpose in the present article to attempt to trace the origins of certain
tendencies in contemporary literature. To persons already familiar with the
field, my explanations will seem rudimentary; but it seems true, at the present
time, for reasons which I shall suggest, that, in general, and even among literary
people, the sources and fundamental principles of the books which are most
discussed are singularly little understood. It is not usually recognized, for
example, that writers such as W. B. Yeats, James Joyce, T. S. Eliot, Gertrude Stein,
Marcel Proust and Paul Valéry represent the culmination of a perfectly self-
conscious and very important literary movement; and even when we become
aware that these writers have something in common, that some sort of
movement exists, we are likely to be rather vague as to what its distinguishing
features are.

We do however, today, as a rule, have a pretty clear idea of the issues which
were raised by the Romantic Movement of the beginning of the nineteenth
century. We still debate Classicism and Romanticism, and when we attempt to
deal with contemporary literary problems, we often tend to discuss them in those
terms. Yet the movement of which in our own day we are witnessing the mature
development is not merely a degeneration or an elaboration of Romanticism, but
rather a counterpart to it, a second flood of the same tide. And even the metaphor
of a tide is misleading: what we have today is an entirely distinct movement,
which takes place under different conditions and must be discussed in different
terms.

Romanticism, as everyone has heard, was a revolt of the individual. The
"Classicism" against which it was a reaction meant, in the domain of politics and
morals, a preoccupation with society as a whole; and, in art, an ideal of objectivity.
In "Le Misanthrope," in "Bérénice," in "The Way of the World," in "Gulliver's
Travels," the artist is out of the picture: he would consider it artistic bad taste to
identify himself with his hero or to betray agitation. But in "René," in "Rolla," in
"Childe Harold," in "The Prelude," the writer is either his own hero, or
unmistakably identified with his hero, and the personality and emotions of the
writer are presented as the sole matter of importance. Racine, Molière, Congreve
and Swift ask us to be interested in what they have made; but Chateaubriand,
Musset, Byron and Wordsworth ask us to be interested in themselves. And they
ask us to be interested in themselves by virtue of the intrinsic value, and
therefore of the rights, of the individual as against society—that is, against

government, morals, conventions, academy or church. The Romantic is nearly always a rebel.

In this connection, it is illuminating to remember the explanation of the Romantic Movement given by A. N. Whitehead in his "Science and the Modern World." The Romantic Movement, Whitehead says, was really a reaction against scientific ideas, or rather against mechanistic ideas. The seventeenth and eighteenth centuries were the great period in Europe of the development of mathematics and physics; and the principal influences upon the literature of the so-called Classical Age were really Newton and Descartes. The poets, like the astronomers and mathematicians, had come to regard the universe as a machine, obeying logical laws and susceptible of reasonable explanation: God figured merely as the clockmaker who must have made the clock. They applied this conception also to society, which, from the point of view of Louis XIV and of the American Constitution alike, had the character of a planetary system or well adjusted machine; and they examined human nature dispassionately, in the same lucid and reasonable spirit, to discover what principles it exemplified. Thus the theorems of the physicist were matched by the geometrical plays of Racine and the balanced couplets of Pope.

But this conception of a fixed mechanical order came eventually to be felt as a constraint: it excluded too much of life—or rather, the description which it furnished did not seem to fit actual experience. The Romantics were becoming acutely conscious of aspects of human experience which could not be analyzed or explained on the theory of a world run by clockwork. The world was not a machine, after all, but something far more mysterious.

> The atoms of Democritus,
>   And Newton's particles of light
> Are sands upon the Red Sea shore,
>   Where Israel's tents do shine so bright!

asserted Blake, in contemptuous contradiction of the scientific theory of his day. And to Wordsworth, the countryside of his boyhood meant neither agriculture nor neo-classic idylls, but a light never seen on land or sea. When the poet looked into his own soul, he beheld something which did not seem to him reducible to a set of principles of human nature such, for example, as La Rouchefoucauld's "Maxims": he beheld mystery, conflict, confusion. And he either set himself, like Wordsworth and Blake, to affirm the superior truth of this mystery and confusion, as a description of reality, to the mechanical universe of the physicists; or, accepting this mechanical universe, like Byron or Alfred de Vigny, as external to and indifferent to man, he pitted against it, in defiance, his own turbulent and insubordinate nature.

In any case, it is, as in Wordsworth, the individual sensibility, or, as in Byron, the individual will, which has come to preoccupy the poet; and he has invented a new language to render its mystery, its conflict and its confusion. The arena of literature has been transferred from the universe conceived as a machine, or from society conceived as an organization, to the individual soul.

What has really taken place, says Whitehead, is a philosophical revolution. The scientists of the seventeenth century who described the universe as a mechanism had given rise to the assumption that man was something apart from nature, something introduced into the universe from outside and remaining alien to all that he finds. But a romantic poet like Wordsworth has come to feel the error of this assumption: he has perceived that the world is an organism, that nature includes planets and people alike, that what we are and what we see, what we hear, what we feel and what we smell; are inextricably related, that they are all parts of the same entity. So that it is Ruskin, after all, and not the Romantics, who were guilty of a "pathetic fallacy" in supposing that there was no intimate connection between the landscape and their personal emotions. There is no real dualism, says Whitehead, between external lakes and hills, on the one hand, and personal emotions, on the other: they are interdependent and developing together in some fashion of which our classical notions of laws of cause and effect, of dualities of mind and matter, or of body and soul, can give us no true idea. The Romantic poet, then, has begun to describe things as they truly are: and a revolution in the imagery of poetry is in reality a revolution in metaphysics.

Whitehead drops the story at this point; but he has provided the key to what follows. In the middle of the nineteenth century, science made new advances, and mechanistic ideas were brought back into fashion again. But they came this time from a different quarter—not from physics and mathematics, but from biology. It was the effect of the theory of evolution to reduce man from the heroic stature to which the Romantics had tried to raise him, to the semblance of a helpless animal, again very small in the universe and at the mercy of the forces about him. Humanity was the accidental product of heredity and environment and capable of being explained in terms of them. This doctrine in literature was called Naturalism, and it was exemplified by novelists like Zola who believed that composing a novel could be accomplished like a laboratory experiment: you had only to supply your characters with a definite heredity and environment and then watch their automatic reactions; and by literary critics like Taine, who asserted that virtue and vice were as much the products of automatic processes as alkalis and acids, and who attempted to account for masterpieces by studying the geographical and climatic conditions of the countries in which they had been produced.

Not, however, that the movement known as Naturalism arose directly from "The Origin of Species." There had already begun, about the middle of the century, quite independent of the theory of evolution, a reaction against the sentimentality and the looseness of Romanticism in the direction of the objectivity and the severity of Classicism again, and this reaction was already characterized by a kind of scientific observation. This movement is seen most clearly in France. The Parnassian group of poets, who made their first appearance in the fifties—Gautier, Leconte de Lisle, Hérédia—seemed to have taken it for their aim merely to picture historical incidents and natural phenomena as dispassionately, as accurately and in verses as perfect as possible. Leconte de Lisle's elephants crossing the desert may be taken as a classical example: he describes the elephants crossing the desert almost as if he were writing natural history, and he leaves it at that.

It is less easy, in English poetry, to give clear examples of the reaction toward

Naturalism: the English did not, after the Romantic Movement, take. much interest in literary methods till toward the end of the nineteenth century. But this reaction was taking place, none the less, and we can see very clearly in Tennyson, who was also preoccupied with the doctrines of evolution, something of the same exactitude of description combined with something of the same severity of verse—though with less hardness and more grace—that we find in the Parnassians:

> Nor wilt thou snare him in the white ravine,
> Nor find him dropt upon the firths of ice,
> That huddling slant in furrow-cloven fells
> To roll the torrent out of dusky doors:
> But follow; let the torrent dance thee down
> To find him in the valley; let the wild
> Lean-headed eagles yelp alone.

And it it interesting to compare Tennyson, in this connection, with Pope on the rare occasions (though not so rare as people sometimes suppose) when he is describing natural objects:

> The silver eel, in shining volumes roll'd,
> The yellow carp, in scales bedropp'd with gold.

These lines have the technical perfection and the precise observation of Tennyson, but they are heavier and more metallic. And Pope is often, as a matter of fact, very close to the Parnassians.

But the highest developments of Naturalism took place, not in poetry, but in prose. The plays of Ibsen and the novels of Flaubert are the masterpieces of this second period of modern classicism, as Racine and Swift are of the first. Their art has become again scrupulously non-personal and objective, insisting on precision of language and economy of form. Compare the lucidity, the logic and the limited number of characters of such a drama of Ibsen's as "Rosmersholm" with the rigorous conventions of Racine; or compare "Gulliver's Travels" with "Bouvard et Pécuchet" or "L'Education Sentimentale." Yet, though the earlier works resemble the later ones in many obvious ways, they differ from them in this: where a seventeenth-century moralist like La Rochefoucauld would have sought to discover and set forth the universal principles of human behavior, a nineteenth-century writer like Ibsen or Flaubert has begun to study man in his relation to his particular environment and time. But in both cases, the point of view may be described as "scientific," as tending to be mechanistic.

Now Flaubert and Ibsen both had been suckled on Romanticism. Flaubert had begun by writing a Romantic "Saint-Antoine" before he chastened it and cut it down to the more sober one which he published; and Ibsen had written in verse his Faustian "Brand" and "Peer Gynt" before he arrived at his realistic plays in prose. Each, beginning in Romanticism, had evolved for himself a new discipline and developed a new point of view. For "Madame Bovary" is not merely arranged and written differently from a novel by Victor Hugo, but it also constitutes an objective criticism of a case of Romantic personality; and Ibsen was occupied all his life with an objective presentation of the conflict between our duty to our neighbor and our duty—that Romantic duty—to ourself.

But in the later prose plays of Ibsen, the trolls and apparitions of his early dramatic poems have begun to creep back into the bourgeois drawing-rooms: the Naturalist has been finally compelled to break his own mold. All that vaporous, confused and grandiose world of Romanticism had been resolutely ordered and compressed; but the technique and the conceptions to which it has answered have begun again to seem too narrow. The reader begins to feel the strain, and the artist begins to betray it. Huysmans described Leconte de Lisle as "the sonorous hardware man": we remember Wordsworth's strictures on Pope. Literature is rebounding again from the scientific-classical pole to the poetic-romantic one. And the name of this second reaction at the end of the nineteenth century, of this counterpart to Romanticism at the end of the century before, was Symbolism.

Now in attempting to write literary history, one most guard against giving the impression that these movements and counter-movements necessarily occur in a punctual and well-generalled fashion—as if eighteenth-century reason had been cleanly put to rout by nineteenth-century Romanticism, which then proceeded to hold the field till it was laid by the heels by Naturalism, and as if Rimbaud and Mallarmé had then blown up Naturalism with bombs. What really happens, of course, is that one set of methods and ideas is not completely superseded by another; but that, on the contrary, it thrives in its teeth; so that, on the one hand, Flaubert's prose has learned to hear, see and feel with the delicate senses of Romanticism at the same time that Flaubert is disciplining and criticizing the Romantic soul; and so that, on the other hand, certain members of a school will continue to practise its methods and to exploit its possibilities further and further, unaffected by new influences in the air, when most of the rest of the world have abandoned it.

I have here purposely been selecting writers who seemed to represent some tendency or school in its purest or most highly developed form. We must, however, now consider some Romantics who, in certain ways, carried Romanticism far further than Chateaubriand or Musset, or than Wordsworth or Byron, and who became the first precursors of Symbolism and were afterwards placed among its saints.

One of these was the French writer who called himself Gérard de Nerval. Gérard de Nerval suffered from spells of insanity; and, partly no doubt as a result of this, tended to confuse his own fancies and feelings with external reality. He was convinced, even in his lucid periods—and no doubt Whitehead would approve his metaphysics—that the world which we see about us corresponds in some more intimate fashion than is ordinarily supposed to the things that go on in our minds, and even to our dreams and hallucinations; and in one of Gérard de Nerval's sonnets he surely goes Wordsworth one better in ascribing eyes to the walls and a soul to the stones.

But a more important prophet of Symbolism was Edgar Allan Poe. It was in general true that, by the middle of the century, the American Romantics—Poe, Hawthorne, Melville, Whitman and even Emerson—seemed, for reasons which it would be interesting to determine, to be developing in the direction of

Symbolism; and one of the events of prime importance in the early history of the Symbolist movement was the discovery of Poe by Baudelaire. When Baudelaire, a late Romantic, discovered Poe in 1847, he "experienced a strange commotion." When he began to look up Poe's writings in the files of American magazines, he found among them stories and poems which he said he had "thought vaguely and confusedly" of writing himself, and Poe became one of his great admirations. In 1852, he published a volume of translations of Poe's tales; and from then on the influence of Poe became one of the most important in French literature. Poe's critical writings provided the first scriptures of the Symbolist Movement, for he had formulated what amounted to a new literary program which corrected the Romantic looseness and lopped away the Romantic extravagance, at the same time that it aimed, not at Naturalistic, but at ultra-Romantic effects. There was, of course, a good deal in common between Poe's poetry and such Romantic poetry as Coleridge's "Kubla Khan," as there was between his poems in prose and such Romantic prose as that of DeQuincey. But Poe, by insisting on and specially developing certain aspects of Romanticism, helped to transform it into something different. "I *know*," we find Poe writing, for example, "that indefiniteness is an element of the true music [of poetry]—I mean of the true musical expression . . . a suggestive indefiniteness of meaning with a view of bringing about a definiteness of vague and therefore of spiritual *effect*." And to approximate the indefiniteness of music became one of the principal aims of Symbolism.

This indefiniteness was accomplished not only by the confusion I have mentioned already between the imaginary and the real; but also by means of a confusion between the perceptions of the different senses.

> *Comme de longs échos qui de loin se confondent.*
> *Les parfums, les couleurs et les sons se répondent,*

wrote Baudelaire. And we find Poe, in one of his poems, *hearing* he approach of the darkness, and writing such a description as the following of the sensations which follow death: "Night arrived; and with its shadows a heavy discomfort. It oppressed my limbs with the oppression of some dull weight and was palpable. There was also a moaning sound, not unlike the distant reverberation of surf, but more continuous, which beginning with the first twilight, had grown in strength with the darkness. Suddenly lights were brought into the room . . . and issuing from the flame of each lamp, there flowed unbrokenly into my ears a strain of melodious monotone."

Now when an English-speaking reader comes to consider French Symbolist poetry, it may be difficult for him at first to understand why it should have created a revolution: he may not even be able to see in what the novelty of Symbolism consisted. The medley of images; the telescoped metaphors; the mixture of irony with passion—of the grand with the prosaic manner; the bold amalgamation of material with spiritual—may all seem to him quite familiar. He has always known them in the English poetry of the sixteenth and seventeenth centuries—they are the language of Shakespeare and of Donne. It may even seem to the English-speaking reader that this sort of thing is the norm against which, in English poetry, the eighteenth century was a heresy and which the Romantics did their best to return to. But we must remember that the development of

French poetry has been quite different from the development of English. Michelet said that in the sixteenth century the fate of French literature hung in the balance between Rabelais and Ronsard, and he regrets that it was Ronsard who triumphed. For Rabelais in France represented a sort of equivalent to our own Elizabethan literature, while Ronsard, who represented to Michelet all that was poorest, dryest and most conventional in the French genius, was one of the fathers of that classical tradition of lucidity, sobriety and purity which culminated in Molière and Racine. In comparison, the English Classical period of the eighteenth century, the age of Dr. Johnson and Pope, was a brief ineffective deviation. And from the point of view of English readers, the most daring innovations of the Romantic revolution in France, in spite of all the excitement which accompanied them, must appear of an astonishingly moderate character. But the age and the strictness of the tradition were the measure of the difficulty of breaking out of it. After all, Wordsworth, Shelley and Keats—in spite of Pope and Dr. Johnson—had only to look back to Milton and Shakespeare, who had thrown their shadows across the scene all along. But to an eighteenth-century Frenchman like Voltaire, Shakespeare was incomprehensible; and to the Frenchman of the classical tradition of the beginning of the nineteenth century, the rhetoric of Hugo was a scandal: the French were not used to such rich colors or to so free a vocabulary; moreover, the Romantics broke metrical rules far stricter than any we have had in English. But Victor Hugo was still very far from the complexity and freedom of Shakespeare. It is enlightening to compare Shelley's "O World! O Life! O Time!" with the poem of Alfred de Musset's which begins *"J'ai perdu ma force et ma vie."* To us, the similarity appears chiefly one of sentiment. Musset, even when sighing, is clear and precise, where Shelley is confused and vague. And it will not be till the advent of the Symbolists that French poetry will become capable of this fluidity and vagueness.

The Symbolist movement broke those rules of French metrics which the Romantics had left intact, and it threw overboard the clarity and precision of the French classical tradition which the Romantics had still largely respected. It was nourished from many alien sources—German, Flemish, modern Greek—and especially, precisely, from English. Verlaine had lived in England, and knew English well; Mallarmé was a professor of English; and Baudelaire, as I have said, had provided the movement with its first programs by translating the essays of Poe. Two of the Symbolist poets, Stuart Merrill and Francis Vielé-Griffin, were Americans who lived in Paris and wrote French; and an American, reading today the latter's "Chevauchée d'Yeldis," for example, may wonder how, when Symbolism was new, such a poem could ever have been regarded as one of the movement's acknowledged masterpieces: to us, it seems merely agreeable, not in the least revolutionary or novel, but like something which might possibly have been written by Thomas Bailey Aldrich, if he had been influenced by Browning. (It is interesting also to note that today, when the pupils of the Symbolists really rule French literature, the French have resurrected and reinstated the solitary seventeenth-century French poet—Maurice de Scèves—who, by reason of his obscure "conceits," corresponded to the "metaphysical" English poets such as Crashaw and Donne: his poetry had always hitherto been rejected as crabbed and unintelligible!)

What made Poe particularly acceptable to the French, however, was what had distinguished him from most of the other Romantics of the English-speaking countries: his interest in esthetic theory. The French have always reasoned about literature far more than the English have; they always want to know what they are doing and why they are doing it: their literary criticism has acted as a constant interpreter and guide to the rest of their literature. And it was in France that Poe's literary theory, to which no one seems to have paid much attention elsewhere, was studied and developed. So that, though the effects and devices of Symbolism were of a kind that was familiar in English, and though the Symbolists were sometimes indebted to English literature directly—the Symbolist Movement itself, by reason of its origin in France, had a deliberate self-conscious esthetic which made it different from anything in English. Its leader, Stéphane Mallarmé, was a figure of a kind very rare in English literature. Paul Valéry says of Mallarmé that, as he was the greatest French poet of his time, he could have been also one of the most popular. But Mallarmé was an unpopular poet: reasoning much over the theory of poetry and proposing to himself the most difficult aims, he became a veritable saint of art. Ridiculed and denounced by the public, who insisted that his productions were nonsense, and yet were irritated by his seriousness and obstinacy, he exercised, from his little Paris apartment, where he held weekly receptions, an influence curiously far-reaching upon the young writers—English and French alike—of the end of the century. Mallarmé taught English for a living, and wrote little and published less: his was a life of singular purity and disinterestedness, given up to the philosophy and practice of poetry. He had applied himself to making poetry do things which it had never—self-consciously at least—undertaken to do before. Mallarmé was, as Thibaudet says, engaged in "a disinterested experiment on the confines of poetry, at a limit where other lungs would find the air unbreathable."

What, then, precisely, was this limit, on the confines of poetry, which the Symbolists were trying to approach? What was the purpose of the Symbolist experiment? I have called attention, in speaking of Poe, to the confusion between the perceptions of the different senses, and to the attempt to make the effects of poetry approximate those of music. And I should add, in this latter connection, that the influence on Symbolist poetry of the music of Wagner was as important as that of any writer; at the time when Romantic music had come closest to literature, literature was attracted toward music. I have also spoken, in connection with Gérard de Nerval, of the confusion between the imaginary and the real, between our sensations and fancies, on the one hand, and what we actually do and see, on the other. It was the tendency of Symbolism—that second swing of the pendulum away from a mechanistic view of nature and a preoccupation with society as a whole—to make poetry even more a matter of the sensations and emotions of the individual than Romanticism had done: it had, indeed, almost the result of making poetry private to the individual.

The peculiar subtlety and difficulty of Symbolism is indicated by the name itself. It may prove misleading to English readers: for the symbols of Symbolism really had little in common with symbolism in the ordinary sense—the sense in which the Cross is the symbol of Christianity, or the Stars and Stripes the symbol of the United States. The symbols of Symbolism were not instruments, like the

Stars and Stripes or the Cross, for reminding us of larger things. It was the assumption of the Symbolists that every feeling or sensation we have is different from every other feeling and sensation; and that it is, in consequence, impossible to render them through the conventional and universal language of ordinary literature. Each poet has his own special language; each moment has its special language. And these languages make use of symbols: what is so special, so fleeting and so vague cannot be conveyed by direct statement or description, but only by a series of images which may serve to suggest it. The Symbolists themselves hoped that these images spoke at once as plainly and as purely as the notes and chords of music. But the words of our speech are not musical notation, and what the symbols of Symbolism really were were metaphors detached from their subjects: one had to guess what these metaphors were being applied to. And Symbolism may perhaps be defined as an attempt by carefully studied means—a complicated association of ideas represented by a medley of metaphors—to communicate unique personal feelings.

The Symbolist Movement, at first, was thus largely confined to France and principally limited to poetry of rather an esoteric kind; but it was destined, as time went on, to spread to the whole western world and its principles to be applied on a scale and in departments of literature which the most enthusiastic of its founders could scarcely have foreseen. "The reaction against the rationalism of the eighteenth century," wrote Yeats in 1897, "has mingled with a reaction against the materialism of the nineteenth century, and the symbolical movement, which has come to perfection in Germany in Wagner, in England in the Pre-Raphaelites, and in France in Villiers de l'Isle Adam, and Mallarmé, and Maeterlinck, and has stirred the imagination of Ibsen and D'Annunzio, is certainly the only movement that is saying new things."

Without some knowledge of the aims and significance of Symbolism, it is impossible properly to understand much of the literature of the present time. And I want to suggest that, if English and American criticism have, in general, shown themselves singularly incompetent to deal with the contemporary literary situation, it is simply because, in spite of the Pre-Raphaelites, who were launched in England by an impulse somewhat similar to that of the Symbolists, the contemporary situation is the result of a revolution which occurred outside English literature, and whose ideas have reached us from France. The case of the Romantic Movement was different: Wordsworth's prefaces were English manifestoes: and Lockhart's attack on Keats and Byron's attacks on Jeffrey were blows struck in an English civil war. But, in spite of the not very clear-headed English "decadent" and "esthetic" movements of the end of the century, the battle of Symbolism has never properly been fought out in English. And I want to suggest that this is the reason that, whereas writers like Paul Valéry and Proust, who have grown out of the Symbolist Movement, are well understood and well appreciated by French literary criticism, the English-writing literary critics, who usually read little French literature, have so often seemed not to know how to deal with similar English-writing writers such as T. S. Eliot and Joyce. Even when these writers have brought back into English literature qualities which are natural to it and resources which it originally possessed, they have returned by way of France and have taken on the complexion of the French mind—critical, philosophical, much occupied with esthetic theory and tending always to aim at particular effects and to study appropriate means.

It has been peculiarly easy for certain of the leaders of contemporary English literature—that is, of the literature since the War—to profit by the example of Paris, because they are themselves not English. Yeats is an Irishman who turns almost as easily toward Paris as toward London; Joyce is an Irishman who has done most of his work on the Continent and who has scarcely lived in England at all; and T. S. Eliot and Gertrude Stein are Americans living abroad. The work of these writers has been largely a continuance or extension of Symbolism. Yeats, who went to Paris in the nineties and who was instructed in Symbolism by Arthur Symons, succeeded in transplanting it to Ireland. T. S. Eliot in his earliest poems seems to have been as susceptible to the influence of French Symbolists such as Tristan Corbière and Laforgue as to the influence of the English Elizabethans. Joyce, a master of Naturalism as great perhaps as Flaubert, has at the same time succeeded in dramatizing Symbolism by making use of its methods for conveying the special and varying states of mind of his characters. And Gertrude Stein, who introduced her first book with an epigraph from Laforgue, has carried Mallarmé's principles so far in the direction of that limit where other lungs find the air unbreathable as finally, perhaps, to reduce them to absurdity. It is true, however, that under proper conditions, these principles remain valid; and the strength and the weakness alike of much of the literature since the War— including Dadaism and Expressionism—derive naturally from the Symbolist poets and may already be studied in their work. The history of the growth of Symbolism, and of its blending with or conflict with Naturalism, is the history of the literature of our time.

WILLA CATHER   APRIL 12, 1922

The Novel Démeublé

The novel, for a long while, has been over-furnished. The property-man has been so busy on its pages, the importance of material objects and their vivid presentation have been so stressed, that we take it for granted whoever can observe, and can write the English language, can write a novel. Often the latter qualification is considered unnecessary.

In any discussion of the novel, one must make it clear whether one is talking about the novel as a form of amusement, or as a form of art; since they serve very different purposes and in very different ways. One does not wish the egg one eats for breakfast, or the morning paper, to be made of the stuff of immortality. The novel manufactured to entertain great multitudes of people must be considered exactly like a cheap soap or a cheap perfume, or cheap furniture. Fine quality is a distinct disadvantage in articles made for great numbers of people who do not want quality but quantity, who do not want a thing that "wears," but who want change,—a succession of new things that are quickly threadbare and can be lightly thrown away. Does anyone pretend that if the Woolworth-store windows were piled high with Tanagra figurines at ten cents, they could for a moment compete with Kewpie brides in the popular esteem? Amusement is one thing; enjoyment of art is another.

Every writer who is an artist knows that his "power of obervation," and his "power of description," form but a low part of his equipment. He must have both, to be sure; but he knows that the most trivial of writers often have a very good observation. Mérimée said in his remarkable essay on Gogol: "L'art de choisir parmi les innombrable traits que nous offre la nature est, après tout, bien plus difficile que celui de les observer avec attention et de les rendre avec exactitude."

There is a popular superstition that "realism" asserts itself in the cataloguing of a great number of material objects, in explaining mechanical processes, the methods of operating manufactures and trades, and in minutely unsparingly describing physical sensations. But is not realism, more than it is anything else, an attitude of mind on the part of the writer toward his material, a vague definition of the sympathy and candor with which he accepts, rather than chooses, his theme? Is the story of a banker who is unfaithful to his wife and who ruins himself by speculation in trying to gratify the caprices of his mistresses, at all reinforced by a masterly exposition of the banking system, our whole system of credits, the methods of the Stock Exchange? Of course, if the story is thin, these things do reinforce it in a sense, any amount of red meat thrown into the scale to make the beam dip. But are the banking system and the Stock Exchange worth being written about at all? Have such things any place in imaginative art?

The automatic reply to this question is the name of Balzac. Yes, certainly, Balzac tried out the value of literalness in the novel, tried it out to the uttermost, as Wagner did the value of scenic literalness in the music drama. He tried it, too, with the passion of discovery, with the inflamed zest of an unexampled curiosity. If the heat of that furnace could not give hardness and sharpness to material accessories, no other brain will ever do it. To reproduce on paper the actual city of Paris; the houses, the upholstery, the food, the wines, the game of pleasure, the game of business, the game of finance: a stupendous ambition—but, after all, unworthy of an artist. In exactly so far as he succeeded in pouring out on his pages that mass of brick and mortar and furniture and proceedings in bankruptcy, in exactly so far he defeated his end. The things by which he still lives, the types of greed and avarice and ambition and vanity and lost innocence of heart which he created—are as vital today as they were then. But their material surroundings, upon which he expended such labor and pains. . . . the eye glides over them. We had had too much of the interior decorator and the "romance of business" since his day. The city he built on paper is already crumbling. Stevenson said he wanted to blue-pencil a great deal of Balzac's "presentation"—and he loved him beyond all modern novelists. But where is the man who could cut one sentence from the stories of Mérimée? And who wants any more detail as to how Carmencita and her fellow factory girls made cigars? Another sort of novel? Truly. Isn't it a better sort?

In this discussion another great name automatically occurs. Tolstoi was almost as great a lover of material things as Balzac, almost as much interested in the way dishes were cooked, and people were dressed, and houses were furnished. But there is this determining difference; the clothes, the dishes, the moving, haunting interiors of those old Moscow houses, are always so much a part of the emotions of the people that they are perfectly synthesized; they seem to exist, not so much in the author's mind, as in the emotional penumbra of the characters themselves. When it is fused like this, literalness ceases to be literalness—it is merely part of the experience.

If the novel is a form of imaginative art, it cannot be at the same time a vivid and brilliant form of journalism. Out of the teeming, gleaming stream of the present it must select the eternal material of art. There are hopeful signs that some of the younger writers are trying to break away from mere verisimilitude, and, following the development of modern painting, to interpret imaginatively the material and social investiture of their characters; to present their scene by suggestion rather than by enumeration. The higher processes of art are all processes of simplification. The novelist must learn to write, and then he must unlearn it; just as the modern painter learns to draw, and then learns when utterly to disregard his accomplishment, when to subordinate it to a higher and truer effect. In this direction only, it seems to me, can the novel develop into anything more varied and perfect than all of the many novels that have gone before.

One of the very earliest American novels might well serve as a suggestion to later writers. In The Scarlet Letter how truly in the spirit of art is the mise-en-scène presented. That drudge, the theme-writing high school student, could scarcely be sent there for information regarding the manners and dress and interiors of the Puritans. The material investiture of the story is presented as if unconsciously; by the reserved, fastidious hand of an artist, not by the gaudy fingers of a showman or the mechanical industry of a department store window-dresser. As I remember it, in the twilight melancholy of that book, in its consistent mood, one can scarcely ever see the actual surroundings of the people; one feels them, rather, in the dusk.

Whatever is felt upon the page without being specifically named there—that, it seems to me, is created. It is the inexplicable presence of the thing not named, of the overtone divined by the ear but not heard by it, the verbal mood, the emotional aura of the fact or the thing or the deed, that gives high quality to the novel or the drama, as well as to poetry itself.

Literalness, when applied to the presenting of mental reactions and of physical sensations seems to be no more effective than when it is applied to material things. A novel crowded with physical sensations is no less a catalogue than one crowded with furniture. A book like The Rainbow by Mr. Lawrence, sharply reminds one how vast a distance lies between emotion and mere sensory reactions. Characters can be almost de-humanized by a laboratory study of the behavior of their bodily organs under sensory stimuli—can be reduced, indeed, to mere animal pulp. Can one imagine anything more terrible than the story of Romeo and Juliet, rewritten in prose by Mr. Lawrence?

How wonderful it would be if we could throw all the furniture out of the window; and along with it, all the meaningless reiterations concerning physical sensations, all the tiresome old patterns, and leave the room as bare as the stage of a Greek theatre, or as that house into which the glory of Pentecost descended; leave the scene bare for the play of emotions, great and little—for the nursery tale, no less than the tragedy, is killed by tasteless amplitude. The elder Dumas enunciated a great principle when he said that to make a drama, a man needed one passion, and four walls.

WILLIAM FAULKNER   MAY 20, 1931

Beyond the Talking

THE ROAD BACK by Erich Maria Remarque. Boston: Little, Brown and Company.

There is a victory beyond defeat which the victorious know nothing of. A bourne, a shore of refuge beyond the lost battles, the bronze names and the lead tombs, guarded and indicated not by the triumphant and man-limbed goddess with palm and sword, but by some musing and motionless handmaiden of despair itself.

Man does not seem to be able to stand very much prosperity; least of all does a people, a nation. Defeat is good for him, for it. Victory is the rocket, the glare, the momentary apotheosis at right angles with time and so doomed: a bursting diffusion of sparks at the last, dying and dead, leaving a word perhaps, a name, a date, for the tedium of children in primary history. It is the defeat which, serving him against his belief and his desire, turns him back upon that alone which can sustain him: his fellows, his racial homogeneity; himself; the earth, the implacable soil, monument and tomb of sweat.

This is beyond the talking, the hard words, the excuses and the reasons; beyond the despair. Beyond that dreadful desire and need to justify the disaster and give it significance by clinging to it, explaining it, which is the proven best way to support the inescapable. Victory requires no explanation. It is in itself sufficient: the fine screen, the shield; immediate and final: it will be contemplated only by history. While the whole contemporary world watches the defeat and the undefeated who, because of that fact, survived.

That's where the need to talk, to explain it, comes from. That's why Remarque puts into the mouths of characters speeches which they would have been incapable of making. It's not that the speeches were not true. If the characters had heard them spoken by another, they would have been the first to say, "That is so. This is what I think, what I would have said if I had just thought of it first." But they could not have said the speeches themselves. And this method is not justified, unless a man is writing propaganda. It is a writer's privilege to put into the mouths of his characters better speech than they would have been capable of, but only for the purpose of permitting and helping the character to justify himself or what he believes himself to be, taking down his spiritual pants. But when the character must express moral ideas applicable to a race, a situation, he is better kept in that untimed and unsexed background of the choruses of Greek senators.

But perhaps this is a minor point. Perhaps it is a racial fault of the author, as the outcome of the War was due in part to a German racial fault: a belief that a mathematical calculation would be superior to the despair of cornered rats. Anyway, Remarque justifies himself: ". . . I try to console him. What I say does not convince him, but it gives me some relief. . . . It is always so with comfort."

It is a moving book. Because Remarque was moved by the writing of it. Granted that his intent is more than opportunism, it still remains to be seen if art can be made of authentic experience transferred to paper word for word, of a peculiar reaction to an actual condition, even though it be vicarious. To a writer, no matter how susceptible he be, personal experience is just what it is to the man in the street who buttonholes him because he is a writer, with the same belief, the same conviction of individual significance: "Listen. All you have to do is write it down as it happened. My life, what has happened to me. It will make a good book, but I am not a writer myself. So I will give it to you. If I were a writer myself, had the time to write it down myself. You won't have to change a word." That does not make a book. No matter how vivid it be, somewhere between the experience and the blank page and the pencil, it dies. Perhaps the words kill it.

Give Remarque the benefit of the doubt and call the book a reaction to despair. Victory has its despairs, too, since the victorious not only do not gain anything, but when the hurrah dies away at last, they do not even know what they were fighting for, what they hoped to gain, because what little percentage there was in the whole affair, the defeated got it. If Germany had been victorious, this book would not have been written. And if the United States had not got back its troops 50-percent intact, save for the casual cases of syphilis and high metropolitan life, it would not be bought (which I hope and trust that it will be) and read. And it won't be the American Legion either that will buy the 40,000 copies, even if there are forty thousand of them that keep their dues paid up.

It moves you, as watching a child making mud pies on the day of its mother's funeral moves you. Yet at the end there is still that sense of missing significance, the feeling that, like so much that emerges from a losing side in any contest, and particularly from Germany since 1918, it was created primarily for the Western trade, to sell among the heathen like colored glass. From beyond the sentimentality, the defeat and the talking, this fact at least has emerged: America has been conquered not by the German soldiers that died in French and Flemish trenches, but by the German soldiers that died in German books.

A Bolt from the Blue

PALE FIRE by Vladimir Nabokov. New York: Putnam.

Pale Fire is a Jack-in-the-box, a Fabergé gem, a clockwork toy, a chess problem, an infernal machine, a trap to catch reviewers, a cat-and-mouse game, a do-it-yourself novel. It consists of a 999-line poem of four cantos in heroic couplets together with an editor's preface, notes, index, and proof-corrections. When the separate parts are assembled, according to the manufacturer's directions, and fitted together with the help of clues and cross-references, which must be hunted down as in a paper-chase, a novel on several levels is revealed, and these "levels" are not the customary "levels of meaning" of modernist criticism but planes in a fictive space, rather like those houses of memory in medieval mnemonic science, where words, facts, and numbers were stored till wanted in various rooms and attics, or like the Houses of astrology into which the heavens are divided.

The poem has been written by a sixty-one-year-old American poet of the homely, deceptively homely, Robert Frost type who teaches at Wordsmith College in New Wye, Appalachia; his name is John Shade, his wife is called Sybil, née Irondell or Swallow; his parents were ornithologists; he and his wife had a fat, plain daughter, Hazel, who killed herself young by drowning in a lake near the campus. Shade's academic "field" is Pope, and his poem, *Pale Fire*, is in Pope's heroic measure; in content, it is closer to Wordsworthian pastures—rambling, autobiographical, full of childhood memories, gleanings from Nature, interrogations of the universe: a kind of American *Prelude*. The commentator is Shade's colleague, a refugee professor from Zembla, a mythical country north of Russia. His name is Charles Kinbote; he lives next door to Shade in a house he has rented from Judge Goldsworth, of the law faculty, absent on sabbatical leave. (If, as the commentator points out, you recombine the syllables of "Wordsmith" and "Goldsworth," you get Goldsmith and Wordsworth, two masters of the heroic couplet.) At the moment of writing, Kinbote has fled Appalachia and is living in a log cabin in a motor court at Cedarn in the Southwest; Shade has been murdered, fortuitously, by a killer calling himself Jack Grey, and Kinbote, with the widow's permission, has taken his manuscript to edit in hiding, far from the machinations of two rival Shadians on the faculty. Kinbote, known on the campus as the Great Beaver, is a bearded vegetarian pederast, who has had bad luck with his youthful "ping-pong partners"; a lonely philologue and long-standing admirer of the poet (he has translated him into Zemblan), he has the unfortunate habit of "dropping in" on the Shades, spying on them (they don't draw theirs) with binoculars from a post at a window or in the shrubbery; jealous of Mrs. Shade, he is always available for a game of chess or a "good ramble" with the tolerant poet, whom he tirelessly entertains with his Zemblan reminiscences. "I don't see how John and Sybil can stand you," a faculty wife hisses at him in the grocery. "What's more, you are insane."

That is the plot's ground floor. Then comes the *piano nobile*. Kinbote believes that he has inspired his friend with his tales of his native Zembla, of its exiled king, Charles the Beloved, and the Revolution that started in the Glass Works; indeed, he has convinced himself that the poem is *his* poem—the occupational mania of commentators—and cannot be properly understood without his gloss, which narrates Zemblan events paralleling the poet's composition. What at once irresistibly peeps out from Kinbote's notes is that he himself is none other than Charles the Beloved, disguised in a beaver as an academic; he escaped from Zembla in a motor boat and flew to America after a short stay on the Côte d'Azur; an American sympathizer, a trustee of Wordsmith, Mrs. Sylvia O'Donnell, has found him a post on the language faculty. His colleagues (read "mortal enemies") include—besides burly Professor Hurley, head of the department and an adherent of *"engazhay"* literature—Professor C., a literary Freudian and owner of an ultra-modern villa, a certain Professor Pnin, and an instructor, Mr. Gerald Emerald, a young man in a bow tie and green velvet jacket. Meanwhile, the Shadows, the Secret Police of Zembla, have hired a gunman, Jakob Gradus, alias Jacques d'Argus, alias Jacques Degré, alias Jack Grey, to do away with the royal exile. Gradus' slow descent on Wordsmith synchronizes, move by move, with Shade's composition of *Pale Fire*; the thug, wearing a brown suit, a trilby, and carrying a Browning, alights on the campus the day the poem is finished. In the library he converges with Mr. Gerald Emerald, who obligingly gives him a lift to Professor Kinbote's house. There, firing at the king, he kills the poet; when the police take him, he masks his real purpose and identity by claiming to be a lunatic escaped from a local asylum.

This second story, the *piano nobile*, is the "real" story as it appears to Kinbote of the events leading to the poet's death. But the real, real story, the story underneath, has been transpiring gradually, by degrees, to the reader. Kinbote is mad. He is a harmless refugee pedant named Botkin who teaches in the Russian department and who fancies himself to be the exiled king of Zembla. This delusion, which he supposes to be his secret, is known to the poet, who pities him, and to the campus at large, which does not—the insensate woman in the grocery store was expressing the general opinion. The killer is just what he claims to be— Jack Grey, an escaped criminal lunatic, who has been sent to the State Asylum for the Insane by, precisely, Judge Goldsworth, Botkin's landlord. It is Judge Goldsworth that the madman intended to murder, not Botkin, alias Kinbote, alias Charles the Beloved; the slain poet was the victim of a case of double mistaken identity (his poem too is murdered by its editor, who mistakes it for something else). The clue to Gradus-Grey, moreover, was in Botkin's hands when, early in the narrative, he leafed through a sentimental album kept by the judge containing photographs of the killers he had sent to prison or condemned to death: ". . . a strangler's quite ordinary-looking hands, a self-made widow, the close-set merciless eyes of a homicidal maniac (somewhat resembling, I admit, the late Jacques d'Argus), a bright little parricide aged seven. . . ." He got, as it were, a preview of the coming film—a frequent occurrence in this kind of case. Projected onto Zembla, in fact, are the daily events of the campus. Gradus' boss,

Uzumrudov, one of the higher Shadows, met on the Riviera in a green velvet jacket is slowly recognized to be "little Mr. Anon.," alias Gerald Emerald, alias Reginald Emerald, a teacher of freshman English, who has made advances to (read in reverse "had advances made to him by") Professor Botkin, and who is also the author of a rude anonymous note suggesting that Professor Botkin has halitosis. The paranoid political structure called Zembla in Botkin's exiled fantasy—with its Extremist government and secret agents—is a transliteration of a pederast's persecution complex, complicated by the "normal" conspiracy-mania of a faculty common room.

But there is in fact a "Zembla," behind the Iron Curtain. The real, real story, the plane of ordinary sanity and common sense, the reader's presumed plane, cannot be accepted as final. The explanation that Botkin is mad will totally satisfy only Professors H. and C. and their consorts, who can put aside *Pale Fire* as a detective story, with the reader racing the author to the solution. *Pale Fire* is not a detective story, though it includes one. Each plane or level in its shadow box proves to be a false bottom; there is an infinite perspective regression, for the book is a book of mirrors.

Shade's poem begins with a very beautiful image, of a bird that has flown against a window and smashed itself, mistaking the reflected sky in the glass for the true azure. "I was the shadow of the waxwing slain|By the false azure of the window pane." This image is followed by another, still more beautiful and poignant, a picture of that trick of optics whereby a room at night, when the shades have not been drawn, is reflected in the dark landscape outside.

"Uncurtaining the night I'd let dark glass
Hang all the furniture above the grass
And how delightful when a fall of snow
Covered my glimpse of lawn and reached up so
As to make chair and bed exactly stand
Upon that snow, out in that crystal land!"

"That crystal land," notes the commentator, loony Professor Botkin. "Perhaps an allusion to Zembla, my dear country." On the plane of everyday sanity, he errs. But on the plane of poetry and magic, he is speaking the simple truth, for Zembla is Semblance, Appearance, the mirror-realm, the Looking Glass of Alice. This is the first clue in the treasure-hunt, pointing the reader to the dual or punning nature of the whole work's composition. *Pale Fire,* a reflective poem, is also a prism of reflections. Zembla, the land of seeming, now governed by the Extremists, is the antipodes of Appalachia, in real homespun democratic America, but it is also the *semblable,* the twin, as seen in a distorting glass. Semblance becomes resemblance.

The word Zembla can be found in Pope's *Essay on Man* (Epistle 2, v); there it signifies the fabulous extreme north, the land of the polar star.

"But where the Extreme of Vice was ne'er agreed.
Ask where's the North? At York, 'tis on the Tweed;
In Scotland, at the Oroades, and there,
At Greenland, Zembla, or the Lord knows where;
No creature owns it in the first degree,
But thinks his neighbor farther gone than he."

Pope is saying that vice, when you start to look for it, is always somewhere else—will-o'-the-wisp. This somewhere else is Zembla, but it is also next door, at your neighbor's. Now Botkin is Shade's neighbor and vice versa; moreover, people who live in glass houses. . . . Shade has a vice, the bottle, the festive glass, and Botkin's vice is that he is an *invert, i.e.,* turned upside down, as the antipodes are, relative to each other. Further, the reader will notice that the word Extreme, with a capital (Zemblan Extremists) and the word degree (Gradus is degree in Russian), both occur in these verses, in the neighborhood of Zembla, pre-mirroring *Pale Fire,* as though by second sight. Reading on, you find (lines 267-268), the following lines quoted by John Shade in a discarded variant:

"See the blind beggar dance, the cripple sing,
The sot a hero, lunatic a king . . ."

The second line is *Pale Fire* in a nutshell. Pope continues (lines 269-270):

"The starving chemist in his golden views
Supremely blest, the poet in his muse."

Supremely Blest is the title of John Shade's book on Pope. In this section of the poem, Pope is playing on the light and shade antithesis and on what an editor calls the "pattern of paradoxical attitudes" to which man's dual nature is subject. The lunatic Botkin incidentally, playing king, *inverts* his name.

To leave Pope momentarily and return to Zembla, there is an actual Nova Zembla, a group of islands in the Arctic Ocean, north of Archangel. The name is derived from the Russian Novaya Zemlya, which means "new land." Or *terre neuve,* Newfoundland, the New World. Therefore Appalachia=Zembla. But since for Pope Zembla was roughly equal to Greenland, then Zembla must be a green land, an Arcadia. Arcady is a name often bestowed by Professor Botkin on New Wye, Appalachia, which also gets the epithet "green," and he quotes *"Et in Arcadia ego,"* for Death has come to Arcady in the shape of Gradus, ex-glazier and killer, the emissary of Zembla on the other side of the world. Green-jacketed Gerald Emerald gives Death a lift in his car.

The complementary color to green is red. Zembla has turned red after the revolution that began in the Glass Factory. Green and red flash on and off in the narrative like traffic signals and sometimes reverse their message. Green appears to be the color of death, and red the color of life; red is the king's color and green the color of his enemies. Green is pre-eminently the color of seeming (the theatrical greenroom), the color, too, of camouflage, for Nature, being green at least in summer, can hide a green-clad figure in her verdure. But red is a color that is dangerous to a wearer who is trying to melt into the surroundings. The king escapes from his royal prison wearing a red wool cap and sweater (donned in the dark) and he is only saved by the fact that forty loyal Karlists, his supporters, put on red wool caps and sweaters too (red wool yarn—yarn comes from Latin "soothsayer"—is protective Russian folk magic) and confuse the Shadows with a multitude of false kings. Yet when the king arrives in America he floats down with a green silk parachute (because he is in disguise?), and his gardener at New Wye, a Negro whom he calls Balthasar (the black king of the three Magi), has a green thumb, a red sweater, and is seen on a green ladder; it is the gardener who saves the king's life when Gradus, alias Grey, appears.

Now when Alice went through the looking-glass she entered a chess game as a white pawn. There is surely a chess game or chess problem in *Pale Fire*, played on a board of green and red squares. The poet describes his residence as "the frame house between|Goldsworth and Wordsmith on its square of green"; the Rose Court in the royal palace in Onhava (Far Away), the Zemblan capital, is a sectile mosaic with rose petals cut out of red stone and large thorns cut out of green marble. There is much stress, in place-descriptions, on framing, and reference is made to chess problems of "the solus rex type." The royal fugitive may be likened to a lone king running away on the board. But in problems of the solus rex type, the king, though outnumbered is, curiously enough, not always at a disadvantage; for example, a king and two knights cannot checkmate a lone king—the game is stalemated or drawn. All the chess games played by characters in the story are draws. The plot of the novel ends in a kind of draw, if not a stalemate. The king's escape from the castle is doubtless castling.

Chess is the perfect mirror-game, with the pieces drawn up confronting each other as in a looking-glass; moreover, castles, knights, and bishops have their twins as well as their opposite numbers. The piece, by the way, called the bishop in English, in French is *"le fou"* or madman. In the book there are two opposed lunatics at large: Gradus and Kinbote. The moves made by Gradus from the Zemblan capital to Wordsmith in New Wye parallel spatially the moves made in time by the poet toward the completion of his poem; at the zero hour, there is a convergence of space and time. What is shadowed forth here may be a game of three-dimensional chess-three simultaneous games played by a pair of chess wizards on three transparent boards arranged vertically. A framed crystal land, the depth-echo of the bedroom projected onto the snow.

The moves of Gradus also hint some astrological progression. The magnum opus of old John Shade is begun July 1, 1959, at the dead center of the year. The poem is completed (except for the last line) the day of Gradus' arrival, July 21, on the cusp between Cancer and Leo. Botkin arrived at Judge Goldsworth's "chateau" on February 5, 1959; on Monday, February 16, he was introduced to the poet at lunch at the Faculty Club; on March 14, he dined at the Shades', etc. The fateful conjunction of three planets seems to be indicated, and the old astrological notion of events on earth mirroring the movements of the stars in the sky.

The twinning and doubling proliferate; the multiplication of levels refracts a prismatic, opaline light on Faculty row. Zembla is not just land but earth—"Terra the Fair, an orbicle of jasp," as John Shade names the globe; a Zemblan feuilletonist had fancifully dubbed its capital Uranograd—"Sky City." The fate of Charles the Beloved is a rippling reflection of the fate of Charles II of England on his travels, of Bonnie Prince Charlie and of he deposed Shakespearean rulers for whom streets are named in Onhava—Coriolanus Lane, Timon Alley. Prospero of *The Tempest* pops in and out of the commentary, like Fata Morgana, to mislead the reader into looking for "pale fire" in Shakespeare's swansong. It is not there, but *The Tempest* is in *Pale Fire:* Prospero's emerald isle, called the Ile of Divels, in the New World, Iris and Juno's peacock, sea caves, the chess game of Ferdinand and Miranda, Prospero's enchantments, his lost kingdom, and Caliban, whom he taught language, that supreme miracle of mirroring.

Nature's imitations of Nature are also evoked—echo, the mocking-bird perched on a television aerial ("TV's huge paperclip"), the iridescent eyes of the peacock's fan, the cicada's emerald case, a poplar tree's rabbit-foot—all the "natural shams" of so-called protective mimicry by which, as Shade says in his poem, "The reed becomes a bird, the knobby twig|An inchworm and the cobra head, a big|Wickedly folded moth." These disguises are not different from the exiled king's red cap and sweater (like the markings of a bird) or the impersonation of an actor. Not only Nature's shams but Nature's freaks dance in and out of the lines: rings around the moon, rainbows and sun dogs (bright spots of light, often colored, sometimes seen on the ring of the solar halo), the heliotrope or sunturner, which, by a trick of language, is also the bloodstone, Muscovy glass (mica), phosphorescence (named for Venus, the Morning Star), mirages, the roundlet of pale light called the *ignis fatuus*, fireflies, everything speckled, freckled, curiously patterned, dappled, quaint (as in Hopkins' poem, "Pied Beauty"). The arrowy tracks of the pheasant, the red heraldic barrings of the Vanessa butterfly, snow crystals. And the imitation of natural effects in manufactures: stained glass, paperweights containing snowstorms and mountain views, glass eyes. Not to mention other curios like the bull's eye lantern, glass giraffes, Cartesian devils. Botkin, the bearded urning, is himself a prime "freak of Nature," like Humbert. And the freakish puns of language ("Red Sox 5/4 on Chapman's Homer"), "muscat" (a cat-and-mouse game), anagrams, mirror-writing, such words as versipel. The author loves the ampersand and dainty diminutives ending in "let" or "et" (nymphet). Rugged John Shade is addicted to "word-golf" which he induces Botkin to play with him. Botkin's best scores are hate-love in three (late-lave-love), lass-male in four (last-mast-malt-male), live-dead in five. If you play word-golf with the title words, you can get pale-hate two and fire-love in three. Or pale-love in three and fire-hate in three.

The misunderstandings of scholarship, cases of mistaken word-identity, also enchant this dear author. *E.g.*, "alderwood" and "alderking" keep cropping up in the gloss with overtones of northern forest magic. What can be alderking be, excluding chief or ruler, which would give king-king, a redundancy?" "Erle" is the German word for alder, and the alder tree, which grows in wet places, has the curious property of not rotting under water. Hence it is a kind of magic tree, very useful for piles supporting bridges. And John Shade, writing of the loss of his daughter, echoes Goethe's "The Erl-King."

"Who rides so late in the night and the wind?
It is the writer's grief. It is the wild March wind. It is the father with his child."

Now the German scholar, Herder, in translating the elf-king story from the Danish, mistook the word for elf *(elle)* for the word for alder. So it is not really the alderking but the elf- or goblin-king, but the word alder touched by the enchanted word elf becomes enchanted itself and dangerous. Goethe's erl-king, notes Kinbote, fell in love with the traveler's little boy. Therefore alderking means an eerie; dangerous invert found in northern forest-countries.

Similar sorcerer's tricks are played with the word stone. The king in his red cap escaping through the Zemblan mountains is compared to a *Steinmann,* which, as Kinbote explains, is a pile of stones erected by alpinists to commemorate an ascent; these stonemen, apparently, like snowmen, were finished off with a red cap and scarf. The *Steinmann*, then, becomes a synonym for one of the king's disguised followers in red cap and sweater (*e.g.*, Julius Steinmann, Zemblan patriot). But the *Steinmann* has another meaning, not divulged by Kinbote; it is the *homme de Pierre or homme de St. Pierre* of Pushkin's poem about Don Giovanni, in short the stone statue, the Commendatore of the opera. Anyone who sups with the stone man, St. Peter's deputy, will be carried off to hell. The mountain that the *Steinmann*-king has to cross is wooded by Mandevil Forest; toward the end of his journey he meets a disguised figure, Baron Mandevil, man of fashion, catamite, and Zemblan patriot. Read man-devil, but read also Sir John Mandeville, medieval impostor and author of a book of voyages who posed as an English knight (perhaps a chess move is indicated?). Finally the stone (glancing by glass houses) is simply the stone thrown into a pool or lake and starting the tremulous magic of widening ripples that distort the clear mirroring of the image—as the word stone itself, cast into the pool of this paragraph has sent out wavelets in a widening circle.

Lakes—the original mirrors of primeval man—play an important part in the story. There are three lakes near the campus, Omega, Ozero, and Zero (Indian names, notes Botkin, garbled by early settlers); the king sees his consort, Disa, Duchess of Payn (sadism; theirs was a "white" marriage) mirrored in an Italian lake. The poet's daughter was drowned herself in Lake Omega; her name (". . . in lone Glenartney's hazel shade") is taken from *The Lady of the Lake*. But a hazel wand is also a divining-rod, used to find water; in her girlhood, the poor child, witch Hazel, was a poltergeist.

Trees, lakes, butterflies, stones, peacocks—there is also the waxwing, the poet's alter ego, which appears in the first line of the poem (duplicated in the last, unwritten line). If you look up the waxwing in the OED, you will find that it is "a passerine bird of the genus Ampelis, esp. A garrulus, the Bohemian waxwing. Detached from the chatterers by Monsieur Vieillot." The poet, a Bohemian, is detached from the chatterers of the world. The waxwing (belonging to the king's party) has red-tipped quills like sealing wax. Another kind of waxwing is the Cedar Waxwing. Botkin has fled to Cedarn. The anagram of Cedarn is nacred.

More suggestively (in the popular sense), the anal canal or "backdoor" or *"porte étroite"* is linked with a secret passage leading by green-carpeted stairs to a green door (which in turn leads to the greenroom of the Onhava National Theater), discovered by the king and a boyhood bedfellow. It is through this secret passage (made for Iris Acht, a leading actress) that the king makes his escape from the castle. Elsewhere a "throne," in the child's sense of "the toilet," is identified naughtily with the king. When gluttonous Gradus arrives in Appalachia, he is suffering from a severe case of diarrhea, induced by a conflict of "French" fries, consumed in a Broadway restaurant, with a genuine French ham sandwich, which he had saved from his Nice-Paris railway trip. The discharge of his bowels is horribly paralleled with the discharge of the automatic pistol he is carrying; he is the modern automatic man. In discharging the chamber of his pistol he is exercising what to him is a "natural" function; earlier the slight sensory pleasure he will derive from the act of murder is compared to the pleasure a man gets from squeezing a blackhead.

This is no giggling, high-pitched, literary camp. The repetitions, reflections, misprints, and quirks of Nature are taken as signs of the presence of a pattern, the stamp or watermark of a god or an intelligence. There is a web of sense in creation, old John Shade decides—not text but texture, the warp and woof of coincidence. He hopes to find "some kind of correlated pattern in the game,/Plexed artistry, and something of the same/Pleasure in it as they who played it found." The world is a sportive work of art, a mosaic, an iridescent tissue. Appearance and "reality" are interchangeable; all appearance, however deceptive, is real. Indeed it is just this faculty of deceptiveness (natural mimicry, trompe l'oeil, imposture), this power of imitation, that provides the key to Nature's cipher. Nature has "the artistic temperament"; the galaxies, if scanned, will be an iambic line.

Kinbote and Shade (and the author) agree in a detestation of symbols, except those of typography and, no doubt, natural science ("H_2O is a symbol for water"). They are believers in signs, pointers, blazes, notches, clues, all of which point into a forest of associations, a forest in which other woodmen have left half-obliterated traces. All genuine works contain pre-cognitions of other works or reminiscences of them (and the two are the same), just as the flying lizard already possessed a parachute, a fold of skin enabling it to glide through the air.

Shade, as an American, is naturally an agnostic, and Kinbote, a European, is a vague sort of Christian who speaks of accepting "God's presence—a faint phosphorescence at first, a pale light in the dimness of bodily life, and a dazzling radiance after it." Or, more concessively, "Somehow Mind is involved as a main factor in the making of the universe." This Mind of Kinbote's seems to express itself most lucidly in dualities, pairs, twins, puns, couplets, like the plots of Shakespeare's early comedies. But this is only to be expected if one recalls that to make a cutout heart or lacy design for Valentine's Day all a child needs is a scissors and a folded piece of paper—the fold makes the pattern, which, unfolded, appears as a miracle. It is the quaint principle of the butterfly. Similarly, Renaissance artificers used to make wondrous "natural" patterns by bisecting a veined stone, an agate or a carnelian, as you would bisect an orange. Another kind of magic is the child's trick of putting a piece of paper on the cover of a school book and shading it with a pencil; wonderfully the stamped title, *Caesar's Gallic Wars*, emerges, as though embossed, in white letters. This, upside down, is the principle of the pheasant's hieroglyph in the snow or the ripple marks on the sand, to which we cry "How beautiful!" There is no doubt that duplication, stamping, printing (children's transfers), is one of the chief forms of magic, a magic we also see in Jack Frost's writing on the window, in jet trails in the sky—an intelligent spirit seems to have signed them. But it is not only in symmetry and reproduction that the magic signature of Mind is discerned, but in the very imperfections of Nature's work, which appear as guarantees of authentic, hand-knit manufacture. That is, in those blemishes and freckles and streakings and moles already mentioned that are the sports of creation, and what is a vice but a mole?

Nabokov's tenderness for human eccentricity, for the freak, the "deviate," is partly the naturalist's taste for the curious. But his fond, wry compassion for the lone black piece on the board goes deeper than classificatory science or the collector's choplicking. Love is the burden of *Pale Fire*, love and loss. Love is felt as a kind of homesickness, that yearning for union described by Plato, the pining for the other half of a once-whole body, the straining of the soul's black horse to unite with the white. The sense of loss in love, of separation (the room *beyond*, projected onto the snow, the phantom moves of the chess knight, that deviate piece, *off* the board's edge onto ghostly squares), binds mortal men in a common pattern—the elderly couple watching TV in a lighted room, and the "queer" neighbor watching *them* from his window. But it is most poignant in the outsider: the homely daughter stood up by her date, the refugee, the "queen," the bird smashed on the window pane.

Pity is the password, says Shade, in a philosophical discussion with Kinbote; for the agnostic poet, there are only two sins, murder and the deliberate infliction of pain. In the exuberant high spirits, the wild laughter of the book, there is a cry of pure pain. The compassion of Nabokov stops violently short of Gradus, that grey, degraded being, the shadow of a Shade. The modern, mass-produced, jet-propelled, newspaper-digesting killer is described with a fury of intimate hatred; he is Death on the prowl. Unnatural Death is the natural enemy of the delicate, gauzy ephemerids who are Nabokov's special love. Kinbote makes an "anti-Darwinian" aphorism: "The Killer is *always* his victim's inferior."

But except for the discussions between the poet and his neighbor and Kinbote's theological justification of suicide, the book is quite free of religion—a remarkable achievement for a work that plays on traditional associations. How was it possible to avoid the Holy Rood, the Trinity, the Harrowing of Hell, the Resurrection, etc.? Among the myriads of references, there seem to be only two to Christian legend: the oblique one to St. Peter as gatekeeper of Heaven and the chess-jesting one to the Black King of the Magi. The book is obstinately, adamantly secular. It flies this fact gallantly like a flag of difference. The author's attitude toward the mystery of the universe is closer to the old botanist's wonder than to the modern physicist's mysticism. His practical morality, like Kant's, seeks to reconcile the Enlightenment with universal maxims of conduct held as axioms. Nabokov's pantheism contains Platonic gleams: Kinbote's "phosphorescence" recalls the cave myth. Kinbote reverts to this notion when he concedes in his final remarks that Shade's poem, for all its deficiencies, has "echoes and wavelets of fire and pale phosphorescent hints" of the real Zemblan magic. This madman's estimate is also the author's apologia for his own work, in relation to the fiery Beyond of the pure imagination—Plato's Empyrean, the sphere of pure light or fire. But Plato's Empyrean is finished, a celestial storehouse or vault of models from which the forms of earthly life are copied. In Nabokov's view (see Shade's couplet, "*Man's life as commentary to abstruse/Unfinished poem*. Note for further use"), the celestial Poem itself is incomplete.

I have not been able to find, in Shakespeare or anywhere else, the source of "pale fire." In the commentary there is an account of the poet burning his rejected drafts in "the pale fire of the incinerator." An amusing sidelight on the question may be provided by the word ingle, used by Kinbote to mean a catamite or boy favorite, but which also means blaze, from the Gaelic word for fire. A Helena Rubinstein product is called Pale Fire. I think too of the pale fire of opals and of Wordsworth, one of the patron saints of the grotesquely named Wordsmith College: "Life like a dome of many-colored glass/ Stains the pale radiance of eternity." Whether the visible world is a prismatic reflection of eternity or vice versa is perhaps immaterial, like the question of which came first, the chicken or the egg. In the game of signaling back and forth with mirrors, which may be man's relation with the cosmos, there is perhaps no before or after, only distance— separation—and, across it, the agitated flashing of the semaphore.

In any case, this centaur-work of Nabokov's, half poem, half prose, this merman of the deep, is a creation of perfect beauty, symmetry, strangeness, originality, and moral truth. Pretending to be a curio, it cannot disguise the fact that it is one of the very great works of art of this century, the modern novel that everyone thought dead and that was only playing possum.

ROBERT LITTELL   OCTOBER 13, 1926

Gogol

In a not even very exacting literary examination paper, the question, Who was Gogol? should rank high. It is sadly to be expected that very few Americans could answer the question at all, and still fewer name a book of his they had actually read. Yet there is something in the best of Gogol which, one would think, ought to have a singular appeal to the American spirit. One can so easily imagine him writing about us, and getting, by the simplest of means if also by the rarest kind of human and literary gifts, to the bottom of us, to that instinct for truth which makes each one of us think, in his heart of hearts and rightly, that he is not like any other human being in all the forty-eight states.

We have little excuse not to know Gogol, now that Mrs. Constance Garnett, the best of translators of Russian fiction, has turned her abilities in his direction. We had from her hand Dead Souls, his masterpiece, and a volume of short stories including that singular, that baffling treasure, The Overcoat, and now we have a third volume of his earliest stories, published about a hundred years ago (Evenings on a Farm near Dikanka. Knopf). Of all three, this volume is the least interesting, the least alluring to strangers, the least characteristic of Gogol as we think of him, and probably the greatest loser by translation. The stories which sprawl under' that vague title scarcely hint what there was to come from him. They bubble, shout and sing with a wild, often sloppy exuberance, with a fantastic peasant fairy-tale carelessness and freshness which is not to be found in any of the other Russians translated into English. For Gogol came from Little Russia—temperamentally a long way from Great Russia, with her northern agonies, her frosts, orgies and disappointments, her heroisms and brutalities, her small people seen through great eyes, and by that themselves made great. Little Russia is the south, a Slavic Italy with full moons, rich harvests, sun, laughter and light-heartedness irrepressible. Also a land of superstition—none of your gaunt wolfish superstitions, but full-fed galloping raids of the imagination into the unknown.

In most respects it is a long way from Evenings on a Farm near Dikanka to The Overcoat, which is surely one of the most remarkable stories ever written. The farcical Little Russian with his tales of witches and midnight revelries is gone, and instead we have a story, not an author. The vast majority of stories are containers, more or less appropriate, more or less concealed, in which the writer packs his people. The people live and change according to their creator's skill, but unless his skill is of the highest, some corner of the box into which he has put them will always show. The Overcoat is a story without a box, without a container. It seems to have grown, like a fruit, in Gogol's mind, from whose branches it was suddenly found hanging down, enormous, mysterious, and all of one piece like an apple.

Some Americans have heard of Dead Souls, and a few have read it. It is a book which the two few of us who are interested in American fiction and the too many who are writing it ought to read. It is not only that we are missing a highly readable book; there are definite reasons why we ought to read it, and know it, too. It is a book curiously parallel with what is waiting to be done for America.

The story of it is well known, and of small importance. Two gifted crooks go about the country buying up serfs who have died, but are still on the rolls. The book stops short, Gogol never finished it, and he might have gone on writing it for ever. The story is only an excuse for presenting the main matter, a collection of some of the most curious, various and living specimens of humanity who were ever coaxed into print. The two partners go, naturally, from one estate to another in search of their non-existent riches. The search for dead souls is the thread on which are strung appallingly voracious and complete descriptions of each estate, and the most humorous presentation of the owners. For anyone who finds fiction rewarding in proportion to the reality of the characters and the respect felt for their individualities by the author, Dead Souls is extraordinarily good reading.

Its greatness is not wholly due to its vitality, nor to its abundance, nor to its extreme vividness, if we may assume one of the vaguest of words to mean something, to denote that quality in writing which makes things and people "real," which makes them stand before our eyes and speak to our ears, which makes us remember them as we do people we have actually known, sometimes a little better. The eye that achieves "vividness" can be of several kinds. It can be reportorial, trusting that out of an accumulation of data a final impression will of itself arise; or it can, from the available facts, reject some and choose others, or it can carefully match facts that exist with others of its own invention. In these, the more literal visions by the eye and the mind's eye, we Americans have done well. We have done well also as caricaturists, cartoonists, exaggerators, and have succeeded in magnifying reality two or three diameters with astonishing results.

But in between this understatement and this overstatement is an ability, which Gogol possessed to a high degree, to distort the person or the thing he is looking at ever so little, so little that one cannot see in what feature distortion has taken place. This is not a conscious gift; the writer cannot say to himself, "Here I will distort, here I will not"; it is a subtle partnership between the eye and the emotions, and whoever is not born with it is hardly likely ever to acquire it. Even the word "distorted" is too gross for the change Gogol works on what he sees.

Of course it is true that his material was quite unlike what we have to deal with. On the surface, and probably below the surface, too, it was much richer. As Gorky says, Russia is full of strange and remarkable people; "in Russia, even the fools are wonderful." Which is more than can be said of America. To the casual glance, and very few glances today are more than casual, we are repellently standardized. The novelist must go deeper, and that is always hard and painful work. The deeper he goes, the less standardized we will turn out to be, the more he will learn that no two of us are alike, and the nearer he will be to doing for America what Gogol did for Russia.

America is here, full of interesting people, and Gogol's method is there for anyone to copy. What could be simpler: a plot which gives the writer the excuse for traveling from place to place and meeting all sorts of people, living in all sorts of different ways, one right after another? The nearest that we have come to Dead Souls is Huckleberry Finn. That was done for a Mississippi that is gone. Our own times cry aloud to be written about in the same way. Everything is present except the man, the eye that can penetrate everywhere and distort, ever so little, the calm sameness of the surface into dozens and hundreds of separate and fascinating human beings.

LOUISE BOGAN   DECEMBER 5, 1923

The Springs of Poetry

When he sets out to resolve, as rationally as he may, the tight irrational knot of his emotion, the poet hesitates for a moment. Unless the compulsion be absolute, as is rarely the case, the excitement of the resolution sets in only after this pause, filled with doubt and terror. He would choose anything, anything, rather than the desperate task before him: a book, music, or talk and laughter. Almost immediately the interruption is found, and the motion diverted, or the poem is begun, and the desperation has its use.

The author of the Poetica recognized this necessary intensity when he wrote that distress and anger are most faithfully portrayed by one who is feeling them at the moment, that poetry demands a man with a special gift for it, or else one with a touch of madness in him. Few poems are written in that special authentic rage because even a poet has a great many uses for grief and anger, beyond putting them into a poem. The poem is always a last resort. In it the poet makes a world in little, and finds peace, even though, under complete focused emotion, the evocation be far more bitter than reality, or far more lovely.

Sometimes the poet does not entirely succeed in diverting his energies. He expresses himself, determined to take a holiday from any emotion at all, being certain that to hear, see, smell and touch, merely, is enough. His hand has become chilled, from being held too long against the ground to feel how it is cold; his mind flinches at cutting down once again into the dark with the knife of irony or analysis.

So he writes a poem at third, fourth, or fifth hand, bred out of some delicate fantastic ruse of the brain. Even though at its best a poem cannot come straight out of the heart, but must break away in some oblique fashion from the body of sorrow or joy,—be the mask, not the incredible face—yet the synthetic poem can never be more than a veil dropped before a void. It may sound, to change the images, in ears uninitiate to the festival, but never to those, who, having once heard, can recognize again the maenad cry.

It would seem best, in order that his temptation to second-rate work be kept negligible, that for long periods the poet himself be his only audience. He has no business with the shifting criteria with which each little year would charge him. He should have no thought of a descending scale of editors to whom his best and his worst may be fed.

One would wish for the poet a stern countryside that could claim him completely, identify him rigidly as its own under the color of every season. He should be blessed by the power to write behind clenched teeth, to subsidize his emotion by every trick and pretense so that it trickle out through other channels, if it be not essential to speech,—blessed too, by a spirit as loud as a houseful of alien voices, ever tortured and divided with itself. And most completely blessed by that reticence celebrated by the old prophetic voice: "I kept silent, even from good words . . . the fire kindled, and at the last I spoke with my tongue." Under the power of such reticence, in which passion is made to achieve its own form, definite and singular, those poems were written that keep an obscure name still alive, or live when the name of their author is forgotten. Speaking thus, as though the very mind had a tongue, Yeats achieves his later work: poems terribly beautiful, in which the hazy adverbial quality has no place, built of sentences reduced to the bones of noun, verb, and preposition.

This is the further, the test simplicity, in the phrase of Alice Meynell, sprung from the passion of which every poet will always be afraid, but to which he should vow himself forever.

How to Criticize a Poem

(In the Manner of Certain Contemporary Critics)

1.

I propose to examine the following poem:

Thirty days hath September,
April, June and November:
All the rest have thirty-one,
Excepting February alone,
Which has only eight and a score
Till leap-year gives it one day more.

2.

The previous critics who have studied this poem, Coleridge among them, have failed to explain what we may describe as its fundamental *dynamic*. This I now prepare to do. The first thing to observe is the order in which the names (or verbal constructs) of the months are presented. According to the prose meaning—what I shall henceforth call the prose-*demand*—"September" should not precede, it should follow "April," as a glance at the calendar will show. Indeed "September" should follow not only "April," it should also follow "June" if the prose-demand is to be properly satisfied. The prose order of the first two lines should therefore read: "Thirty days hath April, June, September and November." That is the only sequence consonant with prose logic.

3.

Why then, we ask ourselves, did the poet violate what educated readers know to be the facts? Was he ignorant of the calendar, believing that September preceded April in the progress of the seasons? It is difficult to imagine that such was the case. We must find another explanation. It is here that the principle of dynamic analysis comes to our aid.

4.

Dynamic analysis proves that the most successful poetry achieves its effect by producing an *expectation* in the reader's mind before his sensibility is fully prepared to receive the full impact of the poem. The reader makes a *proto-response* which preconditions him to the total response toward which his fully equilibrized organs of apperception subconsciously tend. It is this proto-response which the poet has here so sensitively manipulated. The ordinary reader, trained only to prose-demands, expects the usual order of the months. But the poet's sensibility knows that poetic truth is more immediately effective than the truth of literal chronology. He does not *state* the inevitable sequence; he *prepares* us for it. In his profound analysis of the two varieties of mensual time, he puts the *gentlest* month first. (Notice how the harsh sound of "pt" in "September" is softened by the "e" sound on either side of it.) It is the month in which vegetation first begins to fade, but which does not as yet give us a sense of tragic fatality.

5.

Hence the poet prepares us, dynamically, for what is to follow. By beginning his list of the months *in medias res,* he is enabled to return later to the beginning of the series of contrasts which is the subject of his poem. The analogy to the "Oedipus Rex" of Euripides and the "Iliad" of Dante at once becomes clear. Recent criticism has only too often failed to observe that these works also illustrate the dynamic method by beginning in the middle of things. It is a striking fact, hitherto (I believe) unnoticed, that a Latin poem called the "Aeneid" does much the same thing. We expect the author of that poem to begin with the departure of his hero from Troy, just as we expect the author of our poem to begin with "April." But in neither case is our expectation fulfilled. Cato, the author of the "Aeneid," creates dynamic suspense by beginning with Aeneas in Carthage; our anonymous poet treats his readers' sensibilities in a similar fashion by beginning with "September," and then *going back* to "April" and "June."

6.

But the sensibility of the poet does not stop at this point. Having described what is true of *four* months, he disposes of *seven* more with masterly economy. In a series of pungent constructs his sensibility sums up their inexorable limitations: they *All* (the capitalization should be noted) "have thirty-one." The poet's sensibility communicates a feeling to the sensibility of the reader so that the sensibility of both, with reference to their previous but independent sensibilities, is fused into that momentary communion of sensibility which is the final sensibility that poetry can give both to the sensibility of the poet and the sensibility of the reader. The texture and structure of the poem have erupted into a major reaction. The ambiguity of equilibrium is achieved.

7.

Against these two groups of spatial, temporal and numerical measurements— one consisting of four months, the other of seven—the tragic individual, the sole exception, "February," is dramatically placed. February is "alone," is cut off from communion with his fellows. The tragic note is struck the moment "February" is mentioned. For the initial sound of the word "excepting" is "X," and as that sound strikes the sensibility of the reader's ear a number of associations subconsciously accumulate. We think of the spot, the murderous and lonely spot, which "X" has so frequently marked; we remember the examinations of our childhood where the wrong answers were implacably signaled with "X"; we think of ex-kings and exile, of lonely crossroads and executions, of the inexorable anonymity of those who cannot sign their names. . . .

8.

And yet the poet gives us one ray of hope, though it eventually proves to be illusory. The lonely "February" (notice how the "alone" in line four is echoed by the "only" in line five), the solitary and maladjusted individual who is obviously the hero and crucial figure of the poem, is not condemned to the routine which his fellows, in their different ways, must forever obey. Like Hamlet, he has a capacity for change. He is a symbol of individualism, and the rhythm of the lines which are devoted to him signalize a gayety, however desperate, which immediately wins our sympathy and reverberates profoundly in our sensibility.

9.

But (and this is the illusion to which I have previously referred) in spite of all his variety, his capacity for change, "February" cannot quite accomplish (and in this his tragedy consists) the *quantitative* value of the society in which circumstances have put him. No matter how often he may alternate from twenty-eight to twenty-nine (the poet, with his exquisite sensibility, does not actually *mention* those humiliating numbers), he can never achieve the bourgeois if anonymous, security of "thirty-one," nor equal the more modest and aristocratic assurance of "thirty." Decade after decade, century after century, millenium after millenium, he is eternally frustrated. The only symbol of change in a changeless society, he is continually beaten down. Once every four years he tries to rise, to achieve the high, if delusive, level of his dreams. But he fails. He is always one day short, and the three years before the recurrence of his next effort are a sad interval in which the remembrance of previous disappointment melts into the futility of hope, only to sink back once more into the frustration of despair. Like Tantalus he is forever stretched upon a wheel.

10.

So far I have been concerned chiefly with the dynamic *analysis* of the poem. Further study should reveal the *synthesis* which can be made on the basis of the analysis which my thesis has tentatively attempted to bring to an emphasis. This, perhaps, the reader with a proper sensibility can achieve for himself.

VLADIMIR NABOKOV   AUGUST 4, 1941

The Art of Translation

Three grades of evil can be discerned in the queer world of verbal transmigration. The first, and lesser one, comprises obvious errors due to ignorance or misguided knowledge. This is mere human frailty and thus excusable. The next step to Hell is taken by the translator who intentionally skips words or passages that he does not bother to understand or that might seem obscure or obscene to vaguely imagined readers; he accepts the blank look that his dictionary gives him without any qualms; or subjects scholarship to primness: he is as ready to know less than the author as he is to think he knows better. The third, and worst, degree of turpitude is reached when a masterpiece is planished and patted into such a shape, vilely beautified in such a fashion as to conform to the notions and prejudices of a given public. This is a crime, to be punished by the stocks as plagiarists were in the shoebuckle days.

The howlers included in the first category may be in their turn divided into two classes. Insufficient acquaintance with the foreign language involved may transform a commonplace expression into some remarkable statement that the real author never intended to make. *"Bien être general"* becomes the manly assertion that "it is good to be a general"; to which gallant general a French translator of "Hamlet" has been known to pass the caviar. Likewise, in a German edition of Chekhov, a certain teacher, as soon as he enters the classroom, is made to become engrossed in "his newspaper," which prompted a pompous reviewer to comment on the sad condition of public instruction in pre-Soviet Russia. But the real Chekhov was simply referring to the classroom "journal" which a teacher would open to check lessons, marks and absentees. And inversely, innocent words in an English novel such as "first night" and "public house" have become in a Russian translation "nuptial night" and "a brothel." These simple examples suffice. They are ridiculous and jarring, but they contain no pernicious purpose; and more often than not the garbled sentence still makes some sense in the original context.

The other class of blunders in the first category includes a more sophisticated kind of mistake, one which is caused by an attack of linguistic Daltonism suddenly blinding the translator. Whether attracted by the far-fetched when the obvious was at hand (What does an Eskimo prefer to eat—ice cream or tallow? Ice cream), or whether unconsciously basing his rendering on some false meaning which repeated readings have imprinted on his mind, he manages to distort in an unexpected and sometimes quite brilliant way the most honest word or the tamest metaphor. I knew a very conscientious poet who in wrestling with the translation of a much tortured text rendered "is sicklied o'er with the pale cast of thought" in such a manner as to convey an impression of pale moonlight. He did this by taking for granted that "sickle" referred to the form of the new moon. And a national sense of humor, set into motion by the likeness between the Russian words meaning "arc" and "onion," led a German professor to translate "a bend of the shore" (in a Pushkin fairy tale) by "the Onion Sea."

The second, and much more serious, sin of leaving out tricky passages is still excusable when the translator is baffled by them himself; but how contemptible is the smug person who, although quite understanding the sense, fears it might stump a dunce or debauch a dauphin! Instead of blissfully nestling in the arms of the great writer, he keeps worrying about the little reader playing in a corner with something dangerous or unclean. Perhaps the most charming example of Victorian modesty that has ever come my way was in an early English translation of "Anna Karenina." Vronsky had asked Anna what was the matter with her. "I am *beremenna*" (the translator's italics), replied Anna, making the foreign reader wonder what strange and awful Oriental disease that was; all because the translator thought that "I am pregnant" might shock some pure soul, and that a good idea would be to leave the Russian just as it stood.

But masking and toning down seem petty sins in comparison with those of the third category; for here he comes strutting and shooting out his bejeweled cuffs, the slick translator who arranges Scheherazade's boudoir according to his own taste and with professional elegance tries to improve the looks of his victims. Thus it was the rule with Russian versions of Shakespeare to give Ophelia richer flowers than the poor weeds she found. The Russian rendering of

> There with fantastic garlands did she come
> Of crowflowers, nettles, daisies and long purples

if translated back into English would run like this:

> There with most lovely garlands did she come
> Of violets, carnations, roses, lilies.

The splendor of this floral display speaks for itself; incidentally it bowdlerized the Queen's digressions, granting her the gentility she so sadly lacked and dismissing the liberal shepherds; how anyone could make such a botanical collection beside the Helje or the Avon is another question.

But no such questions were asked by the solemn Russian reader, first, because he did not know the original text, second, because he did not care a fig for botany, and third, because the only thing that interested him in Shakespeare was what German commentators and native radicals had discovered in the way of "eternal problems." So nobody minded what happened to Goneril's lapdogs when the line

> Tray, Blanche and Sweetheart, see, they bark at me

was grimly metamorphosed into

> A pack of hounds is barking at my heels.

All local color, all tangible and irreplaceable details were swallowed by those hounds.

But, revenge is sweet—even unconscious revenge. The greatest Russian short story ever written is Gogol's "Overcoat" (or "Mantle," or "Cloak," or "She-nel"). Its essential feature, that irrational part which forms the tragic undercurrent of an otherwise meaningless anecdote, is organically connected with the special style in which this story is written: there are weird repetitions of the same absurd adverb, and these repetitions become a kind of uncanny incantation; there are descriptions which look innocent enough until you discover that chaos lies right round the corner, and that Gogol has inserted into this or that harmless sentence a word or a simile that makes a passage burst into a wild display of nightmare fireworks. There is also that groping clumsiness which, on the author's part, is a conscious rendering of the uncouth gestures of our dreams. Nothing of these remains in the prim, and perky, and very matter-of-fact English version (see— and never see again—"The Mantle," translated by Claude Field). The following example leaves me with the impression that I am witnessing a murder and can do nothing to prevent it:

> Gogol: . . . his [a petty official's] third or fourth-story flat . . . displaying a few fashionable trifles, *such as a lamp for instance*—trifles purchased by many sacrifices. . . .
> Field: . . . fitted with some pretentious articles of furniture purchased, etc. . . .

Tampering with foreign major or minor masterpieces may involve an innocent third party in the farce. Quite recently a famous Russian composer asked me to translate into English a Russian poem which forty years ago he had set to music.

The English translation, he pointed out, had to follow closely the very sounds of the text—which text was unfortunately K. Balmont's version of Edgar Allan Poe's "Bells." What Balmont's numerous translations look like may be readily understood when I say that his own work invariably disclosed an almost pathological inability to write one single melodious line. Having at his disposal a sufficient number of hackneyed rhymes and taking up as he rode any hitch-hiking metaphor that he happened to meet, he turned something that Poe had taken considerable pains to compose into something that any Russian rhymester could dash off at a moment's notice. In reversing it into English I was solely concerned with finding English words that would sound like the Russian ones. Now, if somebody one day comes across my English version of that Russian version, he may foolishly retranslate it into Russian so that the Poe-less poem will go on being balmontized until, perhaps, the "Bells" become "Silence." Something still more grotesque happened to Baudelaire's exquisitely dreamy "Invitation au Voyage" ("*Mon amie, ma soeur, connais-tu la douceur. . . .*") The Russian version was due to the pen of Merejkovsky, who had even less poetical talent than Balmont. It began like this:

> My sweet little bride,
> Let's go for a ride;

Promptly it begot a rollicking tune and was adopted by all the organ-grinders of Russia. I like to imagine a future French translator of Russian folksongs re-Frenchifying it into:

> Viens, mon p'tit,
> A Nijni

and so on, *ad malinfinitum*.

Barring downright deceivers, mild imbeciles and impotent poets, there exist, roughly speaking, three types of translators—and this has nothing to do with my three categories of evil; or, rather, any of the three types may err in a similar way. These three are: the scholar who is eager to make the world appreciate the works of an obscure genius as much as he does himself; the well meaning hack; and the professional writer relaxing in the company of a foreign confrere. The scholar will be, I hope, exact and pedantic: footnotes—on the *same* page as the text and not tucked away at the end of the volume—can never be too copious and detailed. The laborious lady translating at the eleventh hour the eleventh volume of somebody's collected works will be, I am afraid, less exact and less pedantic; but the point is not that the scholar commits fewer blunders than a drudge; the point is that as a rule both he and she are hopelessly devoid of any semblance of creative genius. Neither learning nor diligence can replace imagination and style.

Now comes the authentic poet who has the two last assets and who finds relaxation in translating a bit of Lermontov or Verlaine between writing poems of his own. Either he does not know the original language and calmly relies upon the so-called "literal" translation made for him by a far less brilliant but a little more learned person, or else, knowing the language, he lacks the scholar's precision and the professional translator's experience. The main drawback, however, in this case is the fact that the greater his individual talent, the more apt he will be to drown the foreign masterpiece under the sparkling ripples of his own personal style. Instead of dressing up like the real author, he dresses up the author as himself.

We can deduce now the requirements that a translator must possess in order to be able to give an ideal version of a foreign masterpiece. First of all he must have as much talent, or at least the same kind of talent, as the author he chooses. In this, though only in this, respect Baudelaire and Poe or Joukovsky and Schiller made ideal playmates. Second, he must know thoroughly the two nations and the two languages involved and be perfectly acquainted with all details relating to his author's manner and methods; also, with the social background of words, their fashions, history and period associations. This leads to the third point: while having genius and knowledge he must possess the gift of mimicry and be able to act, as it were, the real author's part by impersonating his tricks of demeanor and speech, his ways and his mind, with the utmost degree of verisimilitude.

I have lately tried to translate several Russian poets who had either been badly disfigured by former attempts or who had never been translated at all. The English at my disposal is certainly thinner than my Russian; the difference being, in fact, that which exists between a semi-detached villa and a hereditary estate, between self-conscious comfort and habitual luxury. I am not satisfied therefore with the results attained, but my studies disclosed several rules that other writers might follow with profit.

I was confronted for instance with the following opening line of one of Pushkin's most prodigious peoms:

Yah pom-new chewed-no-yay mg-no-vain-yay

I have rendered the syllables by the nearest English sounds I could find; their mimetic disguise makes them look rather ugly; but never mind; the "chew" and the "vain" are associated phonetically with other Russian words meaning beautiful and important things, and the melody of the line with the plump, golden-ripe "chewed-no-yay" right in the middle and the "m's" and "n's" balancing each other on both sides, is to the Russian ear most exciting and soothing—a paradoxical combination that any artist will understand.

Now, if you take a dictionary and look up those four words you will obtain the following foolish, flat and familiar statement: "I remember a wonderful moment." What is to be done with this bird you have shot down only to find that it is not a bird of paradise, but an escaped parrot, still screeching its idiotic message as it flaps on the ground? For no stretch of the imagination can persuade an English reader that "I remember a wonderful moment" is the perfect beginning of a perfect poem. The first thing I discovered was that the expression "a literal translation" is more or less nonsense. "Yah pom-new" is a deeper and smoother plunge into the past than "I remember," which falls flat on its belly like an inexperienced diver; "chewed-no-yay" has a lovely Russian "monster" in it, and a whispered "listen," and the dative ending of a "sunbeam," and many other fair relations among Russian words. It belongs phonetically and mentally to a certain series of words, and this Russian series does not correspond to the English series in which "I remember" is found. And inversely, "remember" though it clashes with the corresponding "pom-new" series, is connected with an English series of its own whenever real poets do use it. And the central word in Housman's "What are those blue *remembered* hills?" becomes in Russian "vspom-neev-she-yes-yah," a horrible straggly thing, all humps and horns, which cannot fuse into any inner connection with "blue," as it does so smoothly in English, because the Russian sense of blueness belongs to a different series than the Russian "remember" does.

This interrelation of words and non-correspondence of verbal series in different tongues suggest yet another rule, namely, that the three main words of the line draw one another out, and add something which none of them would have had separately or in any other combination. What makes this exchange of secret values possible is not only the mere contact between the words, but their exact position in regard both to the rhythm of the line and to one another. This must be taken into account by the translator.

Finally, there is the problem of the rhyme. "Mg-no-vain-yay" has over two thousand Jack-in-the-box rhymes popping out at the slightest pressure, whereas I cannot think of one to "moment." The position of "mg-no-vain-yay" at the end of the line is not negligible either, due as it is to Pushkin's more or less consciously knowing that he would not have to hunt for its mate. But the position of "moment" in the English line implies no such security; on the contrary he would be a singularly reckless fellow who placed it there.

Thus I was confronted by that opening line, so full of Pushkin, so individual and harmonious; and after examining it gingerly from the various angles here suggested, I tackled it. The tackling process lasted the worst part of the night. I did translate it at last; but to give my version at this point might lead the reader to doubt that perfection be attainable by merely following a few perfect rules.

Mr. Nabokov's August 4 essay, "The Art of Translation," contains a beautiful example of the Art of Misquotation.

He refers to a line from "L'Invitation au Voyage" as *"Mon amie, ma soeur, connais-tu la douceur . . ."* Poor Baudelaire! The Russian translator didn't do so badly.

Baudelaire wrote:

"Mon enfant, ma soeur,
Songe à la douceur . . ."

New York City   E.W. N*ASH*

I am sorry that a poor memory led me to make a "friend" of that child; but Mr. Nash is quite wrong in assuming that by correcting my quotation he has baudelairized the Russian version: that little joy ride goes on undisturbed.

Palo Alto, Calif.   V*LADIMIR* N*ABOKOV*

Miss Lowell and Things

E ver since Miss Amy Lowell explained the "new manner" in poetry I have
been trying to imagine life lived as she describes it. For she says that there
has been a changed attitude towards life which compels a poet to paint
landscapes because they are beautiful and not because they suit his mood, to tell
stories because they are interesting and not because they prove a thesis. I don't
understand this "externality"; I don't know what it means to be interested in
"things for themselves."

Let Miss Lowell try it some morning and see what happens. I pass over all the
things that might catch her poetic attention between the first sound of the alarm
clock and her appearance at the breakfast table. I assume that her human interest
in breakfast carries her past them, and prevents her from lingering immeasurably
over their color and form and polyphony. So she arrives at breakfast, and beholds
a sliced orange. It fascinates her. She "never tires of finding colors in it," and
sometimes the colors so occupy her that she takes them separately, unrelated to
the sliced orange, as it were. She goes on gazing at "colors, and light and shade, in
planes and cubes with practically no insistence on the substance which produces
them." Says someone at the table, disconcerted: "Eat your orange, Miss Lowell."
"Impossible," is the unhesitating reply. "I am interested in things for themselves.
It is an inevitable change, my dear, reflecting the evolution of life."

My guess is that Miss Lowell does not live at this pitch of externality. I imagine
that among the thousand objects which might attract her attention—oranges,
eggs, umbrellas, dustheaps—she chooses some one about which to write a poem.
And I imagine that she chooses it because it interests her for the particular mood
she happens to be in. And I imagine that she feels she has written a good poem
when her mood has got itself expressed about the object. I imagine she is external
when it interests her to be external. To be sure, if she doesn't choose to be
interested in her own feelings about the objects she selects, that is her affair. But
she shouldn't ask us to believe that she has transcended them, and is now
contemplating the world with the detachment of Aristotle's God. Nobody has
ever yet succeeded in being external to himself, and I doubt whether Miss Lowell
will succeed.

She speaks in her article about the universality of life, and then tells us that
"noble thoughts," are anathema to the modern poet. Of course they are, if you put
them in quotation marks. But there are noble thoughts which poets have not
always ruled out of the universality of life, and those thoughts expressing the

depth and variety of human desire are the elements which Miss Lowell's school somehow seems to avoid.

Much of their work often reminds me of the art collections which museums put in the basement—Persian pottery, a choice array of Egyptian beetles, six hundred and fifty specimens of Roman drinking cups, and a fascinating group of curious watches made at Nuremberg in the sixteenth century. All interesting enough if you have the time to look at them, and if properly distributed, amusing and delightful. A few specialists may be seen poring over the showcases, and an occasional party of tourists comes through bent on seeing all there is to see. But upstairs there is a crowd in front of the Madonna and Child, the famous Venus, and somebody's battle picture. Those are the art works the people remember, and hang photographs of in the parlor. It is the art with which they live.

And I wonder whether they're not more right than Miss Lowell, when they ask the artist to express human responses to the central issues of life and death. If art is a solace and a stimulus to men, are they such utter philistines in saying that the significant artist is not he who deals with things for themselves, but with things in relation to human need? I grant Miss Lowell that there are colors in the dustheaps, but what I'm afraid of is that her horror of noble thoughts has frightened her away from the effort to find color and significance in those more difficult objects about which human life revolves. I'm afraid that Miss Lowell calls a preoccupation with incidentals a brave attempt to be external and universal.

GRANVILLE HICKS   DECEMBER 3, 1930

The World of Robert Frost

COLLECTED POEMS by Robert Frost. New York: Henry Holt and Company.

In one of the poems in his "West Running Brook," Frost says,

I have been one acquainted with the night.
I have walked out in rain—and back in rain.
I have outwalked the furthest city light.

He has known, he would tell us, what the world has to offer of pain and sorrow. He is not unfamiliar with the experiences that make men grieve and despair. If he has kept his sanity, it is not because he has blinded himself to the elements in life that make men mad. But to him as a poet the most important result of his acquaintance with sorrow has been the realization that the exercise of the creative faculties is independent of circumstance—

And further still at an unearthly height
One luminary clock against the sky

Proclaimed the time was neither wrong nor right.
I have been one acquainted with the night.

This is vigorous doctrine in an age that has been fertile in self-analysis and self-commiseration. Frost's credo, however, runs counter to the consensus of opinion of the critics of all ages as well as to the temper of his own era. Matthew Arnold summarized the verdict of most students of letters when he said, "For the creation of a master work of literature two powers must concur, the power of the man and the power of the moment, and the man is not enough without the moment." Wordsworth said something of the same sort, and perhaps came closer to the difficulties of our own time, when he pointed out that facts and ideas have to become familiar to mankind, have to become part of common human experience, before the poet can use them. The poet cannot accept them until they are "ready to put on, as it were, a form of flesh and blood." So much in modern life has not been assimilated to organized human experience, so many of our acts and thoughts are unrelated to any central purpose or unifying hypothesis, so many obstacles stand in the way of the much-discussed modern synthesis, that the poet must grow desperate who looks for the order of ideas, the intellectual and spiritual atmosphere, that Arnold says he needs. It is no wonder that most poets and critics would say that a time may indeed be either wrong or right and that the present time is decidedly wrong.

So strong is the case for this view of literature that we may omit the task of defending it in detail, and, instead, ask ourselves how it is possible for Frost to hold the contrary opinion. The answer is to be found, of course, not in any critical writings of his but in his poetry. "Collected Poems" shows and shows clearly that Frost has written as fine poetry as any living American and that the proportion of first-rate poetry to the whole is greater than that in the work of any other contemporary. This last point is important, not because quantity matters, but because so many American poets, after a brief productive period, have dipped into silence or mediocrity. The fact that Frost's power is not only intense but also sustained forces us either to accept his theory or find some other explanation of his achievements.

What the other explanation may be is suggested when we realize how compact and unified Frost's work is. Instead of writing about this aspect of our civilization and that, instead of yielding himself to the casual inspirations of unrelated phenomena, he has occupied himself with a limited body of experiences. He has, in short, found, for poetic purposes, a world of his own. In so doing he is not, obviously, alone among contemporary poets: Robinson, Aiken, Eliot, each has his own world. But Frost's world is different from the world of any of these other poets, in that it is related to a real world with definite boundaries in time and space. That is why his poetry is more substantial than the poetry of any of the others, why his people are three-dimensional, why his figures of speech are always concrete and non-literary. His world is not an artificial, intellectual abstraction from the real world; it is set apart from the rest of the world by geographical and historical facts. Of course his world is not to be completely identified with the rural New Hampshire of the maps and books of statistics; it is, after all, his world. But it is directly related to rural New Hampshire, as Dante's world was directly related to medieval Europe and Shakespeare's to Elizabethan England.

Let us enter Frost's world and examine its advantages for the poet. What we do not find is perhaps more important than what we do. We find, in the first place, nothing of industrialism, and since at present so many of both the demands and the accomplishments of the machine are unrelated to the permanent hopes and impulses of the human heart, the absence of this phenomenon is significant for the poet. In the second place, we look in vain for evidences of the disrupting effect that scientific hypotheses have had on modern thought. The natives may have heard that

"The trouble with the Mid-Victorians
Seems to have been a man named John L. Darwin."

But the fundamental problems of conduct and destiny are still considered in terms older and richer in emotional connotations than the phraseologies of Darwinian biology and Einsteinian physics:

"Go 'long," said I to him, he to his horse.

Frost, living in that world, can afford to look with amusement on the bewildered modern—

A baggy figure, equally pathetic
When sedentary and when peripatetic.

Finally, to take a third example of the absence in Frost's world of some of the less assimilable factors in our civilization, there is the matter of Freudianism. He is still free to treat love in the language of an era before psychoanalysis was known. When he is in New York he may be told,

"Choose you which you will be—a prude, or puke,
Mewling and puking in the public arms."

But he can reply,

"Me for the hills where I don't have to choose."

It remains to summarize briefly some of the things that can be found in Frost's world. For purposes of his narrative verse he can find not merely pathos but also, because there are certain standards implicit in that world, something close to tragedy. He can find subjects for comedy there, dramatic conflicts, objects of natural beauty. He can treat abnormality and yet keep it in its place, or he can find a theme for as illuminating a commentary on failure as Robinson ever wrote. In the contemplation of nature he can, as scores of lyrics show, find the beginnings of paths that lead straight to the problems that have perennially perplexed the mind of man. He can, in short, find opportunity and stimulus to exercise to the full the poetic imagination.

There is one thing, of course, Frost cannot do: he cannot contribute directly to the unification, in imaginative terms, of our culture. He cannot give us the sense of belonging in the industrial, scientific, Freudian world in which we find ourselves. The very limitations that are otherwise so advantageous make it impossible. That is why no one would think of maintaining that he is one of the great poets of the ages. To that extent the time, even though he refuses to lay the responsibility at its door, is not right. But, if the time is so completely wrong as there is reason to suspect, no poet, however great his genius, could render that ultimate service of the imagination. Every poet today is necessarily a limited poet. Frost's relative greatness lies in the fact that, endowed with the power, he discovered a way to make the time as favorable for the exercise of that power as it could possibly be. He told the story himself when he said of the star in the stone boat—

> Such as it is, it promises the prize
> Of the one world complete in any size
> That I am like to compass, fool or wise.

He compassed it, and we should be considerably the poorer if he had not.

GEORGE SANTAYANA   FEBRUARY 27, 1915

Shakespeare: Made in America

Custom blinds us to the costume of thought. Not until the fashion has entirely changed do we see how extravagant the old costume was. The late middle ages and the renaissance, when modern languages took shape, had a very elaborate and modish dress for the mind as well as for the body. Notice, for instance, how Shakespeare can deck out a Hock sentiment, proper to any schoolboy:

> When in disgrace with fortune and men's eyes
> I all alone beweep my outcast state
> And trouble deaf heaven with my bootless cries
> And look upon myself and curse my fate,
> Wishing me like to one more rich in hope,
> Featur'd like him, like him with friends possess'd,
> Desiring this man's art and that man's scope,
> With what I most enjoy contented least,
> Yet in these thoughts myself almost despising,—
> Haply I think on thee; and then my state,
> Like to the lark at break of day arising
> From sullen earth, sings hymns at heaven's gate:
> For thy sweet love remember'd such wealth brings
> That then I scorn to change my state with kings.

For Shakespeare this sonnet is comparatively plain and direct, yet it is simply encrusted with old-fashioned jewels and embroideries. How much so will become clear if we venture to paraphrase it, scrupulously leaving out every suggestion that could not have had its origin in the twentieth century and in America.

In the first few lines almost every connotation is obsolete and will have to be abandoned. So the idea of falling out of favor at a court where the capricious monarch is Fortune. This mythological Fortune was rather a verbal deity from the beginning and had become merely rhetorical even in Shakespeare's time; for us it is worse, and the unrepublican image is inadmissible. To *beweep* anything is also contrary to our manners; if tears ever escape us it is not ceremoniously nor as a fit accompaniment to magnificent lamentations. As to *men's eyes*, we look through our eyes, but seldom talk through them; and if we wish to shake off an objectionable friend we do not cast withering glances upon him, like the noble savage. We simply avoid the man; or if we are inclined to be offensively demonstrative, we cut him. The word *outcast* is still current; but the background which gave poignancy to that metaphor belongs to a bygone age. No one can be easily excommunicated in our tolerant society. If one circle disowns him he will slip into another, perhaps with relief, and find it no less self-respecting, even in jail; and if he makes bold to flaunt his crime or his heresy, he will excite more interest than loathing, and a party of sympathizers will probably flock to his side.

No less obsolete is the habit of troubling heaven with one's bootless cries. Even the lover in the sonnet, though he might have prayed, would hardly have emitted cries; only in remote antiquity his predecessors in the art of troubling heaven may actually have wailed. Nowadays hardly anybody would pray in the hope of recovering his friends or his property by divine interposition. People certainly have recourse to religion, and often in a more desperate need than ever; but to modern feeling religion opens a second sphere of interest and hope, without being expected to further our worldly hopes and interests.

In the body of the sonnet there are a number of phrases which, without being in the least archaic, have a certain grand sweeping air and *panache* about them quite foreign to our experience. The word *art*, for instance, to most Americans suggests the profession of painting; the intended faculty of doing all things easily and well would have to be called ability or skill, or more pungently and characteristically, *brains*. This single transition from art to brains speaks volumes. Again, while no nation was ever more hopeful than America or more optimistic, to say *rich in hope* is to give the matter a different twist. You are optimistic when you take for granted or religiously assure yourself that the future, whatever it may be, will be all right, and will somehow grow better and better. You are rich in hope when you have great and definite expectations, are heir or aspirant to an exalted position, and can picture in a concrete form the happy future before you. So a bridegroom is rich in hope on his wedding morning, or an expectant mother when making bibs for her first-born; but the optimist may be as poor in hope as in experience.

Similarly the phrase *I look upon myself* expresses something different from our self-consciousness. It describes the shock of suddenly seeing yourself as others see you, as when you unexpectedly come upon yourself in a mirror. The poet is borrowing men's eyes in order to consider and pity himself; he is not retreating into a psychological observation of what is hidden from others in his consciousness.

The eleventh and twelfth lines will have to be sacrificed in their entirety. There are no larks in America. There is no heaven in modern cosmology such that the blue sky in which larks sing should be called the gate of it. And what hymns could the poet have been thinking of? Christmas carols, perhaps, or such as the choir of Magdalen College in Oxford greet the sunrise with on May morning from the top of their lovely tower. In any case they were pre-Puritan hymns, hymns of joyful familiarity with a religion sweetly and humanly miraculous, hymns not associated with drawling tunes, funerals, or a vague sense of constraint and edification. For these two lines, therefore, we must substitute something wholly different, yet as nearly equivalent as possible. I can think of nothing domesticated in America nearer to larks and to bright religion than music is. So orchestral strains shall take the place of larks, with profound apologies; and in speaking of music we may perhaps slightly inflate the poetic bellows, since modern shyness does not attack our souls so much in that invisible wilderness.

As to the final couplet, we may still talk occasionally of being as happy as a king or as drunk as a lord, but whatever seduction there may once have been in those images, they have paled. Something of far greater moment, however, lies submerged here. The unsophisticated reader may pass approvingly over the phrase *thy sweet love*, as if the poet might just as well have written *our sweet love* instead, meaning that mutual, complete, hearty, happy, plebeian love which alone should figure in our revised American version. Yet as a matter of fact the sentiment and pathos of the original are profoundly different, being charged with the most exotic metaphysical overtones. If we compare this sonnet with the rest of Shakespeare's, and consider the W.H. to whom at least by a poetic fiction they were addressed, it becomes evident that *thy sweet love* can only mean *the sweet love of thee*, a love which the poet did not and could not aspire to see returned. That ornate and exuberant age had so much passion to spare that it could think it but graceful adulation for a poet to address the intensest and richest effusions of love to some insipid youth in a high station. And behind that lavish play of expression (for perhaps it was nothing more) we must not ignore the possibility that the passion expressed may sometimes have been real, at least in those who first set this literary fashion; and in that case, seeing that even if graciously tolerated, such adoration could not possibly be mutual, we are at once transported into the dim sanctuary of Platonic love, where youth and beauty, at an aesthetic remove and because of their intrinsic virtue, are reputed to communicate a supreme and sufficient bliss to the worshipper, with all those moral and saving effects which this sonnet, for instance, celebrates. The lover in his infatuation, and in the religious chastening of it, is said somehow to find God. Humbug or philosophy, this Platonic mysticism has long been a classic refuge of hopeless emotion, and Shakespeare's sonnets march conventionally in the devout procession. Such ambiguous mysteries, however, are alien to modern sentiment and to the plain man's experience, and we may shut them out without further parlance.

Plucked of all its Elizabethan feathers, our sonnet might then present somewhat the following appearance:

> When times are hard and old friends fall away
> And all alone I lose my hope and pluck,
> Doubting if God can hear me when I pray,
> And brood upon myself and curse my luck,
> Envying some stranger for his handsome face,
> His wit, his wealth, his chances, or his friends,
> Desiring this man's brains and that man's place,
> And vexed with all I have that makes amends,

Yet in these thoughts myself almost despising,—
By chance I think of you; and then my mind,
Like music from deep sullen murmurs rising
To peals and raptures, leaves the earth behind:
For if you care for me, what need I care
To own the world or be a millionaire?

The reader may laugh, but I have not made the sonnet absurd on purpose; on the contrary I have tried to keep it as good as possible under the conditions imposed. The experiment is not intended to show how an American poet would actually feel or treat Shakespeare's subject, for he would either compose fine imitative literature, with a lapse here and there which he might not be conscious of, or else he would give birth to something entirely novel. The experiment is meant only to make evident how much old finery there is in our literary baggage, and how original an original poet would have to be. Any wise man of Shakespeare's time might have prophesied that ruffs would no longer be worn in three hundred years, but only a genius could have foretold our trousers. So any critic may unfrock Shakespeare, but to dress his thought up again in the costume of a future poetry can be given only to the future poets themselves.

E. M. FORSTER   MARCH 28, 1928

Ibsen the Romantic

"My book is poetry, and if it is not poetry, then it will be."—Ibsen to Bjornson.

I bsen was a poet during the earlier part of his life. He began as a lyricist, and his first plays are either in verse or are inspired by an imaginative contemplation of the past. When he was about forty, a change occurred, the importance of which has been differently estimated. Certain critics, both friendly and hostile, regard it as a fundamental change. They argue that with "The League of Youth" the real or realistic Ibsen begins to emerge, the singer dies, the social castigator is born, the scene clarifies and darkens, and ideas come to the front which do not necessarily contradict previous ideas, but which are given a prominence that entirely alters the dramatic emphasis. We pass from the epic to the domestic. Peer Gynt becomes Hialmar Ekdal, and Brand as Gregers Werle tears the spectacles of illusion from his eyes, and they work out their tragedy not among forests and fjords, but in a photographic studio opening into a sort of aviary. The aviary contains a few dead Christmas trees, also a water trough, some rabbits, but no bears, one wild duck, and that a damaged one. We could not be further from romance, the critics say, and turn, if they are friendly, to the character drawing, the technique, and the moral and social issues; if they are hostile, to the squalor. "Somewhere in the course of the battle of his life," writes Brandes, "Ibsen had a lyric Pegasus killed under him." "Novel and perilous nuisance," wrote the London Daily Telegraph. The critics agree in thinking that the poetry, if ever there was any, has gone.

Has it gone? Can the habits of forty years be set aside? Of twenty years—yes; most people are romantic at twenty, owing to lack of experience. As they grow older life offers various alternatives, such as worldliness or philosophy or the sense of humor, and they usually accept one of these. If, in spite of more solid temptations, they still cling to poetry, it is because a deep preference has to be satisfied. bsen was a poet at forty because he had that preference. He was a poet at sixty also. His continued interest in avalanches, water, trees, fire, mines, high places, traveling, was not accidental. Not only was he born a poet—he died one, and as soon as we try to understand him instead of asking him to teach us, the point becomes clearer.

He is, of course, not easy to understand. Two obstacles may be noted. In the first place he has got the deceptive air of a teacher, there is something in his method that implies a message, though the message really rested on passing irritabilities, and not on any permanent view of conduct or the universe. In the second place, he further throws us off the scent by taking a harsh or a depressing view of human relationships. As a rule, if a writer has a romantic temperament, he will find human relationships beautiful. His characters may hate one another or be unhappy together, but they will generate nobility or charm, they will never be squalid, whatever their other defects. And the crux in Ibsen is, that, though he had the romantic temperament, he found personal intercourse squalid. Sooner or later his characters draw their little knives, they rip up the present and the past, and the closer their intimacy, the better their opportunities for exchanging pain. Oswald Alving knows how to hurt his mother, Rosmer his mistress, and married couples are even more favorably placed. The Helmers, the Tesmans, the Wangels, Solnesses, Allmers, Borkmans, Rubeks—what a procession, equally incapable of comradeship and ecstasy. If they were heroic or happy once, it was before the curtain rose, and only survives as decay. And if they attain reconciliation, like the Rentheim sisters, the curtain has to fall. Their intercourse is worse than unfriendly, it is petty; moral ugliness trespasses into the esthetic. And when a play is full of such characters and evolves round their fortunes, how can it possibly be a romantic play? Poetry might perhaps be achieved if Ibsen's indignation was of the straight hitting sort, like Dante's. But for all its sincerity there is something automatic about it, he reminds us too often of father at the breakfast table after a bad night, sensitive to the defects of society as revealed by a chance glance at the newspaper, and apt to blame all parties for them indiscriminately. Now it is the position of women that upsets father, now the lies people tell, now their inability to lie, now the drains, now the newspaper itself, which he crumples up, but his helpers and servers have to retrieve it, for bad as are all political parties he must really see who got in at Rosmersholm. Seldom can a great genius have had so large a dose of domestic irritability. He was cross with his enemies and friends, with theater managers, professors, and students, and so cross with his countrymen for not volunteering to help the Danes in 1863 that he had to go to Italy to say so. He might have volunteered in person—he was in the prime of life at the time—but this never occurred to him, he preferred instead to write a scathing little satire about a Norwegian mother whose son was safe at the front. And it is (if one may adopt the phrase) precisely the volunteer spirit that is absent from his conception of human relationships. He put everything into them except the strength of his arm.

"Not a great writer . . . almost great, but marred by this lack of generosity." How readily the phrases rise to the lips! How false they are! For this nagging quality, this habitual bitterness—they are essential in his greatness, because they beckon to the poetry in him, and carry it with them under the ground. Underground. Into the depths of the sea. Had he been of heroic build and turned to the light and the sun, his gifts would have evaporated. But he was—thank heaven—subterranean, he loved narrow passages and darkness, and his later plays have a romantic intensity which not only rivals the romantic expansion of their predecessors, but is absolutely unique in literature. The trees in old Ekdal's aviary are as numerous as a forest because they are countless, the water in the chickens' trough includes all the waves on which the Vikings could sail. To his impassioned vision dead and damaged things, however contemptible socially, dwell for ever in the land of romance, and this is the secret of his so-called symbolism: a connection is found between objects that lead different types of existence; they reinforce one another and each lives more intensely than before. Consequently his stage throbs with a mysteriousness for which no obvious preparation has been made, with beckonings, tremblings, sudden compressions of the air, and his characters as they wrangle among the oval tables and pot-plants are not by any means alone, because an unseen power is watching them or slipping between their words.

A weaker dramatist who had this peculiar gift would try to get his effect by patches of fine writing, but with Ibsen as with Beethoven the beauty comes not from the tunes, but from the way they are used and are worked into the joints of the action. "The Master Builder" contains superb examples of this. The plot unfolds logically, the diction is flat and austere, the scene is a villa close to which another villa is being erected, the chief characters are an elderly couple and a young woman who is determined to get a thrill out of her visit, even if it entails breaking her host's neck. Hilda is a minx, and though her restlessness is not as vulgar as Hedda Gabler's it is quite as pernicious and lacks the saving gesture of suicide. That is one side of Hilda. But on the other side she touches Gerd and the Rat Wife and the Button Molder, she is a lure and an assessor, she comes from the non-human and asks for her kingdom and for castles in the air that shall rest on solid masonry; and from the moment she knocks at the door poetry filters into the play. Solness, when he listened to her, was neither a dead man nor an old fool. No prose memorial can be raised to him, and consequently Ibsen himself can say nothing when he falls from the scaffolding, and Bernard Shaw does not know that there is anything to say. But Hilda hears harps and voices in the air, and though her own voice may be that of a sadistic schoolgirl, the sound has nevertheless gone out into the dramatist's universe, the avalanches in "Brand" and "When We Dead Awaken" echo it, so does the metal in John Gabriel Borkman's mine. And it has all been done so competently. The symbolism never holds up the action because it is part of the action, and because Ibsen was a poet, to whom creation and craftsmanship were one. It is the same with the white horse in "Rosmersholm," the fire of life in "Ghosts," the gnawing pains in "Little Eyolf," the sea in "The Lady from the Sea," where Hilda's own stepmother voices more openly than usual the *malaise* that connects the forces of nature and the fortunes of men. Everything rings true and echoes far because it is in the exact place which its surroundings require.

The source of Ibsen's poetry is indefinable; presumably it comes from the same place as his view of human nature, otherwise they would not harmonize as they do in his art. The vehicle in which poetry reached him—that can easily be defined; it was, of course, the scenery of western and southwestern Norway. At some date previous to his Italian journey he must have had experiences of passionate intensity among the mountains, comparable to the early experiences of Wordsworth in the English lakes. All his life they kept returning to him, clothed in streams, trees, precipices, and hallowing his characters while they recriminated. In "Brand" and "Peer Gynt" they filled the stage; subsequently they shrank and concentrated; in the two last plays they again fill the stage and hasten the catastrophes by a shroud of snow. To compare Ibsen with Wordsworth is to scandalize the faithful in either camp, yet they had one important point in common; they were both of them haunted until the end of their lives by the romantic possibilities of scenery. Wordsworth fell into the residential fallacy; he continued to look at his gods direct, and to pin with decreasing success his precepts to the flanks of Helvellyn. Ibsen, wiser and greater, sank and smashed the Dovrĕfjeld in the depths of the sea, the depths of the sea. He knew that he should find it again. Neither his satire nor his character drawing dwelt as deep; neither the problems he found in human conduct* nor the tentative solutions he propounded lay at the roots of his extraordinary heart. There, in that strange gnarled region, a primeval romanticism lurked, frozen or twisted or exuding slime; there was the nest of the Great Boyg. The Great Boyg did not strive, did not die, lay beneath good and evil, did not say one thing more than another:

> Forward or back, and it's just as far;
> Out or in, and it's just as strait.

What do the words mean, and, apart from their meaning, are they meant to be right? And if right, are the prayers of Solveig, which silence them for a moment, wrong? It is proper that we should ask such questions as these when focusing on the moral and social aspect of his work, and they have been excellently asked and answered by Bernard Shaw. But as soon as we shift the focus the questions go dim, the reformer becomes a dramatist, we shift again and the dramatist becomes a lyric poet, listening from first to last for the movements of the trolls. Ibsen is at bottom Peer Gynt. Side-whiskers and all, he is a boy bewitched:

> The boy has been sitting on his mother's lap.
> They two have been playing all the life-day long.

And though the brow that bends over him can scarcely be described as maternal, it will assuredly preserve him from the melting ladle as long as books are read or plays seen.

---

*Wicksteed conveniently summarizes the problem as: "Suppress individuality and you have no life; assert it, and you have war and chaos."

Willa Cather

In 1922 Willa Cather wrote an essay called "The Novel Démeublé" in which she pleaded for a movement to throw the "furniture out of the novel—to get rid, that is, of all the social fact that Balzac and other realists had felt to be so necessary for the understanding of modern charaver. "Are the banking system and the Stock Exchange worth being written about at all?" Miss Cather asked, and she replied that they were not. Among the things which had no "proper place in imaginative art"—because they cluttered the scene and prevented the free play of the emotions—Miss Cather spoke of the factory and the whole realm of "physical sensations." Obviously, this essay was the rationale of a method which Miss Cather had partly anticipated in her early novels and which she fully developed a decade later in "Shadows on the Rock." And it is no less obvious that this technical method is not merely a literary manner but the expression of a point of view toward which Miss Cather had always been moving—with results that, to many of her readers, can only indicate the subtle failure of her admirable talent.

If we say that Miss Cather has gone down to defeat before the actualities of American life we put her in such interesting company that the indictment is no very terrible one. For a history of American literature must be, in Whitman's phrase, a series of "vivas for those who have failed." In our literature there are perhaps fewer completely satisfying books and certainly fewer integrated careers than there are interesting canons of work and significant life stories. Something in American life seems to prevent the perfection of success while it produces a fascinating kind of search or struggle, usually unavailing, which we may observe again and again in the collected works and in the biographies of our writers.

In this recurrent but heroic defeat, the life of the American writer parallels the life of the American pioneer. The historian of frontier literature, Professor Hazard, has pointed out that Cooper's very first presentation of Deerslayer, the type of all pioneers, shows him a nearly broken old man threatened with jail for shooting a deer, a pitiful figure overwhelmed by the tides of commerce and speculation. In short, to a keen observer, the pioneer's defeat was apparent even in 1823. The subsequent decades that opened fresh frontiers did not change the outcome of the struggle. Ahead of the pioneer there are always the fields of new promise, with him are the years of heartbreaking effort, behind him are the men who profit by his toil and his hope. Miss Cather's whole body of work is the attempt to accommodate and assimilate her perception of the pioneer's failure. Reared on a Nebraska farm, she saw the personal and cultural defeat at first hand. Her forebears had marched westward to the new horizons; her own work is a march back toward the spiritual East—toward all that is the very antithesis of the pioneer individualism and innovation, toward authority and permanence, toward Rome itself.

The pioneer, as seen by a sophisticated intelligence like Miss Cather's, stands in double jeopardy: he faces both the danger of failure and the danger of success. "A pioneer . . . should be able to enjoy the idea of things more than the things themselves," Miss Cather says; disaster comes when an idea becomes an actuality. From "O Pioneers!" to "The Professor's House," Miss Cather's novels portray the results of the pioneer's defeat, both in the thwarted pettiness to which he is condemned by his material failures and in the callous insensitivity produced by his material success. "The world is little, people are little, human life is little," says Thea Kronborg's derelict music teacher in "The Song of the Lark." There is only one big thing—desire." When there is no longer the opportunity for effective desire, the pioneer is doomed. But already in Miss Cather's Nebraska youth the opportunities for effective desire had largely been removed: the frontier had been closed.

"A Lost Lady," Miss Cather's most explicit treatment of the passing of the old order, is the central work of her career. Far from being the delicate minor work it is so often called, it is probably her most muscular book, for it derives power from the grandeur of its theme. Miss Cather shares the American belief in the tonic moral quality of the pioneer's life; with the passing of the frontier she conceives that a great source of fortitude has been lost. Depending on a very exact manipulation of symbols, the point of "A Lost Lady" (reminiscent of Henry James's "The Sacred Fount") is that the delicacy and charm of Marian Forrester spring not from herself but from the moral strength of her pioneer husband. Heavy, slow, not intelligent, Forrester is one of those men who, in his own words, "dreamed the railroads across the mountains." He shares the knightly virtues which Miss Cather unquestioningly ascribes to the early settlers; "impractical to the point of magnificence," he is one of those who could "conquer but not hold." He is defeated by the men of the new money interests who "never risked anything"—and the perdition of the lost lady proceeds in the degree that she withdraws from her husband in favor of one of the sordid new men, until she finds her final degradation in the arms of an upstart vulgarian.

But though the best of the pioneer ideal is defeated by alien forces, the ideal itself, Miss Cather sees, is really an insufficient one. In her first considerable novel, "O Pioneers!" she already wrote in an elegiac mood and with the sense that the old ideal was not enough. Alexandra Bergson, with her warm simplicity, her resourcefulness and shrewd courage, is the essence of the pioneering virtues, but she is distinguished above her neighbors because she feels that, if she is to work at all, she must believe that the world is wider than her cornfields. Her pride is not that she has triumphed over the soil but that she has made her youngest brother "a personality apart from the soil." The pioneer, having reached his goal at the horizons of the earth, must look to the horizons of the spirit.

The disappearance of the old frontier left Miss Cather with a heritage of the virtues in which she had been bred but with the necessity of finding a new object for them. Looking for the new frontier, she found it in the mind. From the world of failure which she portrayed so savagely in "A Wagner Matinee" and "The Sculptor's Funeral," and from the world of fat prosperity of "One of Ours," she could flee to the world of art. For in art one may desire illimitably. And if, conceivably, one may fail—Miss Cather's artists never do—it is still only as an artist that one may be the eternal pioneer, concerned always with "the idea of things." Thea Kronborg, of the breed of Alexandra Bergson, turns all the old energy, bogged down in mediocrity, toward music. Miss Cather rhapsodizes for her: "O eagle of eagles! Endeavor, achievement, desire, glorious striving of human art."

But art is not the only, or a sufficient, salvation from the débâcle of pioneer culture. For some vestige of the old striving after new worlds which cannot be gratified seems to spread a poison through the American soul, making it thin and unsubstantial, unable to find peace and solidity. A foreigner says to Claude Wheeler of "One of Ours," "You Americans are always looking for something outside yourselves to warm you up, and it is no way to do. In old countries, where not very much can happen to us, we know that, and we learn to make the most of things." And with the artists, Miss Cather puts those gentle spirits who have learned to make the most of things—Neighbor Rosicky, Augusta and, preëminently, My Antonia. Momentarily betrayed by the later developments of the frontier, Antonia at last fulfills herself in child-bearing and a busy household, expressing her "relish for life, not over-delicate but invigorating."

Indeed, "making the most of things" becomes even more important to Miss Cather than the eternal striving of art. For, she implies, in our civilization even the best ideals are bound to corruption. "The Professor's House" is the novel in which she brings the failure of the pioneer spirit into the wider field of American life. Lame as it is, it epitomizes as well as any novel of our time the disgust with life which so many sensitive Americans feel, which makes them dream of their pre-adolescent integration and innocent community with nature, speculate on the "release from effort" and the "eternal solitude" of death, and eventually reconcile themselves to a life "without delight." Three stories of betrayal are interwoven in this novel: the success of Professor St. Peter's history of the Spanish explorers which tears him away from the frontier of his uncomfortable and ugly old study to set him up in an elegant but stifling new home; the sale to a foreign collector of the dead Tom Outland's Indian relics which had made his spiritual heritage; and the commercialization of Outland's scientific discovery with its subsequent corruption of the Professor's charming family. With all of life contaminated by the rotting of admirable desires, only Augusta, the unquesting and un-questioning German Catholic seamstress, stands secure and sound.

Not the pioneering philosophy alone, but the whole poetic romanticism of the nineteenth century had been suffused by the belief that the struggle rather than the prize was admirable, that a man's reach should exceed his grasp, or what's a heaven for? Having seen the insufficiency of this philosophy Miss Cather must find another in which the goal shall be more than the search. She finds it, expectably enough, in religion. The Catholicism to which she turns is a Catholicism of culture, not of doctrine. The ideal of unremitting search, it may be said, is essentially a Protestant notion; Catholic thought tends to repudiate the ineluctable and to seek the sharply defined. The quest for Moby Dick, that dangerous beast, is Protestant; the Catholic tradition selects what it can make immediate and tangible in symbol and Miss Cather turns to the way of life that "makes the most of things," to the old settled cultures. She attaches a mystical significance to the ritual of the ordered life, to the niceties of cookery, to the supernal virtues of *things* themselves—sherry, or lettuce, or "these coppers, big and little, these brooms and clouts and brushes" which are the tools for making life itself. And with a religious ideal one may safely be a pioneer. The two priests of "Death Comes for the Archbishop" are pioneers; they happen to be successful in their enterprise, but they could not have been frustrated, Miss Cather implies, because the worth of their goal is indisputable.

From the first of her novels the Church had occupied a special and gracious place in Willa Cather's mind. She now thinks with increasing eloquence of its permanence and certainty and of "the universal human yearning for something permanent, enduring, without shadow of change." The Rock becomes her often repeated symbol: "the rock, when one comes to think of it, was the utmost expression of human need." For the Church seems to offer the possibility of satisfying that appealing definition of human happiness which Miss Cather had made as far back as "My Antonia"—"to be dissolved in something complete and great," "to become a part of something entire, whether it is sun and air, goodness and knowledge."

It is toward that dissolvement that Miss Cather is always striving. She achieves it with the "sun and air"—and perhaps few modern writers have been so successful with landscape. She can find it in goodness and in society—but only if they have the feudal constriction of the old Quebec of "Shadows on the Rock." Nothing in modern life, no possibility, no hope, offers it to her. She conceives, as she says in the prefatory note to her volume of essays, "Not Under Forty," that the world "broke in two in 1922 or thereabouts" and she numbers herself among the "backward," unaware that even so self-conscious and defiant a rejection of her own time must make her talent increasingly irrelevant and tangential—for any time.

"The early pioneer was an individualist and a seeker after the undiscovered," says F.J. Turner, "but he did not understand the richness and complexity of life as a whole." Though Miss Cather in all her work has recognized this lack of understanding of complexity and wholeness, and has attempted to transcend it, she ends, ironically enough, in a fancier but no less restricted provincialism than the one she sought to escape. For the "spirituality" of Miss Cather's latest books consists chiefly of an irritated exclusion of those elements of modern life with which she will not cope. The particular affirmation of the verities which Miss Cather makes requires that the "furniture" be thrown out, that the social and political facts be disregarded; the spiritual life cannot support the intrusion of all the facts the mind can supply. The unspeakable Joubert, the extreme type of the verity-seeker says in one of his *pensées:* "'I'm hungry, I'm cold, help me!' Here is material for a good deed but not for a good work of art." Miss Cather, too, is irked by the intrusion of "physical sensations" in the novel.

Miss Cather's later books are pervaded by the air of a brooding ancient wisdom, but if we examine her mystical concern with pots and pans, it does not seem much more than an oblique defense of gentility or very far from the gaudy domesticity of bourgeois accumulation glorified in The Woman's Home Companion. And with it goes a culture-snobbery and even a caste-snobbery. The Willa Cather of the older days shared the old racial democracy of the West. It is strange to find the

Willa Cather of the present talking about "the adopted American," the young man of German, Jewish or Scandinavian descent who can never appreciate Sarah Orne Jewett and for whom American English can never be more than a means of communicating ideas: "It is surface speech: he clicks the words out as a bank clerk clicks out silver when you ask for change. For him the language has no emotional roots." This is indeed the gentility of Katherine Fullerton Gerould, and in large part the result, one suspects, of what Parrington calls "the inferiority complex of the frontier mind before the old and established."

Yet the place to look for the full implications of a writer's philosophy is in the esthetic of his work. "Lucy Gayheart" shows to the full the effect of Miss Cather's point of view. It has always been a personal failure of her talent that prevented her from involving her people in truly dramatic relations with each other. (Her women, for example, always stand in the mother or daughter relation to men; they are never truly lovers.) But at least once upon a time her people were involved in a dramatic relation with themselves or with their environments, whereas now "Lucy Gayheart" has not even this involvement. Environment does not exist, fate springs from nothing save chance; the characters are unattached to anything save their dreams. The novel has been *démeublé* indeed; but life without its furniture is strangely bare.

STARK YOUNG   APRIL 11, 1923

Bernhardt

I can easily say, I think, that of all the players I have seen on the stage Duse is the greatest artist. More than any other, Duse brings to the art of acting the largest and most poignant idea, the profoundest sensitivity, the deepest and most exquisite response to experience. Of all the people in the theatre Duse has most in common with great poetry, great joy and sorrow and beauty, great living. But Duse's acting was, as one saw very quickly, a mere fragment of her; to the making of her art she brought out of her head a lot of old boards, as she said once, comparing herself to Dolmetsch and his method of working old timbers into instruments for music. You got the sense in Duse that her art arose from her life and what she was, as the form of waves and their light and color arise from the large realm of the sea. But whether Duse was the greatest actor in the world of acting—the greatest stage artist—is another matter.

If Duse is the greatest artist I have ever seen on the stage, it seems to me equally clear that Bernhardt was the greatest actor. By that I mean that, endowed as she was with the necessary tremendous gift, however limited in its range, Sarah Bernhardt of all actors was able to give it what came nearest to complete expression.

That Bernhardt was limited is obvious. She had a limited range of ideas, such ideas, for instance, as amorous seduction, pain and anger—the famous rage through tears—and the infinite throes of dying. She had certain type conceptions—limited in range if not in raw force—of the passionate, the ornate, the regal, the comic, the poetic. She had vast monotonies of temperament, however brilliant and strong. Her physical equipment—most of all the immortal voice—was extraordinary but limited in the possibilities of style. With these limitations and ideas she dominated the great classical dramatists; and to these limitations she forced new dramatists—Sardou, Rostand and the rest—to cater and made or wrecked them as the case might be.

But within these limits Bernhardt's expression was complete. So far as her particular needs went she was professionally competent in the last sense of the word. No vagary of mood or temper or circumstances could prevent her getting down to business. The quality and depth of her performance—the mere matter of sincerity hardly concerned it more than sincerity concerns the sun or the wind— varied of course. Her performances sometimes had to depend wholly on their sheer external competency. They descended often into what in another actor would have amounted to idle tricks; they sank often to what she chose merely to throw into them to get the occasion through with and off her hands. But they carried nevertheless to an amazing extent the thing that she meant them to convey. And this genius for the expression of herself carried not only into her hours of acting on the stage but into her relations with her public, her following carried to the press, the news of herself, to her advertisement, the grand rumor of her singularity and fire, to the manner in which she lived from day to day, her hunting tigers, standing on whales, going up in balloons, packing a coffin about with her, her love affairs, her extravagances, her photographs, her fury, her cars, her gifts, her debts, her sculpture and plays and flowers, her superhuman youth and finally her superhuman age. Bernhardt had, too, an undiluted egotism that very often swamped the play, the other actors, everything except the audience's response to herself. To her, art was a passion of self, a splendor of an artist's mood, though to her art was also the only important thing in the world. And it is true that in watching Sarah Bernhardt's acting, there was, as a number of her critics have said, something like the pleasure one gets from watching wild beasts in a cage.

But in saying that, these critics come to the heart of the matter and pay one of the ultimate tributes to her talent. It is precisely in this sense that Bernhardt rose, through her most adequate acting art, into her greatness. Her acting craft was such as might completely convey an enormous endowment of energy, magnetism, power.

It is this power that gave to Bernhardt's acting that fundamental, first, necessary element that all art must have. In art no serious and high intention, no moral bent, no purpose or idea, can take the place of this power, this energy, this abundance of vitality, at its first source.

This fact, however, has about it a biological unescapability that is to most human thinking none too comfortable. Serious realism, with its inclination to set down only the knowable, does not get very far with this endowment which has about it something of the quality of lightning and thunder and the inexplicable force of nature itself. Ibsen's parochialism would have set down Bernhardt's art as a magnificent perhaps but more or less arrant and useless egotism. Bernard Shaw's whole tone when writing of Sarah Bernhardt betrays his incapacity—since he cannot moralize or rationalize or socialize it to his own ends—for judging her complete achievement. And the whole tone of our democracy when it goes in for thought and philosophic explanation, tries, often unconsciously, to dispose of such a superior phenomenon as Bernhardt's talent by speaking of it as hard-working, devoted, persevering, rather than admit a born eminence in power, rather than confront the raw fact of an undemocratic summit in natural gift. But the public nevertheless saw always that Bernhardt was a stupendous event in human enterprises. Sarah Bernhardt amazed, thrilled, defeated them; she dominated even if she bored them; she delighted, exalted and made them shiver with ice on their spines. She established apart from herself, between herself and the moment out of human living that she wrought to her stage purposes, a magnificent whole idea, a popular image vastly entertaining and unforgettable, whatever else it might be, good or bad. And she made herself as an actor indistinguishable from herself as a woman. The public knew that Bernhardt might be limited in her range but they knew also very well that compared to many actors she might be limited somewhat as a star is more limited than a municipal lighting system, a tempest than Mr. Edison, and the express train between Chicago and New York than a Red Cross ambulance serving here and there. Bernhardt had something mythical about her like a volcano. People found in her something they could recognize though they might not be able to moralize it. They could see in her a kind of sheer life principle which they could enjoy without being able to understand, something that the instinct of life in them drove them, toward as a magnificent example of what they sensed to be the source of all our energy and admiration, I mean elemental power.

STARK YOUNG   JUNE 20, 1923

Duse Now

Duse, closer to seventy now than sixty, preserves still her old art of featuring nothing, but only of conveying the necessary truth. If you see one of the occasional performances that she is giving now in Italian theatres, you get the impression neither of a woman remarkably young-looking for her age nor of a woman on whom age has set an absorbingly interesting record. What you get is the impression of a slender woman with an extraordinary, interesting mask, with beautiful hands, gray hair and a low poignant voice.

All through the performance that I saw, Duse did not suggest age so much as she suggested a diminished endurance. There was no question of quality but only one of quantity. That is to say you could see clearly that the actress might not be able to go on for so long or so many performances or for prolonged, violent scenes; but it was also equally clear that for what she does do her body lacks nothing and is entirely adequate in the most exact meaning of the word: Duse's body keeps its old coordination, the flow of lines is still perfect and continuous; there is no sense of stiffness or angularity, or, as happens with age, of that lessening in the capacity of the muscles to carry out the immediate intention of the thought and will. The voice is something less clear and vibrant than once but no less dramatic and poignant. Looking at Duse's figure there on the stage you get pretty much what you always got, the sense of a body that has no existence apart from its idea and that is inseparable from what she means to express. Now as always Duse's art is connected with the external, the visible and audible aspect of her, as music is connected with sound. And the ideas and qualities that Duse expresses show still no sign of fatigue, of grayness, of doting egotism, of drouth, but only the old, quivering, subtle, profound passion of absorption with life and response to it that occurs in human living in its most complete moments whether in art or in other manifestations. . . .

Duse does not exemplify the art of acting so much as she illustrates the fundamentals of all art. All art, obviously, is concerned with the expression of life. To this purpose the artist is the first means, and after the artist the medium, color, words, sound, whatever it may be, that he works in. Duse's art illustrates first of all the principle in art of the necessity of the artist's own greatness, his sensitivity and power in feeling, in idea, in soul, in the education and fine culture of all these. Her art illustrates the necessity for a fierce and subtle and exact connection between the artist's meaning and his expression of it. It illustrates the universal problem of rhythm in art, of line, emphasis, mood, all rhythm. It illustrates supremely the nature of the poetic as it applies not only to poetry but to every art. And it illustrates the nature of realism in general, especially of that best Italian realism which, as it occurs most of all in sculpture, is so capable of rendering by means of only actual or possible external details the inmost idea.

And so it is that you cannot easily get from Duse's acting a pure acting delight. She is not the actor's actor, as Velasquez is the painter's painter, or Spenser the poet's poet. That is to say you cannot delight in her performance as supreme craft, something that delights whether it is deep or flitting, delights because of the perfection of its brush, its tone, its manner, because of its competency, because of its happy application of the art and the possibilities of pleasure in it by reason of its sheer technical purity and perfection, independent, so far as that is possible, of everything in life outside itself. And it is difficult to take any academic delight in Duse's acting. Something in you withholds you from saying what a beautiful gesture that was, what a tone, what a contrivance in that scene, what reading in this, what technical facility. All these things are good in themselves, of course; they too may be almost in themselves a kind of art. They are means of speaking, dialects for ideas; and, after all, art is art not life. Style, however, in the sense of an added elaboration and distinction of method, of something in itself creative and separable, style in that separable aspect of technical felicity or skill or tact, Duse rarely has. Style in the sense of a medium which, like a glass over a laboratory experiment, disappears before the matter which it isolates and exhibits, Duse is never without. It is only slowly and almost unwillingly that Duse's art will allow you a stylistic or academic enjoyment. It will not allow that separation of the craft from the meaning; it will not yield itself to the mere choice judgments of a sophistication in taste. Duse will not grant you that kind of appreciation. It is as if she would accept no love but the love for all herself and the cost that follows.

It is only slowly that you see what labor and skill has gone to make up that creation of Duse's soul in the outer forms of an art. You see her bending over the child, you see her carry the pilgrim's staff, the lines of her long garment, the pity of her hands, the wandering of her hands among the lights on the altar. You see suddenly that dumbness, and then that flutter of life through the body. You see that the entire moment has revealed itself to you. You see what this woman knows; and you wonder whether such a knowledge of the human life and soul resolves itself in her finally into tears or into light. But it is only slowly that you perceive this artist's years of study of the lines of statuary—and especially of sculptors like Mino da Fiesole and Desiderio da Settignana and those more delicate realists of the earlier Renaissance, to discover the inevitable lines of grace and meaning, to learn how to study the rhythms of the form in order to free them of all but that last beauty of its own characteristics. And you gradually observe that Duse suggests perpetually a state of music which must have come from a long love and study of that art. And most of all you will see that such a gradation of emphasis throughout the play and so fine and so elusive but unforgettable a comprehension of the entire meaning of the character and theme could come only from a remarkable ability and association with culture and ideas, combined with a poetic and reflective nature, with a courage of mind, and, finally, with something throughout the personality, quiet and taken for granted, a kind of untouched and unstressed and constant spiritual audacity.

PAUL ROSENFELD   APRIL 14, 1920

Strawinsky

The new steel organs of man have begotten their music in Le Sacre du Printemps. For with Strawinsky, the rhythms of machinery enter musical art. With this, his magistral work, a new chapter of music commences, the spiritualization of the new body of man is manifest. Through Debussy, music had liquefied, become opalescent and impalpable and fluent. It had become, because of his sense, his generation's sense, of the infirmity of things, a sort of symbol of the eternal flux, the eternal momentariness. It had come to body forth all that merges and changes and disappears, to mirror the incessant departures and evanescences of life, to shape itself upon the infinitely subtle play of light, the restless, heaving, foaming surface of the sea, the impalpable racks of perfume, upon gusts of wind and fading sounds, upon all the ephemeral wonders of the world. But through Strawinsky there has come to be a music stylistically wellnigh the reverse of that of the impressionists. Through him, music has become again cubical, lapidary, massive, mechanistic. Scintillation is gone out of it. The delicate sinuous melodic line, the glamorous sheeny harmonies, are gone out of it. The elegance of Debussy, the golden sensuality, the quiet, classic touch, are flown. Instead, there are come to be great weighty metallic masses, molten piles and sheets of steel and iron, shining adamantine bulks. Contours are become grim, severe, angular. Melodies are sharp, rigid, asymmetrical. Chords are uncouth, square clusters of notes, stout and solid as the pillars that support roofs, heavy as the thuds of trip hammers. Above all, there is rhythm, rhythm rectangular and sheer and emphatic, rhythm that lunges and beats and reiterates and dances with all the steely perfect tirelessness of the machine, shoots out and draws back, shoots upward and shoots down, with the inhuman motion of titanic arms of steel. Indeed, the change is as radical, as complete, as though in the midst of moonlit noble gardens a giant machine had arisen swiftly from the ground, and inundated the night with electrical glare, and set its metal thews and joints relentlessly whirring, relentlessly functioning.

And yet, the two styles, Debussy's and Strawinsky's, are related. Indeed, they are complementary. They are the reactions to the same stimulus of two fundamentally different types of mind. No doubt, between the two men there exist differences besides those of their general fashions of thinking. The temper of Debussy was profoundly sensuous and aristocratic and contained. That of Strawinsky is nervous and ironic and violent. The one man issued from an unbroken tradition, was produced by generations and generations of gentlemen. The other is one of those beings who seem to have been called into existence solely by the modern way of life, by express trains and ocean grayhounds, by the shrinkage of continents and vibration of the twentieth century world. But the chief difference, the difference that made Le Sacre du Printemps almost antithetical to Pelléas et Mélisande, is essentially the divergence between two cardinal manners of apprehending life. Debussy, on the one hand, seems to be of the sort of man in whom the center of conscience is, figuratively, sunken; one of those who have within themselves some immobility that makes the people and the things about them appear fleeting and unreal. For such, the world is a far distant thing, lying out on the rims of consciousness, delicate and impermanent as sunset hues or the lights and gestures of the dream. The music of Debussy is the magistral and classic picture of this distant and glamorous procession, this illusory and fantastical and transparent show, this thing that changes from moment to moment and is never twice the same, and flows away from us so quickly. But Strawinsky, on the other hand, is in the very midst of the thing so distant from the other man. For him, the material world is very real, sharp, immediate. He loves it, enjoys it, is excited by its many forms. He is vividly responsive to its traffic. Things make an immediate and biting impression on him, stimulate in him pleasure and pain. He feels their edge and knows it hard, feels their weight and knows it heavy, feels their motion in all its violence. Strawinsky takes an almost frenetic delight in the processes that go on about him. He goes through the crowded thoroughfares, through cluttered places, through factories, hotels, wharves, sits in railway trains, and the glare and tumult and pulsation, the engines and locomotives and cranes, the whole mad phantasmagoria of the modern city, evoke images in him, inflame him to reproduce them in all their weight and gianthood and mass, their blackness and luridness and power. The most vulgar things and events excite him. The traffic, the restlessness of crowds, the noise of vehicles, of the clatter of horses on the asphalt, of human cries and calls sounding above the street-bass, a couple of organ-grinders trying to outplay each other, a brass band coming down the avenue, the thunder of a railway train hurling itself over leagues of steel, the sirens of steamboats and locomotives, the roar of cities and harbors, become music to him. In one of his early orchestral sketches, he imitates the buzzing of a hive of bees. One of his miniatures for string-quartet bangs with the beat of the wooden shoes of peasants dancing to the snarling tones of a bagpipe. Another reproduces the droning of the priest in a little chapel, recreates the scene almost cruelly. And the score of Petruschka is alive marvellously with the rank, garish life of a cheap fair. Its bubbling flutes, seething instrumental caldron, concertina-rhythms and bright gaudy colors conjure up the movement of the crowds that surge about the amusement booths, paint to the life the little flying flags, the gestures of the showmen, the bright balloons, the shooting-galleries, the gipsy tents, the crudely stained canvas walls, the groups of coachmen and servant girls and children in their holiday finery. One can even smell the frying sausages.

For Strawinsky is one of those composers, found scattered all along the pathway of his art, who augment the expressiveness of music through direct imitation of nature. His imagination seems to be free, bound in no wise by what other men have adjudged music to be, and by what their practice has made it. He comes to his art without prejudice or preconception of any kind, it seems. He plays with its elements as capriciously as the child plays with paper and crayons. He amuses himself with each instrument of the band, careless of its customary uses. There are times when Strawinsky comes into the solemn conclave of musicians like a gamin with trumpet and drum. He disports himself with the infinitely dignified string-quartet, makes it do light and acrobatic things. There is one interlude of Petruschka that is written for snare-drums alone. His work is incrustated with cheap waltzes and barrel-organ tunes. He makes the orchestra imitate the quavering of an old hurdy-gurdy. Of late he has written a ballet for eight clowns. And he is reported to have said, "I should like to bring it about that music be performed in street cars while people get out and get in." For he finds his greatest enemy in the concert room, that rut that limits the play of the imagination of audiences, that fortress in which all of the intentions of the men of the past have established themselves, and from which they dominate the musical present. The concert room has succeeded in making music a drug, a sedative, has created a "musical attitude" in folk that is false, and robbed musical art of its power. For Strawinsky, music is either an infection, the communication of a lyrical impulse, or nothing at all. And so he would have it performed in ordinary places of congregation, at fairs, in taverns, music halls, street cars, if you will, in order to enable it to function freely once again. His art is pointed to quicken, to infect, to begin an action that the listener must complete within himself. It is a sort of musical shorthand. On paper, it has a fragmentary look. It is as though Strawinsky had sought to reduce the elements of music to their sharpest and simplest terms, had hoped that the "development" would be made by the audience. He seems to feel that if he cannot achieve his end, the communication of his lyrical impulse, with a single strong motif, a single strong movement of tones, a single rhythmic start, he cannot achieve it at all. So we find him writing songs, the three Japanese lyrics, for instance, that are epigrammatic in their brevity; a piece for string quartet that is played in fifty seconds; a three-act opera performed in thirty minutes.

But it is no experiment in form that he is making. He seems to bring into music some of the power of the Chinese artists who, in the painting of a twig, or of a pair of blossoms, represent the entire springtide. He has written some of the freshest, most rippling, delicate music. Scarcely a living man has written more freshly or incandescently. April, the flowering branches, the snowing petals, the clouds high in the blue, are really in the shrilling little orchestra of the Japanese lyrics, in the green gurgling flutes and watery violins. None of the innumerable Spring Symphonies, Spring Overtures, Spring Songs, are really more vernal, more soaked in the gentle sunshine of spring, are more really the seed-time, than the six naive piping measures of melody that introduce the figure of the Sacre entitled Rondes Printanières. Is any slumber-song really fuller of sleep than the few pages of L'Oiseau de Feu that precede the death of Kastchei the Immortal? No doubt, in venturing to write music so bold and original in aesthetic, Strawinsky was encouraged by the example of another musician, another Russian composer. Moussorgsky, before him, had trusted in his own innocence instead of in the wisdom of the fathers of the musical church, had dared obey the promptings of his own blood and set down chords, melodies, rhythms, just as they sang in his skull, though all the world rise up to damn him. But the penning of music as jagged, cubical, barbarous as the prelude to the third act of Strawinsky's little opera The Nightingale, or as naked, uncouth, rectangular, rocklike, polyharmonic, headlong, as some of that of Le Sacre du Printemps required no less perfect a conviction, no less great a self-reliance. The music of Strawinsky is the expression of an innocence comparable, indeed, to that of his great predecessor. Le Sacre du Printemps is what its composer termed it. It is "an act of faith."

And so, free of preconceptions, Strawinsky was able to let nature move him to imitation. Just as Picasso brings twentieth century nature into his still lives, so the young composer brings it into his music. It is the rhythm of machinery that has set Strawinsky, the artist, free. All his life, he has been conscious of these steel men. Mechanical things have influenced his art from the beginning. It is as though machinery had revealed him to himself, as though sight of the functioning of these metal organisms, themselves but the extension of human bones and muscles and organs, had awakened into play the engine that is his proper body, as though the infection of the dancing, lunging, pumping piston-rods, walking beams, drills, has awakened out of him a response, and given him his power to beat out rhythm. The machine has always fascinated him. One of his first original compositions, written while he was yet a pupil of Rimsky-Korsakof's, imitates fireworks, distinguishes what is human in their activity, in the popping, hissing, exploding, in the hysterical weeping of the fiery fountains, the proud exhibitions and sudden collapses of the pin-wheels. It is the machine, enemy of man, that is pictured by The Nightingale, that curious work of which one act dates from 1909, and two from 1914. Strawinsky had the libretto formed on the tale of Hans Christian Andersen which recounts the adventures of the little brown bird which sings so beautifully that the Emperor of China bids it to his court. Strawinsky's nightingale, too, comes to the palace and sings, and all the ladies of the entourage fill their mouths with water in the hopes of better imitating the warbling of the songster. But then there enter envoys bearing the gift of the Emperor of Japan, a mechanical nightingale that amuses the court with its clockwork antics. Once more, the emperor commands the woodland bird to sing. But it is flown. In his rage, the emperor banishes it from his realm. Then Death comes and sits at the emperor's bedside, and steals from him crown and scepter, till, of a sudden, the nightingale returns, and sings, and makes Death relinquish his spoils. And the courtiers who enter expecting to find the monarch dead, find him well and glad in the morning sunshine.

And in his two major works, Petruschka and Le Sacre du Printemps, Strawinsky makes the machine represent his own person. For the actions of machinery woke first in the human organism, and Strawinsky intensifies consciousness of the body by referring these motions to their origin. Petruschka is the man-machine seen from without, seen unsympathetically, in its comic aspect. Countless poets before Strawinsky have attempted to portray the puppet-like activities of the human being, and Petruschka is but one of the recent, innumerable stage-shows that expose the automation in the human soul. But the puppet-show of Strawinsky is singular because of its musical accompaniment. For more than even the mimes on the stage, the orchestra is full of the spirit of the automaton. The angular wooden gestures of the dolls, their smudged faces, their entrails of sawdust, are in the music ten times as intensely as they are upon the stage. In the score of Petruschka Music itself has become a little manikin in particolored clothes, at which Strawinsky gazes and laughs as a child laughs at a funny doll, and makes dance and tosses in the air, and sends sprawling. The score is full of the revolutions of wheels, of delicate clock-work movements, of screws and turbines. Beneath the music one always hears the regular insistent maniacal breathing of a concertina. And what in it is not purely mechanistic nevertheless completes the picture of the world as it appears to one who has seen the man machine in its comedy. The stage pictures, the trumpery little fair, the tinsel and pathetic finery of the crowds, the dancing of the human ephemera a moment before the snow begins to fall, are stained marvellously deeply by the music. The score has the colors of crudely dyed, faded bunting. It is the symbol of the whole cheap, flimsy, villainous globe.

Le Sacre, on the other hand, is the man-machine viewed not from without, and unsympathetically, but from within. So far, it is Strawinsky's masterwork, the completest and purest expression of his genius. For the elements that make for the originality of style of Petruschka and the other of Strawinsky's representative compositions, in this work attain a signal largeness and powerfulness. The rhythmic element, already fresh and free in the Scherzo of L'Oiseau de Feu and throughout Petruschka, attains virile and magistral might in it, surges and thunders with giant vigor. The instrumentation, magical with all the magic of the Russian masters in the earlier ballets, in Le Sacre begets that sharpness, hardness, nakedness which is originally Strawinsky's. Besides, the latter work has the thing hitherto lacking somewhat in the young man's art—grandeur and severity and ironness of language. In it, he stands completely new, completely in possession of his powers. And in it the machine operates. Ostensibly, the action of the ballet is laid in prehistoric times. Ostensibly, it figures the ritual with which a tribe of stone age Russians consecrated the spring. Something of the sort was necessary, for an actual representation of machines, a ballet of machines, would not have been as grimly significant as the angular uncouth gestures of men, would by no means have as nakedly revealed the human engine. Here, in the choreography, every fluid, supple, curving motion is suppressed. Everything is angular, cubical, rectilinear. The music pounds with the rhythm of engines. It whirls and spirals like screws and flywheels, grinds and shrieks like laboring metal. The orchestra is transmuted to steel. Each movement of the ballet correlates the rhythms of machinery with the human rhythms which they prolong and repeat. The weird orchestral introduction to the second scene has all the oppressive silence of machines at rest at night. And in the hurtling finale the music and the dancers create a figure that is at once the piston and a sexual symbol. For Strawinsky has stripped away from man all that with which specialization, differentiation, have covered him, and revealed him again, in a sort of cruel white light, a few functioning organs. He has shown him a machine to which power is applied, and which labors in blind obedience, no differently from the microscopic animal that eats and parturates and dies. The spring comes, and life replenishes itself, and man, like seed and germ, obeys the promptings of the blind power that created him, and accomplishes his predestined course and takes in energy and pours it out again. But, for a moment, in Le Sacre du Printemps, we feel the motor forces, watch the naked wheels and levers and arms at work, see the dynamo itself.

The ballet was completed in 1913, the year Strawinsky was thirty-one years old. It may be that the work will be succeeded by others even more original, more powerful. Or it may be that Strawinsky has already written his masterpiece. The works that he has composed during the war are not, it appears, strictly new developments. Whatever enlargement of the field of the string quartet the three little pieces, which the Flonzaleys played here in 1915, created, there is no doubt that it was nothing at all to compare with the innovation in orchestral music created by the great ballet. And, according to rumor, the newest of Strawinsky's work, the music-hall ballet for eight clowns, and the work for orchestra, ballet and chorus entitled Les Noces Villageoises, are by no means as bold in style as Le Sacre, and resemble Petruschka more than the later ballet. But, whatever Strawinsky's future accomplishment, there can be no doubt that with this one work, if not also with Petruschka, he has secured a place among the great musicians. It is doubtful whether any living composer has opened new musical land more widely than he. For he has not only minted music anew. He has reached a point ahead of us that the world would have reached without him. That alone shows him the genius. He has brought into music something for which we had long been waiting, and which we knew must one day arrive. To us, at this moment, Le Sacre du Printemps appears one of those compositions that mark off the musical miles.

Progress in Music

I

If western music were, like most of the other arts, supported by a really long tradition, the issue of present and future progress in music would perhaps be less important. If, for instance, there were extensive musical pieces dating back to the time of Euripides, or even going back a thousand years, music as we know it would seem less new. The fact is that only a few fragments have survived the Greco-Roman era. Even the music of the Middle Ages, which can be reconstructed and performed, was left by its composers in such a vague and fragmentary form that the authenticity of its modern interpretations can never finally be proved.

The supreme accomplishment of the Middle Ages in music was the development of a notation, a system of committing sounds and rhythms to the page in writing; all music composed before the perfection of this system is at least partially lost. The development of large, elaborate forms has been predicated on the notational system, which was usable as early as 1400, but very cumbersome. Refinements in style and technique followed refinements of notation consistently, but the earliest really sophisticated styles are not much more than four hundred years old. Because of this, music is the infant of the arts, a recent arrival, hundreds of years behind literature, painting, sculpture and architecture. The classical period of music is not Greco-Roman antiquity: it is the late eighteenth century, and Mozart is its Virgil.

The lack of a long tradition seems to make musicians, especially composers, inordinately jittery about the future. Music is alone among the arts in that its relatively brief history has, in the main, been one of clear and obvious progress. Some musicians feel that the progress reached its zenith in the music of the High Baroque, especially in the work of J. S. Bach, and that subsequent changes have been less progressive in character. Others trace an unbroken line of progress from the Gregorian Chant to the present day, and see that line continuing, unchecked and at the same greatly accelerated speed, into an apparently unlimited future.

We are accustomed to using the word "progress" ambiguously, applying it to either general or personal improvement. To recognize progress in the development of an individual talent is easy; it is more difficult to recognize in music generally. To accept trend as a phenomenon in and of itself progressive is to follow Hegel and the Marxists into that curious (and rosy) view of evolution which considers practically everything a step in the right direction, and which puts all artists at the mercy of historical processes. Arnold Schoenberg, who tended to think of music history as a general onward-and-upward movement, felt that progress was a divinely inspired thing, that the composer who set his own taste higher than the gift of God would end up, like Jonah, inside the whale; Schoenberg preferred to prophesy at the gates of Nineveh.

I suppose that the first criterion of progress is some kind of recognizable improvement. The word "recognizable" here is, of course, dangerous, since not everyone is capable of recognizing a change for the better. However, change is easily discernible, and few would be naïve enough to assert that a chronological accident had made the music of Rossini or Weber superior to that of Mozart or J.S. Bach. The comparison, of course, is unfair at the outset, since Weber and Rossini were not composers of the first rank. The worth of the historical view of progress must be tested be comparing the output of the best composers of different periods.

This issue is generally side-stepped. We like to say that we like Beethoven and Mozart equally in different ways, that Mozart is subtle where Beethoven is sublime, and so on. There is certainly no question that, in his major work, Beethoven introduced a kind of passion and grandeur not to be found in earlier music; at the same time, he introduced a kind of coarseness, an obviousness, an element of the gross, which music could have done without very nicely, and which had to supercede the subtleties of the eighteenth century if the new style were to have the effect for which it was intended. Beethoven's achievement, while not the first of its kind in music, is a superb illustration of the composer-*qua*-Shiva, destroying as he creates.

Since Beethoven's time, the destruction of the past has become a part of the working process of those musicians who feel that they are helping things along to make progress in music in a progressive way. Wagner and Liszt, for instance, expanded harmonic language while making a frontal attack on form. Schoenberg, whose work was aimed, at least in part, on the destruction of a whole system of harmonic and melodic conventions while building up another system of tonal relationships, frequently relied on the most rigid of antique forms. If the evolution from Liszt through Schoenberg is progress in the Hegelian sense, it is a strange brand, since it goes backwards and forwards at the same time.

In that these composers and, especially during the past fifty years, a great many others, have added enormously to the technical resources of music (and, in some instances, actually extended the aesthetic frontiers of the art) they have provided that recognizable improvement which, in spite of the destructive element in their work, could be used to support the historical view. In that their innovations have, in many instances proved to be only an *embarras de richesse*, impeding their work, the innovations would tend to seem actually regressive. The most pathetic example of this auto-frustration is probably that of Schoenberg, whose heart, as he constantly reminded us, was off in *Verklaerte Nacht* a-chasing the deer, while his head was contriving a system to put an end to all such nonsense. The compromise at which he finally arrived, of writing alternately in old and new styles, was one man's tragedy. But his thinking, brilliant and logical as it was, has provoked a catastrophe in the musical art and in the work of dozens of smaller composers. Schoenberg's metaphysics relieves the composer of personal responsibility; it makes him a vessel through which the music simply flows, whether he likes it or not.

It is not Schoenberg's technique which makes this true. Such composers as Alban Berg and Luigi Dallapiccola, to whom Schoenberg's method is subject to their own personal wills, have found their personalities in Shoenberg's technique. Schoenberg himself did not wish to have his method imitated by people who did not understand it, and, unfortunately, this irresponsible imitation is epidemic in the world at present. However, without the onward-and-upward view, composers would not feel the need—indeed, moral responsibility—for adopting styles and methods developed by others, styles which they themselves find abstruse.

The act of musical creation is one of the most personal, private occupations that a human being can undertake. The kind of music anyone writes, or whether he writes at all is, finally, his own business. To assume, as Schoenberg did, that change in musical method is divinely dictated, is to make God party to some outrageous practical joke. To assume that historical processes inexorably dictate change is to dispose, once and for all, of the spiritual nature of music, reducing it to a mechanical operation.

I would suggest that any real progress in music is a private matter, something that evolves in a lively musical mind and constitutes a development of the resources of that mind. Personal advancement takes on general significance only insofar as it becomes part of the experience of the musical community, stimulating and shaping the thought of other minds. Because of this, a responsible composer will find or assimilate into his technique only those elements which he needs for his work; and these elements may as well be drawn from the past—perhaps the remote past—as the present. A revaluation of the past can inaugurate a tremendous personal evolution.

Paul Hindemith, a composer who totally rejects the notion of progress as an historical process, gives particularly eloquent testimony to the case of progress as a personal and private affair. Hindemith's early music sounds like Brahms, and not like very good Brahms, but the elements of his own style are there. Between the end of the first World War and 1922, the main elements of Hindemith's style crystallized. From that date until the early thirties, that style was in a process of continuous refinement, as Hindemith's assimilated the *methods*, minus the manners, of the past.

The perfected style, as we find it in *Mathis der Maler*, has not changed noticeably in twenty years, and it will never change, because Hindemith knows exactly what he is doing and why. A composer as solidly rooted as Hindemith has no more need to change style than Bach or Mozart would. Hindemith is eclectic in the literal and best sense of the word, since his knowledge of the past is so exhaustive that every successful technique ever employed is part of his equipment.

Bela Bartok was eclectic, too, in a rather more limited way. His major influences were Beethoven, Liszt, and the folk musicians of the Balkans. It is probably the folk music which sustained his equilibrium during the Central European musical upheavals of thirty years ago. Again, his evolution was a personal one. It produced a rich, distinguished style, impossible to imitate, but with only a few technical eccentricities (most of them harmonic and rhythmic) which could be of use to other musicians.

To list the composers, from Debussy to Peter Mennin, who have built personal styles on a careful analysis of existing music with a view to preserving existing traditions, is to account for the stylistic richness of this century so far. The lack of a common practice in twentieth century music can be considered a weakness, and in that it encourages charlatanry, it is. But the lack of stylistic orthodoxy encourages the maximum development of the lively mind. Exponents of the historical view of progress feel that our great stylists are outside the mainstream of the art, have divorced music from its mission and its meaning, and are a thoroughly pernicious crew. The stylists tend to believe that the road from Beethoven to Wagner to Schoenberg leads straight to hell. This reminds one, of course, of the old Brahms-Wagner feud, which Wagner seems to have won. At present, there are two camps, armed, neither of which is willing to yield. On the matter of progress, however, there seems to be one point of agreement, which is that progress, whatever it may really be, can not come out of a literal imitation of antique styles.

II

In *The New Year Letter*, Mr. Auden reminds us that every aesthetic discipline carries with it a sin, peculiar to it, to which its exponents are especially prone. The composer whose predilections are conservative is constantly in danger of losing himself in the past; of losing himself so completely that his own development never occurs. One of the delights of a pre-perfected style is that it poses no real problems to the composer; if he follows the simple instructions on the label, he is bound to confect something fairly palatable.

If eclectic composers, like Hindemith and Bartok, may be considered progressive in that they have adopted the techniques of the past but developed personal styles from those techniques, what is the position of a man like Stravinsky? During the past thirty years, Stravinsky has worked in several distinct styles, most of them clearly appropriated from the eighteenth century. But Stravinsky never sounds like an eighteenth century composer. In a work like *The Rake's Progress*, Stravinsky approaches the style of Mozart so closely that at times one chord progression, or even one note could produce a completely antique effect. Yet the dryness of the scoring, the slight alterations of harmonic and rhythmic usages produce a sound which is peculiarly, recognizably Stravinskian and of our century.

Aaron Copland's music poses the same problem. Three works, written within a few years of each other—*El Salon Mexico*, the *Piano Sonata*, and *Appalachian Spring*— are totally different in materials and effect, but they are all obviously the work of the same composer. Again, there is a harmonic and rhythmic consistency which Copland brings to his material by which he is able to transform that material into his own. Stylistically, Copland and Stravinsky seem to be skating on the thinnest possible ice. They have helped to give the word "eclecticism" a pejorative meaning, which is perhaps unfair. To be more conservative is surely to succumb to that sin peculiar to eclecticism, but to have drawn style *from* style, as they have is to have established personality and to have progressed in the personal sense. Anonymity is an abyss into which it is very easy to fall, and one of the easiest ways to do this is to imitate currently fashionable styles. For the past twenty years, there has been a large, miraculously growing body of American composers, conservatory trained, passionately conservative, and motivated solely by the desire to conform to existing fashion. These are the composers who are not embarrassed to write like Stravinsky one year, Hindemith the next, Bartok the next, and Schoenberg the next. In most instances, their work is technically very good, but badly timed and otherwise undistinguished. A composer who has no convictions of his own serves only one function, which is to get in the way. Our best young composers, men like Robert Palmer, David Diamond and William Schuman, have suffered professionally from their refusal to join the noisy crowd on the bandwagon, and even better established men, notably Roy Harris and Walter Piston, have been hurt for the same reason. If there is any single phenomenon impeding a general progress in music, it is the effect of fashion on musical style.

Compared with the fashionable imitators, those few real innovators working at present deserve our respect. But there is a sin peculiar to *their* discipline, too: the assertion of individuality at the expense of standards.

For many years, most of the important experimental work in America has been carried on in New York by the composers associated with John Cage. This work, at its outset, was distinguished by a revaluation of Occidental standards. Cage hoped to introduce certain Oriental values into our conception of music. This involved experimentation with percussion, rhythm, and form.

In effect, this experimentation has produced two different sets of results. Lou Harrison and Alan Hovhaness have adjusted the rich, percussive sonorities to the traditions of the West. Cage himself and Morton Feldman have almost finally divorced themselves from Western traditions. Cage has written music in which radios are the performing instruments, so that the composer has no control over the sounds produced. Feldman has composed pieces on graph paper, in which no notes are written, so that the performer makes up the music as he goes along.

The fact that his music has, conceptually, some relation to the improvisatory practices of India, does not, in itself, constitute an improvement in Western music. One suspects that, because it is less controlled, it is inferior to the Indian original. The fact that Western music can be written down accurately has made its evolution a special thing, and if the element of control is removed, everything peculiarly Western about the music is destroyed, even if familiar instruments are used. And Western standards cannot be imposed on a music which disregards its basis. While it would be unfair to suspect Feldman's sincerity, one can only assume that what standards he has are of his own making, and that no matter how elaborate his rationale is, he has arrived at a musical anarchy. A composer to whom originality and innovation supercede purely musical values must be guilty of husbanding his own talent badly.

The total accomplishment of musical innovation in the twentieth century has been depressingly small. The Italian Futurism of forty years ago has disappeared, almost without a trace. Atonality, as it was thought of forty years ago, has proven to be little more than a tortured extension of Romanticism. Its best apologists not only employ the forms of the past, they constantly compare their music with that of the past, assuring the listener that, once the difficulties of idiom are surmounted, the music will have much the same effect as that of Beethoven or Brahms, as if that in itself is desirable. One might point out that, if the effect is to be the same, the evolution of an elaborate new technique is scarcely necessary. And, if the aesthetic standard is to remain the same, there is no reason to assume that technical change constitutes general progress.

Inversely, real technical innovations, such as the splitting up of the gamut into quarter-tones or the evolution of a music without notes, innovations which strike at the root of the Western aesthetic, are not progressive if one assumes that Western music as such is capable of further development. Real and important as these innovations are to their creators, their general application is terribly limited by the contexts in which they must occur.

If great changes of technique or style are generally so ineffectual against the broad, traditional aesthetic standards of music, one may well wonder why anyone bothers to tamper with common practice or to alter existing methods in any way.

The most valid reason is surely that of purely private need, the need of becoming oneself musically. As he develops, any lively composer will, sooner or later, come face to face with a blank wall, a dead end into which his technique and his preconceptions have led him. Until he has reached this point in his career, no matter how brilliantly or rapidly he has advanced, he cannot have attained that individuality which distinguishes him from everybody else. He must either find his way out of this situation or relax into oblivion and anonymity.

It is at this point that he must develop what Hindemith calls "the crown and glory of technique," which is style, and no matter whose shoulders he is standing on, what influences have gone into his style, what new technical resources it may require for its realization, or what thinking has conditioned his choice, the result will be a new sound, called modern not because its component parts are original in themselves, but because they have been regulated to fit the needs of a single, special individual. Having arrived at this happy condition of being himself, he will show what the theologian calls "the outward signs of an inward grace," not because he has been given this grace, but because he has had the courage to fight for it, to conjure it out of his own mind, spirit, experience and imagination.

Frequently, a generous composer with missionary instincts and abundant good will, will attempt to lead other composers, especially young or unformed ones, through the whole process of development, including the last stage. The unfortunate thing about this is that lively people are difficult to lead. Like horses, they must be broken before they can be made to submit to the will of the master, and once this is realized, there is no further hope for them. I suspect that people of real talent have been destroyed by over-zealous teaching, but the small number which survives the process of indoctrination is heartening.

A gifted composer must, ultimately, find himself through his own resolution. This is why musical progress, in the general sense, has only a superficial meaning and might better be called a change in common practice, based on the idioms and techniques of some powerful figure and enjoyed by a coterie of composers who have not yet been able to assert their individual wills on what they know. Real progress is a private affair, concerning only the individual composer and his art.

FRANCIS HACKETT   MAY 1, 1915

The Movies

There are two ways, after all, of considering any modern invention. One is to consider it in the light of its use, another in the light of its misuse. There is no human contrivance that hasn't certain dire possibilities. A safety match is an admirable little thing, but not when the baby eats it. A laundry pin serves its humble purpose in the world, but not when the baby swallows it. Dynamite can be employed to blow men to smithereens, but it can also be employed to blow rocks to smithereens. One of the ugliest murders in modern times was the Phoenix Park murder, but it was only by a cruel irony that Lord Frederick Cavendish was stabbed to death with the finest surgeons' operating knives. The man who bought those knives had often put similar ones to a purpose diametrically opposite. If the demon in man can pervert his own instruments, it is a feeble argument against the instruments.

There are times when man's machinery seems created to enslave him. Were one a pit-boy at the mines, or a youth in the glass-works, or a shirtwaist maker, or a laundry worker, or a coal-trimmer on a liner, or a fighter in the trenches, one might curse the day that machinery was invented. But man is the deity over it all, over his glass and his sewing-machine and his ocean greyhound and his lyddite, and when he asserts his deity over these, his own creatures, they will glorify, not bestialize, his existence. A "simple life" is not the answer to machinery.

It is understandable, however, that the attempt to adapt a machine process to art should antagonize the conservative. Most conservatives still see the "movie" through the noisy gloom of the first firetrap theatres. The movie, in their eyes, is still a theatrical tintype. They observe its vogue, but they also observe the vogue of chewing gum. And, as they reckon it, the movie is in a class with chewing gum.

To assume a lofty tone about chewing gum would not be sincere on my part. Still, as one of the mortals to whom it was never anything more than an avocation, conducted in timid privacy, I recollect it as perhaps the least delectable of uselessnesses. Combining the maximum of activity with the minimum of effect, it seems to be the supreme example of lost motion, and on that ground alone I disdain it. On similar ground, though they are equally dear to millions of Americans, one criticizes the average moving pictures. Popular though they are, the conservatives are justified in contemning them. Incapable of assimilation, they are, for the most part, mental chewing gum. The objection which holds for one holds for the other. And it is no apology to say that they are "popular." The best test of democracy is often the desire to revise, rather than submit to, the popular. It was once popular to dress like an undertaker in midsummer, to sleep in a stuffy bedroom, to regard a woman who smoked as a prostitute, to be lugubrious on Sunday. A custom or a taste or a prejudice is not entitled to respect because it is popular. If the popularity of bull-fighting in Spain does not vindicate it, the popularity of the vapid movie in America does not vindicate it either. It is perhaps pleasant that our tendency is toward aesthetic insipidities, not brutalities. But that is also open to question. A country that leads the world in domestic homicide cannot lay too much flattering unction to its soul. Perhaps it would be better for us if we killed a few more bulls and a few less men.

But where the conservatives go astray about the movies is in assuming that because the invention has been unsatisfactorily utilized it is not proved capable of the most wonderful utilization. They fail to appreciate the illimitable artistic, the illimitable social, possibilities of the moving picture.

What Bernard Shaw says in the current *Metropolitan* is true. The moving picture is incalculably potential. It is availing of human curiosity and human imagination as no other medium has ever availed before. Speaking the universal language, it is the greatest instrument of popular suggestion that has ever been devised. Capable of pouring the most diverse material into the brain, it is limited only by mental capacity. However inadequately its material has been governed up to the present, its power is unquestionable. To ignore that fact is, for actors or publicists or educators or playwrights, to go on thinking in terms of gas after the discovery of electric light.

Last year nearly ten million feet of film were inspected by the National Board of Censorship. The total cost of the circulated films was probably close on $50,000,000. What this means, as regards the interest created and the time and money consumed, staggers the imagination. That the profits of the regular theatre should be cut in half is only one small proof of the energy diverted to the movies. Most of the energy has come from channels never before tapped for semi-aesthetic amusement. The movies have broken a window into the blank wall of myriad minds. They have spread a thousand worlds at the feet of the simplest spectators.

But, granting its social significance, the question of its artistic significance remains, and it is on this that its ultimate value hinges. Primarily a process for reproducing things seen, the great problem is its potentiality for giving artistic value to the things it reproduces. Can this machine process, in other words, be used to express emotions inexpressible in any other way?

As it exists, the moving picture process is not yet aesthetically enlightened. Its aesthetic possibilities have been ruthlessly sacrificed to the mere crude informative or sensational possibilities. Neither actors nor producers have learned as yet to work within its conventions as the sculptor works within his, controlling their mechanism as he does in the interest of a new, an emotional, result. But, once the aesthetic intention governs the process, and raw reproduction ceases to be the object, the prospects for an art are illimitable.

That an art can lie submerged in mankind, as the Gothic cathedrals lay submerged in the unchiseled rocks of France, is one of the facts which give life its value. It is only of recent years, we may as well remember, that through the genius of Isadora Duncan we became again aware of the possibilities of dancing, and began to recapture the "fair attitude" of Tempe and the dales of Arcady. It is perhaps ambitious to suppose that any machine process could lend itself to any such emotional result, but the experiment beckons us.

Once men begin to think of the camera as an aesthetic instrument, I believe the art of the movies will be vastly subtilized, ramified, developed. There is nothing which the eye of man has seen, nothing in form or color or movement, nothing so delicate, so evanescent, so glorious, nothing from dawn to dawn or from pole to pole, which may not be captured and adapted by its magic. I believe the day will come when people will look back on the present productions as admirers of Coburn and Stieglitz look back on the first tintype. And when that day comes the despised machine will have paid part of its debt to common people.

OTIS FERGUSON   NOVEMBER 24, 1941

Land of Dreams, and Nightmares

To a sizable bulk of our population, Hollywood is where you go when you die, if you're good. To some of our more impatient critics, Hollywood is where you die if you go there. It is a most complex place to report on, and in this series of articles I have surely not even brushed a good third of the business of picture-making, in one respect or another. There are territories left out. There are the endless score sheets in composer's row and the always last-minute hustle over there to get the music out after the film has been made and cut—to get it broken down, sequence by sequence and scene by scene, each shift of mood, place or action timed to the second and written in on a rehearsed master sheet, with its demand of music to fit and get it up, where is it, why not. There are the overtime sessions on the recording stage, when the score has been written, arrangements made and the band tired in shirt sleeves and the director looking at his watch, looking at the control room, waiting for the film to flash on the screen preceded by the metronome beat and numbers shifting with it: 7, 6, 5, 4, 3, 2 *and* in, the men in the band with their single earphone apiece getting the exact tempo for that stretch of action, and then that little stretch of music played once and played again, rephrased here or there and played over, all for just, say, the bridge into a song in a musical, for a strain under the credit titles of the film, for the establishment of a new mood, whether of snow or of city traffic. And the composer sweating, watching his men and the inexorable numbers on the screen, watching the score and the clamped-down faces in the control room.

And there is the quiet and incomprehensible activity of the art department, with its draftsmen and painters and model builders, filling room after room with scheme and replica, running up a coal mine or a wooded hill in the time it would take you to describe it, establishing the key of a scene with charcoal, crayon, watercolor, scaling a point of action down to inches so that the director may study his moves even as the set is being built. The art department starts as soon as a script has been decided on, and it makes so much of the picture in stills and models that its work for any one show could be made a traveling exhibit, of craftsmanship and care and feeling, too, a background for motion, almost alive in itself.

Following these specifications, there are the veterans on the sets, running you up a house or a tree, a gravel drive or a pasture slope, as neat in each case as you please. They are here today, before they or anybody knows what the picture is about, busy with saw and hammers and guy wires to the tying-off position on the parallels, with paint and shrubbery and paper flowers; tomorrow, when the cameras and lights roll up to look at the first scene, over and over, they are gone, leaving their portion of a city or a canyon ready and solid behind them. No amateur who has ever tried to saw and angle without a mitre-box will fail to delight in this fairyland carpentry where men build only for the illusion but with the speed of illusion. A seat is too low for the effect desired, but cannot be mounted on a box that would show in the camera: within twenty minutes the cushion has been taken off and a wooden riser built and fitted to its curves, stained and secured in place, ready. A door has to open without human aid, and in ten minutes a heavy thread is run out and over a pulley and back, and painted dull black so the camera won't pick it up. A director wants a shot from floor level, and before you know it they have sawed through the planking and established a base for the camera on its dolly three feet below. If you have any idea of what you want, all you have to do is ask them.

Of course there are the actors. They are important in pictures, but by the process of identification are made much more important than they should be. Actually they are at the mercy of the story they are put in, the director who uses them to tell it, and in a lesser but still important way they are at the mercy of costume designers, cameramen, etc. But they are the part of Hollywood on which speculation and gossip focuses most brilliantly and their contribution to the art of pictures is immediately visible to all. Pictures demand of them first, that they should have that quality which stands up under the camera eye and lives to project itself out from the shadows of the screen into the imagination of an audience; second, that they have a bounty of patience, of willingness before instruction, above all, of a hardihood of imagination and belief in the fragment that must be run over and over until it is natural and right. You know all about them, or less than nothing about them, by the evergreen life-stories in every kind of journal using movable type. A lot of them are just tired stage actors, doing it the easy way; but some of them are developed for and by the movies, and some of them are very good people. Alongside the flat braveries of Errol Flynn you must put Gary Cooper, to be fair. And you will not forget, I hope, the lank, eager, common-man sweetness of Henry Fonda, whose Abe Lincoln was so high and far above the studied caricature of Raymond Massey that it is not to talk. Sometimes in the movies the free and honest is released as it is nowhere else, needing only a shrewd director and a sensible story; and for every foolish star, exploded into a million dollars by virtue of the public thirst for new personality and new types of brassière, you will find someone plugging along, believing in the thing, worrying over it, trying to do it the best way. They are rarely bright copy but they are there, the movies in their general faceless all-inclusive way having made them because they need them.

The scoring of music is something the movies have not developed to a point where they know what to do about it, and certainly the question is still one of the most difficult, to the composers as well as to the audience. Fanfares, heavy orchestration, lack of imagination obtrude on almost any film story you think of, yet anything in the way of delicacy and restraint is ruled out of most productions on the ground of lack of appeal. Normally intended to underline or even set up a mood, music often comes to have the opposite effect of diverting the attention if not actually pouring over the edge of dramatic necessity into its own puddle of splendor. Composers wrestle sometimes with the demands of the form, but they are too often cut down by some chump from the front office, if not in intention then in the matter of budget, because the front office either knows what it likes or what the whole world likes, as represented of course by some blowsy homebody of a wife.

And there is so little chance of a progressive, continuous and memorable composition in furnishing chords now for a hurricane and next minute for Nelson Eddy, that the boys all too quickly find the easiest course to be that of swimming with the current, giving the boobs what they want, and overloading the microphone at every point of European action by sitting the brass section for the 1812 Overture no more than ten feet away from it. And if a composer does get a score he fancies he can work on in an original way, who is to blame him for pushing the music at the expense of theatre continuity, using the main business of the picture itself as an excuse or suggestion for his themal development, until sometimes a country garden takes on the aspect of a mixture of a Legion convention and the Albert Hall.

Nobody has sufficiently explored this field, though Oscar Levant and Virgil Thomson have dropped a few pertinent and acid notes by the way; nobody has been allowed to; and though no action can seem to happen in its natural silence any more (Fritz Lang got the reputation of reverting to the Ufa days of the silents when he took scenes in "Man Hunt" with nothing but the breathing of people and the trickle of water, as they should exactly be heard for the full effect), most of the picture makers accept as incessant that which should be incidental. There is no near-remedy or answer. We cannot get decent scoring of pictures until we somehow breed a type of man who will have the enormous background and training of a good musician, plus the understanding and appreciation of the film at large.

There are also the nicest people in the world, all the people on the set from actual manual labor to script girls, who make the majority, the majority you have to depend on for pictures if not glamor. It is the place they live and work in, and what if crazy things happen in the papers or even actually? They have their homes, they head out for them at the end of the hard day for supper. Maybe they go to movie, though it is not a movie-mad town and the audiences you find in theatres are a cross between the very wise ("Look at him faking that one, with the tree; the dope forgets it's an elm to start with, look at him, and what's he making a week?") and the unalert or dumb. Most of the technicians have made or seriously wish to make a profession or trade out of it, as you would with machine-tool making or draftsmanship. In it they are happy, and their carefree wisdom in the midst of bewilderment is contagious—I believe it is the main thing, above the money, which makes the long day on the set tolerable. I've said how efficient they are, how unobtrusive in their steady realization of the miracle in such matters as device, weight, time, speed. Hollywood has built up a new ideal in craftsmanship, where to speak a mean word or to be discourteous to the most obvious dope of a stranger, would be an ill thing.

The cameramen there is no space for in any such brief report on an industry so highly technical and ramified. Their mystery is well preserved if only because they have learned the values and intricate means of reproduction of the still camera while appreciating and absorbing the principles of motion, of running emphasis, contrasting moods of fiction. It is said about them simply and finally that you may prefer one man's style to another's, you may have people you do or don't like to work with, but you can't work on an "A" picture and get an "A" cameraman who isn't a veteran in his art, who doesn't know more about what you think you're doing than you do, and who won't turn you in just as good a picture as you are able to see in your mind and pass on to him in the way of communication.

It is always pleasant to speculate about what Hollywood Needs Most and indeed one of the trade magazines makes a yearly feature out of inviting several hundred film reviewers to tell what is wrong and what they think ought to be done. With the industry set up as it is, catering successfully to millions at a profit of millions, there is little to be hoped for in the way of easy miracles, and what energy is at the disposal of reform movements is almost invariably misled, being misinformed in the first place (the most recent large example is the fuss about block-booking: block-booking was done away with and now the very exhibitors who kept the howl going don't like the result; and as for any change in the quality of pictures, don't ask).

The best thing to hope for is a complete shake-up, some basic shock in the financial relation of pictures to public. It would not be an easy cure for anybody and it certainly wouldn't be complete. But it could achieve what you could never get by asking: the low-budget picture as a general rule, and the low-budget picture means junking expensive stars and fantastic story costs. It also means—if it is low enough and imperative enough—the return of ingenuity to the films. The films were in the hardiest period of their growth when directors had to scrabble and make-do under severe handicaps, when they couldn't employ five or six Name writers of no talent but great salary potential, when they weren't carrying the load of a so-called producer whose salary for six months, let alone his bungling, exceeded the necessary cost of the picture. Now and again someone makes a small picture which is also a good one, and he doubles his cost with ease. But the man is running counter to the industry as it normally operates today, and he is retired soon enough from competition by being given a fat job with one of the majors as assistant something in charge of something.

The immediate hope is that the men who are getting a bellyful of the machine set-up, who know a story when they see one and how to go about making a film from it, will get the resolution and the money to come forward with the old United Artists idea, now in decay. They would be directors and director's writers (as opposed to such blown-up nonentities in film as, say, James Hilton or Phil Stong). They would take less money and take more time, and if there were only four or five of them they would turn out a half-dozen moderately good pictures a year. The pictures would be distributed, for only the most ferocious boycott can hold its own with eternal and insistent demand of theatre operators for product, for the thing their neighborhood and all the neighborhoods will lay down their coins to see, whether it has been advertised and premiered or not. There isn't a good director or a good writer in Hollywood who doesn't tear his hair over what the front office has done to his story now, and more because of this than because of the nature of things, the front offices will eventually have to take a back seat. They can't make pictures, and that's the size of it. They can throw millions around and they can draw lackeys like flies, but they can't make the pictures, and without pictures they die. I should not be surprised if there were not going on right now, slowly and with no concerted front, something like the managerial revolution in films. With so many private and expensive egos charging around in their own interests, you can never be sure of any common result; but even without concerted action you can hear a general and rising demand: give the movies back to the people who make them.

MANNY FARBER   1941

Saccharine Symphony

The new Disney cartoon "Bambi" is interesting because it's the first one that's been entirely unpleasant. The robust irrationality of the mouse comedies has been squelched completely by the syrup that has been gradually flowing over the Disney way. In an attempt to ape the trumped-up realism of flesh and blood movies, he has given up fantasy, which was pretty much the magic element. Mickey Mouse and Donald Duck lived in a beautiful escape land, where they flew through the air, swam under water, died a thousand deaths and lived to see the end of each picture. These comedies were perfectly suited to a moving camera; held down by nothing human, they had terrific pace and action. It was a wonderful movie shambles.

But not "Bambi." The animals here behave just as Hollywood thinks we do, and behaving that way it's old stuff and boring because of it. Everything is straight-faced, with feet flat on the ground. The animals give birth, grow up, fall in love, get shot at and killed. Besides, it is moral, starched heavy. The hero is a deer named Bambi, whose mother is killed by the villain, Mr. Man, whose sweetheart is attacked by Mr. Man's dogs, whose terrestrial paradise is destroyed by Mr. Man's fire. There's no harm in Disney's being righteous, unless, as in this picture, the accent is on the cute and pretty rather than on the comedy invention which produced the righteous Donald. Only so much amusement can come from fairylike naïveté, after that it's just one long squirm. Along the way "Bambi" has all the stereotyped mechanisms of the formula movie—the heavy side to the love triangle, the fight for the doe's ("Feline") affections, the wise old king deer whose place Bambi wins over in the closing shots.

In keeping with this new spirit, "Bambi" talks itself dizzy to the exclusion of movement and action. The animals are horribly equipped with human voices, not the neuter piping of Mickey or the incoherent gabbling of Donald, which were so perfectly right, but the cuddly or waspish voices of ladies and gentlemen. Like their counterparts in the regular movies, the animals here gather round and trade chitchat, very sweet, and it is grotesque. And there are songs everywhere, coming out of the mountains, from under the trees, flooding you with the most maudlin sounds a director ever let happen. Example: "Drip, Drip, Drop, Little April Shower."

The bogus art which has been creeping into the Disney pictures is really hammered at you in this one. Again, it is an affectation of reality, like a Maxfield Parrish painting. No more the flat house-paint colors of the early comedies, in which there were no half-tones or dull intensities, with every red the same hot, pure scarlet, every black like coal, and nothing flimsily grayed. The films are now doused in sweet sugary tints, flowery violets, fancy-pants pinks, and he'll waste ten minutes if he can end up with a gold-splashed sunset. Whereas the early color was fresh, simple and in the comedy spirit, this new development is a synthetic reveling in vulgarity. The worst effect of all this artiness is the preference now for cheap painting, the Vanishing American kind you buy in Kress's, in place of the movement which was the main thing before. No longer do the trees and flowers carry on like mad: they are there for pretty; and as the camera moves slowly over them and you drink up all this tinseled loveliness, there is the lone deer on the distant hilltop, a gold aura around him.

Mickey wouldn't be caught dead in this.

Orson Welles:
There Ain't No Way

FALSTAFF (Peppercorn-Wormser)

What makes movies a great popular art form is that certain artists can, at moments in their lives, reach out and unify the audience—educated and uneducated—in a shared response. The tragedy in the history of movies is that those who have this capacity are usually prevented from doing so. The mass audience gets its big empty movies full of meaningless action; the art-house audience gets its studies of small action and large inaction loaded with meaning.

Almost everyone who cares about movies knows that Orson Welles is such an artist. Even audiences who don't know that Welles is a great *director* sense his largeness of talent from his presence as an actor. Audiences are alert to him, as they often were to John Barrymore, and later to Charles Laughton, as they sometimes are to Bette Davis, as they almost always are to Brando—actors too big for their roles, who play the clown, and not always in comedy but in roles that for an artist of intelligence can only be comedy. Like Brando, Welles is always being attacked for not having fulfilled his prodigious promise; but who has ever beaten the mass-culture fly-by-night system of economics for long? What else could Welles do with his roles in *Black Magic* or *Prince of Foxes* or *The Black Rose* or *Trent's Last Case* but play them as comedy? Could one take such work seriously? The mediocre directors and the cynical hacks got money when he couldn't. His ironic playing is all that one remembers from those movies anyway; like Brando, he has the greatness to make effrontery a communicated shared experience—which lesser artists had better not attempt. It takes large *latent* talent to tell the audience that you know that what you're doing isn't worth doing and still do it better than anyone else in the movie.

Waiting for a train in Grand Central Station recently, I was standing next to a group of Negroes. To everything that they talked about, one of them—a young girl—said, "There ain't no way"; and it fit perfectly each time.

Orson Welles' *Falstaff* came and went so fast there was hardly time to tell people about it, but it should be back (it should be around forever) and it should be seen. It's blighted by economics and it will never reach the audience Welles might have and should have reached, because there just ain't no way. So many people—and with such complacent satisfaction, almost, one would say, delight—talk of how Welles has disappointed them, as if he had wilfully thrown away his talent through that "lack of discipline" which is always brought in to explain failure.

309

There is a widespread notion that a man who accomplishes a great deal is thus a "genius" who should be able to cut through all obstacles; and if he can't (and who can?), what he does is far beneath what he should have done to be worth consideration. On the contrary, I think that the more gifted and imaginative a director, the greater the obstacles. It is the less imaginative director who has always flourished in the business world of movies—the "adaptable," reliable fellow who is more concerned to get the movie done than to do it his way, who, indeed, after a while has no way of his own, who is as anonymous as the director of *Prince of Foxes*. And the more determined a man is to do it his way or a new way, the more likelihood that this man (quickly labeled a "troublemaker" or "a difficult person" or "self-destructive" or "a man who makes problems for himself"— standard Hollywoodese for an artist and, of course, always true at some level, and the greater the artist, the more true it's likely to become) won't get the support he needs to complete the work his way. In the atmosphere of anxiety surrounding him, the producers may decide to "save" the project by removing him or adding or subtracting from his work, or finally dumping the film without publicity or press screenings, consigning it to the lower half of double bills. All these things have happened to Welles (*Citizen Kane* was not big enough at the box-office and it caused trouble; he was not allowed to finish his next picture, *The Magnificent Ambersons*). Treatment of this sort, which usually marks the end of great movie careers, was for Welles the beginning. Most of these things have happened to men as pacific as Jean Renoir, whom few would accuse of being "undisciplined." (Renoir turned to writing a novel, his first, last year when he could not raise money to make a movie, though the budget he required was less than half that allotted to movies made to be premiered on television.) And they are still happening to men in Hollywood like Sam Peckinpah. Such men are always blamed for the eventual failure of whatever remains of their work, while men who try for less have the successes (and are forgiven their routine failures because they didn't attempt anything the producers didn't understand). Joseph L. Mankiewicz's *Julius Caesar* was considered a success and Orson Welles' *Othello* a failure. The daring of doing Shakespeare at all was enough for Mankiewicz and his producer, John Houseman, who was to be ritualistically referred to as "the distinguished producer John Houseman" because of this film—not from his early theatre work with Orson Welles—much as George Schaefer is referred to as "the distinguished director" from his specialty of embalming old war horses for television. Mankiewicz's luck held good on *Julius Caesar*; it's perfectly suited to the small screen, where it recently appeared, while Welles' *Othello*—with its disastrous, imperfectly synchronized sound track—isn't even intelligible. How could it be? A movie shot over a period of four years with Welles dashing off periodically to act in movies like *The Black Rose* to earn the money to continue; and then, his cast scattered, trying to make a sound track reading half the roles himself (not only Roderigo, but if my ear is to be trusted, parts of Iago, too), selecting long shots and shots with the actors' backs to the camera to conceal the sound problem. This, of course, looked like "affectation." And his splendid, flawed production—visually and emotionally a near-masterpiece—was a "failure." Earlier, working on a Republic Pictures budget (for Republic Pictures), Welles had shot his barbaric *Macbeth*—marred most by his own performance—in 23 days because "no one would give me any money for a further day's shooting." In the early fifties, Welles, as an actor, was in top flamboyant form; in roles like his Lord Mountdrago in *Three Cases of Murder* nobody seemed to enjoy the sheer physical delight of acting as much as he. Still very young, he played like a great ham of the old school— which was marvelous to watch in his Father Mapple in *Moby Dick* and in *The Roots of Heaven*. This lesser talent that he could live on was a corollary to his great talent. It was a demonstration of his love of (and prowess in) traditional theatre—like the way Vittorio De Sica (also an actor from adolescence) could go from being the romantic singing star of Italian musical comedy to make *Shoeshine* and then back again (he, too, to raise money for his own films) to playing in an ornate style, Gina's lawyer or Sophia's papa, a whole Barzini gallery of glory-ridden, mustachioed Italians. But Welles was beginning to turn into America's favorite grotesque. Like Barrymore and Laughton and Brando, he seemed to be developing an obsession with false noses, false faces. He had once, at least, played a role in his own face—Harry Lime in *The Third Man*, a role he had written for himself; by the sixties he was encased in makeup and his own fat—like a huge operatic version of W. C. Fields. Audiences laughed when he appeared on the screen. He didn't need to choose the role of Falstaff: it chose him.

When Welles went to Europe, he lost his single greatest asset as a movie director: his sound. (He had already lost the company that *talked* together, the Mercury players he had brought to Hollywood—Joseph Cotten, Agnes Moorehead, Everett Sloane, *et al.*—who were now working separately.) Welles had first skyrocketed to public attention on radio, and what he had brought to movies that was distinctively new was the radio sound—with an innovative use of overlapping dialogue—which was used for trick shock purposes, almost playfully, in *Citizen Kane*. But by the time of *The Magnificent Ambersons* he was using this technique for something deeper (the family bickering was startling in its almost surreal accuracy; the sound was of arguments overheard from childhood, with so many overtones they were almost mythic). Welles himself had a voice that seemed to carry its own echo chamber; somehow, in becoming the whiz kid of vocal effects, in simulating so many deep, impersonal voices, he had emptied his own voice of emotion, and when he spoke his credit at the end of *The Ambersons,* audiences laughed at the hollow voice (and perhaps at the comic justice of the *spoken* credit). Ironically, sound—the area of his greatest mastery—became his worst problem as he began to work with actors who didn't speak English and actors who did but weren't around when he needed them (for the post synching which is standard in Europe because the actors don't speak the same language, and is becoming standard here, too, because it saves shooting-time). Welles compensated by developing greater visual virtuosity.

Yeats said "Rhetoric is heard, poetry overheard," and though I don't agree, I think I see what he means, and I think this assumption is involved in much of the rejection of a talent like Welles.' His work is often referred to as flashy and spectacular as if this also meant cheap and counterfeit. Welles is unabashedly theatrical in a period when much of the educated audience thinks theatrical flair vulgar, artistry intellectually respectable only when subtle, hidden. Welles has the approach of a *popular* artist: he glories in both verbal and visual rhetoric. He uses film *theatrically*—not stagily, but with theatrical bravado. He makes a show of the mechanics of film. He doesn't—if I may be forgiven the pun—hide his tracks. Movies gave him the world for a stage, and his is not the art that conceals art, but the showman's delight in the flourishes with which he pulls the rabbit from the hat. (This is why he was the wrong director for *The Trial,* where the poetry needed to be overheard.) I think that many people who enjoy those flourishes, who really love them—as I do—are so fearfully educated that they feel they must put them down. It's as if people said, he's a mountebank, an actor showing off. But there's life in that kind of display: it's part of an earlier theatrical tradition that Welles carries over into film, it's what the theatre has lost, and it's what brought people to the movies.

Welles might have done for American talkies what D. W. Griffith did for the silent film. But when he lost his sound and his original, verbal wit, he seemed to lose his brashness, his youth, and some of his vitality. And he lost his Americanness; in Europe he had to learn a different, more exclusively visual language of film. An enfant-terrible defeated, ages fast. At 51, Welles seems already the grand old master of film, because, of course, everybody knows that he'll never get in the position to do what he might have done. Governments and foundations will prattle on about excellence and American film companies will rush to sign up Englishmen and Europeans who have had a hit, hoping to snare that magic money-making gift. And tired transplanted Europeans will go on making big, lousy American movies, getting financed because they once had a hit and maybe the magic will come back. And Welles—the one great creative force in American films in our time, the man who might have redeemed our movies from the general contempt in which they are (and for the most part, rightly) held—is, ironically, an expatriate director whose work thus reaches only the art-house audience. And he has been so crippled by the problems of working as he does, he's lucky to reach that. The distributors of *Falstaff* tested it out of town before risking Bosley Crowther's displeasure in New York.

You may want to walk out during the first twenty minutes of *Falstaff.* Although the words on the sound track are intelligible, the sound doesn't match the images. We hear the voices as if the speakers were close, but on the screen the figures may be a half mile away or turned from us at some angle that doesn't jibe with the voice. In the middle of a sentence an actor may walk away from us while the voice goes on. Often, for a second, we can't be sure who is supposed to be talking. And the cutting is maddening, designed as it is for camouflage—to keep us from seeing faces closely or from registering that mouths which should be open and moving are closed. Long shots and Shakespearean dialogue are a crazy mix. It's especially jarring because the casting is superb and the performance beautiful. It's not hard to take Shakespeare adapted and transformed by other cultures like Kurosawa's *Throne of Blood,* a *Macbeth* almost as much related to Welles' as to Shakespeare's—but the words of Shakespeare slightly out of synch! This is as intolerable as those old prints of *Henry V* that the miserly distributors circulate— chewed up by generations of projection machines, crucial syllables lost in the splices. The editing rhythm of *Falstaff* is at war with the rhythm and comprehension of the language. Welles, avoiding the naturalistic use of the outdoors in which Shakespeare's dialogue sounds more stagey than on stage, has photographically stylized the Spanish locations, creating a theatrically darkened, slightly unrealistic world of angles and low beams and silhouettes. But when this photographic style is shattered by the cuts necessary to conceal the dialogue problems, the camera angles seem unnecessarily exaggerated and pretentious. But then despite everything—the angles, the doubles in long shots, the editing that distracts us when we need to concentrate on the dialogue—the movie begins to be great. The readings in *Falstaff* are great even if they don't always go with the images—which are often great, too.

Welles has brought together the pieces of Falstaff that Shakespeare had strewn over the two parts of *Henry IV* and *The Merry Wives of Windsor*, with cuttings from *Henry V* and *Richard II*, and fastened them into place with narration from Holinshed's Chronicles (read by Ralph Richardson). Those of us who resisted our schoolteachers' best efforts to make us appreciate the comic genius of Shakespeare's fools and buffoons will not be surprised that Welles wasn't able to make Falstaff very funny: he's a great conception of a character, but the charades and practical jokes seem meant to be funnier than they are. This movie does, however, provide the best Shakespearean comic moment I can recall: garrulous Falstaff sitting with Shallow (Alan Webb) and Silence (Walter Chiari), rolling his eyes in irritation and impatience at Silence's stammer. But Welles' Falstaff isn't essentially comic; W. C. Fields' Micawber wasn't either: these actors, so funny when they're playing with their own personae in roles too small for them, are not so funny when they're trying to measure up. The carousing and roistering in the tavern doesn't seem like such great fun either, though Welles and the cast work very hard to convince us it is. Oddly, we never really see the friendship of Prince Hal—played extraordinarily well by Keith Baxter—and Falstaff; the lighter side in *Henry IV, Part I* is lost—probably well lost, though we must take it for granted in the film. What we see are the premonitions of the end—Hal taking part in games that have gone stale for him, preparing himself for his final rejection of his adopted father Falstaff in order to turn into a worthy successor of his father, the king. And we see what this does to Falstaff, the braggart with the heart of a child who expects to be forgiven everything, even what he knows to be unforgivable— his taking the credit away from Hal for the combat with Hotspur (Norman Rodway). Falstaff lacks judgment—which kings must have.

John Gielgud's Henry IV is the perfect contrast to Welles; Gielgud has never been so monkishly perfect in a movie. Welles could only get him for two weeks of the shooting and the makeshift of some of his scenes is obvious, but his performance gives the film the austerity it needs for the conflict in Hal to be dramatized. Gielgud's king is so refined—a skeleton too dignified for any flesh to cling to it, inhabited by a voice so modulated it is an exquisite spiritual whine. Merrie England? Falstaff at least provides a carcass to mourn over.

Welles as an actor had always been betrayed by his voice. It was too much and it was inexpressive; there was no warmth in it, no sense of a life lived. It was just an instrument that he played, and it seemed to be the key to something shallow and unfelt even in his best performances, and most fraudulent when he tried to make it tender. I remember that once, in *King Lear* on television, he hit a phrase and I thought his voice was emotionally right; it had beauty—and what a change it made in his acting! In *Falstaff* Welles seems to have grown into his voice; he's not too young for it anymore, and he's certainly big enough. And his emotions don't seem fake anymore; he's grown into them, too. He has the eyes for the role. Though his Falstaff is short on comedy, it's very rich, very full.

He has directed a sequence—the battle of Shrewsbury—which is totally unlike anything he has ever done, indeed unlike any battle ever done on the screen before. It ranks with the best of Griffith, John Ford, Eisenstein, Kurosawa—that is, with the best ever done. How can one sequence in this movie be so good? It has no dialogue and so he isn't handicapped: for the only time in the movie he can edit, not to cover gaps and defects but as an artist. The compositions suggest Uccello and the chilling ironic music is a death knell for all men in battle. The soldiers, plastered by the mud they fall in, are already monuments. It's the most brutally somber battle ever filmed. It does justice to Hotspur's great "O, Harry, thou hast robbed me of my youth."

Welles has filled the cast with box-office stars. Margaret Rutherford, Jeanne Moreau, Marina Vlady are all in it (though the girl I like best was little Beatrice Welles as the pageboy). And Falstaff is the most popular crowd-pleasing character in the work of the most enduringly popular writer who ever lived. Yet, because of technical defects due to poverty, Welles' finest Shakespearean production to date—another near-masterpiece, and this time so very close—cannot reach a large public. There ain't no way.

STANLEY KAUFFMANN   SEPTEMBER 12, 1970

Diary of a Mad Housewife

This film is a prototypical contemporary American cultural artifact. It is well finished, well acted, brightly written, with all its assorted talent and technological smartness turned to the varnishing of mediocrity. And it is not about what it thinks it's about.

Eleanor Perry, whose last script was *Last Summer*, wrote the screenplay from a novel by Sue Kaufman. (Which I haven't read.) The story is of a young Manhattan woman, wife of a young successful lawyer, mother of two small girls, chatelaine of an expensive, very *consciously* furnished apartment: her tribulations, her humiliations, her fineness, her first extra-marital affair, her ultimate reliability. (The word "mad" may apply to the novel, not to the film—in either sense. She is rarely angry, and no one thinks she's insane. She goes to group therapy at the end, but, one may almost say, who doesn't?)

The ostensible theme is the New Materialism of Affluence. The husband is a connoisseur—of wine, of clothes, of social status, of business investment. His anxieties about all these things are intended as a picture of the sterilities and false values that lead him to underprize, for instance, his wife. At one point he remembers how different they used to be when they were "young" (he's now in his early thirties!), and he says that all the idealism went out of them when JFK was assassinated. If that passage were meant satirically, it would be the best moment in the film, a statement of the kind of bankruptcy that is relieved to have found an occasion to declare itself. But I think the lines are offered as a deep social perception. Anyway, the husband's present empty busyness has turned him into an urbane nag.

From the very first moment, he is nagging. He nags his wife awake, nags her while she dresses, nags at breakfast, and so on. His nagging is sometimes supposed to be witty, sometimes flattering, sometimes kittenish (when he wants a "roll in de hay"). But underneath his vaudeville, he is nothing but a conceited, nagging boor. And that's not all the wife has to endure. Her children are nasty smart-alecks. Her household work is endless (and unappreciated). Her party-going is dismal—until she virtually solicits attention from a prowling young novelist. She is driven to his bed by her husband's egotism. Subsequently she is literally thrown out by her lover because she wants humanity as well as sex. Then her husband, who has been cleaned out by a snobbish investment in a French vineyard and whose job in his law firm is now threatened, comes to her for comfort, which she gives, aware that new success will again make him what he was. At the last she goes to a therapy group and tells her problem, whereupon she is promptly attacked, by men and women, as spoiled and self-pitying. *Nobody* understands her.

In short, what is presented to us as a devastating picture of modern urban *mores* is in fact a modernized version of a dozen Joan Crawford-Ruth Chatterton films, yet another spayed version of *A Doll's House*. Ibsen gave us the awakening of a woman who has been spiritually brutalized by her marriage and who resolves to break out of it. *Housewife* gives us a woman who is essentially unchanged from beginning to end: she is noble all the way; and she stays with her husband at the end in order to go on being unappreciatedly noble. No other person in the film has anything like her vision or decency—not a shred of it. She is solitary in nobility. And so the film's depiction of male conceit shrinks beside its profounder, unintended depiction of female vanity. I hazard, further, that the Lib ladies will dislike the film because it shows this oppressed woman resolving to persist in her proper place as egotist's helpmeet and brats' ma.

There is something else operating here, too, a larger cultural current of which this picture becomes a tiny part. Here we have an attractive intelligent young woman, a Phi Beta Kappa out of Smith, who allows herself to be treated like an amiable dimwit; whose husband is well-off but who, even with a part-time servant, lets herself be used like a drudge. True, love begets forbearance; true, too, some women like housework and even prospering hubands cannot afford, or get, the household staffs of yore. But from start to finish her husband is abusing or blatantly utilizing her, and she almost always accepts it meekly. She takes a great deal of bullying from her lover, as if it were part of her lot. Why does she accept all this? A sense of inferiority? Her family and intellectual backgrounds are at least the equal of her husband's. Masochism? Not proved. No, there is, finally, only one credible reason for her acceptance of continual abuse. *Because she knows the camera is there.* She has witnesses (us): who know what she is suffering and how fine she is, who are sitting in judgment on her harassers and will reward her—at least with our sympathy and high opinion—for the reticent courage with which she undergoes her trials.

Put literally, this means of course that the film-makers know the camera is there, but the film is told so intensely from the viewpoint of a heroine among besiegers, it is so inexplicable and unbalanced without the other half of the equation, that it has the effect of her conscious autobiography for those who are watching. This effect—a sense that the protagonist of a fiction knows that he (or she) is being watched or read or listened to—has been a familiar one now for two hundred years. With the decline of belief in God, the omnipresent witness, the secret sharer and rewarder, various art-forms have moved to fill the gap left by his departure. These art-forms, subjective and inevitably self-aggrandizing, finally substantiate Hulme's definition of romanticism as "split religion." Mountains of fiction and poetry attest to this phenomenon; now this film is carrying it on. Religion is not mentioned, yet what could be sustaining this woman except some kind of faith that her disregarded virtues are not lost? (The kind of job God used to do.) Imagine her as unwitnessed, and the only thing that would then be credible is her quick flight or quick breakdown.

Much of this confidence in our presence comes from the performance of the role by a newcomer named Carrie Snodgress. She has attractive taciturnity and an unusual voice, reminiscent of Jean Arthur, and, like Miss Arthur, Miss Snodgress is always saying to us privately and winningly, "See?" Even in her bed scenes. Another film newcomer, Frank Langella, known in the New York theater, plays the lover with feline insolence. The husband is Richard Benjamin who again displays his limited, sure gifts of comic inflection and calmly arrogant italicization. The bright rich boy, grown partially up. Any differences between this performance and, say, Danby in *Catch-22* are simply differences in dialogue.

Frank Perry has done his best direction so far. As usual, he is good with his actors, and here he has "staged" things adroitly. For instance, the final quarrel between lover and wife: the man angrily shoves her flat on her back on the sofa and she has to argue upward at him. But Perry has often seemed strained in pure cinema technique, and now he is as smooth and creamy as the best TV commercials—which, technically speaking, is a compliment. The best thing that can be said about his direction is that it is free of those incessant zooms and intercuts which many younger directors think essential to hipness. On the other hand, like so many currently developing directors, Perry's work is devoid of personal style.

This lack of style matches the general chic anonymity of the whole film. Its infinite accurate details do not make for specific truth, only for general recognition. Like *Bob and Carol and Ted and Alice*, it is a product of the very culture it means to examine critically. Its interest is not in any way that it takes us but in the way it can be looked at objectively.

Stripped Bare at the Follies

THE TITICUT FOLLIES
Produced and Directed by Frederick Wiseman (Grove Press, Distributor)

Four years ago a man named Robert Rohner was riding his bicycle late at night when he was spotted by a policeman and stopped. He was in Stoughton, Massachusetts, and on his way to Boston, about twenty miles off. Mr. Rohner didn't feel he should be questioned or thought bizarre because he had selected an unusual time to travel. He protested vigorously, but was arrested and charged with "vagrancy"—whereupon he became "belligerent in violent protest at his arrest." The next day he was brought into Stoughton District Court, still angry and still demanding to be released. The police had him in a straightjacket and the judge ordered him sent to Bridgewater State Hospital for the Criminally Insane for 35 days of observation. Those days turned into years. A psychiatrist recommended "permanent commitment" and Mr. Rohner, a poor man, had no lawyer to fight for him. This year the Supreme Court of Massachusetts ruled that Robert Rohner, and all those who fall into the predicament he did, have a right to legal counsel, and to more than a hearing that is in fact an arbitrary administrative decision by those who run a state hospital.

Robert Rohner's fate at Bridgewater State Hospital was actually far better than Dominic Rosati's. While Mr. Rohner found himself virtually imprisoned for life because he didn't take lightly to gratuitous arrest, Mr. Rosati's stay at Bridgewater was suddenly terminated: not too long ago he was found naked and dead in his cell, a victim of rat poison.

The hospital was investigated by a legislative committee. Both the Massachusetts Bar Association and the Massachusetts Medical Society became concerned. Newspapers all over the state demanded action, changes, reform—as did the hospital's superintendent, Charles Gaughan, a very intelligent and compassionate man who year after year has been pleading for more money, more personnel, better programs, so that his patients would in fact be treated like something more than caged animals living in an 88-year-old institution whose facilities and arrangements prompted one observer to summon the image of a "race horse stable" (where he felt the living conditions were more favorable); another, the brave superintendent himself, talked of a "hencoop." In essence the hospital was charged with allowing dangerous criminals to escape, with providing little or no psychiatric care to its patients, and with keeping its inmates improperly or unfairly—that is, offering them no chance of release, no ability to have their psychiatric and legal status clarified, and no right to a periodic review of their case, done in public, before a judge or other impartial authority with a defending lawyer's presence.

Against such a background a young lawyer, Frederick Wiseman, began to plan doing a documentary of the Bridgewater hospital. He lives in Cambridge, and I suppose it can be said that he has had his "problems." He is not a member of a law firm. He does not spend his days studying the tax laws or helping (with dozens of other lawyers) this or that business solve the various intricacies of its "corporate life." He has not used law as a means of political advancement. After he graduated from law school he became interested in the fate of criminals and the poor: what do *they* do when they get into trouble? Who looks after them—that is, which one of our distinguished law firms, so competitively pursued by aspiring members of the bar? Mr. Wiseman started teaching law students, and in 1958 took them to Bridgewater State Hospital, so that he and they together would see at firsthand what American doctors and lawyers do for some of their fellow citizens.

Apparently that visit, and some others to similar places, "traumatized" Mr. Wiseman. He began to lose interest in "the law" as such. He started wondering about the reasons people end up in places like Bridgewater, never to leave. He started looking at some of our ghettos, too; they are full of desperate, wild, anarchic youths who don't consider the police their defenders, or lawyers and judges men of integrity and righteousness. He made the connection that others have: Bridgewater and sections of Harlem aren't all that different. Ghettos have walls as high as any the state of Massachusetts can build to confine its "criminally insane."

Perhaps the time had come for such a man to seek out psychiatric "care." *Why* was he forsaking a promising career on State Street or Wall Street? *What* made him "identify" or become "involved" with Negroes or severely disturbed people? *How come* he was beginning to commit his energies, his life-work to "them"? Did something in his *past* make him want to sacrifice, do the unconventional, work for the "deprived"? Yes, we all have our sympathies, but wasn't he going *too* far, becoming *unusually* and *unrealistically* worried—over the fate of people who are notoriously poor "treatment risks"? In 1961, apparently still unable to "work things out" and become a "normal self-respecting" lawyer, Frederick Wiseman decided to produce a film. He had read Warren Miller's *The Cool World* and couldn't get out of his mind the particular hellish view of Harlem that the book's text inspired. On an impulse—yes, unexamined—he went to see Mr. Miller, and secured from him the rights to make a movie out of his book. In 1964 it was finished: *The Cool World*, produced by Frederick Wiseman and directed by Shirley Clarke. The reviews were excellent, both here and abroad, but the film lost money, much of it the producer's own savings.

Now he was *really* in trouble. His interests had led him into a new career. Working alongside Shirley Clarke he had learned how to make as well as produce a film; but he was nearly broke, and he had no idea what to do next. How long can an "adult" give himself reign to live in a "dreamworld," build "fantasies," ignore a professional life, throw away money on "losing propositions," on celluloid? Moreover, the Bridgewater he had seen in 1958 came back to haunt him—surely evidence that some kind of "conflict" was under way in his unconscious. He decided to try making a documentary of the place—one that would convey to the viewer what it is like to be sent there, to live there, to die there.

He had to find backers, no easy job in the precarious world of "educational" or essentially "noncommercial" films. Even more difficult, he had to gain access to Bridgewater, to a state hospital under the ultimate jurisdiction of politically sensitive and politically vulnerable men. But Bridgewater's superintendent was desperately anxious for change, for the kind of exposure necessary to enlighten people and move them to action. He himself was going all over the state, pleading with and exhorting audiences, telling them how awful conditions were in his hospital, asking them for help. In 1965, Mr. Wiseman moved ahead in earnest, and secured his shoe-string budget for the film. In the spring of 1966 he started shooting at Bridgewater. Certainly he had proven what determination, what a high degree of "motivation" can do—because somehow he had obtained permission to go ahead and do the job. It is probably fair to say that the hospital's superintendent encouraged his project, and so did the state's attorney-general and former lieutenant governor Elliot Richardson, who is a distinctly superior public official, especially as they come in Massachusetts. Both men now have cause to regret whatever help they gave Mr. Wiseman, whatever interference they ran for him against the bureaucrats of a state fairly well-known for its colorfully vicious politics. Why? What happened to set Mr. Richardson and Mr. Gaughan against Mr. Wiseman?

The film was finished last year and this year it has attracted wide and enthusiastic critical acclaim. One audience after another felt itself shocked, horrified and disturbed; but, by court order, The Titicut Follies cannot be seen in Massachusetts, even though it was shown this September at New York's Lincoln Center film festival and won first prize in West Germany's Mannheim film festival. A look at the film itself is perhaps the best way to find out why it would inevitably stir up a political controversy. The Indians used to call the area around Bridgewater Titicut, and so last year when the guards and inmates of the hospital put on a public benefit show, they called it "Titicut Follies." Mr. Wiseman's 16 millimeter black and white film, 84 minutes long, opens with a scene from that show: eight men in straw hats are on stage singing "Strike Up the Band." Behind them one reads the tinseled sign: Titicut Follies. From a long shot we go to close-ups, first of the performers' faces, sad despite the singing, and then of others, the people "backstage" who spend their days and nights in the hospital, as inmates, prisoners, guards, doctors, nurses, whatever. At the very end Bridgewater's temporary entertainers appear once again—so that if we wish, if we can, everything that went on "in-between" can be forgotten, for that is the privilege of free men. Ironically the film is so effective because it is not another Snake Pit, another brutal and unrelenting exposé of life behind the closed doors of a mental hospital. Yes, there are some scandalous and disgusting moments, but by and large they are not those that offer us the standard "backward" scene, with its shrieks and groans and hilarious desolation or grim excitement. I have seen much worse in other state hospitals that Massachusetts maintains.

Something else is at work to give this film its power, and to unsettle its critics, many of whom are objecting to the nudity allowed or demanding to know why the faces of inmates are used, in clear violation of the right to privacy. (The legislators who are shocked that patients appear live and undisguised in *Titicut Follies* have yet to raise their voices against a book called *Christmas in Purgatory* by Burton Blatt, in which mental patients are also photographed and not always provided with black bands across their eyes. Mr. Blatt's descriptions of the hospitals located in several states, including Massachusetts, make *Titicut Follies* seem like a whitewash job.) If Frederick Wiseman has offended the sensibilities of his fellow citizens he has done it I believe by making them nervous about far more than nudity (in this day of bikinis and miniskirts) or the individual's right to privacy (in this day of wire-tapping, of cleverly manipulative advertising, of espionage that has been into so many things that any number of people can reasonably doubt whose purposes they have served and with whose money).

After a showing of *Titicut Follies* the mind does not dwell on the hospital's ancient and even laughable physical plant, or its pitiable social atmosphere. What sticks, what really hurts is the sight of human life made cheap and betrayed. We see men needlessly stripped bare, insulted, herded about callously, mocked, taunted. We see them ignored or locked interminably in cells. We hear the craziness in the air, the sudden outbursts, the quieter but stronger undertow of irrational noise that any doctor who has worked under such circumstances can only take for so long. But much more significantly, we see the "professionals," the doctors and workers who hold the fort in the Bridgewaters of this nation, and they are all over. We see a psychiatrist interviewing a new patient. We see another one and his staff as they question another patient and then discuss him upside down. In sum, we see ourselves. Even the most callous and cynical politician has a right to become uneasy and fearful when he sees the most respected, educated and "rational" members of *his* world, his middle-class, professional world, behave as they do in this film.

"Why do you do this when you have a good wife?" asks the doctor of a youth driven to molest children. The questions pour out, one after another—crudely put, monotonously asked; the young man is told that he is sick, sick, sick. His frightened, searching face contrasts with the doctor's boredom, his weariness, his vulgarity, his lack of interest in the man he yet feels free to interrogate (feels he has the right and knows he has the power to interrogate). Then there is the staff meeting where another heartbreaking encounter takes place. A young man feels himself driven mad by the hospital, and pleads for a return to a regular jail. Again the questions shoot out at him and in a few minutes shred him to bits. He is given a label, a diagnosis. The faces, the professional faces, smile ever so faintly. They are satisfied. He can go. It is cruel of Mr. Wiseman to have done that to us—all of us who pin names on people in order to brush them aside.

In any event, the film's producer and director is now in court, charged with violating the privacy of patients, and with a "breach of contract." The documentary wasn't supposed to turn out like that, say the men who allowed it to be made. The politicians, who for years ignored Bridgewater's problems, have someone to attack, a movie to vilify. The former lieutenant governor, Mr. Richardson, and Bridgewater's Superintendent, Mr. Gaughan, have to run for cover, run for their lives. And the same politicians also have people to defend: the inmates whose privacy has been invaded.

Titicut Follies is a brilliant work of art, and as such it will not go unnoticed, despite the opposition to it. We are asked not to be outraged at others—a cheap and easily spent kind of emotion—but to look at ourselves, the rich and strong ones whose agents hurt the weak and maimed in the name of—what? Our freedom. Our security. Our civilization. Were men's "rights" violated, or do places like Bridgewater strip men of everything, their "rights," their dignity, their humanity? Does a man like Frederick Wiseman have the obligation to say, tell or show what he saw, or is the state entitled to *its* privacy? If so, how can we move the state to correct its wrongs, to end its evasion or corruption or worse? (A series of newspaper stories over the years have had only a limited effect.) How long will men like Mr. Richardson, Mr. Gaughan and Mr. Wiseman be divided and conquered? They have all three become caught up in a web of accusations meant to gratify some of the more seedy elements in American political life. All the while our Bridgewater State hospitals still stand; and the human beings in them bother us only rarely, when a film like this one comes along or a particularly scandalous story (like the two I mentioned at the beginning) breaks into the news. Anyway, we can even shut out those bothersome events. The inmates of Bridgewater know that, know the limits of our concern. When we see them, that knowledge of theirs, never stated but apparent, unnerves us. For a second *our* privacy is invaded, *we* are stripped bare. Then we compose ourselves, and become angry. The rest is easy and perhaps has been best described by T. S. Eliot:

"We demand a committee, a representative committee, a committee of investigation. Resign Resign Resign."

Notes on the Contributors

Conrad Aiken (1889-1973), poet and novelist, classmate of T.S. Eliot, Walter Lippmann, and John Reed at Harvard, awarded Pulitzer Prize for *Selected Poems* (1932).

Woody Allen (1935-), screenwriter, actor, and director of numerous comic films, including *Take the Money and Run* (1969), *Bananas* (1971), *Love and Death* (1975).

Maxwell Anderson (1888-1959), dramatist, founding member of the Playwrights' Company, author of *Elizabeth the Queen* (1930), *Winterset* (1935), *The Bad Seed* (1955), and with Laurence Stallings, *What Price Glory?* (1924).

Sherwood Anderson (1876-1941), Midwest-born novelist and short story writer, onetime paint business owner. Author of *Windy McPherson's Son* (1916), *Winesburg, Ohio* (1919).

Louis Aragon (1897-), French novelist, poet and essayist, Dadaist, author of *Le Paysan de Paris* (1926), *Les Voyages de l'Imperiale* (1940).

W. H. Auden (1907-1972), British-born poet, long a resident of America, collaborator with Christopher Isherwood, Louis MacNeice, and others. Author of *Look, Stranger* (1936), *The Age of Anxiety* (1947).

Hamilton Basso (1904-1964), southern newspaperman, novelist, and critic, author of *The View from Pompey's Head* (1954), longtime contributor to *The New Yorker*.

Clive Bell (1881-1964), British art historian and critic, brother-in-law of Virginia Woolf, author of *Since Cezanne* (1922), *Proust* (1929), *Account of French Painting* (1931).

Stephen Vincent Benét (1898-1943), poet, short story writer ("The Devil and Daniel Webster"), dramatist, author of several collections of verse, including *Western Star*, published posthumously.

John Berryman (1914-1972), poet, teacher, author of the *Dream Songs* series, *Homage to Mistress Bradstreet* (1956), a biography of Stephen Crane.

Elizabeth Bishop (1911-), New England-born poet, author of *North and South* (1946), and *North and South—A Cold Spring* (1955).

Louise Bogan (1897-1970), poet and critic, her *Collected Poems* won the 1954 Bollingen Prize.

Robert Brustein (1927-), Dean of the Yale School of Drama, contributing editor of *The New Republic*, author of several influential books on the theater, *The Theatre of Revolt* (1964), *The Third Theatre* (1969).

Erskine Caldwell (1903-), southern novelist and screenwriter, author of *Tobacco Road* (1932), *God's Little Acre* (1933), sometime collaborator with his wife, photographer Margaret Bourke-White.

Willa Cather (1876-1947), novelist, writer for *McClure's*, winner of the 1922 Pulitzer Prize for *One of Ours*. Author of *O Pioneers!* (1913), *My Antonia* (1918), *Death Comes for the Archbishop* (1927), *Shadows on the Rock* (1931).

John Cheever (1912-), novelist and short story writer, published his first story at seventeen in *The New Republic*, author of *The Wapshot Chronicle* (1957), *Bullet Park* (1969).

John Ciardi (1916-), poet, teacher, longtime contributor to *Saturday Review*, translator of Dante.

Robert Coles (1929-), psychiatrist, contributing editor of *The New Republic*, student of the American South, author of *Children of Crisis* (1968), *Erik H. Erikson: The Growth of His Work* (1970), *Farewell to the South* (1972).

Malcolm Cowley (1898-), critic and editor, joined the staff of *The New Republic* in 1929 and remained as associate editor until 1944. Author of *Exile's Return* (1934), *After the Genteel Tradition* (1937), *The Literary Situation* (1954), *The Faulkner-Cowley File* (1966), editor of the *Portable* authors series.

Hart Crane (1899-1932), poet, author of *The Bridge* (1930), sporadically employed and productive, dependent on patrons, ultimately drowned himself in the Gulf of Mexico.

e.e. cummings (1894-1962), poet and novelist, author of *The Enormous Room* (1922), an account of his sojourn in a French prisoner-of-war camp during World War I, creator of an influential style of free verse.

Babette Deutsch (1895-), poet, novelist, and critic, author of *Honey Out of the Rock* (1925), *Mask of Silenus* (1933), translator of Russian and German poetry.

John Dos Passos (1896-1970), novelist and essayist, first of the Left, then of the Right, author of *Three Soldiers* (1921), *Manhattan Transfer* (1925), and the USA trilogy, *The 42nd Parallel* (1930), *1919* (1932), *The Big Money* (1936).

Kenneth Evett (1913-), chairman of the Department of Art at Cornell, frequent contributor to *The New Republic*.

Robert Evett (1922-1975), composer and critic, brother of Kenneth Evett, member of *The New Republic* staff, 1952-68, music critic of *The Washington Star*, 1969-1975.

Manny Farber (1917-), artist and critic, faculty member of the University of California at San Diego, coined the term "underground film." Author of *Negative Space* (1971), a collection of movie criticism.

William Faulkner (1897-1962), Mississippi-born novelist and short story writer, onetime Hollywood screenwriter, winner of the 1949 Nobel Prize for literature, preeminent American novelist of his day. Author of *The Sound and the Fury* (1929), *As I Lay Dying* (1930), *Light in August* (1932), *Go Down, Moses* (1942).

Otis Ferguson (1907-1943), pioneer jazz and film critic, longtime contributor to *The New Republic*, killed in World War II. *The Film Criticism of Otis Ferguson* was published in 1971.

Hallie Flanagan (1890-), onetime director of Vassar's experimental theater, associate of George Pierce Baker at Harvard, director of the Federal Theatre Project (WPA) throughout the 1930s.

E.M. Forster (1879-1970), British novelist, author of *A Room with a View* (1908), *Howards End* (1910), *A Passage to India* (1924).

Robert Frost (1874-1963), poet, preeminent New England literary figure, although born in California and first prominent in England. Four-time winner of the Pulitzer Prize, author of *A Boy's Will* (1913), *North of Boston* (1914), *A Further Range* (1936).

John Galsworthy (1867-1933), British novelist, winner of the 1932 Nobel Prize for literature, author of *The Forsyte Saga* series and many plays.

Michael Gold (1894-1967), pseudonym of Irving Granich, novelist and critic, Stalinist proponent of "proletarian" literature, an example of which is *Jews Without Money* (1935).

Robert Graves (1895-), British poet, critic, and historical novelist, first prominent for poems of his experiences in World War I, long resident on Majorca. Author of *Goodbye to All That* (1929), *I, Claudius* (1934), several collections of poetry.

Francis Hackett (1893-1962), founding staff member of *The New Republic*, literary editor, 1914-1922.

Thomas Hardy (1840-1928), English novelist and poet, creator of the fictional county of Wessex, author of *Far from the Madding Crowd* (1874), *The Return of the Native* (1878), *Tess of the d'Urbervilles* (1891). After the poor critical reception of *Jude the Obscure* (1895), he wrote poetry only.

Gilbert Harrison (1915-), editor of *The New Republic*, 1953-1975, essayist and compiler of *Gertrude Stein's America* (1965).

Lillian Hellman (1905-), playright and memoirist, author of *The Children's Hour* (1934), *The Little Foxes* (1939), *Watch on the Rhine* (1941), *Pentimento* (1973).

Ernest Hemingway (1899-1961), novelist and short story writer, winner of the 1954 Nobel Prize for literature, resident of Paris in the 1920s, war correspondent in Spain and during World War II, "Papa" to a generation of imitators. Author of *A Farewell to Arms* (1929), *To Have and Have Not* (1937), *For Whom the Bell Tolls* (1940), *The Old Man and the Sea* (1952).

Granville Hicks (1901-), critic and teacher, staff member of *The New Masses, New Leader, Saturday Review*. Author of *John Reed — The Making of a Revolutionary* (1933), *The First to Awaken* (1940), *Part of the Truth* (1965).

John Hollander (1929-), poet, critic, and teacher, author of *A Crackling of Thorns* (1958), short stories and essays, a frequent contributor to *The New Republic*.

Langston Hughes (1902-1967), pioneer modern black poet, short story writer, and editor, creator of a satirical character collected in *The Best of Simple* (1961).

Randall Jarrell (1914-1965), poet and teacher, author of *Pictures from an Institution* (1954), *A Sad Heart at the Supermarket* (1962).

Robinson Jeffers (1887-1962), poet, pessimist, long resident on the California coast, author of *Cawdor* (1928), *Thurso's Landing* (1932).

James Joyce (1882-1941), Irish novelist and short story writer, long resident on the Continent, creator of a handful of modern classics, including *Ulysses* (1921), *Finnegans Wake* (1939).

Pauline Kael (1919-), film critic for *The New Yorker* since 1968, at *The New Republic*, 1966-1967. Author of *I Lost It at the Movies* (1965), *Kiss Kiss Bang Bang* (1968), *Going Steady* (1970), *The Citizen Kane Book* (1971).

Stanley Kauffmann (1916-), film and drama critic for *The New Republic* since 1967, author of *A World on Film* (1966), *Figures of Light* (1971).

Alfred Kazin (1915-), critic and teacher, onetime literary editor of *The New Republic*, author of *On Native Grounds* (1942), *The Inmost Leaf* (1955), *Contemporaries* (1962), some autobiographical writing.

Stephen Koch, art critic and teacher, author of *Stargazer: Andy Warhol's World and His Films* (1973).

Louis Kronenberger (1904-), essayist, critic, novelist, onetime drama critic for *Time*, teacher at Columbia and Brandeis. Author of *Grand Right and Left* (1952), *Company Manners* (1954), *The Republic of Letters* (1955).

Ring Lardner (1885-1933), humorist, former sports reporter, connoisseur of slang and colloquialisms, author of *You Know Me Al* (1915), *The Round Up* (1929), drinking companion of the Scott Fitzgeralds.

Richmond Lattimore (1906-), poet, teacher, scholar of classical culture, longtime member of the Bryn Mawr faculty, translator of Pindar, *The Iliad, Hesiod*.

D.H. Lawrence (1885-1930), British novelist, poet, short story writer, critic, and painter, son of a Nottinghamshire miner. Author of *Sons and Lovers* (1923), *The Plumed Serpent* (1926), *Lady Chatterly's Lover* (1928).

Vachel Lindsay (1879-1931), poet and troubador, lecturer for the Anti-Saloon League, author of *Rhymes to be Traded for Bread* (1912), *The Eagle That is Forgotten* (1913), *In Praise of Johnny Appleseed* (1921).

Walter Lippmann (1889-1974), journalist and political philosopher, founding editor of *The New Republic*, editorial writer for *The New York World*, syndicated columnist for a generation. Author of *A Preface to Politics* (1913), *A Preface to Morals* (1929), *The Public Philosophy* (1955).

Robert Littell (1896-1963), associated editor of *The New Republic* during the 1920s.

Robert Lowell (1917-), poet and teacher, member of the famous Boston family. Author of *Lord Weary's Castle* (1946), *Life Studies* (1959), several plays.

Archibald MacLeish (1892-), poet and journalist, onetime *Fortune* editor, Librarian of Congress, and Assistant Secretary of State, awarded Pulitzer Prize for *Conquistador* (1932), *Collected Poems* (1953), drama *J.B.* (1958).

Marya Mannes (1904-), journalist, critic, novelist, television commentator, author of *More in Anger* (1958), *They* (1968).

Katherine Mansfield (1888-1923), New Zealand-born short story writer, wife of John Middleton Murry, author of *The Garden Party* (1922), among others.

Edgar Lee Masters (1868-1950), poet, lawyer, sprang from middle-aged obscurity with *Spoon River Anthology* (1915).

T.S. Matthews (1901-), journalist and man of letters, on the staff of *The New*

Republic, 1925-1929, managing editor of *Time*, 1943-1949, and editor, 1949-1953. Author of *The Sugar Pill* (1957), *Name and Address* (1960), *Great Tom: Notes Toward the Definition of T.S. Eliot* (1974).

Mary McCarthy (1912-), novelist and critic, briefly married to Edmund Wilson, author of *The Company She Keeps* (1942), *A Charmed Life* (1955), *The Group* (1963), *Birds of America* (1971).

H.L. Mencken (1880-1956), newspaperman, critic, editor, preeminent American journalist of his time, "the sage of Baltimore," author of several books, onetime editor of *Smart Set* and with George Jean Nathan co-editor of *The American Mercury*, 1924-1933.

Edna St. Vincent Millay (1892-1950), poet, member of the 1920s Greenwich Village-Provincetown Players set, author of plays including *The King's Henchman* (1917) and awarded the Pulitzer Prize for *The Harp Weaver and other poems* (1923).

Lewis Mumford (1895-), historian and teacher, pioneer in city and regional planning, onetime contributing editor of *The New Republic*. Author of *The Culture of Cities* (1938), *The City in History* (1961).

Vladimir Nabokov (1899-), Russian-born novelist, educated in England, taught at Cornell, long resident in Switzerland. Author of *Bend Sinister* (1947), *Pnin* (1957), *Lolita* (1958), *Pale Fire* (1962), *Speak, Memory* (1968), *Ada* (1969).

Dorothy Parker (1893-1967), poet, short story writer, critic, screenwriter (*A Star is Born*, 1937), luminary of the Algonquin Round Table, contributor to *Vanity Fair*, *The New Yorker, Esquire.*

John Crowe Ransom (1888-1974), poet, critic, and teacher, founder of the Fugitive school at Vanderbilt. Author of several volumes of verse and a founder of the *Kenyon Review*.

Kenneth Rexroth (1905-), San Francisco poet, critic, and translator of Chinese poetry, author of *The Phoenix and the Tortoise* (1944), *The Dragon and the Unicorn* (1952).

Edwin Arlington Robinson (1869-1935), poet, three-time Pulitzer Prize-winner, author of several collections of poetry, two plays.

Paul Rosenfeld (1890-1946), music and art critic, author of *Musical Portraits* (1920), *By Way of Art* (1928), contributing editor of *The New Republic*.

Carl Sandburg (1878-1967), poet and folklorist, in later years singer and national sage, author of several collections of poetry and a six-volume biography of Abraham Lincoln.

George Santayana (1863-1952), Spanish-born philosopher, critic, teacher, member of the Harvard faculty where he taught T.S. Eliot and Walter Lippmann, thereafter resident in Rome. Author of *The Life of Reason* (1906), *Platonism and the Spiritual Life* (1927), *The Last Puritan* (1935), *Persons and Places* (1943).

William Saroyan (1908-), Armenian-American novelist, short story writer and playwright, author of *The Daring Young Man on the Flying Trapeze* (1934), *Love, Here is My Hat* (1938), *My Name is Aram* (1940), several plays including *My Heart's in the Highlands* (1939), *The Time of Your Life* (1939), *Love's Old Sweet Song* (1940).

Delmore Schwartz (1913-1966), poet, short story writer, teacher, author of *In Dreams Begin Responsibilities* (1938), *Shenandoah* (1941), *The World is a Wedding* (1948).

Alan Seeger (1888-1916), Harvard-educated poet, killed in World War I, author of "I Have a Rendezvous with Death."

Anne Sexton (1928-1974), poet and teacher, author of *To Bedlam and Part Way Back* (1960), *Transformations* (1971), winner of the 1967 Pulitzer Prize.

Karl Shapiro (1913-), poet, critic, and teacher, gained notice for poems written as a soldier during World War II, author of *V-Letter and Other Poems* (1944), *Beyond Criticism* (1953), onetime editor of *Poetry* magazine.

Irwin Shaw (1913-), novelist and short story writer, author of *The Young Lions* (1948), *Two Weeks in Another Town* (1960), and the televised version (1975) of *Rich Man, Poor Man* (1970).

Theodore Spencer (1902-1949), poet and critic, longtime member of the Harvard faculty. Author of *Death and Elizabethan Tragedy* (1936) and *Shakespeare and the Nature of Man* (1942).

Leo Stein (1872-1947), painter and art critic, brother of Gertrude Stein, claimed to have discovered Cézanne. Author of *Appreciations: Painting, Poetry and Prose* (1947).

Allen Tate (1899-), poet, critic, teacher, a founder of the Fugitive school at Vanderbilt, author of *Mr. Pope and Other Poems* (1928), *Reactionary Essays on Poetry and Ideas* (1936).

Peter Taylor (1917-), novelist and short story writer, author of *The Widows of Thornton* (1954), *Happy Families Are All Alike* (1960).

Dylan Thomas (1914-1953), Welsh poet and playwright, renowned for his tempestuous private life, author of *A Portrait of the Artist as a Young Dog* (1940), the radio play *Under Milk Wood* (1944), and several posthumous collections.

Lionel Trilling (1905-1975), critic and teacher, longtime faculty member at Columbia, mentor of a generation of students of culture. Author of *Matthew Arnold* (1939), *The Liberal Imagination* (1950), *Freud and the Crisis of Our Culture* (1955), and a novel, *The Middle of the Journey* (1947).

Ivan Turgenieff (1818-1883), Russian novelist, onetime civil servant, author of *The Hunting Sketches* (1852), *Fathers and Sons* (1862), *Virgin Soil* (1876).

John Updike (1932-), novelist, short story writer, poet, and critic, graduate of Harvard and longtime contributor to *The New Yorker*, author of *The Poorhouse Fair* (1958), *Rabbit, Run* (1960), *Couples* (1968).

Mark Van Doren (1894-1972), poet and editor, onetime film critic for *The Nation*, awarded Pulitzer Prize for *Collected Poems* (1939).

Robert Penn Warren (1905-), southern-born novelist, poet, and teacher, contributor to *The Fugitive* while at Vanderbilt, author of *All the King's Men* (1946) and several collections of poetry.

Eudora Welty (1909-), Mississippi-born novelist and short story writer, author of *A Curtain of Green* (1941), *Delta Wedding* (1946), *Losing Battles* (1970).

Rebecca West (1892-), British critic and novelist, author of *Black Lamb and Grey Falcon* (1941), *The Meaning of Treason* (1949).

Oscar Williams (1900-1964), poet, onetime advertising man, author of *The Golden Darkness* (1921), *That's All That Matters* (1945), *Selected Poems* (1947).

William Carlos Williams (1883-1963), poet and physician, lifelong resident and practitioner in northern New Jersey, author of *In the American Grain* (1925) and the extended poem "Paterson" (1946,1951).

Edmund Wilson (1895-1972), essayist, critic, historian, editor, novelist, in his day America's preeminent man of letters, staff member of *The New Republic* during the 1920s. Author of *Axel's Castle* (1931), *To the Finland Station* (1940), *Classics and Commercials* (1950), *Apologies to the Iroquois* (1960).

Thomas Wolfe (1900-1938), North Carolina-born novelist, author of *Look Homeward, Angel* (1929), *Of Time and the River* (1935), *The Web and the Rock* (1939), *You Can't Go Home Again* (1941).

Virginia Woolf (1882-1941), British novelist, luminary of the Bloomsbury Group, author of *Mrs. Dalloway* (1925), *To the Lighthouse* (1927), *A Room of One's Own* (1930).

William Butler Yeats (1865-1939), Irish poet and playwright, founder of Dublin's Abbey Theatre, awarded the Nobel Prize for literature in 1923, author of several collections of poetry and memoirs.

Stark Young (1881-1963), poet, playwright, and essayist, on *The New Republic* staff, 1921-1924 and drama critic until 1947. Author of *The Flower in Drama* (1923), *Immortal Shadows* (1948).

Composed in Palatino by The New Republic Book Company, Inc.

Printed on 60-pound Warren's Old Style Laid paper and bound in Holliston Kingston Natural by Halliday Lithograph, West Hanover, Massachusetts.

Designed by Gerard Valerio.